ACTIVE BUSINESS CULTURE

ANGLAIS → B2
BTS 1re & 2e années

Sous la coordination de Christine Pilorget
Professeur agrégé d'anglais
au lycée Fustel de Coulanges (Massy)

Claire Delarocque
Professeur agrégé d'anglais
au lycée Jean Lurçat (Paris 13e)

Béatrice Firobind
Professeur agrégé d'anglais
au lycée Claude Monet (Paris 13e)

Marie-Hélène Fougeron
Professeur certifié d'anglais
au lycée Jean Lurçat (Paris 13e)

Serena Murdoch-Stern
Anglophone, professeur d'anglais en entreprise
et dans les grandes écoles parisiennes

Nathan
TECHNIQUE

Votre manuel

Destiné à être utilisé sur les 2 années de BTS, ce manuel a pour ambition de vous aider à vous entraîner aux examens du BTS et de vous amener à une pratique fluide de l'anglais en vue de votre future formation professionnelle. Il est constitué de 11 chapitres / 11 thèmes liés aux différentes filières de BTS.

Structure d'un chapitre

- **Ouverture de chapitre :** encourager la prise de parole sur le thème du chapitre à partir d'un visuel, de questions et d'une boîte de mots.

- **Starters :** entrer dans le thème par des activités de compréhension et de production orales et écrites.

- **Practice Text • Audio • Video :** travailler à partir d'articles de presse, d'extraits audio et vidéo pour acquérir une méthode de compréhension et d'expression ; se préparer aux épreuves de l'examen et travailler du vocabulaire et des points de grammaire.

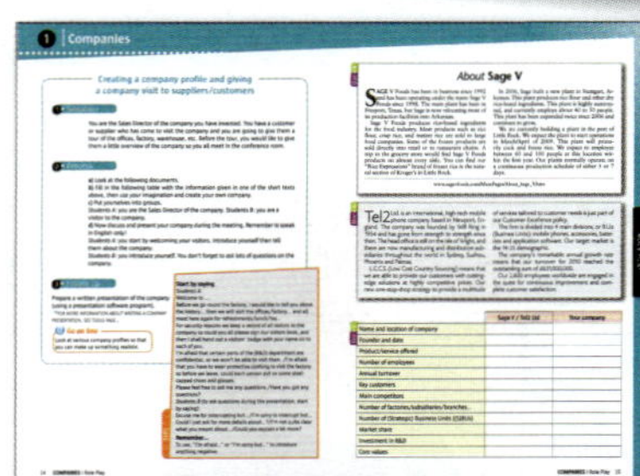

- **Role play :** faire des études de cas à partir de documents professionnels et se mettre en situation de communication professionnelle pour parler en interaction.

- **Active Business Culture :** se forger une culture du monde des entreprises :
  - **Background** : les connaissances et notions essentielles du thème à retenir ;
  - **Focus** : une analyse comparative de deux marchés, deux entreprises, deux secteurs professionnels…

- **Active vocabulary :** apprendre le vocabulaire spécifique du thème et faire des exercices pour s'entraîner à le retenir.

- **Tools for the exam :** des fiches livrant les étapes, la méthode et des conseils à suivre pour se préparer aux épreuves orales et écrites de l'examen de BTS.

- **Grammar :** revoir les règles essentielles pour dépasser les principales difficultés grammaticales et s'exprimer dans un anglais correct.

Zoom sur les pages « PRACTICE • TEXT » et « PRACTICE • AUDIO • VIDEO »

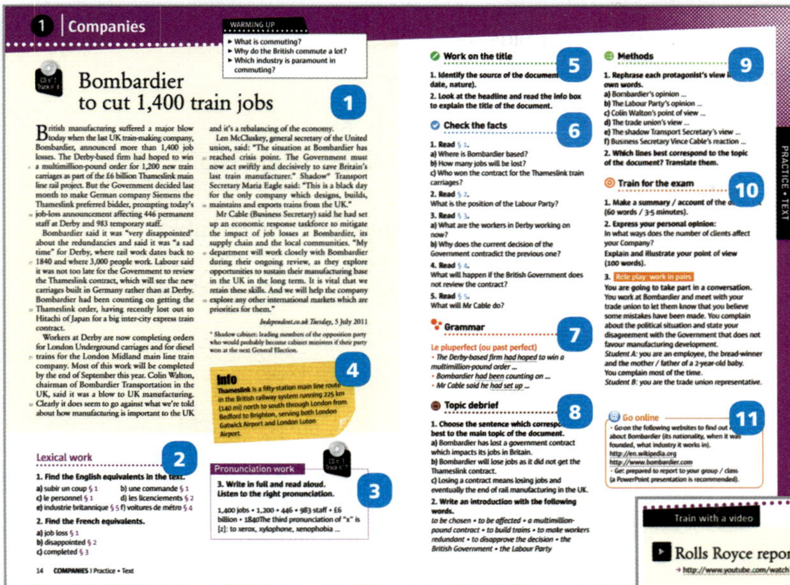

1 Train with a document : travailler à partir d'un document (article de presse ou extrait audio). Tous les documents (écrits et audio) sont enregistrés.

2 Lexical work : rechercher du lexique (équivalents et synonymes) dans le document pour se préparer à la compréhension et pouvoir résumer/rendre compte de son contenu.

3 Pronunciation work : travailler la prononciation de certains mots extraits du document de travail.

4 Info : mieux comprendre certaines références du document grâce à des compléments d'information (sur la société anglo-saxonne, sur les entreprises...).

5 Work on the title : présenter et anticiper sur le contenu du document à partir du titre.

6 Check the fact : lire/écouter progressivement le document et en comprendre les faits et informations majeurs à travers une série de questions.

7 Grammar : repérer un point de grammaire dans le document et revoir la règle qui lui correspond (en fin de manuel).

8 Topic debrief : identifier et présenter le thème du document.

9 Methods : développer une méthode d'écoute et de lecture pour dégager les idées essentielles du document.

10 Train for the exam : s'entraîner à des activités d'expression écrite et orale comme à l'examen :

- **Account/summary :** rendre compte/résumer le document ;
- **Expressing yourself :** donner son opinion à propos d'une idée développée dans le document ;
- **Comment :** discuter et illustrer par des exemples les enjeux du document ;
- **Role play :** s'entraîner à des activités de communication (en groupes ou à deux) et se mettre en situation pour parler et écrire en interaction.

11 Go online : faire des recherches sur Internet et rendre compte de l'information collectée.

12 Train with a video : se préparer à l'épreuve de compréhension orale d'anglais à partir d'une vidéo (à consulter sur Internet) à l'aide d'un guidage pour décrypter son contenu.

Sommaire

Sommaire

- **Direction éditoriale :** Christine Asin
- **Edition :** Camille Delenclos-Ledoux
- **Conception graphique et mises en pages :** Sophie Bensaci et Alinéa
- **Couverture :** Sophie Bensaci
- **Iconographie :** Laëtitia Jannin et Valérie Delchambre
- **Fabrication :** Pascal Mégret
- **Coordination artistique :** Evelyn Audureau
- **Relecture :** Lisa Barnett

Nathan • 21 avenue Pierre de Coubertin
75211 Paris Cedex 13

ISBN 978-2-09-162002-2

Crédits photographiques :
Couverture : Getty images France/Kutay Tanir.
Page 7 : The Kobal Collection, 8hg et hd : Fotolia/Yuri Arcurs, 8md : Fotolia/Goodluz, 8b : Graphics Hunt, 12 : Ted S. Warren/AP/SIPA, 19 : Pool for Yomiuri/NBC/AP/SIPA, 23 : REA/Zuma/The Bakersfield Californian, 24 : REA/Pascal Sittler, 27g : Fotolia/ra2 studio, 27d : BIS/Ph. Coll. Archives Larbor © Adagp, Paris 2012, 28g : Fotolia/Monkey Business, 28mg : Fotolia/Edyta Pawlowska, 28md : Fotolia/ra2 Studio, 28d : Fotolia/Chlorophylle, 32 : Groupon, 40 : Fotolia/Onidji, 43 : REA/Zuma/London News Pictures, 44 : Amazon, 47 : Lisa Maree Williams/Getty IMAGES /AFP, 48g : Photo12/Alamy/Andre Jenny, 48mg : Photo12/Alamy/Eric James, 48md : Photo12/Alamy / WDA Bravo, 48d : Photo12/Alamy/Chris Howes, 49h : Shirley J, 49b : Plush Chocolates, 53 : AIJAZ RAHI/AP/SIPA, 67 et 68 : Fotolia/Henry Bonn et Apple Inc., Champion, American Express, Converse, Goldman Sachs, Kellog's, Sony, MTV, Dell, Pzizer, Ben & Jerry's, Toyota, Starbucks coffee, Google, Ford, Nikon, Black & Decker, Nescafé, Nike, Ikea, 69gmd : The Advertising Archive Collection, 72 : KidStock/Blend Images/Corbis, 82 : Converse, 87 : Droits réservés, 88hg : Fotolia/Edelweiss, 88hd : REA/Benoît Decout , 88bg : Fotolia/ra2 Studio, 88bd : Fotolia/Cybrain, 89h : REA/Benoît Decout, 89b : AFP/Attila Kisbenedek, 90 : Facebook, 92 : Angry birds, 93 : Starbuck coffee, 99 : David Levenson / Alamy, 103 : Reuters, 104 : REA/Kim Kulish, 107 : Fotolia/TheModernCanvas, 108hm : Fotolia/Yuri Arcurs, 108 hd : Fotolia/Lucastor, 108bg : Fotolia/Alexander Raths, 108bd : Fotolia/Deshacam, 121 : Fotolia/Yuri Arcurs, 129 : Source : Affiche 9 May 2011 Europe Day, http://europa.eu, © Union européenne, 1995-2012, 130 : Fotolia/Adamgolabek, 134 : Istock/Baris Simsek, 135 : Istock/Mike Bentley, 137 : AFP/Gérard Malie, 145 : Fotolia/Brad Pict, 146bg : Shutterstock/Roman Sigaev, 146hd : Shutterstock/Psamtik, 146bd : AFP/Jacques Collet , 147 : AFP/Getty/Sean Gallup, 151 : Droits réservés, 160 : Istock/Ruslan Ivantsov, 165 : Fotolia/Nikola Bilic, 171 : Shutterstock/VectorForever, 172 : www.euinfrastructure.com, 176 : Paul Sancya/AP/SIPA, 185 : Fotolia/Giovanni Rinaldi, 186 : Fotolia/Christophe Fouquin, 188 : Ford, 187 : Tata Motors, 191g : Fotolia/Lunamarina , 191d Fotolia/devianART, 192g : Fotolia/Worachat Sodri, 192mh et mb : Fotolia/Zerotwolab, 192d : Fotolia/Lilya, 196 : Fotolia/Ynamaku, 205ht : Fotolia/GIS, 205hg : Fotolia/Yri Arcurs, 205hgm : Fotolia/Mateei, 205hgm Fotolia/Pavel Losevsky, 205hm : Fotolia He2, 205hmd Fotolia/Nyul, 205bg : Fotolia/Vaditto, 205bd : Fotolia/Sbrisov, 205b: Fotolia/Beboy, 207 : Getty/Bloomberg, 208 : AFP/Getty/Bruno Vincent, 211 : WWF, 212hg : Bios/Chamnanrith/UNEP/Still Pictures, 212hm : REA/Frédéric Lelan, 212hd : REA/Zuma/Imaginechina , 215 : Fotolia/Michel Bazin, 217 : Biswaranjan Rout/AP/SIPA, 227 : Fotolia/Rafa Irusta, 228 : Fotolia/Chengas et 229 : Shutterstock/Buriy.

1

Companies

Updating, restructuring... outsourcing?

Question

How can small companies resist?

WORD BOX

commercial centres • high street consumers • department stores • profit • corporate responsibility • business ethics

1 | Companies

1 • Look and discuss

Look at the pictures about dress codes in companies and say to which category of dress code these people belong: *business formal – business casual – casual*. Then discuss in class.

2 • Read and understand

a) Read the following text and look at the cartoon.

Casual Friday
The dot.com revolution of the 90s with all its computer geeks making the world go round at Silicon Valley (California) launched a Friday wear trend which is referred to as casual Friday. It allows the employees to depart a little from the formal company dress code just before the weekend.
Some guidelines for casual Friday:
– Casual doesn't mean unprofessional. Avoid wearing clothing with advertising or messages that are inappropriate for the workplace.
– Clothing should be clean and in good repair.
– Always check your company's policy on what is appropriate for casual Friday.
– Jeans are not always allowed.
– Don't show any more skin than you would do on a normal workday.
– Flip-flops are never appropriate office wear unless you're having a beach party at work.

b) Answer the questions.

1. What are "inappropriate advertising messages"? Give examples and explain.
2. Why are jeans sometimes banned even on casual Fridays?
3. How much skin can be shown? Give examples.
4. What does the cartoon tell us about casual Friday?

3 • Read and write

a) Why is it so important to have a clear organisation chart? Write three sentences using the following words.

to show • where • employees • fit into • business • new career • to assess • employees • current • plan • advancement • who reports to whom • who is responsible for what • to define

b) These people work for BBP Ltd. Fit all the people (underlined) into the organisation chart.

The CFO (Chief Financial Officer) reports to the CEO (Chief Executive Officer), who runs the company.
The Chief Accountant is accountable to the CFO, who is head of the finance department.
The PA (Personal Assistant) assists the CEO.
The Sales Director is in charge of the sales department with the help of the Sales & Marketing Manager, who is responsible for the sales executives.
The Procurement Manager, who reports to the Sales Director, is assisted by the Procurement Officer.
The Training Manager and the Salaries & Wages clerk work directly under the HR Director.

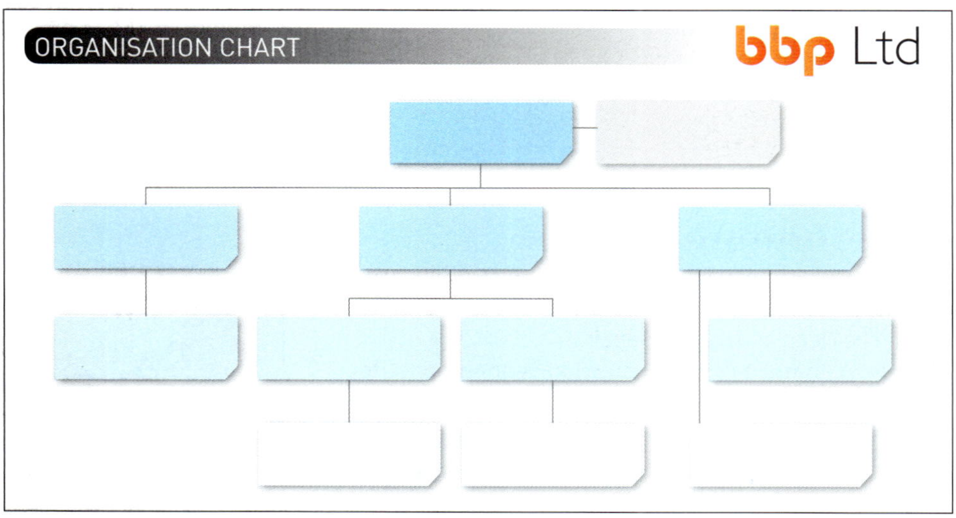

TIPS
The French term "un responsable" cannot be directly translated into English. Use "is responsible for / in charge of / head of ..."

4 • Listen and understand

CD n° 1 Track n° 1

a) What is Bill worried about?
b) Is Bill going to report the new employee to the boss?
c) What would you do under the circumstances?

WARMING UP

- Who are the "successful entrepreneurs" you've heard about?
- How have they become legends?

CD n° 1 Track n° 2

Red Bull's billionaire maniac

Little known outside of his native Austria, Dietrich Mateschitz is one of the most successful entrepreneurs of our age, a man who single-handedly changed the landscape of the beverage industry by creating not just a new brand but a whole new category: the energy drink. As the visionary who brought the world Red Bull, affectionately known as "speed in a can" or even "liquid cocaine," Mateschitz, 67, has been a patron saint for more than two decades to late-night partiers, exam-week undergrads, long-haul truckers, and, above all, extreme-sports athletes everywhere.

In return for his sickly sweet innovation, the world has made him very, very rich. Last year the privately held company, also named Red Bull, says it sold 4.2 billion cans of its drink, including more than a billion in the U.S. alone. That represents a 7.9 percent increase over the year before, and revenues jumped 15.8 percent to $5.175 billion. Mateschitz runs an efficient enterprise that has yet to trip on its rapid growth: At the end of 2004, he had just 2,605 employees; in 2010, Red Bull employed 7,758 people – which works out to more than $667,000 in revenue per person.

Now he's set his sights on media. On May 15, subscribers to the *Los Angeles Times, Chicago Tribune, Miami Herald, Houston Chronicle,* and *New York Daily News* found a magazine called *Red Bulletin* inserted in their Sunday papers. The 98-page glossy magazine features a cover story on San Francisco Giants ace Tim Lincecum, as well as pieces on Bob Dylan, graffiti art, and Russian BASE jumper Valery Rozov. Billed as "an almost independent monthly," the magazine is a product of Red Bull Media House, a subsidiary media company launched in Austria in 2007 that expanded with a Los Angeles outpost this January.

Mateschitz calls the multimedia assault "our most important line extension so far. As a major content provider, it is our goal to communicate and distribute the 'World of Red Bull' in all major media segments, from TV to print to new media to our music record label." He hopes Red Bull Media House will turn a profit, but, as with his sports teams, he's willing to wait. "In literal financial terms, our sports teams are not yet profitable, but in value terms, they are," he says. "The total editorial media value plus the media assets created around the teams are superior to pure advertising expenditures."

Business Week, May 19, 2011

Lexical work

1. Find the English equivalents in the text.

a) seul / tout seul § 1
b) le paysage § 1
c) le secteur des boissons § 1
d) une marque § 1
e) une décennie § 1
f) douceâtre § 2
g) posséder une entreprise § 2

2. Find the French equivalents.

a) to feature § 3
b) a subsidiary media company § 3
c) outpost § 3
d) to turn a profit § 4
e) a goal § 4
f) an asset § 4
g) expenditures § 4

Pronunciation work

CD n° 1 Track n° 3

1. Listen and observe the pronunciation of "wh".

whole • who • which

2. Listen to these words that you may find difficult and repeat with the right stress.

a) single-handedly • long-haul truckers
b) sickly sweet innovation • subsidiary media company • advertising expenditures

Info
Red Bull is an energy drink sold by the Austrian Red Bull GmbH, created in 1987 by the Austrian entrepreneur Dietrich Mateschitz.

Work on the title

1. Identify the source of the document (title, date, nature).

2. Look at the headline and read §1 to find out who is alluded to.

Check the facts

1. Read § 1.
a) What did Dietrich Mateschitz create?
b) What are the nicknames of this energy drink?

2. Read § 2.
a) How many cans were sold in 2010?
b) How successful has the company been?

3. Read § 3.
a) What is *Red Bulletin*?
b) What can you read in it? What is its aim?

4. Read § 4.
a) Why has the company Red Bull diversified?
b) What does the CEO hope to achieve with this magazine?

Grammar → p. 233

Le superlatif
- *He is one of the most successful entrepreneurs of our age.*
- *He is one of the wealthiest entrepreneurs in the world.*

Topic debrief

1. Choose the sentence which you think corresponds best to the main topic of the document.
a) The energy drink is expanding its business.
b) A booming company is diversifying.
c) Red Bull goes to America.

2. Write an introduction to the document by using the following words.
underline • entrepreneur • a patron saint • late-night partiers successfully • magazine • energy drink • multinational

Methods

1. Identify these two sentences in the document and translate into French.
a) He has set his sights...
b) The 98-page glossy magazine features a cover story on Tim Lincecum.

2. Analyse the function of the words in the following sentences and translate into English.
a) Nos équipes de sport ne nous rapportent pas.
b) Il est prêt à attendre.
c) Il y avait seulement 2 605 employés à la fin de l'année 2004.
d) En 2007, une filiale de presse fut lancée.

Train for the exam

1. Make a **summary / account** of the document (60 words / 3-5 minutes).

2. Comment: find an answer to the following questions. Discuss and give examples (100 words / 3-5 minutes).
a) How would you rate the part played by the CEO in a company?
b) What turned Red Bull into a successful company?

3. Role play: work in pairs
You are going to take part in a meeting.
The managers of "Lemon Fresh" company have organised a meeting in order to decide whether they will invest more in the media industries.
Student A: you are one of the managers. You want to expand in the media industry after having heard of Red Bull's success.
Student B: you are another manager. You think that expanding in the media industry is really a waste of money and you think it will not bring your company more customers.

Go online
- Go online and find out more about:
  – *Red Bulletin*
  – Graffiti art and the San Francisco Giants.
- Get prepared to report to your group / class (a PowerPoint presentation is recommended).

Train with an oral document

WARMING UP

► What do you know about low-cost companies?

CD n° 1 Track n° 4

Is Southwest here to stay or is competition so tough that it will clip Southwest's wings?

Info

Southwest Airlines Co. is an American low-cost airline based in Dallas, Texas. The airline was established in 1967, adopting its current name in 1971, and as of June 5, 2011 is the largest airline in the United States based upon domestic passengers carried.

Southwest Airlines planes are shown at McCarran International Airport in Las Vegas.

Lexical work

Match the following words.

fares • prices • to praise • to face • profitability • competition • to expand • foot hold • to return to • to offer • hub and spoke services • to skyrocket

Pronunciation work

CD n° 1 Track n° 5

1. Listen and observe:

injured • expert • transport • learn • passenger • merger • offer • carrier • better

Listen to the British accent and the American accent.

In British English the letter -r in the above words is mute.

2. Listen, pronounce and underline the stressed syllable.

passenger • investigation • departure • carrier • transportation

3. Listen to these words that you may find difficult.

scheduled air transportation • extra seat • checked-in luggage • low-cost carrier

Work on the title

1. Look at the title of the document.

2. Rephrase it with the following words.
Southwest ... tough competition which ... clip ... wings.

Check the facts

1. Listen to part 1.
a) What happened to a Southwest jetliner between Phoenix and Sacramento?
b) When did it happen?
c) What did the pilot do?
d) Why was an investigation by the National Transportation Safety Board conducted?
e) What did Southwest ask two heavy passengers?

2. Listen to part 2.
a) Why is Southwest so popular?
b) When was it created?
c) When did Southwest merge with AirTran?
d) How does the airline industry want to return to profitability?

3. Listen to part 3.
a) What has happened to oil prices?
b) How will it affect passengers and airlines?
c) How many aircrafts has Southwest got? How many cities does it serve?

Topic debrief

1. Choose the sentence which you think corresponds best to the main topic of the document.
a) Southwest is losing customers because of its numerous problems.
b) Southwest is America's favourite airline although it has faced a few problems.
c) Southwest is expanding by taking over other airline companies.

2. Write an introduction to the text by using the following words.
passengers • low-cost carriers • fuel • soaring cost • budget airline • rivals • to operate • to charge • to inspect • to consolidate / to take over • fares • to switch dates • domestic airlines

Methods

1. Complete the following sentences with your own words to prepare your account.
a) Southwest is still popular although there was a problem ... .
b) Southwest has become America's largest low-cost carrier with the merger ... .
c) Southwest is America's favourite airline as it ... .
d) Southwest asked two passengers to ... .

2. Rewrite the sentences above by using linking words.

Train for the exam

1. Use your notes to make an oral presentation about this American low-cost company which is the darling of its American customers and record yourself (3-5 minutes).

2. Comment: find an answer to the following question. Discuss and give examples (100 words / 3-5 minutes).
Is the increase of oil prices a real threat for air companies?

3. Role play: work in groups
You are going to take part in a conversation between 3 people in an airport.
Student A: you are a loyal Southwest passenger. However, last time you flew with the company, you arrived 4 hours late. You are not satisfied with the services.
Student B: you represent the company and you reply to the passenger.
Student C: You are a passenger. You are still happy with the company.

Go online
- Find as much info as you can on a low-cost company.
- Get prepared to report to your group / class (a PowerPoint presentation is recommended).

WARMING UP

- What is commuting?
- Why do the British commute a lot?
- Which industry is paramount in commuting?

CD n° 1 Track n° 6

Bombardier to cut 1,400 train jobs

British manufacturing suffered a major blow today when the last UK train-making company, Bombardier, announced more than 1,400 job losses. The Derby-based firm had hoped to win a multimillion-pound order for 1,200 new train carriages as part of the £6 billion Thameslink main line rail project. But the Government decided last month to make German company Siemens the Thameslink preferred bidder, prompting today's job-loss announcement affecting 446 permanent staff at Derby and 983 temporary staff.

Bombardier said it was "very disappointed" about the redundancies and said it was "a sad time" for Derby, where rail work dates back to 1840 and where 3,000 people work. Labour said it was not too late for the Government to review the Thameslink contract, which will see the new carriages built in Germany rather than at Derby. Bombardier had been counting on getting the Thameslink order, having recently lost out to Hitachi of Japan for a big inter-city express train contract.

Workers at Derby are now completing orders for London Underground carriages and for diesel trains for the London Midland main line train company. Most of this work will be completed by the end of September this year. Colin Walton, chairman of Bombardier Transportation in the UK, said it was a blow to UK manufacturing. Clearly it does seem to go against what we're told about how manufacturing is important to the UK and it's a rebalancing of the economy.

Len McCluskey, general secretary of the United union, said: "The situation at Bombardier has reached crisis point. The Government must now act swiftly and decisively to save Britain's last train manufacturer." Shadow* Transport Secretary Maria Eagle said: "This is a black day for the only company which designs, builds, maintains and exports trains from the UK."

Mr Cable (Business Secretary) said he had set up an economic response taskforce to mitigate the impact of job losses at Bombardier, its supply chain and the local communities. "My department will work closely with Bombardier during their ongoing review, as they explore opportunities to sustain their manufacturing base in the UK in the long term. It is vital that we retain these skills. And we will help the company explore any other international markets which are priorities for them."

Independent.co.uk Tuesday, 5 July 2011

* Shadow cabinet: leading members of the opposition party who would probably become cabinet ministers if their party won at the next General Election.

Info
Thameslink is a fifty-station main line route in the British railway system running 225 km (140 mi) north to south through London from Bedford to Brighton, serving both London Gatwick Airport and London Luton Airport.

Lexical work

1. Find the English equivalents in the text.

a) subir un coup § 1
b) une commande § 1
c) le personnel § 1
d) les licenciements § 2
e) industrie britannique § 3
f) voitures de métro § 3

2. Find the French equivalents.

a) job loss § 1
b) disappointed § 2
c) completed § 3

Pronunciation work

CD n° 1 Track n° 7

Write in full and read aloud.
Listen to the right pronunciation.

1,400 jobs • 1,200 • 446 • 983 staff • £6 billion • 1840

Work on the title

1. Identify the source of the document (title, date, nature).

2. Look at the headline and read the info box to explain the title of the document.

Check the facts

1. Read § 1.
a) Where is Bombardier based?
b) How many jobs will be lost?
c) Who won the contract for the Thameslink train carriages?

2. Read § 2.
What is the position of the Labour Party?

3. Read § 3.
a) What are the workers in Derby working on now?
b) Why does the current decision of the Government contradict the previous one?

4. Read § 4.
What will happen if the British Government does not review the contract?

5. Read § 5.
What will Mr Cable do?

Grammar

→ p. 233

Le pluperfect (ou past perfect)
- *The Derby-based firm had hoped to win a multimillion-pound order ...*
- *Bombardier had been counting on ...*
- *Mr Cable said he had set up ...*

Topic debrief

1. Choose the sentence which best corresponds to the main topic of the document.
a) Bombardier has lost a government contract which impacts its jobs in Britain.
b) Bombardier will lose jobs as it did not get the Thameslink contract.
c) Losing a contract means losing jobs and eventually the end of rail manufacturing in the UK.

2. Write an introduction with the following words.
to be chosen • to be affected • a multimillion-pound contract • to build trains • to make workers redundant • to disapprove the decision • the British Government • the Labour Party

Methods

1. Rephrase each protagonist's view in your own words.
a) Bombardier's opinion ...
b) The Labour Party's opinion ...
c) Colin Walton's point of view ...
d) The trade union's view ...
e) The shadow Transport Secretary's view ...
f) Business Secretary Vince Cable's reaction ...

2. Which lines best correspond to the topic of the document? Translate them.

Train for the exam

1. Make a summary / account of the document (60 words / 3-5 minutes).

2. Express your personal opinion:
In what ways does the number of clients affect your Company?
Explain and illustrate your point of view (100 words).

3. Role play: work in pairs
You are going to take part in a conversation.
You work at Bombardier and meet with your trade union to let them know that you believe some mistakes have been made. You complain about the political situation and state your disagreement with the Government that does not favour manufacturing development.
Student A: you are an employee, the bread-winner and the mother / father of a 2-year-old baby.
You complain most of the time.
Student B: you are the trade union representative.

Go online

- Go on the following websites to find out more about Bombardier (its nationality, when it was founded, what industry it works in).
http://en.wikipedia.org
http://www.bombardier.com
- Get prepared to report to your group / class (a PowerPoint presentation is recommended).

PRACTICE • TEXT

1 | Companies

Train with an oral document

WARMING UP

- Do you go to Starbucks cafés? Why / Why not?
- Do you know other new-style cafés?
- Which changes have you noticed at Starbucks?

CD n° 1 Track n° 8

Starbucks: a company on the move

Lexical work

1. Find the odd word out.

a) fast food restaurants – fine restaurants – espresso bars
b) flavours – tastes – drinks
c) drinking slowly – sipping – spitting
d) comfortable environment – deep armchairs – broken chair
e) available – in stock – out of stock
f) commitment – involvement – disinterest

2. Work on figures: write in full and read aloud.

the year 1971, 1982, 2009 • 900 stores • from 1987 to 1992

Pronunciation work

CD n° 1 Track n° 9

1. Listen and observe.

Observe the letter "x". How do you pronounce it in the alphabet? How is it pronounced in the following words?
experience • luxury • expert • expanding

2. Listen and fill in the grid according to the words' pronunciation. Then pronounce them.

exceed • taxes • exploit • exercise • luxurious • exact • examine • exhaust

[ks]	[gz]

The third pronunciation of "x" is [z]: to xerox, xylophone, xenophobia...

Work on the title

1. Look at the title of the document.

2. For a company, what is meant by being "on the move"?

Check the facts

1. Listen to part 1.

a) When and where was Starbucks founded?
b) What did Howard Schultz import from Italy?
c) What is "specialty coffee"?

2. Listen to part 2.

a) What happened in 2009?
b) What did Starbucks decide to do in 2002?
c) What is said about the logo?
d) How can you pay for your *latte*?
e) Why has Starbucks been criticized?

Topic debrief

1. Choose the sentence which you think corresponds best to the main topic of the document.

a) Starbucks or how a company was born.
b) Starbucks has turned 40 and has had to revamp itself several times.
c) Since its birth in 1971, Starbucks has gone smoothly through ups and downs.

2. Rephrase the correct sentence in order to make a short introduction to the document.

Methods

1. Listen to the document and write down the linking words you've heard.

2. Write four key sentences about the document by using the linking words you have picked up.

Train for the exam

1. Use your notes to make an **oral presentation** about the document and record yourself (3-5 minutes).

2. Comment on this sentence from the text: "Coffee has been turned into a luxury product". Discuss and give examples (100 words / 3-5 minutes).

3. Role play: work in pairs

You are going to take part in a conversation between two people working in a small espresso bar.

Student A: you are an employee. You must find what could make your store a better place.

Student B: you are the manager. You want your coffee store to compete with Starbucks.

TIPS

You should use your notes in order to present a realistic conversation. Don't read them, look up.

You can:

- record the conversation (at the multimedia lab or with your own MP4 recorder; the recording should last between one and two minutes at most);
- videotape the scene and show it to the class;
- act out the scene in front of the class;
- listen to your classmates' recordings and write what you have understood in a short and structured paragraph.

Go online

- Go online and find out about Second Cup and Starbucks in the United Kingdom.
- Get prepared to report to your group / class.

PRACTICE • AUDIO • VIDEO

Train with a video

Rolls Royce reports most sales ever for 2011

→ http://www.youtube.com/watch?v=1FsOjBOaHml

9 January, 2012

Look at this video on the Internet about luxury goods sales

Check the facts	Methods
1. What is the main topic of this video?	• Which companies are mentioned?
2. Why are these companies profitable?	• Why are people attracted by Rolls Royce? • How much is a car? • Is the company British owned?
3. What are the essential qualities required by the companies?	• Who is the Rolls Royce's CEO? What is his nationality? • What are his values? • For him, where does growth come from?
4. Which other luxury companies benefit from the same trend?	• What are the newly rich countries? • Why do they buy British products?
5. **Issues ...** – Who is newly attracted by British luxury? – What are the consequences for the British companies?	• What happened on the site where Rolls Royce was born? • What has the British government decided to do?

WARMING UP

- Which global car companies do you know?
- Which Japanese firms do you know?

CD n° 1
Track n° 10

Toyota expects 31% profit slump

Toyota Motor said Friday that it expected its annual net profit to fall almost a third from the previous year, hurt by production disruptions after the earthquake and tsunami that struck Japan in March.

The company's prediction of a 31 percent decline in net profit to 280 billion yen, or $3.5 billion, for the year ending in March 2012 was gloomier than expected. Analysts had been anticipating a profit forecast of about 422 billion yen, according to a survey by Bloomberg. But Toyota's forecast also projected a strong recovery in the coming months as the automaker made progress in repairing its supply chain.

Even with a recovery, Toyota is still likely to lose its title as the world's biggest automaker by sales to General Motors and be passed by Volkswagen as well, giving up its crown after just three years. Toyota now expects to sell 7.24 million vehicles for the year through March 2012, down from 7.31 million vehicles in the previous year.

"We don't see it as necessary to be the largest automaker in the world," said Satoshi Ozawa, Toyota's executive vice president.

Toyota executives have tended to avoid talking about global market share, especially after the company's embarrassing succession of recalls in 2009, saying that customer trust and safety were more important. Also weighing on production at Toyota are electricity shortages in Japan, since the accident at the Fukushima Daiichi nuclear plant.

Japanese automakers, together with other manufacturers, are being asked to reduce their electricity use 15 percent this summer. Toyota officials have said they will do their best to cut electricity use, moving some shifts to the weekends to avoid peak times. The higher costs of producing cars in Japan has raised the question of how long Toyota can continue to base so much of its production in its home country.

Even compared with its peers, Toyota stands out in the number of cars it still manufactures in Japan, then ships overseas – a setup that has become a drag on its profitability. In 2010, Toyota made 43 percent of its cars in Japan, while Nissan made 28 percent and Honda 27 percent. Akio Toyoda, Toyota's president and a member of its founding family, has repeatedly said the company remains committed to keeping production and jobs inside Japan. But Friday, Mr. Ozawa hinted that Mr. Toyoda's thinking might be changing.

The New York Times, June 10th, 2011

Lexical work

1. Find the English equivalents in the text.

a) interruptions § 1
b) le tremblement de terre § 1
c) s'attendre à § 2
d) prévision § 2
e) un sondage § 2
f) une reprise § 2
g) les ventes § 3
h) sa couronne § 3

2. Find the French equivalents.

a) to tend to § 5
b) recalls § 5
c) trust § 5
d) electricity shortage § 5
e) shifts § 6
f) peak times § 6
g) to stand out § 7
h) a setup § 7

3. Work on figures: write in full and read aloud.

280bn yen • $ 3.5bn • 31% decline • 7.24m vehicles • 1/3

CD n° 1
Track n° 11

Pronunciation work

1. Listen and observe.

production • disruption • prediction • succession

For the words ending in "-tion" or "-sion", the stressed syllable is the previous syllable.

2. Listen and pronounce.

automaker • safety • electricity • setup • profitability

Work on the title

1. Identify the source of the document (title, date, nature).

2. Look at the headline. How can you explain why the Japanese car maker has lost so much profit?

Check the facts

1. Read § 1.
What can explain Toyota's fall in profits by almost a third?

2. Read § 2.
a) Did Toyota expect such a bad figure?
b) What is the good news?

3. Read § 3.
a) How many cars will Toyota sell up to March 2012?
b) Which title will it lose?

4. Read § 4, 5.
a) What is not necessary for the company?
b) What happened in 2009 that was embarrassing for Toyota?

5. Read § 6.
How do electricity shortages affect production?

6. Read § 7.
Why is Toyota more affected by the nuclear accident in Fukushima than other Japanese car-makers?

Grammar

→ p. 233

Le discours rapporté

• *"We don't see it as necessary to be the largest automaker in the world", said S.O.*
• *Toyota officials have said they will do their best to cut electricity use.*

Topic debrief

Read § 3, 4 and complete the following sentences.
a) In 2010 the world's biggest car-maker was ....
b) In 2011 the world's biggest car-maker will be ....
c) In 2011 Toyota will rank ... after ... and ....
d) From March 2011 to March 2012 Toyota will sell ..., fewer ... than ....
e) Ozawa thinks that Toyota ....

Methods

1. Find a key sentence in each paragraph and rephrase it.

2. Connect these sentences by using linking words.

Train for the exam

1. Make a **summary / account** of the document (60 words / 3-5 minutes).

2. Comment on the following sentence: "Natural catastrophes have an economic impact on companies". Explain and illustrate your point of view (100 words).

3. Role play: work in groups
You are going to create a questionnaire from the following sentence: "Customer trust and safety (are) more important than global market shares".
You have to divide your questionnaire in two parts / points of view:
– Did Japanese companies such as Mitsubishi, Fujitsu, Mazda, etc. suffer from the March 2011 tsunami and nuclear accident?
– How do the consumers look at Toyota after Fukushima? What do they expect in terms of comfort, safety, reliability? (Make your own research.)

Info
On March 11, 2011 Japan was struck by the most powerful earthquake ever known. The Tsunami which followed caused a number of nuclear accidents at 3 reactors in the Fukushima nuclear power plant.

The Unit 4, 3, 2, and 1 (R-L) reactor buildings of the troubled Fukushima No. 1 nuclear plant are seen through bus windows in Okuma, Fukushima Prefecture on Nov. 12, 2011.

Creating a company profile and giving a company visit to suppliers / customers

1 • Situation

You are the Sales Director of the company you have invented. You have a customer or supplier who has come to visit the company and you are going to show them around a tour of the offices, factory, warehouse, etc. Before the tour, you would like to give them a little overview of the company so you all meet in the conference room.

2 • Process

a) Look at the following documents (on the next page).
b) Fill in the table with the information given in one of the short texts above, then use your imagination and create your own company.
c) Get into groups.
Students A: you are the Sales Director of the company. *Students B:* you are a visitor to the company.
d) Now discuss and present your company during the meeting. Remember to speak in English only!
Students A: you start by welcoming your visitors. Introduce yourself then tell them about the company.
Students B: you introduce yourself. Don't forget to ask lots of questions about the company.

3 • Follow up

Prepare a written presentation of the company (using a presentation software program). Look at the Document A and Document B to find inspiration.

Go online

Look at various company profiles so that you can make up something realistic.

TIPS

- **Start by saying**

Students A:
Welcome to ...
Before we go round the factory, I would like to tell you about the history ... then we will visit the offices / factory ... and will all meet here again for refreshments / lunch / tea ...
For security reasons we keep a record of all visitors to the company so could you all please sign our visitors book, and then I shall hand out a visitors' badge with your name to each of you.
I'm afraid that certain parts of the R&D department are confidential, so we won't be able to visit them. / I'm afraid that you have to wear protective clothing to visit the factory, so before we leave, could each person put on some steel-capped shoes and glasses?
Please feel free to ask me any questions. / Have you got any questions?
Students B (to ask questions during the presentation:
Excuse me for interrupting but... / I'm sorry to interrupt but ... Could I just ask for more details about ... ? / I'm not quite clear what you meant about ... / Could you explain a bit more?

- **Remember to use...**

I'm afraid ... or *I'm sorry but* ... to introduce anything negative.

Doc • A

About Sage V

SAGE V Foods has been in business since 1992 and has been operating under the name Sage V Foods since 1998. The main plant has been in Freeport, Texas, but Sage is now relocating most of its production facilities into Arkansas.

Sage V Foods produces rice-based ingredients for the food industry. Most products, such as rice flour, crisp rice and instant rice, are sold to large food companies. Some of the frozen products are sold directly into retail or to restaurant chains. A trip to the grocery store would find Sage V Foods products on almost every aisle. You can find our "Rice Expressions" brand of frozen rice in the natural section of Kroger's in Little Rock.

In 2006, Sage built a new plant in Stuttgart, Arkansas. This plant produces rice flour and other dry rice-based ingredients. This plant is highly automated, and currently employs about 40 to 50 people. This plant has been expanded twice since 2006 and continues to grow.

We are currently building a plant in the port of Little Rock. We expect the plant to start operations in March / April of 2009. This plant will primarily cook and freeze rice. We expect to employ between 60 and 100 people at this location within the first year. Our plants normally operate on a continuous production schedule of either 5 or 7 days.

Doc • B

Tel2 Ltd. is an international, high-tech mobile phone company based in Newport, England. The company was founded by Will Ring in 1954 and has gone from strength to strength since then. The head office is still on the Isle of Wight, and there are now manufacturing and distribution subsidiaries throughout the world in Sydney, Suzhou, Phoenix and Palmas.

LCCS (Low-Cost Country Sourcing) means that we are able to provide our customers with cutting-edge solutions at highly competitive prices. Our new one-stop-shop strategy to provide a multitude of services tailored to customer needs is just part of our Customer Excellence policy.

The firm is divided into 4 main divisions, or BUs (Business Units): mobile phones, accessories, batteries and application software. Our target market is the 14-35 demographic.

The company's remarkable annual growth rate means that our turnover for 2010 reached the outstanding sum of £631,000,000.

Our 2,600 employees worldwide are engaged in the quest for continuous improvement and complete customer satisfaction.

	Sage V / Tel2 Ltd.	Your company
Name and location of company		
Founder and date		
Product / service offered		
Number of employees		
Annual turnover		
Key customers		
Main competitors		
Number of factories / subsidiaries / branches ...		
Number of (Strategic) Business Units ((S)BUs)		
Market share		
Investment in R&D		
Core values		

ROLE PLAY

1 | Companies

Background

A company is an economic and social structure which brings together human, material, immaterial (services) and financial means which are organised to provide goods or services to customers in a competitive (the market) or non-competitive (a monopoly) market. A company is a legal entity (→ SEE "STARTERS" PAGE 8)***, which depends on the legal and regulatory framework in force.***

1 How is a company organised?

When the company is founded, there is usually one unit (a factory for a production company). This is where the **headquarters** is based. The company can then expand by creating **subsidiaries**, either in the same country or abroad (often in low-cost countries like China to reduce production costs). The company can also **take over** another firm, or **merge** with another business. Certain parts of the production or service process can also be **outsourced** (or subcontracted) to other companies.
Companies are divided into BUs (Business Units / divisions), and then again into departments.

Types of companies:
- Small and medium sized companies (SMCs) / enterprises (SMEs).
- Single / sole proprietorship: one owner, unlimited liability.
- Partnership: 2-20 owners, unlimited liability.
- Private limited company (Ltd.): shareholders, not quoted on the stock exchange, limited liability.
- Public limited company (Plc.): shareholders, quoted on the stock exchange, limited liability.

2 Who are the people involved in a company?

The key resources of any company are all the **stakeholders** (all the people who have a role to play in a company). Firstly of course those who are directly involved in the everyday running of the business which includes all the members of the staff. Every one of them has their importance in the hierarchical organisation (→ FOR AN EXAMPLE OF AN ORGANISATION CHART, SEE "STARTERS" PAGE 9). Each **team** consists of several people of each level who often share an office.
Less directly involved is the Board of Directors, whose role is to protect the interests of the employees and the shareholders, and oversee the general running of the company.
In most cases, the capital is provided by the shareholders who invest a certain amount of money in shares in the company, and in return are paid annual dividends which depend on the **profit**.
Each year, an AGM (Annual (General) Meeting) brings together the Board of Directors and all the shareholders to elect the Board of Directors and inform the shareholders about company activity and **forecasts**.

3 What are the aims of a company?

The main objective of a company is the bottom line. A good **turnover** is possible when overheads, social contributions and taxes are kept to a minimum, which allows a decent profit.
This money is used to pay the dividends and also reinvested in R&D for innovative developments to the product and to management tools and systems.
Another target in company **growth** is sustainable development (→ SEE CHAPTER "ENVIRONMENT" PAGE 226) and respect for the local and global environment.
The key to a successful business is efficient management, a quality service or product, a good marketing mix (→ SEE CHAPTER "MARKETING" PAGE 62) and employee well-being.
Faulty products can destroy the reputation of the most well-known companies, and an ill-adapted marketing strategy (→ SEE CHAPTER "MARKETING" PAGE 62) means the product will just not sell well. The **competition** is hard and companies have to adapt to an ever-changing business landscape.
Turnaround can be brought about in several ways:
- Streamlining, to make the processes and procedures more efficient and involve less waste;
- Updating existing equipment and IT systems, and retraining staff;
- Implementing new business or marketing strategies.

Less popular are:
- Restructuring, which can lead to job losses;
- Relocating to a low-cost country to cut costs.

→ SEE CHAPTER "WORK" PAGE 122.

Questions

- Do you know the names of any big multinational companies?
- Do you know anything about how the company is run?
- Would you like to work for a big international company?

Focus

Wal-Mart, Carrefour: is the secret to growth consisting in getting smaller?

Up to now Wal-Mart was known for its football-field-sized Supercenters located far away from the dense urban markets. But with a two-year decline in U.S. comparable-store sales, Wal-Mart has decided to roll out smaller stores. Moreover, with the suburbs and rural towns saturated with Supercenters, the biggest grocer in the U.S. has had to find new markets. Carrefour is also moving to town centres. Are small stores the answer to growth? In the United States? And abroad?

Wal-Mart Stores Inc.

Figures

- The biggest retail store worldwide.
- Founded in 1962 in Bentonville, Arkansas, by Sam Welton.
- The third biggest employer, with 2.1 million employees worldwide, after the U.S. Department of Defense (3.2 million employees) and the Chinese Army (2.3 million employees). McDonald's is the fourth biggest employer, with 1.7 million employees.
- Each week, about 100 million customers, nearly one-third of the U.S. population, visit Wal-Mart's U.S. stores.
- The average size of Wal-Mart's Supercenters is about 185,000 square feet (roughly the size of a football field).
- Number of stores in the U.S.: 4,000 in Sept. 2010.
- Known for its low prices at all times.

A strategy on the move: getting smaller

Wal-Mart is shifting to smaller formats with:

- Neighborhood Marketplace is a store of 75,000 to 80,000 square feet. (There were almost 200 Neighborhood Markets in Sept. 2010.)
- Walmart Express is a store of about 15,000 to 25,000 square feet (or Marketside).
- Walmart on Campus: Walmart Express stores will open in both urban and rural areas.
- Since 2008, Wal-Mart has been testing smaller stores, called Marketside (15,000 square feet).

Reasons for moving to smaller outlets

- Wal-Mart is facing stiff competition in the U.S. from dollar chains and drug stores.
- Sales have been falling for at least a year.
- Wal-Mart generates more than half its revenue from grocery sales.
- Moving into vacant storefronts does not require any city planning department reviews.

Info

- Increased globalisation has led to the creation of many **Multinational Corporations and globalised charities** such as "Médecins du Monde" ("The French doctors' charity"), WWF ... However, the first MNC was the British East India Company, founded in 1600!
- A **start-up** is a fledgling company with high risk and growth potential. Many of them are Internet or "dot-com" companies.

Questions

- Explain: "One size doesn't fit all".
- Why do food retailers open urban stores?
- Is there an urban market and a rural / suburban market?
- Do the smaller-sized stores come with new features?
- Are the goods, the design, services the same as in the huge "box"?
- Will Walmart Express and Market be more upscale?

ACTIVE BUSINESS CULTURE

1 | Companies

Focus

Carrefour stores

Figures

- The French world challenger and the European leader in the retail industry and the second largest retail company worldwide.
- Headquartered in Levallois-Perret, France. Founded by Marcel Fournier and Louis Defforey in 1959.
- 1,395 hypermarkets at the end of 2009.
- 2,900 Carrefour Markets in 19 countries.
- 10,300 stores in France and abroad.
- It has 436,000 employees.

A strategy on the move: getting smaller

- Carrefour is shifting to smaller formats.
- It is undergoing a national rebranding.
- Carrefour is moving from the basic grocery items to fresh ingredients and choice with its smaller convenience stores.
- Some convenience stores could be located in emerging residential developments in the United Arab Emirates or Qatar, Oman and Kuwait.
- Carrefour will roll out Carrefour-branded grocery items.

Reasons for moving to smaller outlets

- Sales have been falling for at least a year.
- Moving into vacant storefronts does not require any city planning department reviews.
- Carrefour has been struggling in other markets around the world: Carrefour is pulling out of crisis-hit Russia.

Questions

- What are the reasons for building huge hypermarkets?
- Is the size of the stores related to the country the company is from?
- What does the size of the stores imply in terms of geographic locations?
- Does the size of the store impact on the consumer?

Express your point of view

You and your family go grocery shopping in one or many different shops. How did you make the decision? Has the size of a supermarket an impact on your shopping habits?

Perspectives

The two major players in the retail industry are not alone in targeting dense urban areas and moving to town centres. It seems that Tesco and Target are also adopting the same strategy. Target, an American grocer, is testing smaller stores in urban markets. It opened its first store in Manhattan in July 2010. But with Target, moving to town centres is not as new as it is for Wal-Mart or Carrefour. Target and Wal-Mart have hit a wall in suburban and rural areas and to keep growing both of them have had to change strategies.

However, unlike Carrefour, Wal-Mart has decided to infiltrate the dense urban markets in the United States, but has not changed its tack abroad. In China, Supercenters are still the craze. Carrefour's policy is somewhat different, as it has decided to adopt the same strategy in France as well as abroad.

To be in downtown areas as well as in suburban and rural areas will allow Carrefour, Wal-Mart, Tesco and Target to grab even more food and grocey sales market share. However, one should keep in mind that operating in dense urban environments is different: the assortment of goods must be chosen carefully.

@-Go online

- Carrefour and Wal-Mart have the same objective, to expand, but they proceed differently. Carrefour is selling Carrefour-branded grocery items whereas Wal-Mart is not. Carrefour has opened smaller stores in France as well as abroad, whereas Wal-Mart has not.
- Go online to find out what motivated these choices. • Are Carrefour and Wal-Mart targeting the same customers? Is Carrefour more upscale than Wal-Mart?
- Read more: http://www.time.com/time/business/article/0,8599,1605388,00.html#ixzz1hFzPQtPE

Test yourself

Try to use your memory – do not look at the vocabulary list!

1 MISSING LETTERS

Put in one or two vowels to complete the underlined word(s) in the sentence.

a) The company had to cl-s- d-wn recently because it was badly mismanaged and went b-nkr-pt.

b) An increase in demand in our c-r- m-rk-t has led the company to -xp-nd its product range.

c) We f-r-c-st remarkable gr-wth during the next quarter*.

d) We need to -mpl-m-nt our new quality p-l-cy as quickly as possible.

e) The m-rg-r between PPB and ATA has been highly successful, and we expect to increase our m-rk-t sh-r- by at least 10%.

f) We have managed to cut down our -v-rh--ds by --ts--rc-ng to a new low-cost s-ppl--r.

g) The workers are c-m-ng --t -n str-k- because we had to str--ml-n- production, so there will be job losses.

h) The sp-k-m-n for the w-rk-rs' c--nc-l has complained about the company's b-s-n-ss str-t-gy.

i) The Helpers' S-c--ty is a non-profit ch-r-ty that is s-bs-d-s-d by the state.

j) The m-n-g-m-nt will r-str-ct-r- the f-rm to s-v- money.

---

* Quarter: *trimestre*

3 MATCH THEM UP

Take the first half of a word from list A and match it with the second half in list B.

A:	B:
turn	cast
stake	holder
head	roll
chair	source
pay	man
fore	over
out	quarters

TIPS

In English we talk about the *management* and not the *direction*.

2 HEADLINES

Match the headline to the sentence.

1. modernisation will lead to greater profits
2. legal and equitable trading – the group's new catchword
3. shaky stock exchange
4. streamlining to increase net income
5. beware of breakthroughs in nanometric-sized devices
6. e-business ethics
7. upsurge on its way for smaller companies
8. investment in new premises

a) Shareholders have expressed their worries about the current extremely volatile share prices.
b) A new code of business is seeing the light of day due to the ever-increasing presence of global Internet companies.
c) PMP Inc. is to build a new plant, warehouse and after-sales service near the company headquarters to reduce labour costs and improve customer service efficiency.
d) As part of the quest to increase profitability, logistics tools are to be upgraded and the IT system will be updated.
e) A remarkable boom is forecast for SMEs in the tertiary sector as from the second quarter of the year.
f) The closure of certain subsidiaries and the merger of several departments will have a positive impact on the company's turnover.
g) The group is planning to set up a fair trade business unit, with goods ranging from foodstuffs to clothing.
h) Competitors in the field should be wary of new developments in the nanotechnology sector and focus on domain expertise and cutting-edge R&D output.

1 | Companies

Words

"Every company has two organisational structures. The formal one is written on the charts; the other is the everyday relationship of the men and women in the organisation." (Harold S. Geneen)

Acquire (to): faire l'acquisition de
After-sales service: SAV
Assembly line: chaîne de montage
Bankrupt (to go): faire faillite
Based (to be): qui se trouve à
Board of Directors: conseil d'administration
Bottom line: dernière ligne du bilan / résultat
Business: affaire, entreprise
Business strategy: stratégie des affaires
Business unit: unité commerciale
Branch: agence / succursale
Capital: capitale
CEO (Chief Executive Officer): PDG
Chairman: président
Charity: organisation caritative
Close down (to): fermer
Code of business: déontologie des entreprises
Company / corporation / firm: entreprise
Compete (to) / competition: concurrencer / concurrence
Competitor: concurrent
Core market: marché principal
Corporate: d'entreprise
Customer service: service client
Department: service, département
Dividends: dividendes
Domain expertise: expertise dans un domaine
E-business: affaires en ligne
Executive: cadre
Expand (to): se développer, s'étendre, se diversifier
Factory / plant: usine
Fair trade: commerce équitable
Field: domaine
Focus (to): se concentrer sur
Follow up: suivi clients
Forecast (to) / forecast: prévoir / prévision
Found (to): fonder
Funds: fonds
Global: mondial
Growth: croissance
Headquarters / head office: siège social
Human resources: ressources humaines
Implement (to): mettre en œuvre
Invest (to): investir
Investment: investissement
IT (information technology): informatique (computer technology)
Labour costs: coûts de main d'œuvre
Low-cost country: pays à faible coût
Management: direction, gestion
Market share: part du marché
Merge (to) / merger: fusionner / fusion
Management tools: outils de gestion
Net income: revenu net
NGO (non-governmental organisation): ONG
Office: bureau
Operate (to): (faire) fonctionner
Operating income: compte d'exploitation
Organisation chart: organigramme
Outsource (to): externaliser
Overheads: frais généraux
Payroll: masse salariale
Policy (company): politique (de l'entreprise)
Premises: locaux
Primary sector: secteur primaire
Procurement department: service dépassement des achats
Profits: bénéfices
Profitability: rentabilité
Profitable: rentable
Public / private sector: secteur public / privé
Purchasing department: service des achats
Quoted (to be): être coté (bourse)
R&D (research and development): recherche & développement
Range from ... to ...: aller de ... à...
Restructure (to): restructurer
Run (to): diriger
Sales: ventes
Save (to): economiser
Secondary sector: secteur secondaire
Sell (to): vendre
Set up a business (to): monter une affaire
Share: action
Shareholder: actionnaire
SME (small & medium-sized enterprises): PME
Spokesman / person: porte-parole
Stock exchange: bourse
Stocks: actions, titres
Stakeholder: partie prenante
Streamline (to): rationaliser, dégraisser
Strike (to be on): être en grève
Subsidiary: filiale
Subsidise (to): subventionner
Supplier: fournisseur
Takeover: rachat
Team: équipe
Tertiary sector: secteur tertiaire
Tool: outil
(Trade) Union: syndicat
Turnover: chiffre d'affaires
Update (to): mettre à jour
Warehouse: entrepôt
Work council: comité d'entreprise
Workforce: main d'œuvre

2

Consumers

Consumers and goods are changing

Questions

Are shopping habits changing?
Why is e-commerce so successful?

WORD BOX

consume (to) • consumer • addict • consumer survey • customer • demanding • mass consumption • spend (to) • brick and mortar • click and mortar

2 | Consumers

1 • Look and discuss

a) Read the definition and look at the pictures.

> **What is a consumer profile?**
>
> A consumer profile includes significant demographic and psychographic* details about the user of a particular product. The data includes information such as the user's age category, marital status, income level, education, occupation, sex, area of residence and purchase behavior patterns. Consumer profiles are key information for marketing and advertising campaigns.
>
> ---
> * Psychographics = the use of demographics to study and measure attitudes, values, lifestyles and opinions.

b) Give a name to the different demographic profiles in the photos and think of other profiles.

c) Which do you think is currently the biggest consumer profile – and why? Discuss in class.

2 • Read and understand

a) Read the following text and answer the following question: Why are disposable goods the environmentalists' nightmare?

> **The different types of goods**
>
> **FMCGs:** (fast-moving consumer goods) goods which do not remain long on supermarket shelves; they are the goods bought by consumers on a regular basis (that is why they are "fast-moving").
> **Disposable goods:** goods which are thrown away after use. They concern an increasing amount of products and are environmentalists' nightmares.
> **Durable goods:** goods bought to last.
> **A big ticket item:** a product which is expensive, whose price is expressed at least with a three-digit number (hence the "big ticket" metaphor).
> **A small ticket item:** a product with a small price.

b) Here is a list of goods. Choose the right product category and the right price category. Beware: some products can belong to more than one category.

vegetables • sneakers • sugar • shampoo • nappies / diapers • cars • smartphones • razors • cameras • TV screens • cereals • dishwashers

c) Read the following text and answer the questions.

A guide to understanding today's consumer's expectations

Today's consumer:
- wants access to the product at all times, and as fast as possible;
- wants to see all the feedback, negative and positive, about the product;
- expects a quick customer response;
- expects companies to show some ethics;
- wants to be treated like an informed consumer;
- expects the product to be updated on a regular basis;
- expects to get a full refund if not satisfied with the product.

1. Do you recognise yourself in these expectations?
2. Are there any other elements that you would add?
3. Make your own list with your expectations as a consumer.

3 • Look and write

Use the clues to write five sentences describing the graph showing how the average consumer spends his money.

1. *graph shows • complete range • consumer's expenditures • average American consumer unit*
2. *most • annual budget • spent on housing • food bills • transportation*
3. *see • pie chart • entertainment • one of • smallest spending sectors*
4. *graph reveals • people put • money • information • used • create consumer profiles*
5. *purpose • graph • encourage people • spend less money*

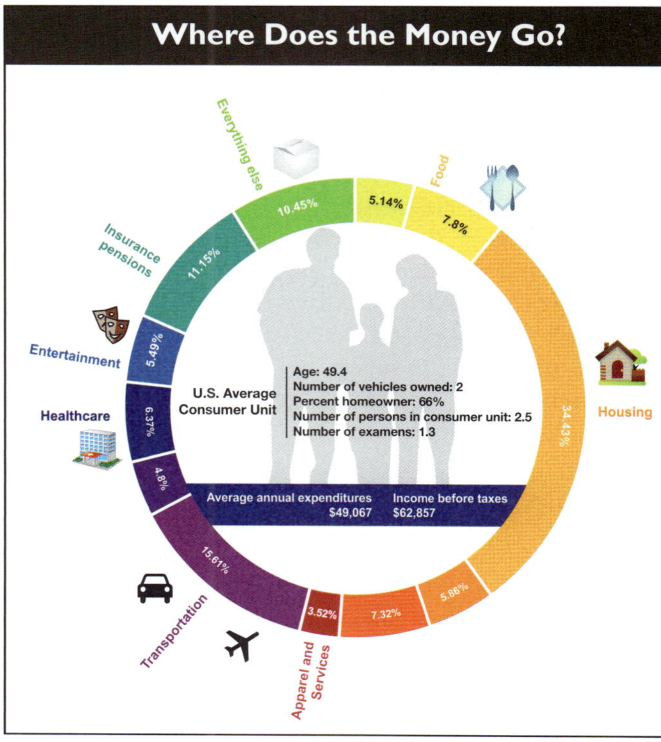

How the average Americans spend their money.

4 • Listen and understand

CD n° 1 Track n° 12

a) What kind of company is the consumer complaining about?
b) What is marked on the packaging?
c) Do you ever complain in a shop or restaurant? What do you complain about?

2 | Consumers

WARMING UP

- Are you a shopaholic?
- Which shops are your favourite ones?
- When do you get the feeling that you are saving money while shopping?

CD n° 1 Track n° 13

Basket cases

Bob McDonald, the boss of Procter & Gamble (P&G), promised that P&G was still on track to have 5 billion customers by 2015. But it is a struggle, as many of the economies in which P&G operates are still recovering from recession.

But there is something else happening, too. Basic consumer goods were long assumed to be more or less recession-proof. Shoppers may not be able to afford Dior dresses or Cartier watches, went the argument, but they still need loo paper and detergent. Yet people are finding ways to save money even on daily necessities.

They are shopping less and with more purpose. Some people deliberately pick up a basket rather than collect a trolley in supermarkets, to prevent themselves from buying too much. Some buy smaller packets, which are cheaper, or huge ones, which are better value. Many make do without air fresheners, hair conditioner and other fripperies once deemed essential. Many scour the Internet for special deals.

Many have traded down name-brand to store-brand products. Alarmingly for, say, Kellogg's or Heinz, lots have discovered that Tesco's cornflakes and WalMart's baked beans taste no worse. A survey of 2,500 American households by Consumer Edge Research found that supermarkets' own labels have become increasingly popular, especially for staples such as milk, peanut butter, bottled water and cooking oil. Store-brand goods are especially popular in Spain, the Netherlands and Germany.

Consumers are also trading down from one name-brand to another: for example, from Lindt chocolates to Cadbury's. Some 18% of packaged-goods buyers switched from a premium brand to a cheaper one during the recession, according to McKinsey, another consultancy.

Terrified consumer-goods firms have cut costs and slashed prices. P&G launched a less expensive "basic" version of its Tide brand of washing powder, but then withdrew it because it was too popular. Many firms are pushing "three for the price of two" deals and the like. Some see opportunities amid the gloom. As people eat out less, Kraft Foods, an American firm, sells more macaroni and cheese and other ready-made meals. As hedonists cut back on spas and beauty salons, P&G sells more beauty products to be applied at home.

Companies with a strong presence in emerging countries have the rosiest prospects. Shoppers in China and Brazil are trading up to foreign brands. But what if this recession teaches consumers that supermarket brands are just as good?

The Economist, October 16th, 2010

Lexical work

1. Find the English equivalents in the text.

a) être sur la bonne voie **§ 1**
b) insensible / imperméable à la récession **§ 2**
c) article de première nécessité **§ 2**
d) considérer ; parcourir / fouiller **§ 3**
e) casser les prix **§ 6**

2. Find the French equivalents.

a) loo paper **§ 2**
b) air freshener **§ 3**
c) fripperies **§ 3**
d) cooking oil **§ 4**

Pronunciation work

CD n° 1 Track n° 14

1. Listen and observe. Which syllable is stressed in …?

a) economies
b) recovering
c) recession
d) detergent
e) supermarkets

2. Work on figures: write in full and read aloud.

5 billion customers • a survey of 2,500 American households • some 18% of packaged-goods buyers

Work on the title

1. Identify the source of the document (title, date, nature).

2. In the 3rd paragraph, look for a repetition of the words which form the headline then explain the headline.

Check the facts

1. Read § 1.
What does P&G's boss expect to have by 2015?

2. Read § 2.
a) What are the daily necessities referred to?
b) When there is a recession, what do customers usually stop buying?

3. Read § 3, 4, 5.
Find out how consumers proceed to buy less (4 elements).

4. Read § 6.
a) How do companies react to these new consuming patterns?
b) Which consumers are mentioned and why?

5. Read § 7.
Who is not affected?

Grammar → p. 233

Les noms et les adjectifs composés

- *... were long assumed to be more or less recession-proof.*
- *Many have traded down name-brand to store-brand products.*
- *... and other ready-made meals.*

Topic debrief

Write an introduction to the document by using the following words (40 words).
economic crisis • economic slowdown / downturn • to face problems • to adapt oneself to • affordable • less often • a shopping list • to change • to behave • consumers • differently

Methods

1. Which paragraph best sums up the new shoppers' strategies in the current economic crisis?

2. List these strategies.

Train for the exam

1. Make a **summary / account** of the document by using the word bank (60 words / 3-5 minutes).
to make do without: faire sans • *to deem:* considérer • to scour: fouiller • *to trade up to foreign brands:* remplacer par des marques étrangères plus chères • *to trade down name-brand to store-brand goods:* remplacer par des marques de magasins moins cher

2. Comment: find an answer to the following questions. Discuss and give examples (100 words / 3-5 minutes).
How can companies learn from the way consumers behave? What is their goal?

3. Role play: work in groups

You want to find out how shoppers shop. You ask students in your class to tell you why and how they have chosen the articles in their trolley.

a) Make a questionnaire to find out about the shopping practices or consuming habits of the students. Examples: When do you go shopping? How often? Do you go shopping for a special item? Where do you go? Do you take advantage of promotions, special offers? Do you pay attention to discounts? Are you a loyal consumer? Have you got a store card? Do you decide how much you want to spend? Do you buy fewer articles if they are more expensive? Do you buy online? Do you compare prices before buying? Do you go to discount shops?

b) Ask four people in the class then give an oral report about your findings.

TIPS

You should use your notes in order to present a realistic conversation. Don't read them, look up.
You can:
- do the same with shoppers in your supermarket;
- record the conversation (the recording should last between one and two minutes at most);
- videotape the scene and show it to the class;
- act out the scene in front of the class;
- listen to your classmates' recordings and write what you have understood in a short and structured paragraph.

Train with an oral document

WARMING UP

► When did you last buy on the Internet? What are the advantages of buying online?

CD n° 1 Track n° 15

The fastest growing Group-online

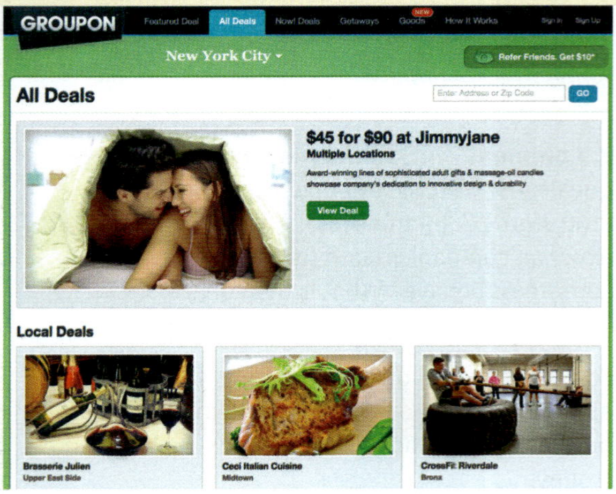

Lexical work

1. Underline the odd word out.

a) decreasing – rising – growing
b) curse – problem – godsend
c) clothes shops – grocery – bakery
d) growth – boom – recession

2. Find the right English equivalents.

a) manpower ... (workforce / labour cost)
b) labelled ... (called / mentioned)
c) eager to ... (keen on / depressed)
d) rush ... (hurry / slow down)

3. Work on figures: write in full.

83m • 2010 • $15 billion • 75% discount

Pronunciation work

CD n° 1 Track n° 16

1. Listen and observe.

a) Shops have been badly hit by the economic downturn. **b)** It has been very successful. **c)** It will have to move fast.
The auxiliary is stressed when it conveys information. Practice repeating these sentences.

2. Key words of "Consumers"

discount • company • services • promote
a) Listen and observe.
b) Practice repeating these words aloud – don't forget to stress the right syllable.

3. Listen to these regular verbs. They have an [-ed] ending in English and are pronounced [d] or [t] or [ɪd]. Place the following words in the right box.

invited • labelled • helped • created

[d]	[t]	[ɪd]

Work on the title

1. Look at the title of the document.

2. There is a pun (play on words) with a famous company. Find which.

Check the facts

1. Listen to part 1.
a) Explain the name Groupon.
b) What does the company do?
c) What do suscribers do?
d) What is required if you want to benefit from a deal?
e) How do you explain Groupon's success?
f) Groupon's history: when was it founded? Who is the chief executive?
g) Figures: what was its revenue in 2010?
h) Is it successful everywhere?

2. Listen to part 2.
a) When did Google make an offer?
b) How much did Google offer?
c) What happened to it?
d) Why is Groupon so expensive?
e) How much is it?
f) Who are Groupon's competitors?
g) What is compared with Groupon?
h) What happened in March 2011?
i) What is Groupon fatigue? What is Groupon anxiety?

Topic debrief

Write down three sentences to introduce the document by using the following words.
online company • special offers • to subscribe • competitors • online retailing • rivals • to be in the lead • emerging countries • economic recession • a takeover • special deals

Methods

Use the information about the companies mentioned in the document to fill in the chart / table.

Company	Targets	Achievement / Success

Train for the exam

1. Use your notes to make an **oral presentation** about the document and record yourself (3-5 minutes).

2. Comment: find an answer to the following question. Discuss and give examples (3-5 minutes / 100 words).
What could be the limits of daily offers to the consumer?

3. Role play: work in pairs
You are going to take part in a conversation.
Student A: you are a Groupon subscriber, and you are convinced that it is absolutely fantastic because you pay less money and discover places you would never have visited. You try to convince your partner that it is a good way to have the best deals.
Student B: you don't know anything about Groupon.

• You should use your notes in order to present a realistic conversation. Don't read them, look up.
You can:
– record the conversation (the recording should last between one and two minutes at most);
– videotape the scene and show it to the class;
– act out the scene in front of the class;
– listen to your classmates' recordings and write what you have understood in a short and structured paragraph.

TIPS

• How to read dates and figures

1. Observe and remember

a) Dates
In March 2011= in March twenty eleven / in March two thousand and eleven
On 12 march 2011 = on the 12th of March twenty twelve
On March 12 2012 = on March the twelfth two thousand and twelve

b) Money
$ 15 billion/bn = 15/fifteen billion ø dollars
$ 175 m = one hundred and seventy-five million ø dollars
£ 50.35 = fifty thirty-five pounds

c) Percentage
Less than 9% = less than nine percent
A 75% discount = a seventy-five percent discount
A 8.6% unemployment rate= an eight point six percent unemployment rate (8,6%)

2. Practise
a) Say it aloud: *I was born on 30 July 1998. There was a 3.5% price increase.*
b) Write in full: *3 milliards d'euros.*

• Graphs
Histogram (histogramme), *run chart* (graphique), *pie chart* (camembert), *bar chart* (histogramme), *scatter plot* (diagramme / nuage de points)...

Go online

• Find out more about Groupon: where is it located? Is it still offering the same deals?
• Get prepared to report to your group / class (a PowerPoint presentation is recommended).

WARMING UP

- Say what you understand by "purchasing power" and "standard of living".
- Are you personally attracted by slogans such as "buy one get one free"?

CD n° 1 Track n° 17

The incredible shrinking shopping baskets

A host of familiar grocery products are getting smaller while their price stays the same. Why?

Tough times might be weighing heavily on UK shoppers, but one burden, at least, is becoming lighter: their shopping trolleys. With the cost of getting products onto the shelves rising higher and higher, some suppliers are reducing the size of their goods while maintaining the same retail price.

Imperial Leather soap is the latest item to shrink. Manufacturer PZ Cussons said it was reducing the size of its bars from 125 g to 100 g, citing a steep rise in the cost of ingredients like palm oil, to avoid a rise in the amount charged to customers. In February, Cadbury's Dairy Milk bars went down from 140 g to 120 g – the equivalent of two chunks – while the recommended retail price remained unchanged. At the same time, Toblerone bars became one triangle shorter to ensure the Poundland chain could carry on selling them for £1, blaming "increases in cost bases".

To producers, it is a rational strategy. To consumer advocates, it has all the hallmarks of a rip-off[1]. But what both sides could agree on is that the trend offers an insight into the psychology of shopping.

At its heart lies the question of why it makes better business sense to reduce the size of products rather than simply charge more at the till. Certainly, there is little doubt that manufacturers have had their margins squeezed by rising commodity prices[2]. Cadbury said it cut the size of Dairy Milk to ensure it was still offering "a very affordable treat" even though the cost of cocoa beans has more than doubled in five years. "The price point has become more important than the size of the product," he added. "Consumers only have a certain amount of money in their pockets and are paying more for fuel and other items, so I'm sure they would rather have this than the price going up."

However, not everyone agrees that the strategy is reasonable. Shopping baskets are getting lighter – but so are our wallets. A 2010 report by the BBC's *Watchdog* programme[3] suggested that some firms had been less forthcoming about size reductions, keeping their size dimensions and packaging unchanged. Martyn Hocking, editor of the consumer magazine *Which?*, argues that the tactic is more about confusing the shopper than providing what they want. "We think this an underhand way of raising prices," he says. But regardless, those lighter shopping baskets will mean a heavier burden on our purses and wallets.

BBC NEWS Magazine, 06/06/2011

1. *a rip-off*: c'est du vol 2. *commodity prices*: prix des produits de base / matières premières 3. *Watchdog programme*: comité / programme de surveillance

Lexical work

1. Find the English equivalents in the text.

a) un poids / un fardeau § 2
b) le même prix au détail § 2
c) une forte augmentation § 3
d) prix conseillés § 3
e) les associations de consommateurs § 4
f) une façon sournoise / détournée § 6

2. Find the French equivalents.

a) tough times § 2 **b)** a chunk § 3 **c)** wallets § 6

Pronunciation work

CD n° 1 Track n° 18

1. Listen to the words and place them according to their pronunciation [ɪ] or [aɪ].

rip-off • size • price • rise • little • item • milk • triangle • still • editor

2. Listen to these words that you may find difficult. Watch out! One consonant is not pronounced.

tough • palm • psychology • could • doubt

Info

The BBC's *Watchdog* programme wants to raise consumer awareness. The title of the text copies the title of the film *The Incredible Shrinking Man* (1957).

Work on the title

1. Identify the source of the document (title, date, nature).

2. Does the headline remind you of a movie?

3. Two sounds are repeated in the headline. Which effect is produced?

Check the facts

1. Read § 1, 2, 3.
a) What is happening to some grocery products?
b) List the products that have shrunk: 3 elements.

2. Read § 3, 4.
a) What are the reasons for reducing the size of some grocery products?
b) What are the two points of view?

3. Read § 5.
What are the two possibilities a producer has? Illustrate your point of view with Cadbury's strategy.

4. Read § 6.
Write down what the BBC's *Watchdog* programme suggested.

Grammar

→ p. 233

Les comparatifs

• *The price point has become more important than the size of the product.*

Topic debrief

1. Focus on § 2 and complete the following sentences with your own words.
In the UK, ... are buying ... grocery products for the ... price. In other words, they spend as ... money as in the past except that the product is not as ... as before.

2. Rephrase the paragraph in order to make a short introduction to the document.

Methods

Word bank

packaging • identical • to buy • the same thing • to get less • price increases • noticeable • to closely inspect weights and measurements • not to compare everything • price of raw materials • to be on the rise • manufacturers • honest • suppliers • to be up-front (frank) *• to sneak smaller products • without saying*

1. Focus on § 3 and § 5. Complete the two following sentences which sum up the two sick's positions by using the word bank.
As far as suppliers are concerned, what is important is ...
However, consumers would rather have ...

2. Use the word bank in order to make a list of arguments informing consumers about the manufacturers' strategies.

Train for the exam

1. Make a **summary / account of the document** (60 words / 3-5 minutes).

2. **Write** a letter of complaint (100-150 words).
You are a consumer advocate at a consumer magazine and strongly believe that consumers are being cheated. Make a list of arguments to inform consumers and give the reasons provided by manufacturers.

3. **Role play: work in pairs**

You are going to take part in a conversation.
Student A: you are a British consumer and a keen chocolate addict. Your favourite bar is the Toblerone bar. You want to meet the Toblerone Marketing Manager (in the UK) to tell him that you are not pleased with the smaller size of your favourite chocolate bar.
Student B: you are the Toblerone Marketing Manager (in the UK).

Go online

• Cadbury is mentioned in the text. Find out about this company: it used to be a famous British chocolate maker and has been taken over recently. Find out which company bought it, if the products are the same and if they are more expensive and where they are made.
• Get prepared to report to your group / class (a PowerPoint presentation is recommended).

Train with an oral document

WARMING UP

- Why do people shop online?
- What do they buy?

CD n° 1
Track n° 19

Online shopping is booming

Lexical work

1. Underline the odd word out.

a) coupons • rewards • losses
b) parenting • family • accessories
c) worries • problems • insurance
d fitness • sports • mobile phones

2. Find the right English equivalent.

a) from scratch (from nothing / from experience)
b) to catch up with (try to equal a competitor / lag behind)
c) quoting (reporting / forgetting)
d) exceeded (did more / did less)

3. Work on figures: write in full.

£71 • £12.6m • £10.9m • 62% • 2002 (the year) • 600,000 customers

Pronunciation work

CD n° 1
Track n° 20

1. Listen and observe.

topics • statistics • strategic
The stress is on the last but one syllable for the words with an -ic ending, except for *Catholic* and *heretic*.

2. Key words of "Consumers"
online • shopping • retailer • customer • e-commerce • to launch
a) Listen and focus on intonations: when asking a question, the intonation rises, but it falls at the end of an assertion.
b) Practise repeating these words aloud.

Work on the title

1. Look at the title of the document.

2. Anticipate the contents. What is a boom? Think of the Baby Boom.

Check the facts

1. Listen to part 1.
a) Which country is famous for buying online?
b) How much does the average Briton spend online?
c) Why do Britons go online?
d) How much was spent in May 2011?
e) What do they spend their money on? Find out four types of products: health, new technologies, food, cars, insurance ...
f) When are British shoppers more likely to buy?

2. Listen to part 2.
a) What is Morrisons?
b) How much has Morrisons invested in Internet business?
c) Which companies did Morrisons invest in?
d) What are the reasons for investing in an online grocer?
e) What about prices at UK supermarkets?
f) Which event boosted sales in the first half of 2011?

Topic debrief

Write an introduction to the document by using the following words (40 words).
clothes • perfume • food • bargains • cars • auto parts • insurance • e-commerce • the royal wedding • inflation • a slowdown • to provide online services • a retailer

Methods

1. Take the example of Morrisons, its non-existent online shopping operations and its investment in a New York online grocer. Write a presentation of this company.

2. Write key phrases about the document.

Train for the exam

1. Use your notes and key phrases to make an **oral presentation** about the document and record yourself (3-5 minutes).

2. Comment: find an answer to the following question. Discuss and give examples (100 words / 3-5 minutes).

Is online shopping a complement to High Street shopping or a rival?

Go online

- Go online to find out about Morrisons and its 3 major competitors. You should know a few facts: when Morrisons was founded, where its supermarkets are located, how many customers it has, etc.
- Get prepared to report to your group / class (a PowerPoint presentation is recommended).

3. Role play: work in pairs

You are going to take part in a conversation.
You have shopped online and have received a book you never ordered. Prepare a telephone conversation.

Student A: you ask for the right department and the right person. Explain the problem (title of the book). Stay polite.

Student B: you answer the phone call but have another customer holding the line. It is late in the afternoon and you have had a very busy day. Take notes. React to the problem. Stay polite.

PRACTICE • AUDIO • VIDEO

Train with a video

American Girl doll store sells innocence and mothers are buying

→ http://www.youtube.com/watch?v=feS_3m-gFw0

26 December, 2011

Look at this video on the Internet about a very young consumer

Check the facts	Methods
1. What is the main subject of this video?	• Look at the girl and her doll. • What are their names? • What is striking?
2. Who is the "consumer" in this video?	• When did this girl get her first American Girl doll? • What does the girl want?
3. Where is she doing her shopping? What for?	• What can you say about the doll's hairstyle?
4. What is the story of American Girl doll?	• Why is it significant to show a doll designed during the American economic Depression? • Why are consumers given the opportunity to buy books with the dolls?
5. Issues ... – Which type of consumer is shown in this video? – How do they justify their dolls purchase? – What is the social impact of such purchases?	• How much do the dolls cost? • How many dolls does the girl have? • Are the dolls role models? • How does the little girl picture herself in the future?

2 | Consumers

WARMING UP

- Do you buy plastic bags to carry your groceries?
- Do you prefer organic food to "regular" food?
- Do you read the labels before buying?

CD n° 1 Track n° 21

Shoppers' green fatigue hits refill revolution

Green fatigue among shoppers has set back Britain's long-awaited refillable bottle revolution, with the latest attempts to persuade supermarket customers to reuse containers ending in failure.

Twelve years after one supermarket chain first began testing ways to encourage shoppers to refill detergent bottles rather than buy new ones, the group is no nearer to launching a national scheme across its stores. Asda admitted this weekend that sales of the two own-brand fabric conditioners used in the trial barely hit half of its projections with the exception of the first two weeks the machines were installed.

Environmentalists had hoped other retailers would embark on similar schemes but that now looks unlikely. Sainsbury's has already admitted it does not see much merit in store-based refill systems. The Body Shop used to offer a shampoo refill service, but stopped in 2002 because only 1 percent of its customers used it.

On the supplier front, Dairy Crest has cut down on its packaging by selling some of its milk in pouches; Sainsbury's and Waitrose sell its Jugit milk jug. And Kenco, which is owned by Kraft, has sold coffee refills since 2009.

A survey by the market research group Mintel found that only 33 percent of consumers would be prepared to pay more for environmentally friendly products in 2009, compared with 39 percent in 2005.

So far, the biggest factors deterring customers from refills are inconvenience, mess and cost. But some people are happy to use refills if they like the product. Refills are a really valuable area and should not be dismissed too early.

A spokesman for the British Retail Consortium said Asda's experience "goes to show the challenge we have in reducing packaging". But he added: "This may not have been as successful as people may have liked, but that doesn't mean the journey is not continuing." All the major retailers have pledged to cut the carbon impact of packaging by 10 percent and packaging waste in the supply chain by 5 percent by next year, in line with a Government-based campaign.

Independent.co.uk, Sunday, 30 January 2011

Lexical work

1. Find the French equivalents in the text.

a) to set back § 1
b) the latest attempts § 1
c) failure § 1
d) a scheme § 2
e) fabric conditioners § 2
f) the trial § 2

2. Find the English equivalents in the text.

a) improbable § 3
b) un système de remplissage § 3
c) diminuer / réduire § 4
d) dissuader / décourager § 6
e) pagaille / saleté § 6
f) un porte-parole § 7

Pronunciation work

CD n° 1 Track n° 22

1. Listen to these words that you may find difficult and repeat with the right stress.

scheme • launching • pouches

2. Listen and underline the stressed syllable.

fatigue • attempt • machine • embark • survey • prepare • campaign • impact

Work on the title

1. Identify the source of the document (title, date, nature).

2. Look at the following word groups: "a green revolution", "a green activist". What are the positive aspects conveyed?

3. With "green fatigue", the headline seems to be contradictory. Explain why.

Check the facts

1. Read § 1.
What do customers not want to do?

2. Read § 2.
a) What did the supermarket Asda introduce twelve years ago?
b) Does Asda sell its two own-brand fabric conditioners?

3. Read § 3.
What will Sainsbury's not do? What did The Body Shop do?

4. Read § 4.
What did suppliers do to be more eco-friendly?

5. Read § 5.
Compare the two figures.

6. Read § 6.
List the three reasons for not wanting to use refills.

7. Read § 7.
What will retailers do to reduce the carbon footprint?

Grammar

→ p. 234

Le gérondif (la forme en -ing)

- *... with the latest attemps (to persuade supermarket customers to reuse containers) ending in failure.*
- *... the group is no nearer to launching a national scheme...*
- *..., Dairy Crest has cut down on its packaging by selling some...*

Topic debrief

1. Choose the sentence which you think corresponds best to the main topic of the document.
a) British shoppers no longer want to spend their money on environmentally friendly products.
b) British shoppers are fed up with companies not offering eco-friendly products.
c) British shoppers are not willing to support the environment if it means using messy refills.

2. Write an introduction to the document by using the following words (40 words).
the document • to be entitled • to be published • to deal with • to be tired of • to reuse / recycle bottles / containers • to like • supermarkets • Britain

Methods

1. Find a key sentence in each paragraph and rephrase it.

2. Connect these sentences by using linking words (first, then, however).

Train for the exam

1. Make an **account / summary** of the document (60 words/3-5 minutes).

2. Comment: find an answer to the following question. Discuss and give examples (100 words / 3-5 minutes).
Responsible consumption: whose responsibility is it, the manufacturers' or the consumers'?

3. Role play: work in groups
You are going to take part in an interview between three people.
Student A: you are Asda's head of corporate sustainability and want to find out if your own-brand fabric conditioners used in five stores across the UK has been successful. You decide to ask two shoppers (male / female, young / elderly) what they think of your revolutionary refill scheme.
Student B: you will be asked questions about the refill service. You are in favour of the scheme.
Student C: you will be asked questions about the refill service. You are against the scheme.

Go online

- Choose one company mentioned in the text and find out: its activity, number of employees, type of retailer (department store, supermarket, etc.), its nationality, headquarters / location, problems it might have encountered, etc.
- Get prepared to report to your group / class (a PowerPoint presentation is recommended).

Consumer feedback survey

1 • Situation

You work at Safelockscams (Document A). You have received a letter of complaint from a consumer support group.

2 • Process

a) Read the letter of complaint (Document B).
b) Get into groups of four students. You decide to investigate before taking any action. Together you write up a consumer survey (or use the ideas from Document C) to find out what certain consumer groups think of this product and whether it should be withdrawn from the market.
c) Once your survey is complete, synthesise the results in your group.
d) Now discuss with another group and try your survey out on them. Remember to speak in English only! Decide whether the product is to be withdrawn or whether you are going to write a letter to answer the complaint.

3 • Follow up

You work for Safelockscams Ltd.
Depending on the results of your survey:
– either write a letter to the public, informing them that the product is to be withdrawn from the market and any products which have already been sold to be recalled;
– or write a letter to Consup-G explaining that you are not going to withdraw the product for certain reasons, with an apology to Mrs. Whine.

Go online

Look on the Internet to find more examples of letters of complaint and responses to the letters.

TIPS

Start by saying
Excuse me. Could you spare me a minute to answer the questionnaire?
Excuse me. Would you mind if I asked you a few questions?

Remember...
Excuse me is used when you interrupt someone. *Sorry* is used to apologise (for example if you tread on someone's toe). *I'm sorry but* ... or *I'm afraid that* ... is used to begin a sentence which will be negative (for example, *I'm sorry to be late but* ..., or *I'm afraid that I cannot come to the meeting* ...).

Doc • A

NEW

NEW, SAFE, EASY-TO-USE PACKAGING PROTECTION

Tried and tested by consumer groups of all ages from elderly to toddlers, our new **Safelock system®** will prevent accidental consumption of medicines (pills & potions) or hazardous products (cleaning products, bleach, etc.).

Just transfer any of your risky household items into one of our **Safelock® packages** and you can leave grandparents and grandchildren alike alone at home.

To order, just visit our website on **www.safelockscams.com**

SAFELOCK

Doc • B

CONSUP-G - Consumer Support Group

www.consup-G.org

Mr. Rookie Swindle
Safelockscams Ltd.
84 Goldbrick Lane

24th July 2011

Dear Mr. Swindle
Re: Problems with Safelock® packages

We are writing on behalf of several consumers who have filed complaints about their experience with your Safelock® packages. Because of the risks entailed in using your product we feel the time has come to take action. Please find below an example of one such letter of complaint, sent to you by Mrs. Whine, on 15th May 20--:
"On 14th January 20--, I bought a pack of various sizes of Safelock® packages (reference number: 004461 / AB) online and received delivery of said products one week later.
Unfortunately, the product does not comply with the advertisement and has not performed well. As promised, my elderly aunt was not able to get into her pill bottle, however neither myself nor my husband were able to open the Safelock® either, and had to resort to using a hammer to smash the plastic, causing damage to my husband's thumb, in order to give my aunt the medicine she so badly needed. However, my grandson (aged 5) had no problem at all in opening the bleach bottle ("safely" tucked away in a Safelock® bag) which was under the sink. As you can see, the Safelock® did not work at all as promised, and I am very disappointed. I have sent you several e-mails, but have never received any answer.
To solve the problem, I would like you to take your product off the market as it is dangerous and does not live up to your promises. I am looking forward to your reply and a solution to this problem. If I do not hear from you within the next two weeks, I shall be obliged to seek help from a consumer protection agency. Please contact me at the above address or by phone on 00 44 1644 786 554.
We would be grateful for a prompt response to our letter and the immediate recall of all your products.
Yours sincerely,
Helping you challenge corporate power since 2002

Do you need help getting fair treatment from a small or large corporation?
Just call our helpline on 0821843 843 for free advice and support (lines open 24/7)

Doc • C

CONSUMER FEEDBACK SURVEY - SAFELOCK® (Tick box where applicable)

Age group: ❑ over 65 ❑ 50-64 ❑ 25-49 ❑ under 24

Regular user of Safelock®: ❑ Yes ❑ No

If "Yes", size of Safelock® package preferred: ❑ small ❑ medium ❑ large

If "No", would you be interested in using Safelock®? ❑ Yes ❑ No

If "Yes", what would you use Safelock® for? (Please write in capital letters) ....

....

Have you had / heard about any problems with Safelock® products? ❑ Yes ❑ No

If "Yes", what were the problems? (Please write in capital letters) ....

....

If "Yes", do you think Safelock® should be taken off the market? ❑ Yes ❑ No

Would you like to try an upgraded version of Safelock®? ❑ Yes ❑ No

Thank you for giving us a bit of your time.

SAFELOCK

ROLE PLAY

2 | Consumers

Background

A consumer is the person who pays for a product or service for their own personal use rather than for manufacture or resale. This involves a decision-making process which can be influenced by advertising and marketing, current trends and financial aspects.

→ SEE CHAPTER "MARKETING" PAGE 62 AND CHAPTER "BRANDS" PAGE 82.

1 Why is it important to understand the consumer?

Marketing strategies, and therefore potentially increased sales of goods, services and ideas, can be improved by the study of **consumer behaviour**. It is important to know:
– How consumers think and feel and analyse. How will they make the choice between one product and another?
– How vulnerable is the consumer to outside influences (culture, family, media...)?
– Does consumer behaviour change depending on the group or organisation they are with at the moment of **purchase**?
– How does the consumer behave when in the store or shopping online?
– How much does the consumer need to know and understand in order to make a decision?
– How does the consumer use and dispose of the product?
– Whether the same decision-making process takes place for products of different levels of importance (cost, status, **lifestyle**, etc.).
– And as a result, how should the marketing campaign be run to reach the consumer efficiently?

→ SEE CHAPTER "MARKETING" PAGE 62.

2 What is consumer protection?

The idea of protecting the consumer dates back to the 1870s in America, became rife in the 1950s, and in the 1960s President John Kennedy introduced the Consumer Bill of Rights to ensure that the right of consumers "to be safe, to be informed, to choose, and to be heard" was respected. The bill was the response to public concern about consumer rights, the honesty of advertising and the quality of **consumer goods**. Well-known for **consumer advocacy** is Ralph Nader, who published *Unsafe at Any Speed* in 1965, claiming that car manufacturers sold goods with little thought for consumer safety, which led to laws being passed for compulsory seatbelts, for example. In 1971 he set up the NGO Public Citizen, which has led to many other consumer organisations which lobby for tougher laws against the pressures of advertising (especially for children) and the vicious spiral of over-consumption. 1966 saw the American "Truth in Packaging" bill, and the compulsory Surgeon General's warning about the dangers of cigarettes.

Questions

- What are the questions which help you understand your target consumer?
- What are the alternatives to the current trend of over-consumerism?
- Do you consider yourself as an ethical or green consumer?

3 What are the alternatives to consumerism as we know it?

Anti-consumerism: The commitment to consuming less and thus reducing wasteful consumption. Happiness is not to be equated with material possessions.
Ethical consumerism: The choice to purchase goods from a company which is known to be ethically sound (it respects human rights, animal rights, does not get involved in arms dealing, etc.). The ethical consumer is on the rise.
Green consumerism: The decision to purchase "environmentally friendly" goods or services which are less damaging to the ecosystem (re-usable instead of disposable goods, local products, less packaging, etc.).

→ SEE CHAPTER "ENVIRONMENT" PAGE 226.

Info

Many other factors can change consumer habits:
- Economic recessions will cause consumers to look for the best quality-price ratio.

→ SEE CHAPTER "BRANDS" PAGE 82 AND CHAPTER " MARKETING" PAGE 62.

- The political situation – governments can pass legislation which may influence consumer habits.
- Legal issues against a company can put consumers off buying from them.
- Technological developments will render a product or even a consumer outlet obsolete.

Focus Brick & mortar? Online retailers? Click & mortar? What has the future in store for the consumer?

Buying online and / or buying in a "brick & mortar" store – where is the consumer more likely to do his or her shopping? What about retailers? Have they already chosen to add online services to their brick and mortar operations?

Consumers' buying habits on the move?

Do "Brick and mortar" retailers remain an absolute necessity?

When buying fruit, customers want to be able to handle the produce and smell how fresh it is. With some items of clothes, customers are more likely to go to the store to try them on, feel the fabric. So grocery shops such as Tesco, Sainsbury's, etc. are there to stay. There are products that can only be purchased in a store. Goods whose quality you cannot judge until you experience them are called "experience goods", such as haircuts or Thai meals. So hairdressers and restaurants will not go but what about clothes shops? Can they not offer an online service and have High Street stores at the same time?

Aren't we moving towards the best of both worlds?

If the local store is better suited for food products, and if sizing is required, some items are better bought in person. But once a size from a brand is known, online shopping becomes possible. Aren't we talking about mail-order buying? There are even some food

producers – speciality foods such as donuts – that will ship food all over the world and have been doing it for years. So the type of product comes into the equation. However, online purchasing is great for general items, such as CDs, records, software, computers, train tickets or plane tickets, concert tickets or even online discounts with companies such as Groupon. But buying patterns are not changing so much, customers make their purchasing choices according to criteria such as pricing, variety, convenience, delivery, warranty, returns and safety. So customers will take advantage of both online and brick and mortar retailers. For customers, online shopping means no longer having to queue, having 24-hour access. Returning an item bought online can be risky but it is generally safe if dealing with companies with return and / or exchange policies.

Questions

- What goods would not sell so well online?
- What do customers expect from their retailers?
- What is online shopping compared to?

@-Go online

Tesco and Amazon are two types of retailers who do not sell the same things but might have the same customers. Look at their online sites to find out the services each one offers.

ACTIVE BUSINESS CULTURE

Focus → **Retailers: rethinking the way they do business**

Why online retailers?

Online companies are doing business differently and it is often less costly: they rent premises at a lower price. They also have access to customers that live far from a brick and mortar storefront. It is not as expensive to have a larger collection online and more efficient and faster to promote products online than for an in-store product. So on the Web, retailers are ready to supply cheaper products as a consequence of reduced overheads. In addition, your online retailer can be located far away, even in a foreign country. Proximity is no longer an issue.

Brick & mortar on the move

Brick & mortar are adapting to the digital revolution by offering online ordering and delivery but also by using IT to help shoppers with their shopping. Smartphones offer applications that make shopping easier: discounts are displayed on your mobile, new items may be displayed for you to discover and some applications offer the customer the possibility of knowing the type of ingredients used in food products. Shoppers allergic to gluten, for instance, will be able to find out with new applications the type of products they should avoid.
South Korea is testing out a virtual supermarket that you access with a smartphone to do your shopping. Here you just need to shop with your mobile by entering codes or pictures. Products will no longer be displayed in the shops. Are we also heading that way?

Questions

- Which criteria are likely to influence shoppers on their purchasing choices?
- How will these criteria determine where they shop?
- Are we not dealing with a different shopping experience?
- Express your point of view.
- You probably do not do your shopping like your parents or even like your grand-parents. Make a comparison and explain the reasons for buying from different types of retailers. In your eyes, what is the future of High Street stores?

Perspectives

Who will win? Who will lose out? Consumers are certainly the winners. In fact far from being left with fewer options, consumers are dictating what companies do: consumers have become very happy with the choices both brick & mortar shops and online retailers offer, and some companies have morphed into click & mortar shops. There are even online retailers that are planning to have a physical storefront. But retailers have also won by targeting new clients, and moving to a new business model. Convenience goods, shopping goods, specialty goods and unsought goods: that is to say, the type of goods we purchase determines where we shop. But on the whole, having access to the Internet will not change the basic criteria that consumers have in mind when shopping. Consumers have been experiencing online shopping. They have chosen to retain or not this new way of shopping and have matured. Window shopping will continue and customers will not be deprived of their local stores with the familiar faces of their shopkeepers, who are happy to help out in making decisions. The digital revolution is only re-forming, re-shaping the way we shop, but not more.

Test yourself   Try to use your memory – do not look at the vocabulary list!

1 NEW-TYPE OR TRADITIONAL SHOPPERS?

Match a word to the type of socio-economic group (which can be part of a consumer profile).

a) single people
b) green consumers
c) the homeless
d) the affluent
e) divorcees
f) middle-income families
g) the overweight
h) senior citizens
i) kids

1. synonym for children
2. were once married but no longer
3. not married
4. need somewhere to live
5. not big but not small incomes
6. usually retired and living on a pension
7. those with high incomes
8. environmentally friendly
9. carry excessive weight

2 CONSUMER BEHAVIOUR

Complete the sentences by using the following words.

complaint • quality-price ratio • over-consumption • boycott • demanding

a) ... will lead to shortages in the long term.

b) Consumers ... companies for several reasons including animal welfare, use of chemicals, etc.

c) An unhappy consumer will not hesitate to make a ... .

d) Consumers are becoming more ... and want to know more about what they purchase.

e) Most consumers seek a fair balance between the price and the quality, or ... .

3 STARTS WITH AN "F"

Fill in the gaps in the following paragraph – each word (or acronym) begins with an "F".

It would appear that for our market the F _ _ _ good F _ _ _ _ _ was a F _ _ which is beginning to fade. A report shows that following the distribution of a F _ _ _ _ / _ _ _ _ _ to each consumer, and the F _ _ _ _ _ _ _ from the survey, we have to stop selling expensive, high quality goods, and rely on the F._._._. sector (goods such as supermarket food, toiletries, etc.).

4 CONSUMERISM

Look at the definition and make compound nouns, each beginning with the word "consumer".

A	The leverage or influence consumers have on the producers of a product or service.	Consumer-...
B	An indicator of inflation (or deflation)	Consumer-...
C	Counsel given to consumers	Consumer-...
D	The typical way in which consumers purchase goods or services	Consumer-...
E	The degree of optimism expressed by consumers	Consumer-...
F	The amount of money spent by households	Consumer-...
G	Consumer watchdogs (individuals or groups)	Consumer-...
H	The "why, when, how & where" study of individuals or a group of consumers	Consumer-...
I	The extent to which people can afford to purchase	Consumer-...
J	A society where buying, selling and owning is important	Consumer-...

VOCABULARY

2 | Consumers

Words

"More and more products are coming out in fiercely protective packaging designed to prevent consumers from consuming them. These days you have to open almost every consumer item by gnawing* on the packaging." (Dave Barry)

***Gnaw** (to): ronger

Addict: accro / toxicomane
Addiction: accoutumance
Affluent: riche, aisé
Ageing / aging: vieillissant
Beverage: boisson
Binge drinker: quelqu'un qui boit pour se saoûler
Boycott (to): boycotter
Brown goods: l'électronique
Cautious: qui fait attention / prudent
Commodity: matière première
Complaint: réclamation
Consume (to): consommer
Consumer: consommateur
Consumer advice: conseils aux consommateurs
Consumer advocacy / protection: défense des consommateurs
Consumer behaviour: comportement du consommateur
Consumer buying pattern: structure des comportements d'achat
Consumer confidence: confiance du consommateur
Consumer fragmentation: fragmentation de la consommation
Consumer goods / products: biens de consommateur
Consumer power: le pouvoir du consommateur
Consumer society: société de consommation
Consumer spending: dépense des consommateurs
Consumer survey: enquête auprès des consommateurs
Consumerism: consumérisme
Consuming habit: habitude de consommation
Consumption pattern: mode de consommation
Convenience food: plat préparé
Convenience goods: produits courants
Convenience store: épicier du coin
Core customer: clientèle principale
CPI (consumer price index): indice des prix à la consommation
Customer: client
Damage (to): porter préjudice à, endommager
Demand (to): exiger
Demanding: exigeant
Disposable: jetable
Durables: biens durables
Elderly: âgé(e)
Fad: mode, lubie, tendance
Feedback: retour d'informations
Feel-good factor: indice de satisfaction
FMCGS (fast-moving consumer goods): biens de consommation à rotation rapide
Free sample: échantilllon gratuit
Garner (to): rassembler
Hazardous product: produit dangereux
High Street spending: les dépenses en centre ville
Home delivery: livraison à domicile
Homeless: sans abri
Household: foyer
Life expectancy: espérance de vie
Lifestyle: mode de vie
Mass appeal: succès populaire
Mass consumption: consommation de masse
Middle-income: à revenu moyen
Non-durables: biens non-durables
Over consumption: surconsommation
Overweight: en surpoids
Packaging: conditionnement / emballage
Plastic money: cartes de crédit
Pre-paid goods: marchandises prépayées
Purchase (to): acheter
Purchase influencer: personne qui influe sur un achat
Purchasing power / buying power: pouvoir d'achat
Quality standard: norme de qualité
Quality-price ratio: rapport qualité-prix
Recall (to) / withdraw (to): retirer de la vente
Semi-durables: biens semi-durables
Senior citizen: personne du troisième âge
Single: célibataire (adjectif)
Spend (to): dépenser
Wealthy: riche, aisé
White goods: l'électroménager

3

Marketing

The magic mix

Beach marketing: beachgoers books from 30 red Ikea Billy bookcases lined up to form the world's longest outdoor bookcase to celebrate the 30th birthday of the brand's furniture piece...

Questions

What do marketers appeal to?
When and where?

WORD BOX

cheap • buy (to), purchase (to) • expensive • dear • sell (to) • sales target • trade • target • appeal (to)

3 | Marketing

1 • Look and discuss

a) Look at the following pictures.

b) Discuss in class.

1. What are all the different kinds of retail outlets? Choose from the following list.
baker's • butcher's • charity shop • convenience shop • corner shop • delicatessen • department store • flagship store • factory outlet • furniture store • grocer's • hard discounter • off-licence • specialist shop • thrift shop • vending machine
2. Which kind of shop do you go to most?
3. Do you buy food in a supermarket or at a smaller grocery shop or delicatessen?
4. Discuss the pros and cons of large retail outlets compared with smaller boutiques.

Info

• The expression "The customer is always right" was coined by Harry Gordon Selfridge (1857-1947), an American who founded Selfridges department store, London (1909). Of course, it has much the same meaning as the expression "The customer is never wrong" ("Le client n'a jamais tort"), which is credited to César Ritz (1850-1918) in 1908.
• Customising is gaining momentum and consists in tailoring a product or service for a specific consumer as if he / she were unique.

2 • Read and understand

What are their tasks and duties? Match the job title to a job description.

shop assistant • buyer • shopwalker • store manager • merchandiser

1. A .... is responsible for:
– Running a shop on a day-to-day basis, including managing the staff and handling the finances.
– Dealing with customer complaints or compliments.
– Ensuring the shop is efficient and effective and makes as much profit as possible.
– Checking the inventory and paying for the goods.
– Handling promotion and advertising.

2. A .... assists customers, supervises the sales staff and helps with customer problems.

3. A .... purchases the goods for the store.

4. A .... is in charge of:
– Presenting the product in the best way to attract the customers' attention.
– Analyzing customer behaviour and the needs of the store.
– Deciding upon decoration, signage[1], POS advertising[2], bags and packaging.

5. A .... provides assistance and customer service to the customers.

1. *Signage*: signalisation du magasin 2. *POS advertising*: PLV

3 • Look and write

a) Look at the following examples of packaging.

b) Packaging and you: answer the following questions by writing a few sentences.

1. Does packaging influence your purchases?
2. What do you think "good packaging" is?
3. Create your own packaging for a product of your choice. Don't forget to give the necessary details on your packaging.

4 • Listen and understand

CD n° 1
Track n° 23

a) Is Mrs. Bean a first-time customer or a customer who has been to the store before?
b) How many shirts did Mrs. Bean want to look at – 12 or 20?
c) What do you think? Should customers be able to behave as they like, even rudely?

3 | Marketing

CD n° 1
Track n° 24

A new look to boost sales

WARMING UP

- Can you give two coffee brands' names?
- How did you get to know them?
- Is coffee a popular product?

Tassimo – a division of Kraft Canada – has brewed[1] a new brand image that includes a package redesign for its personal hot beverage maker. The new look was inspired by global research and will be applied in all markets, creating a unified, easily identifiable look, said Luke Cole, product manager for Tassimo. In the research, consumers said the coffee aisle is a sea of sameness – with packaging that often includes dark rich colours, images of beans[2] or steaming cups of coffee, said Cole.

Tassimo was looking to emphasize its key point of difference – the fact that the machine reads a barcode on each hot beverage "T-Disc" and adjusts everything from water temperature, water amount and brew time to make the optimal beverage. This is the first time Tassimo has undergone a redesign since the brand was launched five years ago. While the UK-based brand design firm Turner Duckworth handled the effort, Kraft Canada worked to incorporate the Canadian-only coffee labels into the new design. Before, the colour of the package changed with each beverage brand. For instance, the Nabob pack was green. The packages are now light silver with the outline of overlapping "T-Discs" in dark silver, arranged as a flower, which is meant to represent the wide range of brands and beverages available within Tassimo, said Cole.

An image of a coffee cup also appears at the bottom right-hand corner of the pack, with the handle turned outwards towards the consumer, said Cole. From a design perspective, the new look clearly communicates the brand's personality: uncomplicated, clever, intuitive and very approachable, said Cole.

Tassimo announced the package redesign in a newsletter to consumers, and continues to support the new look on its website, Facebook page, and through point-of-sale materials including on-pack stickers. The new design will be included in the next advertising campaign, which Tassimo typically launches around festive and gift-giving occasions such as Mother's Day and Christmas.

Marketing Magazine, June 10, 2011

1. Brew: *le verbe* to brew *au sens propre est un terme culinaire qui signifie « infuser » lorsqu'il s'agit d'une boisson comme le thé ou la tisane. Ici le journaliste l'utilise au sens figuré qui dans ce contexte lui permet de jouer sur les deux sens du mot. C'est un procédé très fréquent en journalisme.* 2. Bean (coffee beans): *grains de café*

Lexical work

1. Find the English equivalents in the text.

a) une nouvelle image de marque § 1
b) une nouveau concept d'emballage § 1
c) quantité d'eau § 2
d) temps d'infusion § 2
e) la gamme étendue de marques § 2
f) disponible § 2
g) la personnalité de la marque § 3
h) point de vente § 4
i) campagne publicitaire § 4

2. Find their French equivalents.

a) beverage § 1
b) package § 1
c) range § 2
d) advertising campaign § 4
e) launch § 4
f) point-of-sale § 4

Pronunciation work

CD n° 1
Track n° 25

1. Listen and observe.

support • corner • before • launch • water
the sound [ɔ] may come from different letters: o, au, a.

2. Listen to these words that you may find difficult and repeat.

identifiable • aisle • emphasise • incorporate • advertising

Info
Kraft Canada is an American confectionery, food and beverage conglomerate. It markets many brands, such as Lu, Cadbury and Milka, in more than 170 countries.

Work on the title

1. Identify the source (title, date, origin, nature).

2. Look at the headline. Which marketing "P" is dealt with in this article?

Check the facts

1. Read § 1.
Are the coffee packages varied in the coffee aisle?

2. Read § 2.
a) What makes Tassimo beverages different from the others?
b) What was the packaging like before?

3. Read § 3.
What qualities does the new design communicate?

4. Read § 4.
What strategy did Tassimo adopt to catch consumers' attention?

Grammar

→ p. 234

Le passif
- *The new look was inspired by global research ...*
- *The new design will be applied in ...*

Topic debrief

1. Complete the following sentences to get a full summary of the article.
Tassimo is a ... owned by one of the biggest food ... in the world. Tassimo was ... five years ago on the Canadian market. It offers a wide ... of hot ..., such as coffee, cappuccino, tea, etc.
Tassimo has changed its ... to create a ... easily recognisable by all its consumers. Tassimo will communicate this innovation in its next .... The products will also be promoted on the ..., thanks to ... which will remind customers that many tastes are ....Tassimo hopes to ... sales thanks to its new ....

2. Use the following linking words to connect the sentences in the paragraph above.
first / firstly • *then / after* • *moreover / in addition* • *however* • *actually* • *in fact* • *finally* • *eventually*

Methods

1. Find out which paragraph best sums up the company's new strategy.

2. What has Tassimo decided to do?

3. Make a sentence which explains the importance of clear product packaging.

4. Make a sentence showing the designers' role in selling a product.

Train for the exam

1. Make a **summary / account** of the document (60 words/3-5 minutes).

2. Comment: find an answer to the following questions. Discuss and give examples (100 words / 3-5 minutes).
What do you think of the name "Tassimo"? What is its origin? Why is it adapted to the product? Find another example.

3. Role play: work in pairs
You are going to take part in a conversation.
A sales rep from Tassimo is explaining to one of his / her customers why the new look is better than the old one. The client is the manager of a High Street supermarket.
Student A: you play the customer.
Student B: you play the part of the sales representative.

Go online
- Find information about another company's successful marketing strategy. Examples of companies you can search: Kimberley Clark, Zara, Apple, Red Bull, Unilever, Ikea, etc.
- Get prepared to report to your group / class (a PowerPoint presentation is recommended).

3 | Marketing

Train with an oral document

WARMING UP

- Have you ever tasted Indian food?
- Is it influenced by religions? Which?

CD n° 1
Track n° 26

International restaurant chains head to India

Info
Mumbai, formerly known as Bombay in English, is the capital of India.

A woman walks past a Pizza Hut outlet advertising its vegetarian menu in Bombay.

Lexical work

1. Match the following words according to their meanings.

a) today	**1.** point of sales
b) outlets	**2.** currently
c) dining out	**3.** well-known
d) affluent	**4.** saw
e) leisure	**5.** free time
f) notorious	**6.** going to the restaurant
g) noticed	**7.** foreign
h) overseas	**8.** mistakes
i) blunders	**9.** rich
j) grab a bite	**10**. eat
k) Western	**11**. occidental

2. Find their English equivalents (part 1).

a) point de vente	**f)** aisé (riche)
b) pénétrer (un marché)	**g)** disponible
c) marque étrangère	**h)** loisir
d) auditeurs / public	**i)** classe
e) dehors	**j)** moyenne

Pronunciation work

CD n° 1
Track n° 27

Listen and observe the liaisons between the words.

the Indian market • most of • some of India's people • more and more • go out • have a good time • break away • with a movie • eating out

Work on the title

1. Look at the title of the document.

2. There are two international restaurant chains in the document. Which are they?

Check the facts

1. Listen to part 1.

a) What is Bahumathi Mahal's job and country?
b) Which company does he represent?
c) What is the situation of the Indian consumers?
d) What are the changes in their eating habits?
e) What will be the consequences for Bahumathi Mahal's company in the near future?

2. Listen to part 2.

a) What brands are already present in India?
b) Which brands are ready to tap the Indian market?
c) What products are they planning to sell?
d) Which obstacles will they have to handle?
e) Which mistake should be avoided?
f) What is the role of Pizza Hut and others?
g) What is the state of the Indian market?

Topic debrief

1. Choose the sentence which you think corresponds best to the main topic of the document.

a) All the famous global fast food brands are already operating on the Indian market and are trying to adapt to Indian traditions and religions in this huge country counting over 1 billion people.
b) Some fast food brands are operating in India while others are ready to enter the market. They are quite optimistic as there's a thriving Indian middle class attracted by Western habits.
c) Pizza Hut's Indian manager is worried about the arrival of other Western competitors on the Indian market which is already saturated.

2. Rephrase the correct sentence in order to make a short introduction to the document.

Methods

1. Write ten key words you identified while listening to the document.

2. Use these words to write three key sentences to illustrate the tradition gap in India.

Train for the exam

1. Use your notes to make an **oral presentation** about what you heard (3-5 minutes).

2. Comment: find an answer to the following question. Discuss and give examples (100 words / 3-5 minutes).
Why may going to a restaurant be considered as a Westernisation of Indian life?

3. Role play: work in pairs

You are going to take part in a conversation.
Student A: you are an Indian entrepreneur who wants to open a McDonald's outlet in Mumbai.
Student B: you are his uncle, a traditional Indian restaurant owner and strongly opposed to the "invasion" of Western food in India.

TIPS

You should use your notes in order to present a realistic conversation. Don't read them, look up. You can:
– record the conversation (the recording should last between one and two minutes at most);
– videotape the scene and show it to the class;
– act out the scene in front of the class;
– listen to your classmates' recordings and write what you have understood in a short and structured paragraph.

Go online

- Find out information about western brands operating in India.
- Get prepared to report to your group / class (a PowerPoint presentation is recommended).

CD n° 1
Track n° 28

Online grocery sales will double within five years

WARMING UP

▸ How do you or your family buy grocery products?

Britain's Internet grocery market will double to £9.9bn by 2015, research group IGD* forecast on Thursday as Morrisons became the latest supermarket to make a move into online sales.

IGD said sales online continue to grow at a faster rate than any other sector in the grocery market, with growth of 21.4% in 2010 to £4.8bn. One in four food and grocery manufacturers is considering creating its own e-store, IGD's report found, with 43% of manufacturers anticipating that more than 10% of their total revenue will come from online sales by 2015.

Morrisons, Britain's fourth-largest grocery chain, announced on Thursday that it plans to start selling food online in the next two years. It's the only one of the main UK supermarket chains – including Tesco, Sainsbury's and Asda – which has yet to build an online presence. "The company is beginning to advertise its online offering niche, which will gain more importance as shopping habits equalise between physical and virtual visits to the stores," Richard Hunter, an analyst at Hargreaves Lansdown, told Bloomberg.

The online grocery market, which accounted for 3.2% of total grocery spending in the UK last year, is projected to increase to 5.4% by 2015, IGD said. Its monthly Shopper Track survey found that 13% of Britons expect to use online grocery shopping more in the next year, rising to 24% among 18 to 34 year olds. Joanne Denney-Finch, IGD chief executive, said: "The world around us is changing and technology is leaping ahead. You only need to look at the last 10 years to see that the digital age is evolving at an incredible pace.

The strong growth predicted for the online grocery channel presents an opportunity for companies of all sizes and types – retailers, manufacturers, local producers – to meet the needs of today's multi-channel shopper. It is encouraging to see manufacturers looking to flex their business models, participate in the digital explosion and engage with consumers in different ways.

As the market is constantly changing, it's still difficult to predict exactly what online grocery retailing will look like in the next few years. What is exciting, however, is how the digital revolution will evolve and shape our industry in the years to come." IGD interviewed 169 retailers and manufacturers between November 2010 and January 2011.

The Telegraph, 10 June 2011

* IGD: the Institute of Grocery Distribution.

Lexical work

1. Find the English equivalents in the text.

a) plus récent **§ 1**
b) croissance **§ 2**
c) déclarer **§ 3**
d) augmenter **§ 4**
e) fabricants **§ 5**
f) producteurs locaux **§ 5**
g) épicerie **§ 5**
h) révolution numérique **§ 6**

2. Find the French equivalents.

a) Britain's fourth-largest grocery chain **§ 3**
b) This company has yet to build an online presence. **§ 3**
c) The online grocery market accounted for 3.2% of total grocery spending. **§ 4**

Pronunciation work

CD n° 1
Track n° 29

1. Listen to these words that you may find difficult and repeat.

anticipating • evolving • incredible

2. Work on figures: write in full and read aloud.

21.4% in 2010 to £1.8bn • 5.4% by 2015

Work on the title

1. Identify the source of the document (title, date, nature).

2. The key word of the document is repeated 10 times in the article. Find it to explain the headline.

Check the facts

1. Read § 1, 2.
Why has Morissons decided to sell online?

2. Read § 3.
a) What is the difference between Morrisons and the other British stores?
b) What strategy will Morrisons use to strengthen its online presence?

3. Read § 4.
a) At what rate is the online grocery market expected to grow in 2015?
b) Which age group will have seen the strongest increase?
c) What can account for the change in today's world?
d) What have the last ten years taught us?

4. Read § 5, 6.
a) What types of companies will benefit from the growth of the online market?
b) What strategies will they have to follow if they want to thrive in this new niche?
c) What will be the impact of the digital revolution?

Grammar

→ p. 234

L'expression du futur

- ... *will double within five years ...*
- ... *which will gain more importance as shopping habits equalise ...*

Topic debrief

1. Choose the sentence which you think corresponds best to the main topic of the document.
a) Online sales are growing for all types of products except for some brands which did not take into account the change in consumers' habits.
b) Supermarkets have understood that their future lies in online trade, that is why the major retailers are rushing to get hold of this niche.
c) The digital revolution will generate deep changes in trade in the years to come, and we already have a precise idea of what the future will be like.

2. Rephrase the correct sentence in order to make a short introduction to the document.

Methods

1. Which paragraph sums up the expectations of the online grocery market?

2. Pick out the main element of information in this paragraph and try to rephrase the paragraph in English.

Train for the exam

1. Make a **summary / account** of the document (60 words / 3-5 minutes) with the following elements:
– the reasons why online sales are increasingly important;
– the advantages they offer the company.

2. Write an e-mail (50-70 words).
You are an expert on online sales and you give strategic advice to store managers wishing to sell online.

3. Role play: work in pairs
You are going to take part in a conversation.
Student A: you are a small retailer. You set up your own business 10 years ago and you are not very computer-skilled. You need your trainee's help.
Student B: you are a trainee who studies marketing and sales and you explain the advantages of going online and how it is vital for the retail business.

Go online

- Asda, Sainsbury, Tesco and Morrisons are part of the UK retail landscape. You can choose one or several of these retailers and carry out a Web search.
- Get prepared to report to your group / class (a PowerPoint presentation is recommended).

Train with an oral document

CD n° 1 Track n° 30

Tencent, the march of the Chinese high-tech penguins

WARMING UP

- Is the Internet as free in China as in other countries?
- Which Chinese Internet companies do you know?

Lexical work

1. Match the following words according to their meanings.

a) challenger	**1.** competitor
b) instant messaging	**2.** texting
c) dubbed	**3.** opponent
d) copycat	**4.** fake
e) rival	**5.** unnoticed
f) ignored	**6.** called
g) user-friendly	**7.** easy to use

Pronunciation work

CD n° 1 Track n° 31

1. Listen and underline the stressed syllable. Then practise repeating these words.

surprise • enough • expert • compete

2. Listen to these words that you may find difficult and repeat.

peers • here • reporter • headquarters

Work on the title

1. Look at the title of the document.

2. Find out who is represented by the penguins.

Check the facts

1. Listen to part 1.

a) What are the names of the brands mentioned in part 1?
b) Are today high-tech brands successful or not?
c) What are the characteristics of the expert interviewed?
d) What kind of software is QQ?

2. Listen to part 2.

a) What did you understand about Tencent's size?
b) Why is this company criticised?
c) What advice is given to Western high-tech companies?

3. Listen to part 3.

a) What have some American companies decided to do?
b) What is the origin of the new company's growing success?
c) What is the CEO's personality?
d) From the comparison between QQ and its Western counterparts (Facebook, MSN, etc.), what do you understand?

Topic debrief

1. Choose the sentence which you think corresponds best to the main topic of the document.

a) The American Internet giants control the Chinese sites.
b) Thanks to its mascot, Tencent has become very popular and can't be ignored on the global market.
c) Too much pressure from government is slowing Tencent's growth.

2. Rephrase the correct sentence in order to make a short introduction to the document.

Methods

1. Write 5 key words you identified while listening to the document.

2. Write 5 key sentences showing the contents of the document.

Train for the exam

1. Use your notes to make an **oral presentation** about the document and record yourself (3-5 minutes).

2. Comment: find an answer to the following question. Discuss and give examples (100 words / 3-5 minutes).
Do you think that the use of new technologies has weakened or strenghtened the relocation process to emerging countries?

3. Role play: work in groups

You are going to create a questionnaire.
Your manager wants to improve the company's competitivity.
You have to inquire about multitasking practices among your colleagues and report to the manager about your results.

Go online

- Find out information on the "Silicon Valley guys" and their companies.
- Get prepared to report to your group / class (a PowerPoint presentation is recommended).

PRACTICE • AUDIO • VIDEO

Train with a video

Coca-Cola outdoor interactive advertising campaign

→ http://www.youtube.com/watch?v=RoN_xxGcXzk&feature=related

4 September, 2010

Look at this video on the Internet about advertising

Check the facts	Methods
1. What does the video deal with?	• Why do you see 5 bottle caps? • Why were they essential?
2. Who is mostly targeted in this video?	• How old are the participants shown in the video?
3. Where is the video shot? Is it in a quiet place?	• Do you see a rural or an urban environment?
4. What was necessary to achieve the ad's goals?	• How did Coca-Cola match sight and sound?
5. Issues ... – What are the elements that appeal to young people in this ad? – What do you think of the use of new technologies?	• Do you think the video is still advertising, or is it becoming "brainwashing"? • What are the most efficient elements? The music? The colours?

3 | Marketing

WARMING UP

- What do you know about Desigual? What can you say about this company's concept?
- Would you like Desigual fashion items to be unique?

CD n° 1 Track n° 32

Desigual

Barcelona-based Desigual's website states that its fashion range is created "without a glance at the current trends." Luckily for its owners, the same can be said for the company itself, which has enjoyed 60% year-on-year growth since 2002, and a turnover increased by 85% in 2009 to €250m. This year, Adell (CEO) says it will exceed €450m, adding that there is no reason why this shouldn't continue and that the potential for growth remains "enormous".

Fun, says Adell, is at the heart of Desigual, which was created in 1984 by a young Swiss designer, Thomas Meyer, who spent his summers making T-shirts in Ibiza. Now in-house designers create around 1,000 garments for each collection every season, all with a colourful neo-hippy aesthetic. "We are a young brand, but we try to appeal to a wide audience." So far it seems to be succeeding. There are almost 8,000 points of sale in 72 countries.

More than half of Desigual's business is now international and the largest market outside Spain is France, which, with Germany, is the focus of 2010. Last year the company opened its first German shop, in Berlin. Desigual also broke the record paid for a prime spot on London's Oxford Street.

Each store is customised to reflect local tastes, and staff are encouraged to paint the space and write graffiti on the walls. Other marketing tactics include the "Kiss Tour" gatherings – in which people are encouraged to, well, kiss – and store opening parties where music, sitting around on bean bags and eating fresh fruit all play a part. In the Paris flagship, which opened in June near the Opéra National, the store was mobbed.

"It isn't one of the cheapest, but our products are not an expensive or premium brand. Our product strategy lies in our quality-price ratio and what we transmit, which is a colourful world full of patchwork and graphic design. We are positive and happy and have a sense of humour, which is all part of our product philosophy," says Adell.

The other reason for the company's success, which he says is just as important, is how it has created its teams. "We recruit talent and train people in accordance with our corporate culture. The average age of our employees in this central office in Barcelona is 27, and in the company itself is 24. Our team is also international and includes 30 or more nationalities in the central office alone. In all, we are 1,700. Eight years ago, we were 40.

CNBC business, September 2010

Lexical work

1. Find their English equivalents in the text.

§ 1 **a)** mode **b)** tendances **c)** actuelles
§ 3 **a)** objectif **b)** place de choix
§ 4 **a)** personnalisé **b)** employés **c)** magasin vedette
§ 5 **a)** marque haut de gamme **b)** rapport qualité-prix
§ 6 **a)** en accord avec **b)** culture d'entreprise

2. Find the French equivalents.

turnover § 1 • points of sale § 2 • gathering § 4 • average § 6

Pronunciation work

CD n° 1 Track n° 33

1. Listen and fill in the grid according to the words' pronunciation.

that • this • there • aesthetic • growth

[ð]	[θ]

2. Work on figures: write in full and read aloud.

60% year-on-year • since 2002 • by 85% in 2009 • €450m • we are 1,700

Work on the title

1. Identify the source of the document (title, date, nature, origin).

2. Look at the headline. Desigual means "unequal". Read the 4th paragraph and find out if this name is appropriate.

Check the facts

1. Read § 1.
a) What is Desigual's home country?
b) What does it market?
c) How was it created?
d) What can be said of the brand's growth since 2002?
e) What are its future prospects?

2. Read § 2.
a) When was the brand created and by whom?
b) What audience does the brand wish to target?
c) What style of clothes is created?
d) How many countries is Desigual present in and how many stores have already been opened?

3. Read § 3.
a) What are the brand's two largest foreign markets?
b) Where are they going to open a store?
c) What is special about the price of this location?

4. Read § 4.
a) What information can you give about Desigual's stores layout?
b) What about the brand's other marketing tactics?
c) When and where did Desigual open its flagship store?
d) How do we know it was a big success?

5. Read § 5.
a) How are Desigual's products positioned in terms of price?
b) What is the brand's philosophy?

6. Read § 6.
What is the other reason for Desigual's success?

Grammar → p. 235

Le prétérit

- *... which was created in 1984 ...*
- *... who spent his summers making T-shirts in Ibiza.*

Topic debrief

1. Choose the sentence which you think corresponds best to the main topic of the document.
a) Desigual's marketing success is due to its capacity to stick to present trends and its ability to target a young audience all over the world.
b) Desigual is a new brand present in just a few countries, but they hope to improve and expand in the years to come.
c) Desigual's concept, designed over twenty years ago, has become one of the fastest-growing clothes brands thanks to an all-embracing marketing strategy.

2. Rephrase the correct sentence in order to make a short introduction to the document.

Methods

1. Give a title to each paragraph.

2. Give examples of other strategies used by retailers to attract customers and establish customer loyalty.

Train for the exam

1. Make a **summary / account** of the document (60 words / 3-5 minutes).

2. Comment: find an answer to the following questions. Discuss and give examples (100 words / 3-5 minutes).
Has Desigual invented a new concept?

3. Role play: work in pairs
You are going to take part in a job interview.
Student A: you have applied for a sales assistant job at Desigual's London store. You should be able to explain your motivations for being hired as a member of the Desigual's staff in London.
Student B: you are the recruiter interviewing student A about his / her motivations. You should check how much student A knows about the brand and give him / her information about the brand's strategy and spirit.

Go on line
- Find further information about Desigual's flagship stores in Paris or in London.
- Get prepared to report to your group / class (a PowerPoint presentation recommended).

PRACTICE • TEXT

Marketing sportswear: online and offline shopping

1 Situation

You work in the sales and marketing department of a sports clothes retailer. Sales are regular in the retail outlets but you have to decide whether you should sell online as well.

2 Process

a) Look at the statistics about online shopping and the comments about offline shopping (Documents A et B).
b) Get into groups.
Students A: you would like to sell your product in a retail store.
Students B: you would like to sell your product online.
c) You have to prepare a meeting to discuss the advantages and disadvantages of selling in retail stores and / or online. Prepare your arguments in each group. You can use ideas from Document C.
d) Now discuss and share your points of view. Remember to speak English only! Delegate the job of running the meeting to one of the group. Another person should take notes.
At the end of the meeting you will have to decide whether or not to sell your goods on a website.

3 Follow up

Depending on the outcome of your meeting:
– either write a short report for your boss, explaining whether you have decided to use online selling or not, and why;
– or design a home page for your company's website.

@ Go online

For more information about meetings with different cultures, look at this website: www.culturecrossing.net/index.php

TIPS

Start by saying

The main / most important advantage of ...
One advantage of ...
An additional / further advantage of ...
The pros outweigh the cons.

The main disadvantage of ...
One disadvantage of ...
An important drawback is ...
... but ...

Remember

• Anglo-Saxons don't sit too close to each other in a meeting – they like their space, so leave about two metres between each person. Little or no physical contact (touching) is recommended.
• It is not necessary to shake hands with everyone you know when you enter a meeting room. Shaking hands is only used the first time you meet someone.
• Good eye contact is seen as a sign of respect, but staring is rude.
• Punctuality is important so don't be late for meetings or appointments. Don't waste time because meetings (or even the time you have to participate in one) are often timed. Remember, "time is money"!

Doc • A

Doc • B

What are the reasons you might do more shopping OFF-line this holiday season?

Fear of things going wrong with online transactions (merchant not shipping on time, etc.). 43.2%

Lack of confidence that I can select the best gift online. 22.4%

Preference for familiar stores OFF-line. 32.0%

Greater confidence in being able to return goods to traditional stores. 36.0%

Procrastination… I can shop at the last minute OFF-line. 34.4%

Doc • C

Here are some ideas to get you going ...

TRADITIONAL SHOPPING	ONLINE SHOPPING
You can only shop at specific times of the day.	You can shop all day and all night if you wish.
You have to move to get to the shop.	You can shop from your armchair.
You have to carry (heavy) goods.	Your shopping is delivered. (Beware of shipping and handling costs!)
You can touch and feel what you want to buy.	You can only see what you want to buy.
You can try on clothes.	You have to hope that the size and shape are right.
You can inspect for defects.	You have to trust the seller.
It is harder to compare prices.	It is easy to compare prices on different websites.
The range is limited to what the shop has in stock.	You can easily browse through several sites so the range is probably wider.
You can see and talk to other people.	You have no social experience.
Your ideas ...	Your ideas ...

3 | Marketing

Background

Marketing has been described as "the management process responsible for identifying, anticipating and satisfying customer requirements profitably" (www.cim.co.uk). In other words, market research, consumer research and marketing research followed by the creation of a marketing strategy, and operational marketing or communication.
➔ SEE CHAPTER "BRANDS" PAGE 82.

1 What are market research and marketing research?

In order to introduce a product or service efficiently onto a market, managers need factual information about their target market (➔ SEE CHAPTER "CONSUMERS" PAGE 42) to base their strategy on. **Market research** looks at a specific market (what is the competition, who are the players) and is part of a more overall "**marketing research**", which includes looking into new products, new markets or new modes of distribution, especially online marketing at the moment. ➔ SEE CHAPTER "NEW TECHNOLOGIES" PAGE 102.
Marketing research will guide the overall marketing strategy. ➔ SEE CHAPTER "COMPANIES" PAGE 22.

2 What are the 7Ps?

The 7Ps or "Extended **Marketing Mix**" (people, process and physical evidence have recently been added) is a strategic marketing framework. The 4Ps (promotion, price, place, product) have long been used for the products industry, whereas the 7Ps have developed in line with the development of the service industry.

For the products industry alone, process and physical evidence can be replaced by "packaging" (the visual element of the product and a key part of building brand image) and "positioning" (what the consumer thinks of your product and how they talk about it).

3 Is there a difference between promotion and advertising?

Promotion and **advertising** are both marketing tools which are used everywhere in the modern world and there is often overlap between the two.
Promotion: Targets distributors as well as end-users / consumers. Promotion aims at building sales in the short term and can include in-store events, two-for-one offers, coupons, special discounts and free samples. A technical support service is another way of promoting a product. This involves indirect costs. One more way to promote a product or service is to get a local or national newspaper to write an article about your company / product – which is of course completely free!
Advertising: Targets the end-user and usually involves buying radio or television spots, paying for advertising space in magazines or newspapers, billboard or poster campaigns. It is a long-term strategy to gain customer loyalty and strengthen the brand image. ➔ SEE CHAPTER "BRANDS" PAGE 82.

Questions

There are different selling strategies. For example, intensive (as many retailers and wholesalers as possible), selective (the number of outlets is limited) and exclusive (a single outlet).

- Which is the most appropriate for the following products? Printer paper, high-brand-loyalty clothing, niche market goods, chewing gum, sports equipment, off-the-rack* clothing.
- What kind of direct marketing do you prefer? Personalised mail or e-mail, phone calls or reply coupons? Is it intrusive?
- Which of the 7Ps is the most important, and why?
- What is the impact of new technologies on marketing?

*Off-the-rack: *prêt à porter*

Info

Product life cycle: there are 6 key stages:
- **Development**: Design & testing. 20% of products may not get to the next stage. This is only a cost.
- **Introduction**: Product launch on the market. Low sales and high costs = little or no profit.
- **Growth**: Costs decrease with economies of scale and the product starts to be profitable.
- **Maturity**: Growth in sales slows down and competitors launch similar products on the market.
- **Saturation**: Sales start dropping due to increased competition.
- **Decline**: Lack of sales due to competition and changes in consumer requirements. The product is withdrawn or an extension strategy is implemented (an updated version, new packaging, advertising, new markets, etc.).

Focus

Marks and Spencer: the downs and ups of an iconic UK brand

An iconic retailer, Marks and Spencer can boast over a hundred years of presence in its UK homeland. The brand's notoriety was made possible thanks to Marks and Sparks's* unique strategy centred on British core values. But in the 1990s, the fast pace of changes caught the brand by surprise; Marks and Spencer increasingly lost market share and eventually closed all of its foreign stores in 2001, allegedly to refocus on its home market.
And yet today, Marks and Spencer is thriving again and the opening of a flagship store on the Champs Elysées in December 2011 is the most conspicuous sign of the company's spectacular recovery. How was the brand able to successfully work its way through two decades of hardships?

*Marks and Sparks is the nickname given to Marks and Spencer by its British customers.

A marketing downfall 1990-2001

Info

- Marks & Spencer is one of the UK's leading retailers, with over 21 million customers visiting its stores every week. Marks & Spencer sells clothing, home products and food.
- It was founded in 1884, in Leeds (West Yorkshire) by Michael Marks and Thomas Spencer.
- Headquarters located in London, City of Westminster.
- 1,010 stores worldwide.
- The retailer sources its products responsibly from 2,000 suppliers around the world. Over 76,000 people work for Marks & Spencer, both in the UK and in 42 territories overseas.

Description

- The 1990s: Marks and Spencer refused to acknowledge the need to adapt to market changes, unlike its competitors.
- The retailer preferred to stick to tradition, i.e, none of its stores accepted payment by credit or debit cards.
- Marks and Spencer's clothes line was considered expensive and out of fashion.
- The brand's executives were afraid of change and had no innovative spirit.
- They believed that current trends would pass and that their customers would come back to "reason".
- Marks and Spencer was hit by falling sales, loss of market shares and declining profitability.
- To reduce costs, an inadequate strategy was adopted: floor staff was kept to a minimum, leading to a decrease in customer service, leading to further decline.
- 2001: Marks and Spencer left France and closed all its foreign outlets.
- The French staff and customers in Paris were taken by surprise, as Marks and Spencer's Paris main store was the group's most successful store with the one in Marble Arch (London).

Questions

- Several factors were at the origin of M&S's slump in the 1990s. Can you briefly list them?
- Did the French expect M&S to leave? Why?
- What was the French government's reaction? Why?
- Why did they close all their foreign stores?

Analysis

A near diplomatic incident: Marks and Spencer's departure from France

- When Marks and Spencer closed their 18 French stores in 2001, it caused a general uproar, not only among the staff and the unions, but also among the French government members, who joined the unions' protests against what they considered as an abrupt and unjustified closure.
- The French government talked about "brutal methods" with the lay off of 1,700 French employees, and warned the British that they would bring the case to the EU as, according to the French Minister of Labour, "legal obligations had not been respected".

Focus → The path to recovery 2000-2011 (and beyond)

Description

- M&S had understood that a change of policy was necessary, but was very slow in taking the right measures.
- M&S eventually realised that the policy of "one thing at a time" change was not sustainable.
- M&S started streamlining and closing down unprofitable units to refocus on core activities.
- Payment by credit and debit cards was implemented in all the stores.
- M&S started focusing on the customers' new needs.
- M&S offered 30% discount on clothes in factory outlet malls.
- M&S entered a partnership with a renowned clothing designer.
- By 2002 they had already got back to growing sales results.
- They managed to rediscover the fundamentals of the past and make them relevant in the present.
- Marks and Spencer is ready to reconquer the French customers it had abandoned years before.
- It opened a 3-floor flagship store on the Champs Elysées on November 24, 2011.

Analysis

Marks & Spencer's triumphant return to France

- Today, French people seem to have forgotten how angry they had been when Marks and Spencer had decided to close its 18 stores in France in 2001.
- Indeed, without apparently the slightest grudge, the French consumers, mostly from Paris and around, crowded in front of the new M&S store when it opened its doors in the French capital on November 24, 2011.
- French consumers love to shop for special occasions at M&S's food hall; they also find quite exhilarating the men's and women's wear departments which offer affordable quality clothes from the smallest to the largest sizes. Yet, some M&S fans complain that the 2001 location, right across the street from the notorious Galeries Lafayette, was much better than the new one.
- Apart from this flagship store, the UK retailer has opened general stores in shopping centres around the French capital, together with a number of Simply Food outlets.

Express your point of view

- Do you think it was the right move for M&S to leave the Continent in 2001?
- Do you think that the Champs Elysées is an adequate location for a brand like M&S?
- What brands can you find on the Champs Elysées? Why?

Questions

- What measures did M&S take to reconquer the market?
- What shows that the retailer has recovered from its past financial troubles?
- What are the innovative moves that make M&S stand out today?
- What is the situation of M&S in Paris today?
- Were the French reluctant to accept M&S 10 years after the brand had left France?
- Why are French consumers huge fans of M&S?

Perspectives

Innovative strategic moves
2006: M&S introduced the Look Behind the Label marketing campaign. The aim of the campaign was to raise customers' awareness about ethical and environmental issues. M&S engaged in fair trade and sustainable development.
2011: M&S bacame the greenest UK retailer, along with CO-OP, by becoming carbon neutral, by sending no waste to landfill, by extending sustainable sourcing, by helping improve the lives of people in their supply chain and by helping customers and employees live a healthier life.

@ Go online

- Investigate into Marks and Spencer corporate culture by logging on the Internet. Investigate the consequences of • Marks and Spencer's departure from France.

Test yourself Try to use your memory – do not look at the vocabulary list!

1 HOW DO YOU SHOP?

Replace the underlined by a word or compound noun from the vocabulary list.

a) As I haven't got a lot of money, I usually look at the displays without buying anything.

b) He just loves going to junk shops and buying items which have been used before.

c) Her Dad gave her £500, so she went on a binge to buy lots of clothes.

d) "Can I help you?" "No thank you, I'd just like to have a look around."

e) As the shop is closing down, they are having a sale to get rid of all their stock.

f) She's been caught taking things from the shop without paying for them.

g) He always follows his shopping list carefully and never gets into buying on the spur of the moment.

h) They run a business which does orders and deliveries through the mail.

i) They run a restaurant, so they go to the wholesaler and buy in large quantities.

j) She loves designer clothes and bought a lovely shirt at a price below the original selling price.

2 COMPLETE THE STORY

Put the following story into the right order.

... Then I went to the checkout where the sales assistant swiped my card and I entered my PIN code.

... In one shop, there were a lot of end-of-range clothes on the rack.

... My daughter didn't like the shirt so a week later I took back the shirt and asked for a refund.

... I went to the sales in the High Street last week.

... I chose a very eye-catching shirt for my daughter.

... As it was a present, I asked the sales assistant to wrap it up.

... There were also cheap clothes on display on the shelves.

3 TRUE OR FALSE?

Are the following statements true or false? If they are false, can you correct them?

a) Prices are usually slashed during the sales.

b) Franchising is when the franchisee receives a licence fee and in return the owner of the brand has the right to use the business brand.

c) You don't have to pay for a sample, which is free of charge.

d) QPR (quality-price ratio) is often used to rate how good a wine is compared to the price.

e) The feel-good factor after a special event (like the Royal Wedding) can boost consumer confidence and set off a spending spree.

f) Getting the right store layout makes no difference in customer traffic flow.

g) One-stop shopping is a term used for retail outlets and marketing and distribution which offer a multitude of products or services in one place.

h) A loss leader is sold at a higher price than the cost price to attract customers and stimulate sales.

4 COMPOUND WORDS

Choose from the 3 columns to make a compound word.

Point	of / and / to	distribution
End	of / and / to	mortar
Brick	of / and / to	charge
Door	of / and / to	range
Channel	of / and / to	mortar
Free	of / and / to	living
Click	of / and / to	sale
Cost	of / and / to	door

VOCABULARY

3 | Marketing

Words

"To satisfy our customers' needs, we'll give them what they want, not what we want to give them." (Steve James)

Aisle: allée
Amount to (to): se monter à
Around-the-clock shop: boutique ouverte 24/24h
Brick and mortar shop: magasin avec des murs (réel, opposé au magasin virtuel)
Browse (to) / look around (to): flâner
Bulk purchase: achat en gros
Bulky: encombrant
Buy (to), purchase (to): acheter
Buying / purchasing power: pouvoir d'achat
Cardboard: carton
Cash register: caisse enregistreuse
Central buying office: centrale d'achat
Chain store: grand magasin, grande surface
Channel of distribution: canal de distribution
Checkout: caisse de sortie
Clearance sale: liquidation
Click and mortar: qui associe vente en magasin et vente en ligne
Container: conteneur
Cost of living: coût de la vie
Crate: caisse, cageot
Delivery boy: livreur
Department: rayon
Direct selling: vente directe
Display (on): à l'étalage
Distributor: distributeur
Doorstep / home delivery: livraison à domicile
Door-to-door: porte à porte
Draw (to): attirer
End of range: fin de gamme
Expensive / dear: cher
Eye-catching: qui attire l'œil
Feel-good factor: indice de satisfaction
Franchise: franchise
Franchising: système de franchises
Free-of-charge: gratuit
Generics: produits génériques
High Street spending: dépenses faites dans les magasins
High Street, Main Street (USA): rue commerçante
Home party: vente à domicile
Home shopping: télé-achat
Impulse buying: achat d'impulsion
In stock (to have): avoir en stock
Invaluable: inestimable (cher +++)
Layout: agencement, disposition
Licensed dealer: revendeur agréé
Lose ground (to): perdre du terrain
Loss leader: produit vendu à perte
Marketer: responsable de commercialisation
Marketing mix: plan de marchéage
Marketing play: stratagème marketing
Mass market: grand public
Mass marketing: commercialisation de masse
Mass consumption: consommation de masse
Merchandise: marchandise
Middleman: intermédiaire
Off-label: dégriffe
One-stop shopping: concentration des achats sur un seul lieu
Online shopping: achats en ligne
Opening hours: heures d'ouverture
Outlet: point de vente
Pay upfront (to): payer à l'avance
Point of sale (POS): point de vente
Price markdown: démarquage
Rack: portant
Range: gamme
Refund: remboursement
Regulation: réglementation
Retailer: détaillant
Sales: ventes, soldes
Sales representative: commercial
Sales target: objectif de vente
Sample: échantillon
Second-hand: deuxième main / d'occasion
Sell (to): vendre
Shelf (shelves): étagère, rayonnage
Shelf storage: mise en rayon
Shop / store: magasin / boutique
Shoplifting: vol à l'étalage
Shopping centre, mall (USA): centre commercial
Shopping list: liste de courses
Shopping spree / binge: fièvre acheteuse, débauche d'achats
Showcase: vitrine
Slash (prices) (to): réduire (les prix) de beaucoup
Sports apparel: articles de sports
Standard of living: niveau de vie
Staple goods: les produits de base
Subscribe (to): s'abonner
Swipe (to): passer (une carte magnétique)
The sales: soldes
Town centre, downtown (USA): centre-ville
Trade (to): vendre, faire du commerce
Valueless: sans valeur
Wholesaler: grossiste
Window shopping: lèche vitrine
Wrap (to): envelopper / emballer

4

Brands

A powerful communication means

Question

What makes brands attractive / successful?

WORD BOX

a sense of belonging • loyalty cards • a logo • a slogan • a label • a trademark

4 | Brands

1 • Look and discuss

a) Look at the following logos and read the text.

> **Info**
> Brand recognition is an important part of marketing and communication for a product. The fact that people automatically recognise a brand and know its reputation encourages brand loyalty and better sales.
> Don't confuse the word "brand" with the word "logo". Logo is the image, the visual identity of a product. Branding calls for a "brand plan" or "brand strategy" with long-term vision.

b) Discuss in class.

1. Do you know what products these logos represent?
2. Now think of famous brands of:
Frozen foods (surgelés) • *Convenience foods* (plats preparés) • *household appliances* (appareils ménagers) • *leisure activities* (loisirs) • *soft drinks* (boissons non-alcoolisées) • *clothing* (vêtements) • *white products / electrical goods* (gros électroménager)

c) Choose one of the above brands (either from the pictures or from the list you made), and answer the following questions.

1. What company / product / service does the brand represent?
2. What makes the product different from competitors? Why is it a great product?
3. What are the special attributes of the company / product / service?
4. What demographic (target audience) does the brand appeal to?
5. Are there any downsides (negative aspects) to the brand? How could it be improved?

2 • Read and understand

a) Read the following text.

Drink ads aimed at young in the UK

Ministers charged with delivering the Olympic Games have vowed to protect young people from binge drinking after figures showed a rise in liver disease across the North East.
Department for Culture, Media and Sport (DCMS) officials reaffirmed their commitment to ensuring alcoholic drinks are not targeted at young people after doctors called for new curbs on alcohol advertising. "There are strict criteria which mean that broadcast advertising for alcoholic drinks cannot be targeted at young people or encourage immoderate consumption and which prevent alcohol advertisements from being placed in any programme made for children or likely to appeal to under-18 audiences."

b) Complete the sentences with the following words taken from the extract above.

commitment • advertising • binge drinking • targeted • prevent • audience • broadcasting • advertisements

1. The initials BBC stand for British ... Corporation.
2. ... is a real problem in the UK; many youngsters in their early teens indulge in it once a week.
3. ... for alcoholic drinks should be banned. Governments should show more ... in their fight against alcoholism.
4. Children are a profitable ... for companies, and it is almost impossible for parents to ... their children from being exposed to ads. That is why children shouldn't be ... by advertisers.
5. The latest ... campaign for mixed drinks corresponded to a peak in alcohol consumption.

3 • Look and write

a) Look at the following ads.

b) Answer the questions by writing a few sentences.

1. How sexist can ads be? Comment on the two ads.
2. What tools do these ads use to attract audiences?

4 • Listen and understand

CD n° 2
Track n° 1

a) Does Marjory privilege particular brand names?
b) What is the name for changing brands regularly?
c) What about you? Are you influenced by a brand when you buy a product?

WARMING UP

▸ Who is your best celebrity? Best royal? Does he / she influence your fashion choices?

CD n° 2
Track n° 2

Kate, queen of shops, boosts Britain's retailers by making the buzz

She may be the Duchess of Cambridge but she's also the queen of Britain's shops. The girl once called Kate Middleton is undeniably a fashion icon with huge influence – and now she's got cash tills ringing at retailers right across the United Kingdom.

Economists credit the 29 year old with helping to boost consumer confidence figures, released in the UK Friday, while April retail sales also grew as women across the nation scrambled to get the Kate look. Everything she wears – seemingly everything – is scrutinized, analyzed and promptly sells out within hours. It's a dream come true for the sales department. For example, the blue dress the Duchess wore to announce her engagement to Prince William helped to boost sales by 45 percent for the London brand Issa.

This week, unprecedented demand for a flesh-toned satin number she wore to meet the U.S. President and First Lady crashed the website of its maker Reiss. The garment retails at just $300 – a pretty penny, certainly, but hardly an extravagance for one so wealthy. It was also reportedly several times cheaper than the designer outfit chosen by Michelle Obama, showing it's hard to put a price on elegance. The Middleton effect is worth big money.

And no British fashion chain has benefited more from the Duchess's patronage than Reiss. The company began with just one menswear store on the fringes of London's financial district, known as the City. Today, it's a multi-billion-dollar business, with 106 stores around the world. Reiss now employs 1,500 people and has branches in 10 countries, including the burgeoning economies of China, Russia and the United Arab Emirates.

That's good news because Middleton mania is a truly global phenomenon. The dress the Duchess wore this week is now completely sold out on both sides of the Atlantic. The Middleton effect has been "absolutely phenomenal" for the brand. "She is one of the most watched women in the world at the moment, so anything she wears is bound to have an impact," a Reiss spokeswoman said. "Of course it will have an impact on sales but it also introduces us to a completely different type of customer."

Kate may now be married but the Middleton boost lives on in the form of her younger sister Pippa, who was also in the limelight at the royal wedding and who is now making waves for her wardrobe, too. A blue blazer she wore after the big day sent fashion bloggers into a frenzy. As you can imagine, that's likely to be good news for its maker Zara, owned by Spain's textile giant Inditex.

CNN, May 28th, 2011

Lexical work

1. Find the English equivalents in the text.

Titre **a)** stimuler **b)** faire le buzz

§ 1 **a)** mode **b)** énorme **c)** caisses enregistreuses

§ 2 **a)** publier **b)** se précipiter **c)** se vendre jusqu'à épuisement des stocks **d)** un rêve devenu réalité

§ 3 **a)** saturer / planter un site Internet **b)** vêtement

§ 4 **a)** prêt à porter pour hommes **b)** filiales

§ 5 **a)** phénomène mondial **b)** épuisé **c)** porte parole

§ 6 **a)** l'effet Middleton **b)** continuer **c)** garde robe

Pronunciation work

CD n° 2
Track n° 3

1. Listen and observe.

Kate [ei] • icon [ai] • year [ɪə] • mania [ei] • now [aʊ] In English, some vowels are pronounced with a sound called "diphtong", two following vowel sounds.

2. Listen to these word groups that you may find difficult and repeat with the right stress.

• Kate may now ... • in the limelight • That's likely to be good news.

Work on the title

1. Identify the source of the document (title, date, nature).

2. Look at the headline. What is meant by "queen"? Find an answer in the first sentence of the document.

Check the facts

1. Read § 1.
a) What are the titles given to Kate Middleton?
b) How is she considered by retailers across the UK?

2. Read § 2.
a) How old is Kate Middleton?
b) What is her impact on women across the nation?
c) Which brand had its sales boosted? Why?

3. Read § 3.
a) What is Michelle Obama's other name?
b) What was Kate's dress's impact when she met the First American Couple?
c) How much did this dress cost?
d) Which designer outfit was more expensive?

4. Read § 4.
Which company benefited more from Kate Middleton's outfits?

5. Read § 5.
a) Is the Kate Middleton effect a British phenomenon?
b) What are the consequences of the Kate Middleton effect? (2 answers)

6. Read § 6.
a) Which other celebrity is also involved in the buzz?
b) How is she related to Kate Middleton?
c) Which outfit was at the origin of a frenzy on the Net?
d) Which company designed it?

Grammar

→ p. 235

L'auxiliaire modal : *may*

- *She may be the Duchess of Cambridge but ...* : (elle a beau être ... mais) / even if she is ...
- *Kate may now be married but ...* : (elle est peut être ... mais) / *though she is married ...*

Topic debrief

1. Choose the sentence which you think corresponds best to the main topic of the document.
a) The Kate Middleton phenomenon is costly to women consumers because they can't afford her style.
b) The Duchess has become a celebrity though her outfits are less expensive than Michelle Obama's.
c) Kate Middleton has initiated a global phenomenon, boosting fashion chain sales.

2. Rephrase the correct sentence in order to make a short introduction to the document.

Methods

1. Write a key sentence for each paragraph.

2. Which paragraph best sums up the document? 2, 5, 6?

3. List all the companies mentioned in the document and write a short sentence about them.

4. List all the information you have about Reiss.

Train for the exam

1. Make a **summary/account** of the document (60 words/3-5 minutes).

2. Express your personal opinion:
What do you think of the fashion craze about celebrities?
Explain and illustrate your point of view (100 words / 3-5 minutes).

3. Role play: work in pairs
You are going to take part in a conversation.
Student A: you want to buy the same dress as Kate Middleton's but it is sold out.
Student B: you are a shop assistant and your mission is to sell another dress.

Go online

- Find information about other celebrities who have an impact on the fashion world.
- Get prepared to report to your group / class (a PowerPoint presentation is recommended).

PRACTICE • TEXT

Train with an oral document

CD n° 2
Track n° 4

Boomers: an advertising challenge

WARMING UP

- Have you heard of the 60s generation?
- What are they called?
- Why is this age group interesting for some companies?

Lexical work

1. Match the words to find their equivalents.

a) conseil	**1.** take a few steps back
b) atteindre	**2.** share
c) la plupart	**3.** increasing
d) croissant(e)	**4.** most
e) prendre du recul	**5.** advice
f) personnel	**6.** target
g) inquiétant	**7.** hire
h) conscient(e)	**8.** age gap
i) fossé de génération	**9.** aware
j) recruter	**10**. worrying
k) cibler	**11**. staff
l) partager	**12**. advice

2. Work on figures: write in full and read aloud. 20 • 30 • their 50s • 60s • 70s

Pronunciation work

CD n° 2
Track n° 5

1. Listen and observe.

Well, I'd say → Well, I would say
I'd be very worried → I would be very worried
Remember the rule:
I'd: [aid] + verb is a contraction of I would: I would be worried.
I'd: [aid] + past participle is a contraction of I had: I had worried.

2. Listen, write in full, then pronounce.

a) I'd never say such a thing: ...
b) I'd never mentioned their age: ...
c) I'd never push the door of an ad agency: ...
d) I'd never market this product to a late teen: ...
e) I'd better focus on the products' features: ...

Work on the title

1. Look at the title of the document.

2. Who are the boomers? What are the main characteristics of this age group?

Check the facts

1. Listen to part 1.
a) What is the first mistake companies should avoid when targeting boomers?
b) How old are boomers today?
c) What should ad agencies focus on?
d) What sort of message do boomers not want to hear from admen?

2. Listen to part 2.
a) What is the impact of the advertising revolution on marketeers?
b) What's the average age of ad agencies' staff?
c) What must marketeers do in order to reach their target audience?
d) Why is it a problem?
e) What is the final advice given by the expert?

Topic debrief

1. Choose the sentence which best corresponds to the main topic of the document.
a) Boomers shouldn't be addressed as a different consumer niche because they still play an active role in the community.
b) Most marketeers do not use the right strategy to address boomers because they aren't really interested in this market.
c) Companies have trouble finding the right way to address boomers mostly because they have not yet grasped the consequences of the advertising revolution.

2. Rephrase the correct sentence in order to make a short introduction to the document.

Methods

Listen again to part 1 and complete the sentences by using the following words.
advice • target (2) • avoid • agencies • consumer niche • old • companies • aging • issues • features (2) • benefits • mistake • smart • admen • focusing
a) R: Nuck, what ... would you give to ... wishing to ... boomers.
b) NC: The first ... to ... is to address them as an ... group, distant from everyday life ....
c) R: Would you say that most ... today understand how to target this specific ... ?
d) NC: Instead of ... on the age of their ..., they had better focus on the product's ... and ....
e) Boomers are ... enough to imagine how these ... apply to them; they don't need the ... to spell out for them: You're ..., so this product is for you.

Train for the exam

1. Use your notes to make an **oral presentation** about the document and record yourself (3-5 minutes).

2. Comment: find an answer to the following question. Discuss and give examples (100 words / 3-5 minutes).
Why do boomers not want to be told "you're old, so this product is for you"?

3. Role play: work in pairs
You are going to take part in a conversation.
Student A: you are in charge of the advertising department of a firm; your mission is to launch an advertising campaign for a new phone designed especially for boomers.
Student B: you are an advertiser in charge of student A's advertising campaign.
You both discuss the best strategy to make a successful advertising campaign.

TIPS
You should use your notes in order to present a realistic conversation. Don't read them, look up. You can:
– record the conversation (the recording should last between one and two minutes at most);
– videotape the scene and show it to the class;
– act out the scene in front of the class;
– listen to your classmates' recordings and write what you have understood in a short and structured paragraph.

Go online
• Inquire about other consumer niches and find the best way to target them.
• Get prepared to report to your group / class (a PowerPoint presentation is recommended).

WARMING UP

- Are you an energy drink consumer?
- What do you think about this sort of drink?

CD n° 2 Track n° 6

Chilled drinks[1]

After the heavily manufactured energy drinks boom, a soothing[2] alternative to Red Bull and its peers has become a $500m business. And it is going to get much bigger.

Welcome to the latest, rapidly growing sector of the beverage market – relaxation drinks, designed to relax us, much like the energy drinks so popular during the past couple of decades were concocted to stimulate us.

"We live in crazy times, with technology driving an ever faster pace of life and the demand for instant gratification on the rise. There's a need for products that are more balancing, that allow consumers to take a step back," says Paul Fuegner, marketing head at Marley Beverage Company, which launched last year the Marley's Mellow Mood range, which come in several tea flavours, all featuring singer Bob Marley on their cans and bottles.

"As there are a lot of companies getting very excited about the potential of relaxation drinks, what is going to separate them, apart from taste and effectiveness, is the branding," says Fuegner, a former marketing chief at Skyy Vodka. A portion of the profits from Marley Beverage go to 1Love.org, the Marley's non-profit organisation, which funds charities that "promote youth, protect the planet and strive for global peace".

"The energy drinks market took time to build its huge size – nobody really understood what they were for and acceptance had to grow. That ground has been paved now. Relaxation drink brands have to be faster to market and with a very clear message," Fuegner adds. "The Marley brand means starting on a secure base with a message that resonates."

The winners of this competition will, he adds, both be among the first to market – as Red Bull was – and those that can best stand out on innovative drinks launches: competing for space on the shelves of corner shops and convenience stores. "In this market it's brand name, packaging and position that will get it noticed in the first place," say Weber.

"Every detail counts in shaping a brand, because there are just so many products in such a small space offering to do much the same thing," says Mark Bair, whose relaxation drink Blue Cow was the first to tap the market in the U.S., in 2004. The name is more than an obvious joke – an ironical reference to Red Bull – says Bair, who used to work in Coca-Cola's business.

CNBC business, 11 May 2011

1. a chilled drink: *une boisson relaxante.*
2. soothing: *apaisant.*

Lexical work

1. Find their English equivalents in the text.

a) décennie § 2
b) gamme • représenter § 3
c) lancer § 3
d) création de la marque § 4
e) se concurrencer § 6
f) étagères § 6
g) se différencier § 6
h) magasins de proximité (2 expressions) § 6
i) emballage § 6
j) pénétrer (un marché) § 7

2. Find the French equivalents.

a) taste and effectiveness § 4
b) non-profit organisation § 4
c) a corner shop § 6
d) shaping a brand § 7

Pronunciation work

CD n° 2 Track n° 7

1. Listen and observe.

"i" can be pronounced: [ɪ] drink; [aɪ] life; [ə] first

2. Listen and fill in the grid according to the pronunciation of the "i".

chilled • designed • driving • rise • third

drink [ɪ]	life [aɪ]	first [ə]

Work on the title

1. Identify the source of the document (title, date, nature).

2. Identify the type of market involved from the headline and the first paragraph.

Check the facts

Say if each of the following statement is true or false (T / F). Support your choice with passages from the article.

1. Read §2.
A new brand of energy drink has been launched on the market. T / F

2. Read §3.
a) Today's consumers need soothing drinks. T / F
b) The new brand Marley has nothing to do with the singer Bob Marley. T / F

3. Read §4.
Experts think this new type of drink has no real potential on the soft drink market. T / F

4. Read §5.
Relaxation drink brands have to be marketed faster than energy drinks were. T / F

5. Read §7.
a) Shaping a brand is easy because there is no competition. T / F
b) Former Coca-Cola employee named his relaxation drink Blue Cow to make fun of the most famous brand of energy drinks. T / F

Grammar

→ p. 235

L'article défini : *the* or Ø

- *After the heavily manufactured energy drink boom ...*
- *We live in Ø crazy times ...*

Topic debrief

1. Choose the sentence which you think corresponds best to the main topic of the document.
a) Energy drinks is not a decreasing market.
b) Featuring singer Bob Marley on the cans and bottles suggest they are made out of drugs.
c) Chilled drinks is a fast-growing market.

2. Rephrase the correct sentence in order to make a short introduction to the document.

Methods

1. Complete the sentences with some of the following words (they do not appear in the order of the paragraphs).
company • income • charity • carry out • allowing • successful • shape • winners • competition • huge • succeed • feature • packaging • drinks • launched • iconic brand • communication • relaxation • points of sales • strategy • stand out • issues

It seems that consumers today need products ... them to "take a break". Marley Beverage is a ... which chose to ... Bob Marley on their ... . Moreover, Marley brand gives back part of its ... to a ... promoting environmental ... among others. If relaxation drink companies want to ..., they must ... a persuasive communication strategy, and pay attention to all the details allowing to ... a brand.

2. Which paragraph best sums up the document?

3. What are the main characteristics of Paul Fuegner's company? List them.

Train for the exam

1. Make a **summary / account** of the document (60 words / 3-5 minutes).

2. Comment: find an answer to the following question. Discuss and give examples (100 words / 3-5 minutes).
What is the impact of the use of an iconic figure on product packages?

3. Role play: work in groups
You are going to create an ad.
Group A: is preparing a new ad campaign for Red Bull. Choose an advertising media and create your own ad.
Group B: is preparing a new ad campaign for Blue Cow. Choose an advertising media and create your own ad.
Confront the campaigns in class and debate.

Go online

- Inquire about: http://charityoflove.org/. When was it founded? What are its main activities?
- Get prepared to report to your group / class (a PowerPoint presentation is recommended).

4 | Brands

Train with an oral document

WARMING UP

► Give some examples (ad and other forms of communication) in which a brand is linked to a celebrity.

CD n° 2 Track n° 8

Celebrity endorsement

Lexical work

Match the following words to find their equivalents.

Part 1

a) cohérence	**1.** behaviour
b) engagement	**2.** consistency
c) stratégie à long terme	**3.** commitment
d) savoir / connaissance	**4.** monitoring
e) comportement	**5.** target audience
f) surveillance	**6.** long-term strategy
g) audience cible	**7.** knowledge

Part 2

a) presse à scandale	**1.** grab in its fall
b) entraîner (quelque chose / quelqu'un) dans sa chute	**2.** tabloids
c) des deux côtés	**3.** both sides
d) appariement	**4.** matching
e) sans risque	**5.** safe
f) à risque	**6.** communication channels
g) faire du mal	**7.** non-safe
h) dopage	**8.** advertising strategy
i) stratégie publicitaire	**9.** overshadowing
j) domination	**10.** harm
k) canaux de communication	**11.** doping

Pronunciation work

CD n° 2 Track n° 9

1. Listen and observe.

guest • considering • knowledge • should

These words contain a letter that is not pronounced. Cross out the letter and practice pronouncing them.

2. Key words of "Brands".

a) Listen and focus on long words containing a primary and a secondary stress.

dedicated • celebrity • responsibility • communication

b) Practise repeating these words aloud.

Work on the title

1. Look at the title of the document.

2. What does the word "endorsement" mean?

Check the facts

1. Listen to part 1.

a) What are the two major requirements necessary for endorsing a brand?

b) Why are these requirements indispensable?

c) What should the qualities of an ideal endorser be?

d) Why is the endorser constantly monitored by the company?

2. Listen to part 2.

a) What will happen if an endorser misbehaves?

b) What will happen to the endorser if the brand has image problems?

c) What sector is the safest for brand endorsement?

d) Who are the celebrities quoted as brand endorsers?

e) Why can't the expert give examples of non-safe endorsers?

f) What sector is the most unsafe one?

g) Why should brand endorsement be profitable?

h) What can happen between the brand and the celebrity endorsing it?

Topic debrief

1. Choose the sentence which you think corresponds best to the main topic of the document.

a) Brand endorsement is a both a short-term and safe communication strategy that can rake in a lot of money for the endorsed brand.

b) Brand endorsement is the best strategy for brand owners but it is very expensive and some companies can't afford the cost in their advertising budget.

c) Brand endorsement is one among other aspects of advertising and is not always a win-win situation if something negative happens to one side.

2. Rephrase the correct sentence in order to make a short introduction to the document.

Methods

1. What should the ideal endorser be? Why?

2. What are the dangers in the field of sports?

Train for the exam

1. Use your notes to make an **oral presentation** about the document and record yourself (3-5 minutes).

2. Express your personal opinion:
What are the advantages and drawbacks of brand endorsement?
Explain and illustrate your point of view (100 words / 3-5 minutes).

3. Role play: work in pairs
You are going to take part in a conversation.
Student A and student B: you work in the communication department of a famous brand. You are trying to choose a celebrity to endorse the brand.

a) Define the sector A and B are working in.

b) Choose a real or fictitious brand and celebrities.

c) Find arguments to propose or reject this or that celebrity.

d) Make sure the brand's communication strategy is made clear.

PRACTICE • AUDIO • VIDEO

Train with a video

Nokia Interactive Advertising – "New Conversations"

→ http://www.youtube.com/watch?v=6zkmi_AXACw

10 June, 2009

Look at this video on the Internet about advertising and mobile technology

Check the facts	Methods
1. What does the video deal with?	• Which communication devices are shown?
2. Who are the people involved? – at the beginning – in the second part	• Are they on their own? In groups? In family gatherings?
3. Where does the action take place? – at the beginning – in the second part	• Are they at home? At their workplace?
4. When do you notice a change in the video? Why?	• Which word is repeated all the time? • What can be said about the music, rhythm, colours of the video?
5. **Issues...** In part 2, which message is conveyed about our modern world? Do you agree with it?	• Do you think the video is still advertising, or is it becoming "brainwashing"? • Which is the most effective?

4 | Brands

WARMING UP

- Have you been to the London's West End? What is particular in the West End at night?
- Have you been to New York? Why is New York called "the city that never sleeps"?

CD n° 2 Track n° 10

Piccadilly Circus and globalisation

Bright lights, world city: The stories told by a dazzling London landmark

They are an instantly recognisable symbol of London, but, perhaps appropriately for such a global city, the advertising lights at Piccadilly Circus, first switched on in 1908, have mostly been a pathway for foreign brands, rather than domestic ones. Now Sanyo, which has flashed its name at the site since 1978, is to make way for Hyundai, a South Korean car-maker, which will pay Land Securities, the firm that owns the electronic billboards, around £2m ($3.3m) a year for a central spot.

For the past century, the glittery displays have reflected shifts in international influence in business and beyond. British and European brands predominated until after the Second World War: Perrier, a French drink firm, was the first to spell its name in lights; Guinness, Bovril and Schweppes, three other beverage makers, were also early presences. Yet the London landmark has not hosted a British company for 40 years.

By the 1960s Americans were well established: Coca-Cola has been adding life to the lights since 1955; other American torchbearers have included Budweiser and McDonald's. As Asian companies began to conquer global markets in the 1970s, so Japanese businesses started to colonise the Piccadilly boards. Canon led, followed by Fuji and TDK. The South Koreans came next. The illuminations in New York's Times Square, which feature multiple American brands and also advertise shows, are comparatively limited.

As the geographical spread has tellingly shifted, so has the mix of products on display. Disposable incomes rose, consumers became more ambitious and the cheap and easy pleasures of Player's cigarettes and Skol and Double Diamond beer gave way to the new opiates of the masses: Kodak cameras, Philips Hi-Fis and Panasonic colour televisions, as well as the aspirational pull of the Volkswagen Beetle and foreign air travel.

The lights have sometimes reflected momentous events, as well as commercial trends. Though overrun with American GIs, Piccadilly Circus was dark throughout the Second World War, lighting up again only in 1949. The signs have since been dimmed for the funerals of Winston Churchill in 1965 and Princess Diana in 1997. With the rise of LED displays* and decline of neon, the lights are now brighter than ever. But they may yet need to find greener hues in their multicoloured glory: they generate 1.9m kg of carbon dioxide a year, equivalent to the emissions of around 2,000 of Hyundai's bestselling cars. That is a lot of gas for a set of streetlights.

* LED (light emitting diode): *diode électroluminescente.*

The Economist, June 11th, 2011

Lexical work

1. Find the French equivalents.

§ 1 **a)** international **b)** road **c)** signs **d)** location
§ 2 **a)** arrangements **b)** changes **c)** drink companies
§ 3 **a)** flagship brands **b)** show
§ 4 **a)** purchasing power **b)** be replaced
§ 5 **a)** important **b)** fashion **c)** crowded **d)** during

2. Find the English equivalents.

§ 2 **a)** brillant **b)** au-delà
§ 3 **a)** conquérir **b)** laisser la place
§ 5 plus lumineuse

Pronunciation work

CD n° 2 Track n° 11

1. Listen and observe.

advertisement: [ɪ] for British English.
advertisement: [aɪ] for American English.

2. Underline the stressed syllable, then listen to check the right answer.

recognisable • international • disposable • geographical • aspirational • commercial

3. Listen to these words that you may find difficult and repeat with the right stress.

foreign brands • domestic ones • Asian companies • advertising lights

Work on the title

1. Identify the source of the document (title, date, nature).

2. Look at the headline, then focus on the first sentence to find out which London landmark it deals with.

Check the facts

1. Read §1.
a) Find who or what the following words refer to: l1 they – l4 ones – l7 its – l8 which.
b) What Asian brands are mentioned in §1?
c) How long has London been an advertising landmark?
d) Which company owns the billboards? How much does it get paid for a central advertising location?

2. Read §2.
a) What were the predominant brands before and after WWII?
b) What can you say about British brands? When was the last time a British brand was advertised in Piccadilly Circus?

3. Read §3.
a) What are the names and nationalities of the famous brands present from the 1950s onward?
b) What happened in the 1970s?
c) Which place has mostly products advertised, Piccadilly Circus or Times Square?

4. Read §4.
What effect did the rise in purchasing power have on the products advertised?

5. Read §5.
a) How do the advertising signs in London reflect current events or trends? Give examples from the text.
b) What technology has replaced neon today?
c) What are the negative effects of these advertising billboards?

Grammar → p. 235

Le present perfect / Le prétérit

- *Coca-Cola has been adding life to the lights since 1955.*
- *Japanese businesses started to colonise the Picadilly boards.*

Topic debrief

1. Choose the sentence which you think corresponds best to the main topic of the document.
a) The lights in London vary according to the events; this has been the case since 1908.
b) City lights in London represent a problem for the environment because of the carbon dioxide they generate.
c) London's advertising lights reflect the changes in global trends and tastes, with little or no space for the home brands.

2. Make a short introduction to the document by using the word bank (40 words).
Picadilly Circus • *lights* • *reflect* • *events* • *momentous* • *shift* • *foreign prices* • *international influence*

Methods

1. Paragraph 3 mentions Times Square.
a) Make 2 sentences to explain where it is situated (country / city / district).
b) What comparison is made with Picadilly Circus?

2. Translate paragraph 5 into French. What are the issues raised in this paragraph?

Train for the exam

1. Make a summary / account of the document (60 words / 3-5 minutes).

2. Express your personal opinion:
Are you for or against the profusion of advertising lights?
Explain and illustrate your point of view (100 words / 3-5 minutes).

3. Role play: work in pairs
You are going to take part in a conversation.
Student A: you work for a lobby whose role is to preserve the interests of British brands. You want to obtain central spots for British ads in London.
Student B: you are a Land Securities executive.
Imagine the negotiation between the two: think about the arguments the two parties would develop, as well as the handling of objections on both sides.

Making a brand visible to the public

1 • Situation

You work in the sales and marketing department of a company. You have to work out the best way to make your brand visible to the public.

2 • Process

a) Look at the following documents (on the next page).
b) Get into pairs or small groups. Choose one of the following products (or anything else you would like): *clothing – a ballpoint pen –biscuits – a soft drink – smartphone ...*
All students: invent a brand, logo and catchphrase of your own. Try and make your product as realistic and saleable as possible.
c) Now discuss together what you can do to make your brand visible to the public. Remember to speak in English only! The objective is to come up with some practical ideas for communicating your brand so that it becomes a household name.
d) Finally, summarise your ideas and present them to the class.

3 • Follow up

Write a short report for your boss explaining what decisions you have made.

Go online

Look on the Internet and find examples of product placement, use of SEO, retail planograms, etc. SEO (search engine optimisation) is the process of website creation using key words and terms to increase visibility and have a good position on search engine result pages. See Document B.

TIPS

- **Start by saying**

I would have thought that ...
As I see it ...
On the whole ...
One reason is ..., and another is ...
For one thing ... and for another ...
It seems to me that ...
I'm convinced that ...
In most cases ...
To start with ... and on top of that ...
The main thing is that ...

- **Here are some ideas to get you going:**

Target audience: Decide who the end users are and what kind of message they will listen to.
USP: Your Unique Selling Point makes your brand different from the competition and gives the brand a value.
Visual communication: Use your brand name on every document which comes out of your office – e-mails, letters, envelopes, business cards, sales literature, labels, etc.
Personal communication: Everyone in your company has to be involved in the brand image as they represent the brand. Certain companies even require a certain dress code (or short haircuts, no earrings, etc.).
Consistency and repetition: They are key to brand-building.

Doc • A

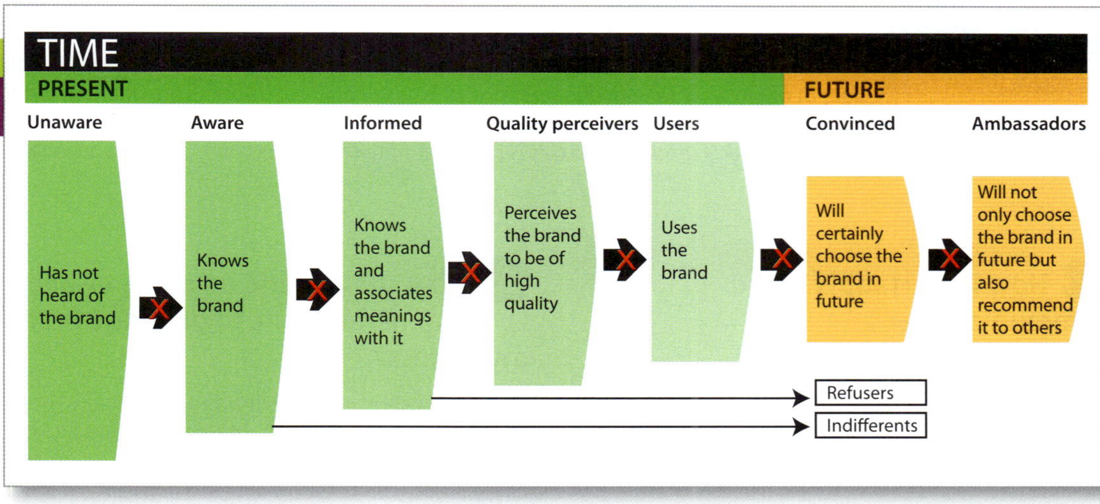

Doc • B

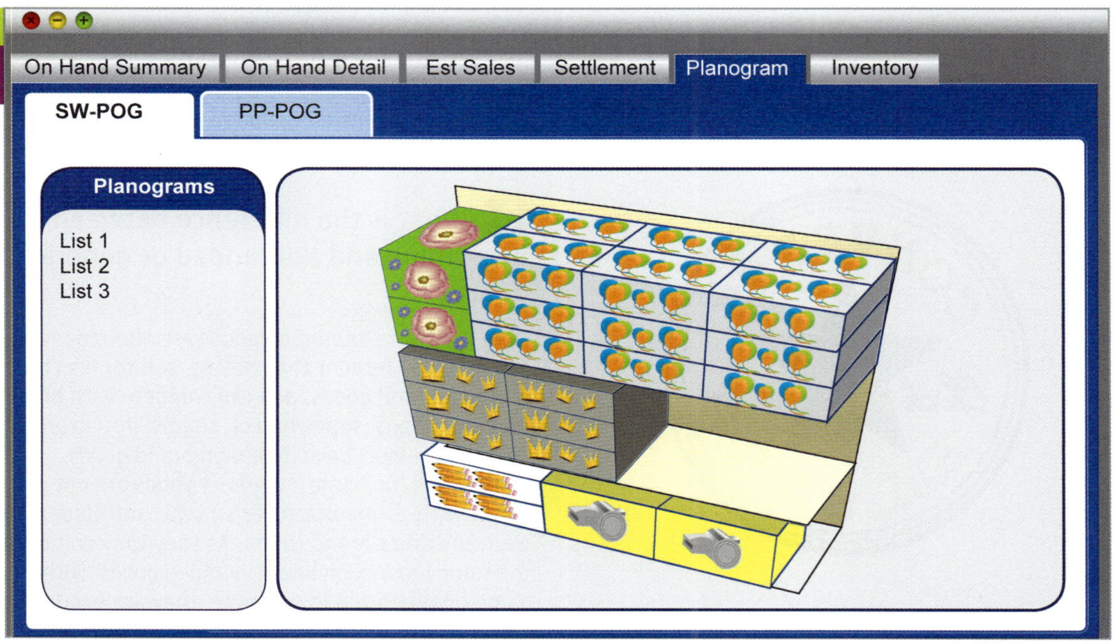

Doc • C

ATWOODZ

Embedded Marketing

What is product placement?

Product placement, or **embedded marketing**, is a form of advertisement where branded goods or services are placed in a context usually devoid of ads, such as movies, the storyline of television shows or news programmes. The product placement is often not disclosed at the time that the goods or services are featured.

We can help

Atwoodz can help you with all of your product placement needs. Whether it is film, television or Web…

www.atwoodz.com

ROLE PLAY

4 | Brands

Background *A brand is a part of marketing which helps in commercialising a product. Communication, in the form of advertising and various kinds of publicity tools, is the moment when the public comes in contact with the brand.* (→ SEE CHAPTER "MARKETING" PAGE 62) ***It is vital to grab the public's attention, as this is the beginning of brand building, and brand loyalty.***

1 How important is brand communication?

Essential. Every time a customer interacts with a brand, brand communication takes place. Brand communication is a carefully planned strategy using eye-catching images to make an impact, create a positive experience, affect consumer behaviour and build a creative two-way dialogue between the company and its customers. A brand not only communicates the product quality but the company's ethics and core values as well. A well-communicated brand image will stick in the customer's mind and be difficult to replace; they are therefore unlikely to switch brand loyalty.

Questions

- Do you know any examples of product endorsement?
- Some brand names have become common terms, for example "Kleenex" instead of paper handkerchief. Do you know of any others?
- Would you say you are a "fashion victim", buying goods because of their brand image and because they are a current fashion? Are you easily influenced by what other consumers say about a brand?
- Should there be strict ethical controls over brand communication strategies (for example, targeting young children, misleading advertising, etc.)?

2 How can a brand be made visible to the general public to generate brand awareness?

The main way is advertising and promotion (→ SEE CHAPTER "MARKETING" PAGE 62). Other techniques include:
Brand extension (or stretching): an established product name is used for a new product in a different category, e.g. Virgin (airplanes, records, mobile phones ...);
Co-branding: when two or more brands work together to enhance current products or create an entirely new product. The Sports Kit by Nike and Apple is just one example.
Endorsement: a celebrity (often a sports star) makes a public statement in support of a particular product.

3 What is the difference between own-brand and unbranded or generic goods?

Own-brand or store-brand goods are often manufactured by the retailer themselves, sell for less than national-brand goods, and can compete with **brand leaders**. Many supermarket chains (for example Tesco, Carrefour) have their own-brand goods.
Unbranded (no name / generic) goods are not marketed with a manufacturer's name and undersell even the store-brand items. As they may come off the same production line as branded goods, with the same quality but a lower price, they are becoming increasingly popular, especially for FMCGs.

Info

The word "branding" originally meant marking your cattle, to make sure your cow stood out among all the others. Then in the 19th century, companies "branded" containers to identify them for shipment, and the same is true today. Branding by a name, logo, symbol or catchphrase makes a seller's product stand out among others and can be seen as a guarantee of quality compared to **copycat brands** / logos.
As global competition gets harder day by day (→ SEE CHAPTER "GLOBALISATION" PAGE 166), it is more and more important to make branding a key part of your marketing strategy.

Focus

Lobbying and shock advertising: two effective and controversial communication tools

Lobbying consists in the attempt to influence government decisions on all sorts of issues. Lobbies can represent a variety of interests: corporations, NGOs, advocacy groups, etc. Some lobbies are so powerful that their influence is extremely difficult to counter; it is the case for the fossil fuel lobby (representing major oil companies) which does everything in its power to prevent governments from taking drastic but necessary measures to cut carbon emissions and turn to alternative energies. The various environmental lobbies, among which WWF and Greenpeace, do not always have the financial means to compete. Are consumers ready for another helping of shock advertising? Today, an advertising campaign has got to make a "buzz" if it wants to attract consumers' attention in a world where ads are gaining ground. In this ultra-competitive context, Benetton has chosen to resort to what it does best, i.e shock advertising.

Lobbying

Corporate lobbies

- They are extremely powerful; their influence is huge on legislators and other decision-makers.
- Corporate lobbies are everywhere critical decisions are made. They can have an enormous impact on key decisions involving major issues such as health or sustainability.
- The junk food lobby in the U.S. is a typical example: Food giants such as Coca-Cola, Pepsi and Kraft have successfully pressed U.S. regulators to weaken the regulations that bar junk food advertisements aimed at children and younger teens.
- The energy lobby, aka fossil fuel lobby, represented by Exxon, Total, Shell, BP, etc., puts all its power into preventing further anti-pollution measures.
- In the U.S., the energy lobby contributes millions of dollars to political campaigns, whereas the alternative energy lobbies only contribute around half a million dollars.

Questions

- To what extent are lobbies powerful? What part do they play in the decision process?
- Quote at least two powerful corporate lobbies in the U.S.
- Why is their influence so important?
- What is the GWPF?
- When was it created? What is its role?
- What are big corporations' claims to the European Commission?
- How do you understand the subhead: David against Goliath?

Lobbying for the planet

The GWPF: a struggling European lobby

- The GWPF stands for the Global Warming Policy Foundation.
- It was launched in 2009 in the UK in the run up to the Copenhagen climate summit.
- The GWPF is funded entirely by voluntary donations from a number of private individuals and charitable trusts. In order to make clear its complete independence, it does not accept gifts from either energy companies or anyone with a significant interest in an energy company.
- Its main focus is to analyse global warming policies and their economic and other implications.
- Its aim is to provide strong and reliable economic analysis and advice.
- It seeks to inform the media, politicians and the public on the subject in general and warn them against the misinformation they are currently subjected to.

David against Goliath

- In 2011 the GWPF desperately called for a series of actions to maintain high emission allowances on companies contributing to global warming.
- 19 giant companies, among which Shell, Tesco and others, are lobbying the European Commission to lower the allowances on carbon emissions.
- The GWPF is pessimistic as to the outcome.

Focus

Advertising: Benetton is back!

Description

- Benetton is a global Italian-based fashion retailer present in 120 countries with 5,000 stores worldwide, created in 1965.
- The brand hired Olivero Toscani, a photographer, as its creative director in 1984.
- From this period onwards, the brand became both famous and controversial for its advertising campaigns based on shocking images addressing current issues: peace, racial integration, AIDS, the death penalty, etc.

The aim of the brand

- The aim of the brand was to raise the level of public awareness.
- It encouraged an advertising revolution through a new concept: shock advertising.
- The campaigns received either praise or loathing but never left indifferent.
- Oliver Toscani said in 1991: "We are a little bit in advance of everyone not by what we say, but by using advertising as communication on a broad range of social, political and environmental issues."
- According to him, "... advertising is the richest and most powerful medium existing today".
- He added, "I feel responsible to do more than to say, 'Our sweater is pretty'."

Focus on two campaigns

- In 2000, the ad "We, On Death Row" made the group realise that even the borders of unconventional advertising had been crossed.
- Surveys showed that some loyal customers had been put off by this campaign.
- Olivero Toscani resigned immediately after this campaign.
- After the departure of Toscani, Benetton's campaigns were hardly noticed.
- The 2011 campaign called "Unhate" was back to shock advertising: it depicted world leaders kissing each other on the mouth.
- This campaign outraged a number of conservative groups worldwide.
- Benetton claimed its "Unhate" campaign was aimed at fostering tolerance.
- It came straight from the Unhate Foundation launched by the Benetton group which seeks to contribute to the creation of a new culture of tolerance, to combat hatred, building on Benetton's values ...
- Benetton's goal has been reached, the buzz is on again.

Questions

- What was advertising like before Benetton?
- Who was Benetton's creative director?
- What are his points of view on advertising?
- Why did he leave the group?
- What campaign was at the origin of his resignation?
- Which groups were outraged by the 2011 campaign and why?
- What is the Unhate Foundation's goal?
- How do you understand the last sentence: "Benetton's goal has been reached, the buzz is on again?"

Express your point of view

- Do you think lobbies play a positive or a negative role in the world's organisation?
- If you had to create a lobby, what would you call it and what types of issues would you like to influence?
- Are you shocked by Benetton's "We, On Death Row" campaign? Why?
- What do you consider as the most efficient communication tool? Explain why.

@ Go online

- Investigate Benetton's other shock campaigns and try to analyse why they were considered shocking.
- Investigate the part the energy lobby played in the Kyoto Protocol (1997), the Copenhagen Conference (2009) and the Durban Conference (2011).

Test yourself

Try to use your memory – do not look at the vocabulary list!

1 COMPOUND NOUNS

Take a word from column (1) and another one from column (2) to make a compound noun. Some words are not in the vocabulary list as a compound noun so you may have to put two words together. The compound noun could also be elsewhere in the unit.

1	Brand	A	time
2	Advertising	B	card
3	Misleading	C	switching
4	Loyalty	D	market
5	Shelf	E	advertising
6	Reply	F	watchdog
7	Comparative	G	rate
8	Response	H	coupon
9	Mass	I	study
10	Field	J	advertising
11	Awareness	K	mix
12	Brand	L	life
13	Prime	M	rate
14	Marketing	N	market

2 POINT OF SALE FLOOR PLANS, DISPLAYS AND LAYOUTS

Look at the recommendations for a shop layout. Fill in the missing words.

end display • *eye level* • *gift* • *skyrocket* • *hand out* • *packs* • *position* • *store-brand / own-brand* • *unbranded* • *voucher*

Dear Sir

Following our visit to your store on March 14th, 20–, I would like to make the following recommendations:

More attention should be paid to the **a)** _ _ _ _ _ _ _ _ of your key products.

You should put the goods you wish to sell most at **b)** _ _ _ _ _ _ _ _ so that they catch the customers' eye better.

c) _ _ _ _ _ _ _ _ _ _ products should be placed near private-label products, but in bigger quantities. However, **d)** _ _ _ _ _ _ _ _ _ products are better on the bottom shelf.

You should make better use of your **e)** _ _ _ _ _ _ _ _ _ _ – it is one of the most visible parts of a display unit.

To encourage people to try new products, you could **f)** _ _ _ _ _ _ _ free samples or a **g)** _ _ _ _ _ _ _ (which the customer has to fill in), for a free trial. You could also try giving out a free **h)** _ _ _ _ with **i)** _ _ _ _ _ of over 10 items, for example a pair of running socks with sugary soft drinks.

I am sure that if you follow these recommendations, your sales will **j)** _ _ _ _ _ _ _ _ _.

Yours faithfully,

3 FIND THE OPPOSITE

Find the word in the vocabulary list which is the antonym to the word in the list.

1	Deregulate		6	No benchmark	
2	Be honest		7	Genuine	
3	Give no notice		8	Make happy / loyal	
4	Flawless		9	Maintain / keep	
5	Pleasing / respectful		10	Succeed	

VOCABULARY

4 | Brands

Words

"It is a pretty recognizable brand name. Originally it was 'Jerry's Guide to the World Wide Web' but we settled on 'Yahoo'." (Jerry Yang)

Ad / advert / advertisement: publicité
Advergaming: publicité dans les jeux vidéo
Advertainment: publicité divertissante
Advertise (to): faire de la publicité
Advertiser: publiciste
Advertising: la publicité
Advertising agency: agence de publicité
Advertising blitz: matraquage publicitaire
Advertising campaign: campagne publicitaire
Advertising media: supports de publicité
Advertising space: espace publicitaire
Advertising spending: dépenses de publicité, budget publicitaire
Aim at (to): cibler
Alienate (to): aliéner
Appeal to (to): faire appel à, séduire
Attract (to): attirer
Audience: public
Awareness campaign: campagne de sensibilisation
Billboard: panneau d'affichage
Body copy: texte (dans une publicité)
Brainwash (to): faire un lavage de cerveau
Brand: marque
Brand awareness: notoriété de la marque
Brand extension: extension de la marque
Brand image: image de marque
Brand leader: leader du marché
Brand loyalty: fidélité à la marque
Brand name: marque déposée
Branded goods: produit de marque
Catchphrase: accroche
Close-up: gros plan
Commercial / spot: spot publicitaire
Comparative advertising: publicité comparative
Conspicuous: visible
Convince (to): convaincre
Coupon: coupon
Customised advertising: publicité sur mesure
Deter from (to): dissuader, décourager
End-display: tête de gondole
Endorsement: promotion assurée par une célébrité
Event: événement
Exhibition: exposition, salon
Eye level: à hauteur de vue
Fair: foire, salon
Feature : caractéristique
Feature (to): figurer, faire figurer
Field study: étude sur le terrain
Gift: cadeau
Hand out (to): distribuer
Hard-sell tactics: stratégie de vente agressive
Hype: battage médiatique
Iconic: emblématique
Indirect advertising: publicité indirecte
Informercial: publicité informative
Junk mail: courrier indésirable
Launch (to): lancer
Leaflet: dépliant, prospectus
Life cycle: cycle de vie
Listener: auditeur
Lure (to): attirer par la ruse, séduire
Luxury brand: marque de luxe
Market leader: leader sur le marché
Market research: étude de marché
Market segment: segment de marché
Market share: part de marché
Merchandising: marchandisage
Misleading advertising: publicité mensongère, trompeur/euse
Own-brand: de marque propre
Pack: paquet, emballage
Position (to): positionner
Poster: affiche
Prime time: heures de grande écoute
Promote (to): promouvoir
Publicity: publicité gratuite
Publicise (to): rendre publique
Ratings system: audimat
Regulate (to): réglementer
Reply coupon: coupon réponse
Response rate: taux de réponse
Shock tactics: tactique destinée à choquer
Sponsor (to): sponsoriser
Spread (to): répandre
Store-brand product: produit à la marque de l'enseigne
Supply and demand: l'offre et la demande
Switch (to): changer
Tap (to): exploiter
Target (to): cibler
Teasing: accrocheur
Trade fair: exposition, salon
Trademark: marque de fabrique
Trailer: bande-annonce
Unbranded: sans marque
USP (unique selling point): argument clé de vente
Voucher: bon
Warning: avertissement

5

New technologies

A faster world = a better world?

Question

What is the impact of new technologies on people's lifestyles?

WORD BOX

to surf the Net • to download • upload • new acronyms • to have a headache • social networks • complex world • to be brainwashed into

5 | New technologies

1 • Look and discuss

a) Look at the following pictures.

b) Discuss in class.

1. What are the items above?
2. What do you think is the most amazing item?
3. Which item has had the most effect on people's everyday lives?
4. What are the upsides and downsides of new technologies?
5. Are you addicted to new technologies? How would you feel if you had to do without your computer or your smartphone for 24 hours? Would you like to try, and then tell everyone about how you felt?

2 • Read and understand

Match the word to the definition.

brainwave • *prototype* • *groundbreaking* • *pioneering* • *patent* • *discovery* • *time-saving* • *setback* • *revolutionary* • *breakthrough*

1. Markedly innovative and comes from breaking the ground for a new building project: ...
2. Shortening the length of time required to do something. No time wasted: ...
3. An unexpected dramatic and important discovery or development: ...
4. A first model of a new machine or device, to be copied for mass production afterwards: ...
5. An unplanned problem which prevents or reverses progress: ...
6. Exclusive rights (national or international) granted to an inventor for an invention: ...
7. A sudden brilliant idea: ...
8. Finding out something which was unknown before, (or a U.S. aerospace shuttle): ...
9. Bringing about a major change: ...
10. Venturing into new areas of thought, research and development: ...

3 • Look and write

a) Look at the pictures and read the text.

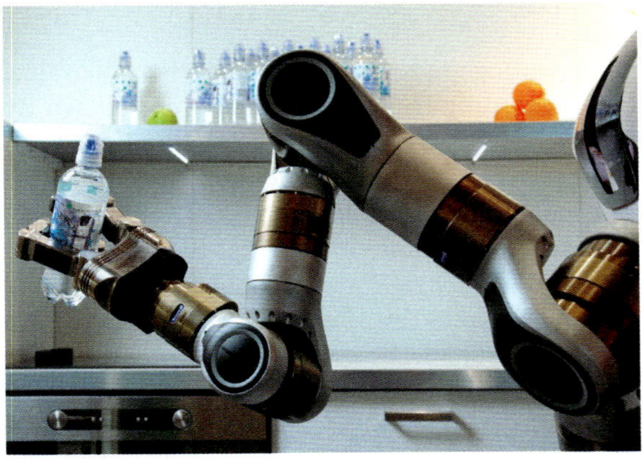

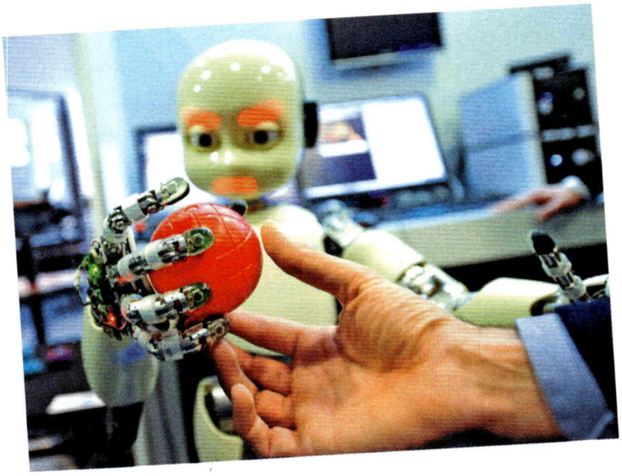

Fabulous Fab Labs (100 worldwide)
A Fabrication Laboratory (Fab Lab) is a small digital workhop offering customised fabrication. The famous Massachussets Institute of Technology (MIT) is at the origin of this extraordinary workshop you can use to manufacture an increasing variety of 3-dimensional objects, thanks to computer-controlled tools.
Some experts think that in the near future, Fab Labs will give us the possibility to make anything!

b) Answer the questions by writing a few sentences.

1. How have the objects (pictures) been made?
2. Imagine Fab Labs are now a feature of your daily life. What objects would you create with it and why? To what purpose?

4 • Listen and understand

CD n° 2
Track n° 12

a) True or False? You need to use your fingertips to get the information from a smartphone.
b) True or False? The boy enjoys getting text messages and e-mails all the time.
c) What do you suppose the solution is?

5 | New technologies

WARMING UP

- Do you belong to a social network? Why / Why not?
- Which one?

CD n° 2 Track n° 13

Facebook fans and fighting social media fatigue

One of the great things about social media is that it's allowed people to feel more connected to the world around them. And while there are many advantages of living in a connected world, the one major downside is that it can sometimes feel quite overwhelming because, despite what you've been told, the world is still a pretty big place. With lots of stuff happening. At the same time. All the time.

When Facebook took over the world, there were groups of people that set out to get as many Facebook friends as possible. But after years of having to scroll through hundreds of updates from people they hardly know on a daily basis, developers have begun to realise that the human brain can only handle a limited amount of information before feeling burnt out. Enter Facebook's "Edge Rank" algorithm, serving to filter interactions to only display posts from people and events you are more engaged with. Like it or not, social media fatigue has begun to set in for lots of people and the friend-ing, like-ing, share-ing trend is hard to achieve without presenting the Facebook user with tangible value.

According to a study recently conducted by Global Web that compared Facebook usage in July 2009 to July 2011, the frequency of several Facebook activities has declined. Some of these activities include messaging friends, joining groups, searching for new contacts and installing apps. Despite this, Facebook is still one of the most popular websites on the Internet. What this tells us is that people aren't actually using social networking sites less. They're just using them differently.

With so much happening online, many users are becoming more selective with what they're engaging with. As a result, they are becoming less likely to "like", "comment" on and "share" a lot of content. This is particularly bad news for brands, especially for brands that have yet to establish a social media presence. If a brand hasn't started yet to engage into a social network, it may be even further behind than it thinks.

FGX Studios, 1 Sept. 2011

Lexical work

1. Find the English equivalents in the text.

§ 1 **a)** le principal inconvénient **b)** cela peut sembler écrasant **c)** beaucoup de choses

§ 2 **a)** s'emparer **b)** dérouler **c)** mises à jour **d)** à peine e) se sentir épuisé **f)** lassitude **g)** s'installer

§ 3 **a)** applications **b)** malgré

§ 4 **a)** à même de **b)** contenu

2. Find the French equivalents.

lots of stuff § 1, display § 2, trend § 2, actually § 3, further behind § 4

Pronunciation work

CD n° 2 Track n° 14

1. Listen and observe.

It's allowed people to feel more connected.
aloud / allowed: these two words have the same sound.

2. Listen and find two other examples.

know / no • for / four

Work on the title

1. Identify the source of the document (title, date, nature).

2. Say what "social media fatigue" may mean.

Check the facts

1. Read § 1.
a) What is Facebook's major positive aspect?
b) What is its negative aspect?

2. Read § 2.
a) In what way is the human brain limited?
b) What was Edge Rank invented for?
c) Who suffers from media fatigue?

3. Read § 3.
a) What happened to Facebook usage between 2009 and 2011?
b) Do people spend less time on Facebook?

4. Read § 4.
For what brands is it bad news?

Grammar → p. 236

Les quantifieurs

- *There are many advantages ...*
- *With so much happening online ...*

Topic debrief

1. Choose the sentence which you think corresponds best to the main topic of the document.
a) Facebook is not the most popular social network, its fans want new activities.
b) The frequency of some Facebook activities have declined and people use social networking sites less.
c) Facebook is still the most popular social network though its users have become more selective.

2. Rephrase the correct sentence in order to make a short introduction to the document.

Methods

1. Find a title or a key phrase for each paragraph in order to understand which paragraph best illustrates the topic.

2. Translate it.

3. Complete the sentences with the following words.
connected • *fatigue* • *display* • *social network* • *updates* • *developers* • *engage* • *Edge Rank* • *handle* • *events*

Facebook is a ... thanks to which people can feel .... But people cannot ... too much information; that's why today Facebook ... are worried about what they call social media .... In order to help people with all their ..., Facebook has launched a new algorithm called .... It helps to ... posts about the people and the ... you really ... with.

Train for the exam

1. Make a summary / account of the document (60 words / 3-5 minutes).

2. Express your personal opinion:
Explain and illustrate your point of view (100 words / 3-5 minutes).
What are the dangers of social networking?

3. Role play: work in pairs
You are going to take part in a debate. You have opposite views on Facebook.
Student A: you are a Facebook fan.
Student B: you are not on Facebook because you think it can be dangerous.

TIPS

Arguments to develop
Student A / advantages of Facebook:
– very useful to stay connected to friends
– to organise special events in one click
– to remind you of birthdays
– to ask and get help from friends
– to exchange videos, photos, ideas ...
Student B / drawbacks of Facebook:
– it is a threat to your private life
– anybody can see who you are
– bosses can fire employees who criticise them
– you can be a victim of cyber bullying
– hackers can use your account to spread lies
– you can become a cyber addict

Go online
Find information about various social networks (Linkedin, Viadeo, Twitter, etc.).
Get prepared to report to your group / class (a PowerPoint presentation is recommended).

5 | New technologies

Train with an oral document

WARMING UP

- What do you know about Starbucks?
- Say whether or not you have heard about Rovio.

CD n° 2 Track n° 15

Virtual birds to fly to Starbucks

Angry Birds, mobile game

Lexical work

1. Find the odd word out.

a) a spokesman – a representative – a game
b) entertainment company – fast food company – film industry
c) a game – a player – stuffed animals

2. Match the right definition.

a) partnership	**1.** permit
b) allow	**2.** working together
c) top-scoring players	**3.** very good

3. Work on figures: write in full and read aloud.

350m times • 1m animals

Pronunciation work

CD n° 2 Track n° 16

1. Listen and observe.

to entertain → an entertainment
to engage → an engagement
to commit → a commitment
-ment is used to make nouns from the above verbs. This ending is never stressed.

2. Find the appropriate noun and pronounce it.

to state → ...
to disappoint → ...
to encourage → ...

3. Key words of "New technologies": pronounce the following words, then listen to check the right pronunciation.

a smartphone • a craze • to download • a device • to spotlight • competitive • tablet's apps

Work on the title

1. Look at the title of the document.

2. What could virtual birds be? How can they fly to Starbucks?

Check the facts

1. Listen to part 1.
a) What sort of programme is it?
b) Who is being interviewed?
c) What is the name of the partner company?
d) What is the name of the game referred to?

2. Listen to part 2.
a) What are the advantages for the partner company?
b) What are the rules of the game?
c) What are Rovio's further plans?
d) What are the new online offers?
e) How does the company explain its energetic marketing strategy?
f) What secret would the company like to keep?
g) What will be the topic of next week's programme?

Topic debrief

1. Choose the sentence which you think corresponds best to the main topic of the document.

a) A Starbucks executive is being interviewed about the company's plan to establish a partnership with Rovio in order to create a specific Starbucks app on smartphones.

b) Rovio's spokesman is revealing the intention of the firm to strike a deal with Starbucks to allow its game to be shared by gamers inside Starbucks outlets.

c) Rovio, the company which launched "Angry Birds", intends to diversify but they do not know yet how and with what companies they plan to establish partnerships.

2. Write an introduction to the document by using the word bank.

games • smartphones • download • partnership • Starbucks • Rovio • players • scores • products • PC • Pac-Man • similar

Methods

1. Write four key sentences in order to prepare your presentation of the document (two sentences for each part).

2. Then try to answer these questions to conclude your presentation.

Will Starbucks new clients change the cafe's concept? What could be the dangers?

Train for the exam

1. Use your notes to make an **oral presentation** about the document and record yourself (3-5 minutes).

2. Comment: find an answer to this question. Discuss and give examples (100 words / 3-5 minutes).

Are screen-to-screen exchanges dangerous for our society? Use the following words and add others:

comfort • smooth • atmosphere • nervous • competition • scores • aggressive • readers • enjoy

3. Role play: work in pairs

You are going to take part in a phone conversation.

Student A: you are a smartphone addict ready to come to Starbucks to play your favourite game and compete with other players.

Student B: you are a Starbucks manager. You have received many letters of complaint from customers who want to enjoy the quiet atmosphere of Starbucks outlets. Find other alternative solutions and tell the smartphone addict.;

TIPS

You should use your notes in order to present a realistic conversation. Don't read them, look up. You can:

- record the conversation (at the multimedia lab or with your own MP4 recorder; the recording should last between one and two minutes at most);
- videotape the scene and show it to the class;
- act out the scene in front of the class;
- listen to your classmates' recordings and write what you have understood in a short and structured paragraph.

Go online

Find information about Rovio's and its blockbuster game.

Get prepared to report to your group / class (a PowerPoint presentation is recommended).

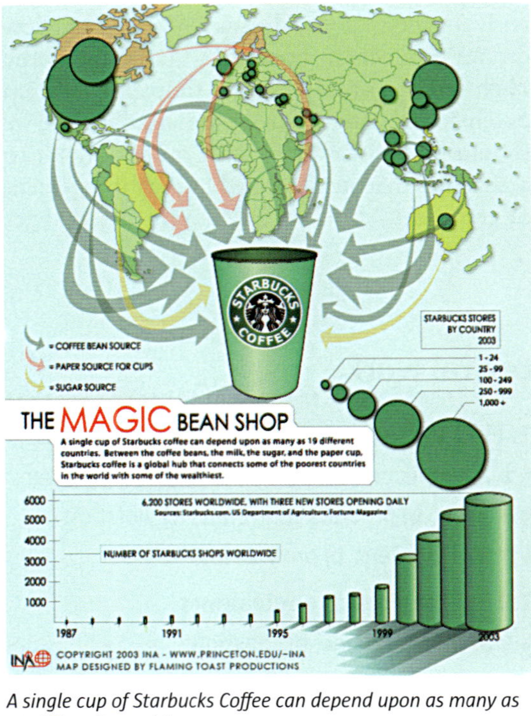

A single cup of Starbucks Coffee can depend upon as many as 19 different countries.

5 | New technologies

WARMING UP

▸ What various forms of cyber crime do you know?

CD n° 2 Track n° 17

Jeremy Hunt urges Web firms to join anti-piracy effort

Jeremy Hunt wants Net firms to do more to prevent access to pirate sites. UK Culture Secretary Jeremy Hunt has delivered a hard-hitting speech, calling on Net firms, advertisers and credit card companies to cut ties with websites that link to unlawful content. In a speech to the Royal Television Society, he said he wanted to make it harder for such sites to prosper. Ideally the government would like to see Google remove pirate sites from its search engine completely. But Google's response suggested this was not necessary. "Without a court order, any copyright owner can already use our removals process to inform us of copyright-infringing content and have it removed from Google Search," the firm said in a statement.

It may not be enough for Mr Hunt, who appeared to be on an anti-piracy crusade. In his speech, he denied that blocking access to pirated content was an attack on Net neutrality. "Unlawfully distributing copyrighted material is theft – and a direct assault on the freedoms and rights of creators of content to be rewarded fairly for their efforts," he said. "We do not allow certain products to be sold in the shops on the High Street, nor do we allow shops to be set up purely to sell counterfeited products. Likewise we should be entitled to make it more difficult to access sites that are dedicated to the infringement of copyright," he added. Many of the changes announced by Mr Hunt are destined for the new Communications Act which is due to become law towards the end of the current Parliament in 2015.

Suggested measures include:

– A cross-industry body, perhaps modelled on the Internet Watch Foundation, to be charged with identifying infringing websites against which action could be taken.

– A streamlined legal process to make it possible for the courts to act quickly.

– A responsibility on search engines to take reasonable steps to make it harder to access sites that a court has decided contain unlawful content or promote unlawful distribution of content.

– A responsibility on advertisers to take reasonable steps to remove their advertisements from these sites.

– A responsibility on credit card companies and banks to remove their services from these sites.

For its part, Google said that it felt that its current anti-piracy policies were sufficient. It operates a takedown process in which it removes links identified as infringing copyright. Last year it removed three million items from its search engine. Jim Killock, chief executive of the Open Rights Group, said the proposals set a dangerous precedent. "It is pretty dangerous to ask credit card companies or Google to decide who is guilty," he said.

BBC News, 14 September 2011.

Lexical work

1. Find the English equivalents in the text.

§ 1 **a)** empêcher **b)** contenu illégal **c)** supprimer

§ 2 **a)** vol **b)** produits contrefaits **c)** violation

§ 3 **a)** polyvalent **b)** promouvoir

2. Find the French equivalents.

§ 1 **a)** search engine **b)** copyright

§ 2 **a)** law **b)** rewarded **c)** current

§ 3 **a)** advertisement **b)** credit card

Pronunciation work

CD n° 2 Track n° 18

Listen and observe.

necessary • firm • search • delivered • certain • companies • services

a) Pay attention to the difference between letters and sounds.

b) Fill in the grid according to the pronunciation of the vowel sound.

[ɜ:]	[ə]

Info
Copyright infringement is the unauthorised or prohibited use of works under copyright, infringing the copyright holder's exclusive rights, such as the right to reproduce or perform the copyrighted work, or to make derivative works.

Work on the title

1. Identify the source of the document (title, date, nature).

2. Read the headline and lines 1-2 to explain J. Hunt's wish.

Check the facts

1. Read § 1.
a) Find who Jeremy Hunt is.
b) What sectors are asked to make efforts?
c) Which company in particular is targeted by the British government and why?
d) What did this company say in its defence?

2. Read § 2 and § 3.
a) Explain in your words what is considered as "theft" by Mr Hunt.
b) What is forbidden in High Street shops and allowed on the Net?
c) What new law is being prepared in the UK? When will it be passed?
d) Rephrase in a short paragraph the measures included in the new Communications Act.

3. Read § 4.
Who is Jim Killock and what is his opinion on the measures suggested?

Grammar → p. 236

Les propositions infinitives

• *Jeremy Hunt wants net firms to join the anti-piracy effort.*

Topic debrief

1. Choose the sentence which you think corresponds best to the main topic of the document.
a) The UK Culture Secretary in a television address said he was thankful for Web firms' recent anti-piracy measures aiming at protecting copyright.
b) Jeremy Hunt thinks it is high time for global Net firms to take efficient measures to block access to pirated content.
c) Global Net firms disagree with Jeremy Hunt in his efforts to reduce copyright infringement on the Net because the Internet should remain a place of complete freedom.

2. Write an introduction to the document by using the word bank.
speech • Jeremy Hunt • pirate sites • Net firms • unlawful • credit card company

Methods

1. Give a title to each paragraph.

2. Which paragraph best sums up the topic of the document?

3. Translate it.

Train for the exam

1. Make a summary / account of the document (60 words / 3-5 minutes).

2. Comment: find an answer to this question. Discuss and give examples (100 words / 3-5 minutes).
Since the Pentagon site was pirated, do you think that there can be any total Internet security? Explain why / why not.

3. Role play: work in groups
You are going to take part in a debate.
Group A: you think downloading material from the Internet is not a crime, therefore it shouldn't be punished by law. You search arguments in favour of piracy.
Group B: you think the opposite, that is to say that copyright infringement should not be tolerated on the Internet either. You search arguments against piracy.

TIPS
Group A / in favour of piracy: the Web is a public space, open and free; banning illegal downloading aggravates the digital gap; some artists release their work on the Net for free; impossible to monitor, control the Internet; it would cost more to chase pirates than to let them be, etc.
Group B / against piracy: theft, crime, illegal, impact on creators' and artists' income, kills original ideas, can be dangerous (ex.: pirated medicine, etc.), safety standards not respected, etc.

5 | New technologies

Train with an oral document

WARMING UP

▸ Say what you know about:
– Amazon
– Kindle Fire
– the IT market

CD n° 2 Track n° 19

Is Amazon's Kindle to set fire to the IT market?

Lexical work

1. Match the words with their equivalents.

a) release	**1.** craze
b) latest	**2.** amazing
c) hype	**3.** gadget addict
d) affordable	**4.** you can buy
e) Gizmo specialist	**5.** launched
f) surprising	**6.** most recent

2. Find the opposite words.

a) light	**1)** single
b) huge	**2)** reality
c) science fiction	**3)** heavy
d) unanimous	**4)** increase
e) slash prices	**5)** small

3. Work on figures: write in full and read aloud.

$179 • $400 iPad

Pronunciation work

CD n° 2 Track n° 20

1. Listen and observe.

[ɪə]: here	[i:]: be
peers • career • here	trainee • free • screen

Diphthongs correspond to two sounds referring to one or more vowels.

Repeat these words with the right pronunciation.

2. Key words of "New technologies".

release • hype • date • e-book • to improve • to be on the watch for

a) Focus on words that may be used in French and pronounce them in good English.
b) Practise repeating these words aloud and stress the right syllable.

Work on the title

1. Look at the title of the document.

2. Explain the play on words in the title.

Check the facts

1. Listen to the introduction.
a) What happened during the night?
b) What are the new product's features?
c) Which company is launching it?
d) What is the product price?
e) What are the other company and product mentioned?

2. Listen to part 1.
a) Who is speaking?
b) What do the people interviewed think about the product? Write down the words you identify from what they say.
speaker 1 ...
speaker 2 ...
speaker 3 ...
speaker 4 ...
speaker 5 ...
speaker 6 ...
speaker 7 ...

3. Listen to part 2.
a) What is the new device compared to?
b) What are its Asian competitors asked to do about it?
c) Why haven't other companies expected this new product's success?
d) What film is this new challenge compared to?

Topic debrief

1. Choose the sentence which best corresponds to the main topic of the document.

a) A new IT device has been launched on the market, but it has hardly a chance to challenge Apple's iPad because it is manufactured by a brand which is not an IT brand.

b) Apple's leadership in IT is being challenged by many brands around the world including Amazon, but Apple is constantly on the watch for new competitors and is ready to respond.

c) Amazon has just launched a new, affordable e-pad which could challenge Apple's immensely popular iPad because it is both affordable and high tech.

2. Rephrase the correct answer to present the topic of the document.

Methods

1. Write two sentences for each part of the document.

2. List all the advantages and disadvantages of reading on a tablet.

Train for the exam

1. Use your notes to make an **oral presentation** about the document and record yourself (3-5 minutes).

2. Comment: find an answer to the following questions. Discuss and give examples (100 words / 3-5 minutes).

a) Do you think we are to see the end of regular books very soon?

b) With a light tablet you feel free to enjoy many activities wherever you are, but what are the problems of always being kept busy with an electronic device?

3. Role play: work in pairs

You are going to take part in a conversation.

Student A: you are a customer who is looking for a tablet, and you hesitate between Apple's iPad or the new Amazon Kindle Fire.

Student B: you are a sales assistant in an IT store whose mission it is to promote Amazon's new tablet and sell it.

PRACTICE • AUDIO • VIDEO

Train with a video

New Sony Crystal LED display

→ http://www.youtube.com/watch?v=5dxXUtx2RN0

10 January 2012

Look at this video on the Internet about a new technology

Check the facts	Methods
1. What is the main topic of the video?	• Where are the two journalists standing?
2. What are the main characteristics of this new device?	• What does LED mean? • What is meant by energy-efficient?
3. Where does this fair take place?	• Use a map. What is this place famous for? What is the CES?
4. When will this product be available? Will it be compatible with other products? Why not?	• Why do new technology brands want to be present at this fair?
5. Issues ... – Is this device only a gadget or is it necessary to our daily lives? – Will it change people's lives? Why? / Why not?	• Find the meaning of: "to keep up with the Joneses". • Why would you want the latest item as far as new technologies are concerned?

WARMING UP

- How do you use the Internet? What do you use most to surf the Net? Your mobile phone? Your PC?
- Which devices do you enjoy best?

CD n° 2 Track n° 21

iConsumers: technology's changing landscape

The technology industry loves buzz phrases and one of those in vogue at the moment is "the consumerisation of IT". This refers to the fact that consumers are now carrying ever more powerful electronic gizmos, from smartphones to tablet computers, and are using them to access an ever broader range of digital services at home, in the office and anywhere else that they are connected to the Internet.

In a new report on what she calls "a post-PC world", Sarah Rotman Epps of Forrester, a research firm, notes that there has been a proliferation of electronic devices beyond the traditional personal computer (PC). Although laptop and desktop PCs are unlikely to disappear – indeed, Forrester predicts that their sales will grow significantly over the next five years, even in relatively mature markets such as America – people will increasingly use other devices for computing, too. According to Ms Rotman Epps, almost 80m American consumers owned three or more connected devices in 2010 and 4.5m owned nine or more.

Some companies such as Apple are helping to drive this change. Whenever he unveiled a new pod, phone or pad, late Apple's boss Steve Jobs used to seize the opportunity to prophecy the post-PC era, much to the annoyance of firms like Microsoft and Hewlett-Packard (HP). Among the biggest beneficiaries of a PC world, they and other companies are now scrambling to adapt to changing times. HP, for instance, is rolling out new e-printers that can print from any connected device, not just a tethered desktop or laptop. And Microsoft is trying to build on the success of systems such as its Xbox gaming console and its Kinect motion-sensing device to create a broader range of gadgets and services that will appeal to users.

One of the consequences of consumerisation has been an explosion of video consumption over the Internet. Much of this involves folk watching content downloaded from services such as Netflix, which stream video over the Web. Video traffic has also been spurred on by Internet phone- and video-calling services such as Skype, which was snapped up by Microsoft last week for $8.5 billion.

The Economist, May 17th, 2011.

Info

"To create the buzz" means to attract media and consumers' attention. What is referred to as "marketing buzz" is a product or an event which has succeeded in becoming famous through its target audience, thanks to word of mouth advertising. For example, the game "Angry Birds" is creating the buzz among iPhone users and beyond.

Lexical work

Match the words with their equivalents.

1) in vogue	**a)** wider
2) broader	**b)** people
3) predict	**c)** attract
4) device	**d)** forecast
5) scramble	**e)** struggle
6) unveil	**f)** launch
7) folk	**g)** gizmo
8) appeal	**h)** trendy
9) user	**i)** generate
10) spur	**j)** consumer

Pronunciation work

CD n° 2 Track n° 22

1. Listen and underline the sound [z].

buzz • phrases • electronic games • digital services • seize the opportunities

2. Key words of "New technologies": pronounce the following words, then listen to check the right pronunciation.

gizmo • a range • digital • to be connected • a laptop • desktop • to spur

Work on the title

1. Identify the source of the document (title, date, nature).

2. Find various devices whose name starts with "I".

Check the facts

1. Read § 1.
a) What is the buzz phrase of the moment?
b) Give examples of how consumers today use new IT.

2. Read § 2.
a) Will traditional computers disappear?
b) What sort of market is the American market?
c) What do many American consumers own?

3. Read § 3.
a) What annoyed other IT firms about Apple's late boss's predictions?
b) Give examples of what they do to remain competitive.

4. Read § 4.
What are the two consequences of consumerisation?

Grammar → p. 236

L'expression du contraste

• *Although laptop and ... are unlikely to disappear, Forrester predicts that ...*

Topic debrief

1. Choose the sentence which you think corresponds best to the main topic of the document.
a) The technology industry is changing its strategies to gain older consumers.
b) The number of new devices have rocketed at Apple and Microsoft.
c) Consumers own more powerful devices so they can have access to a broader range of services.

2. Rephrase the correct sentence in order to make a short introduction to the document.

Methods

1. Give a title to each paragraph.

2. Focus on the following paragraph and translate it into English.
Les ventes d'ordinateurs vont continuer à augmenter dans les prochaines années, malgré l'essor des autres technologies. Apple est l'entreprise la plus avancée dans ce domaine avec sans cesse de nouveaux dispositifs qui aident ou qui divertissent les utilisateurs.

Train for the exam

1. Make a summary / account of the document (60 words / 3-5 minutes).

2. Express your personal opinion:
Explain and illustrate your point of view (100 words / 3-5 minutes).
– Are you a PC or an Apple user? Why?
– Do you think all the new gadgets on smart-phones and e-tablets are necessary for the consumers' comfort?

3. Role play: work in groups
You are going to take part in a debate.
Group A: work on the advantages of new technologies in students' daily lives. Find examples.
Group B: work on the drawbacks the extensive use of new technologies generates in the students' daily lives. Find examples.
When the two groups have gathered enough material, start the debate.

Go online

Find controversies in the way the media reacted after Steve Jobs's death. Was there any reproach of Steve Jobs's admiration / mania?
Get prepared to report to your group / class (a PowerPoint presentation is recommended).

Purchasing new management software

1 • Situation

You work for a manufacturing company of your choice. The company was founded some time ago, and has been run on a traditional basis up to now. It is time for change and you would like to improve efficiency and customer service by investing in an ERP system (enterprise resource planning: *progiciel de gestion integré*).

2 • Process

a) Look at the diagram (Document A) and explain where you can use the software. Then look at the advertisement (Document B).
b) Get into groups.
– *Groups A:* you are the managers of the manufacturing company.
– *Groups B:* you are the managers of the ERP salespeople.
c) Now discuss.
– *Groups A:* you have to list arguments in favour of the state-of-the art software.
– *Groups B:* you have to list and develop arguments to meet the needs of the company's managers.

3 • Follow up

– *Groups A:* write a summary for the General Manager explaining which ERP software you have chosen, and why.
– *Groups B:* write a letter to the purchaser making a commercial proposal.

→ FOR MORE INFORMATION ON HOW TO WRITE A LETTER / COMMERCIAL PROPOSAL, SEE "TOOLS" PAGE 246.

@ Go online

Find out more about ERP on the Internet.

TIPS

• **Start by saying**

Groups A: *Are you sure your solution meets our needs? How long will it take to develop and implement? Why should we choose you rather than the competitor? What is better about your system?*

Groups B: *The key features are ... / The main advantage of this is ... . The main difference between this and the former / the competitor's software is ... . Yet another improvement is ... / It has the edge on ... / It is far ahead of ... .*

• **Remember...**

• Don't rush into deciding which supplier to choose.
• Take your time and don't be afraid to ask all the questions you have.
• Don't let yourself be pressured into buying something you are not sure about.

Doc • A *You can use it in every department of the company.*

Doc • B

THINK ERP

Enterprise Resource Planning

The complete and integrated IT package for the manufacturing industry.
Off-the-shelf or customised software.
A user-friendly and cutting-edge software package for manufacturing and service industries alike.

Ready-to-install and ready-to-run.
Includes all you need to run manufacturing, procurement, accounts and warehousing.

For more information: www.thinkerp.com

ROLE PLAY

5 | New technologies

Background

Information and communication technology (ICT) includes all the innovations applied to data storage volumes and the speed of data processing, and transport due to digital technology and new means of communication (fibre optics, cable, satellite, wireless). Their impact is felt in many sectors, especially our lifestyles and the economy.

1 What is NBIC?

NBIC stands for Nanotechnology, Biotechnology, Information Technology and Cognitive Science. These are the four main currently emerging new technologies.

Nanotechnology is engineering on a very, very small (atomic and molecular) scale used in medical, manufacturing, computing and many other fields. Thanks to nanotechnology, **smartphones** for example are getting smaller and cheaper, with more applications and greater speeds.

Biotechnology is the use of living micro-organisms or biological substances by humans to enhance crops, fuels, medical treatment and many other products. It is a controversial subject, because it covers issues such as gene therapy, GM food and cloning.

Information technology could be defined as "the study, design, creation, utilisation, support and management of computer-based information systems, especially software applications and computer hardware".

Cognitive science is basically the study of the mind, to explain perception, thinking and learning. The mind is seen as an information processor, like a computer.

→ For more information, link up to Nano-Bio-Info-Cogno (NBIC) on Facebook.

2 What has changed or progressed in certain sectors thanks to information technology?

Developments in ICT (information and communications technology) are metamorphosing:

Education: OLPC (one **laptop** per child) and "anywhere anytime" teaching using mobile **devices** such as smartphones or tablets is changing the face of the teaching world, and helping to base pedagogy on more individualised **P2P** teaching.

Health: eHealth means doctors can access patient records and test results, and deliver prescriptions without delay. Patients with certain conditions such as diabetes can be monitored in real time.

Transport: Safety and security have been improved in transport systems thanks to **embedded** video surveillance systems. Other areas of improvement include electronic ticketing and dynamic passenger information. The future is looking to unmanned public transport systems in urban areas.

→ SEE CHAPTER "TRANSPORT" PAGE 226.

3 What is the environmental impact of new technologies?

According to the IEA (International Energy Agency), 4% of the world's energy consumption in 2008 was due to so many people using ICT. It is estimated that this figure will reach 40% by 2030. Add to this the rise in demand for high-technology gadgets in homes, and the rapid growth of factories with high toxic emissions and energy requirements in newly industrialised countries, the carbon footprint caused by new technologies is an issue which urgently needs to be addressed. Certain ICT companies are working on "greener technology" to reduce the harmful effect computers and associated technologies are having on the environment. → SEE CHAPTER "ENVIRONMENT" PAGE 226.

"Frugal- / Eco-innovation" means designing high-tech goods so that they are cheap, strong and user-friendly and use few raw materials to reduce their impact on the environment.

Questions

- What are the four main areas of high-tech developments at the moment?
- Do you think the developments in the fields of education, health and transport are an improvement?
- Do you pay attention to computer security advice and back up your data regularly?
- Can you think of any negative aspects of ICT?

Info

Increased use of new technologies has led to a new branch of computer technology: Computer Security (or Information Security) for both computers and **networks**.
Beware of viruses, worms, Trojan horses, spam, hackers and phishing.

Focus

Steve Jobs: walled gardens versus Richard Stallman: open gardens

The premature death of Steve Jobs, the iconic founding father of Apple, triggered a relentless series of mostly laudatory articles in the media worldwide. And yet among the apparently unanimous praise, words of dissent were uttered by less high profile, hi-tech geeks who up to now have tried to make of the World Wide Web a place people should be free to use and share.
One of these respected figures is Richard Stallman, the creator of the GNU project whose aim was to offer a free operating system for all computer users.

Richard Stallman, a software freedom activist

Bio info

- He was born in 1953 in the USA.
- He became a top computer programmer.
- He launched the GNU project in 1983 (General Public License for software).
- He initiated the free software movement.
- He pioneered the concept of "copyleft" (see below) which he thought should prevail against copyright.

His views and influences

- Software users should be free to share the software they use with anyone; they should also be free to make changes in the original version. This is referred to as "copyleft".
- Freedom is vital for users and is a non-negotiable moral value.
- He became the number one enemy of Microsoft and Apple, which wanted proprietary software (copyright) to prevail (and still do).
- 1991: was followed by a Finnish student Linus Torvalds who created Linux, the free software currently competing with Microsoft Windows and Apple Mac OS.
- 2006: persuaded the Governor of the Indian state of Keral to abandon Microsoft and adopt a free operating system for all the 12,500 state-run high schools.
- He thinks that the U.S. government encourages cloud computing to probe into users' privacy without the need for a search warrant.
- He said of Steve Jobs: "Steve Jobs is the pioneer of the computer as a jail made cool, designed to sever fools from their freedom."

Questions

- Who is Richard Stallman?
- What is his core value?
- Why is he against mainstream software brands?
- What is Linux?

ACTIVE BUSINESS CULTURE

5 | New technologies

Focus

Steve Jobs, an idea man or a remix artist?

Bio info

- Steve Jobs was born an orphan in 1955 in San Francisco, California, USA.
- He was adopted by Paul and Sarah Jobs.
- In 1972 he dropped out of college with no particular talents but befriended a computer genius, Steve Wozniak, in Silicon Valley.
- He exploited Wozniak's talents, which led to the creation of the first Apple computer.
- Apple II dominated the U.S. market until 1981.
- In 1985, Jobs resigned from Apple, which was losing market share.
- In 1986, he acquired Pixar Animation Studios (*Toy Story*) and ran it until Pixar was taken over by Disney in 2006.
- 1987, he set up a new company, NEXT, thanks to which he reconquered Apple in 1998 with the help of his outstanding sales and marketing genius.
- He fathered the iMac, the iBook, iTunes, the iPhone, the iPad and the ePad, which turned out to be such blockbusters.
- He was at the top of his power when he died on October 5th, 2011, with Apple's profits over 3 billion dollars and 200 million iTunes subscribers.

His views and influences

- He was reputed to be hardworking and ruthless as an employer and team worker.
- He knew how to anticipate consumers' needs but was not a high-tech geek.
- He thrived thanks to high-tech geniuses' talents whose names are unknown.
- He was not a scientific innovator.
- He was hated by free software developers, who saw him as the creator of "walled gardens of information".
- He is attacked for obliging online Apple users to have access only to data exclusively provided by Apple software and hardware.

Questions

- What company did Steve Jobs run?
- Quote the most popular products he marketed.
- Who was Wozniak?
- Why can't Steve Jobs be considered as an inventor?
- What happens to the people who invent the technology?
- What reveals Apple's tremendous success?
- Why is he referred to by some as the creator of walled gardens?
- Who are the fools who accept to have their freedom severed from them?
- Compare Steve Jobs's and Richard Stallman's views on software use.

Express your point of view

Should the digital world be a walled garden or an open garden? Investigate further to find more arguments.

Perspectives

Today with Steve Jobs's death and Bill Gates's withdrawal from current computer affairs, the IT world is faced with an alternative: pulling down the walls of Apple and Microsoft's gardens, allowing people to browse, share and travel freely in the realms of the digital world, or maintain the walls or even build thicker ones, which would turn all free users into forced customers by locking software and apps for the benefits of one or two powerful computer companies.

@-Go online

Carry out your own research in order to find more about free Internet software activists.
You can log on to:
www.theanonymous.net/

Test yourself

Try to use your memory – do not look at the vocabulary list!

1 ALL KINDS OF "-ICS"

Match the word to the right definition.

biometrics • domotics • spintronics • photonics • avionics • productics • biogenetics • electronics • robotics • connectics

a) ... is another word for home automation.

b) ... is the science of altering the genetics of a living cell or organism.

c) ... is the study and application of electromagnetic energy for fibre optics, lasers, etc.

d) ... is also known as connector technology for electronic equipment.

e) ... is the development of electronic equipment to be used in aeronautics.

f) ... is the technology which deals with the development of robots.

g) ... involves the design of circuits using microchips and transistors.

h) ... is electronics on a nano scale, using electron spin in electronic devices.

i) ... is the measurement and statistical analysis of biological data (e.g. for passports).

j) ... is another word for automated manufacturing engineering.

> **TIPS**
> These nouns ending in "-ics" take a single verb. "Computer graphics" takes a plural verb.

2 CHOOSING A COMPUTER

Put the words into the right place in the conversation.

laptop • data • virus • download • broadband • click • scan • hard disk • computer game • screen • personal computer • burn • hardware • extra-flat

Shop assistant: Good morning. How can I help you?

Customer: I'm looking for an ..., extra-light ... .

SA: Well, I'm sure I can help you. First of all, I would suggest a .... We specialise in state-of-the-art ... (and software, of course), with a cutting-edge ... (better for your eyes), high capacity ... for data storage, built-in ... protection to protect from bugs, and ...

C: I don't need anything too sophisticated. I just need to store ..., ... things off the Internet, ... copies of my photographs onto CDs, play a few ..., things like that. Oh, and I'll need to ... some documents too.

SA: It's the games which are going to cost you! How about this one? It says you can do everything with just one ... !

C: So how much is that going to put me back? Don't forget I have to pay for ... access too.

SA: Well, we have some very good deals on at the moment. Of course if you take too long to decide ...

3 NOTHING BUT PROBLEMS

Translate the underlined words into French.

a) "My wireless connection doesn't seem to work." "Why don't you ring your ISP for some help?"

b) "I'm fed up. My boyfriend spends his time browsing. He's a complete webaholic." "He sounds like a real "nerd" – try unplugging his computer!"

c) "I've got much too much in my e-mail box – it's completely saturated" "Just delete everything."

d) "I've completely forgotten my password so I can't log in to anything." "Don't you back up all of your important information on a USB stick?"

e) "This program is really complicated!" "I agree. When they sold us the software they told us it was really user-friendly." "I suppose you have to be really computer literate to use it then!"

> **TIPS**
> *Courrier électronique* se dit *e-mail* et pas *mail* (qui est le nom pour courrier postal aux États-Unis). La boîte de messagerie se dit donc *e-mail box* avec *inbox* pour boîte de réception et *outbox* pour boîte d'envoi.

5 | New technologies

Words

"The first rule of any technology used in a business is that automation applied to an efficient operation will magnify the efficiency. The second is that automation applied to an inefficient operation will magnify the inefficiency." (Bill Gates)

Access point: point d'accès
Adware: logiciel publicitaire
Avionics: avionique
Bandwidth: la bande passante
Biogenetics: biogénétique
Biometric: biométrique
Biometrics: biométrie
Biotechnology: biotechnologie
Broadband / ADSL: ADSL
Browse (to): surfer
Built-in: intégré
Burn (to): graver
CCTV (closed circuit TV): télévision en circuit fermé
Cell phone (USA) / mobile (UK): téléphone portable
Chat (to): discuter, chatter
Chip: puce (élecronique)
Click (to): cliquer
Computer: ordinateur
Computer crime: délit informatique
Computer file: fichier informatique
Computer game: jeu électronique
Computer graphics: infographie
Computer literacy: compétence en informatique
Computer literate: initié en informatique
Computer nerd / geek: surdoué / fou d'informatique
Computer programming: programmation informatique
Computer virus: virus informatique
Computer-assisted: assisté par ordinateur
Conference call: téléconférence
Connectics: connectique
Copy and paste: copier-coller
Copyright: droits de reproduction
Crack (to): déchiffrer par effraction
Damage (to): endommager
Data: données
Delete (to): supprimer
Device: mécanisme
Digital: numérique
Digitise (to): numériser
Domotics / home automation: domotique
Download (to): télécharger / téléchargement
Electronic surveillance tag: étiquette de surveillance électr.
Electronic wallet: portefeuille électronique
Electronics: électronique
Embedded: gravé / inséré
Enter (to): entrer / saisir
Extra-flat: extra-plat
Extra-light: ultra-léger
Fibre-optic: la fibre optique
File sharing: partage de fichier
Fingerprint: empreinte digitale
Font: police de caractères
Freeware: gratuiciel / logiciel gratuit
Game console: console de jeux
Hack (to) / hacker: pirater / pirate
Handheld: tenu à la main
Hard disk: disque dur
Hardware: matériel informatique
High technology: haute technologie
Host (to): héberger
Hotspot: point d'accès WiFi
IT (information technology): informatique
Internet service provider (ISP): fournisseur d'accès Internet
Laptop: ordinateur portable
Lock (up) (to): verrouiller
Login: identification
Multiplayer: multi-joueurs
Nanotechnology: nanotechnologie
Network: réseau
Obsolete: dépassé
Online: en ligne
P2P / peer-to-peer: P2P / d'utilisateur à utilisateur
Password: mot de passe
Personal computer (PC): ordinateur
PIN Number (personal identification number): code PIN, numéro d'identification personnel
Phishing: piratage des cartes de crédit en ligne
Processing: traitement
Productics: productique
Radio frequency: fréquence radio
Remote control: télécommande
Robotics: robotique
Saturate (to): saturer
Scan (to): scanner
Screen: écran
Search engine: moteur de recherche
Secure: sans risque
Shareware: partagiciel / logiciel partagé
Smartphone: téléphone intelligent (multifonction)
Software: logiciel
Spyware: logiciel espion
State-of-the-art: dernier cri
Technical: technique
Technology / technological: technologie / technologique
Text message / SMS: SMS
Tool: outil
USB stick / flash drive / thumb drive: clé USB
User: utilisateur
User-friendly: convivial, facile à utiliser
Video conference: visioconférence
Website: site Internet
Wireless: sans fil

6

Work

New working trends

Question

What has changed in our working patterns?

WORD BOX

to set up a business • to be successful • to take risks • to come up with new ideas • to grow businesses • apply for a job (to) • type of product • to meet the clients' needs • to work hard

6 | Work

1 • Look and discuss

a) Look at the following pictures.

b) Discuss in class.

1. What are these people's jobs? Would you like to be in their position?
2. What is your dream job? What are you planning to do to make your dream come true? What skills will you need?
3. Read the following quotation. Do you agree with it? Write a few lines to say what you think the most important thing in a job is. Could it be job satisfaction?
"I feel sorry for the person who can't get genuinely excited about his work. Not only will he never be satisfied, but he will never achieve anything worthwhile." (Walter Chrysler)

2 • Read and write

Answer the following questions by writing a few sentences.

1. Do the above company regulations suit you? Why?
2. What would be the ten most ideal regulations for employees? Imagine them. Write a list. Use the headings in exercise 4 for ideas.

3 • Listen and understand

CD n° 2
Track n° 23

a) True or false? Since the change in working hours, people are expected to arrive very early.
b) True or false? Sandra wrote about her phones on the social network.
c) Do you think it is right that companies can look at your social networking pages and that you could lose your job because of it?

4 • Read and understand

a) Read the following text.

<u>Rules for new employees</u>

Welcome to the company. Please read the following rules carefully and sign on the dotted line at the bottom of the page to show your agreement. Any violation of the company rules and regulations will lead to immediate dismissal[1].

The following rules and regulations shall apply to all employees of the company while on the company's premises[2] at all times, including break times, overtime[3] and work done on off-days, rest days and paid public holidays.

1. Clothing: Employees shall dress in a professional manner commensurate to their position in the company. Jeans and cotton shirts are authorised on Fridays only (Friday wear). Piercing and tattoos are subject to the agreement of the CEO upon inspection.

2. Punctuality: All employees are required to report to work on time. Biometric time clocks are available at all company entrances to avoid employees clocking in or clocking out[4] for colleagues.

3. Confidentiality: Each employee is to sign and adhere to a non-disclosure agreement[5].

4. Working hours: Each employee is expected to fulfill a 10-hour working day. One hour maximum is allowed for lunch breaks. You are entitled to a timed 10-minute rest break mid-morning and another mid-afternoon to go to the "rest area" for refreshments, and use the toilet facilities.

5. Days off: Each employee is entitled to 2 weeks paid leave and is expected to fulfill all personal obligations within these 2 weeks. We do not expect employees to request parental leave[6] or sick leave[7].

6. Food and drink: The consumption of food or beverages at desks or work stations is forbidden. The consumption of alcohol and / or smoking is strictly prohibited on the premises.

7. Company materials: Employees may not use company equipment, stationery[8] or materials for personal use. Employee Web use is monitored[9].

8. The following are forbidden: Trade union membership[10] and any complaints about working conditions.

Please note: Internal whistleblowing[11] is greatly encouraged and rewarded.

Employee name (in caps): .... Signature: ....

1. Dismissal: *renvoi* 2. Premises: *locaux* 3. Overtime: *heures supplémentaires* 4. Clock in / out: *pointer* 5. Non-disclosure agreement: *clause de confidentialité* 6. Parental leave: *congé parental* 7. Sick leave: *congé maladie* 8. Stationery: *papeterie* 9. Monitor: *surveiller* 10. Trade union membership: *appartenance à un syndicat* 11. Whistleblower: *dénonciateur*.

b) Answer by true or false.

1. Employees are likely to be fired if they do not adhere to all the rules when they are at work.

2. Managers should be dressed in steel-capped shoes and overalls, and factory workers should wear a suit and tie.

3. Employees are allowed to punch in and out at the time clock for a friend.

4. Employees can choose, within reason, what time they get to work, and what time they leave.

5. Employees can take one hour and twenty minutes off during the day at the utmost.

6. Employees are encouraged to have a cup of tea or coffee, or even a glass of wine, at their desk.

7. The company keeps an eye on how employees use the Internet.

8. The company is likely to give a bonus to someone who reports misconduct, wrongdoings or malpractices within the company.

WARMING UP

► Do you think it is possible for a company to avoid discrimination (gender / age / ethnic ...)?

CD n° 2 Track n° 24

Parents, non-parents compete for time off

New york • With schools around the country back in session, parents who work at small businesses will be asking for and receiving time off for soccer games and class plays – possibly leading to some friction because other workers don't have such powerful reasons for leaving early.

Business owners and human resources executives say companies can avoid such problems with equitable time-off policies – in other words, by recognizing that all employees regardless of their personal circumstances need a work-life balance. Encouraging an atmosphere of mutuality and goodwill among co-workers can also head off conflicts and resentments when one staffer leaves early.

Colleen Haviland, founder and president of Xsell Resources Inc. and Ready to Hire, two businesses in Willow Grove, Pennsylvania, sees no difference between giving parents time off for a child's game and giving childless workers time to go to sporting or theatrical events. "No matter if it's children or any type of other commitment, we all have a real life outside of work," Haviland said. "Everyone needs to support each other in their real life in order to have synergy in the workplace."

She sees this kind of approach as an integral part of fostering good relationships with staffers."If they're a good employee, when they're here they give 110 percent, so you should make exceptions for them," Haviland said.

At Kel & Partners, a Hopkinton, Massachusetts, marketing services agency, "We don't limit flexibility to parents," President Ginny Pitcher said, noting that some staffers need time off to care for elderly parents or grandparents. "We've built a mutual foundation of respect between employees." Pitcher said employees who need time away from the office make sure they get their work done, and they don't dump responsibilities on co-workers. As a result, she said, when a parent takes time off for a child's baseball game, other staffers are likely to be asking the next morning, "How did Justin do? Did he pitch well?"

Similarly, another staffer who needs time to care for an ill grandparent is likely to be asked, "Can I help you out?" she said. Pitcher said staffers don't try to take advantage of the situation – they'll be checking e-mail later in the day to see what they might have missed.

Bonnie Beirne, director of service operations for Administaff Inc., declared, "Typically, when you have a PTO plan, (paid time off) employees can take time off for any reason – it doesn't really require any justification," Beirne said. Paid time off allows employees to feel they're being treated equally, and also relieves an owner or manager from having to be an arbiter of what is a reasonable request for time away from work. Employees need to feel "they're treated in a consistent way and they have the same opportunity as other employees to request time off for personal needs," Beirne said.

Feldman noted that without a policy, employers could inadvertently be discriminating against some staffers when granting time off. For example, she noted, if mothers are allowed to leave early because of children's needs but male staffers don't receive similar treatment, there could be a perception of discrimination – a violation of federal law.

Associated Press, 6 September 2011

Pronunciation work

CD n° 2 Track n° 25

1. Listen and observe.

employee / trainee
Remember the rule: words in [-ee] are stressed on the last syllable.

2. Listen to these words that you may find difficult and repeat.

leaving early • personal circumstances • synergy • time off • checking e-mail later

Lexical work

1. Find the French equivalents of the following words.

§ 1 animosity
§ 2 **a)** fair **b)** limit (v) **c)** employee
§ 3 **a)** office **b)** encourage
§ 5 old **b)** throw away
§ 6 **a)** profit (v)
§ 7 **a)** fairly **b)** exonerate (v) **c)** time off **d)** appropriate **e)** ask (v)
§ 8 **a)** accidentally **b)** give (v)

2. Find the English equivalents in the text.

§ 1 **a)** petite entreprise **b)** football
§ 2 **a)** poltique du temps libre **b)** quitter plus tôt
§ 3 **a)** engagement **b)** lieu de travail
§ 4 encourager
§ 5 **a)** parents âgés **b)** déverser / décharger
§ 6 tirer profit
§ 7 une demande § 8 accorder

Work on the title

1. Identify the source of the document (title, date, nature).

2. Look at the headline and read paragraph 1. Why could parents and non-parents compete?

Check the facts

1. Read § 1.
What do some parents ask their employers?

2. Read § 2.
How can companies avoid friction?

3. Read § 3.
Which time-off policy is presented in paragraph 3?

4. Read § 4.
What is said about employees who need time off?

5. Read § 5, 6.
What do managers do in order to be flexible?
In which consequences?

6. Read § 7.
What is a PTO (paid time off) plan?

7. Read § 8.
How could employees be discriminated against?

About Work ...

Do you know other types of workplace discrimination?

Grammar

→ p. 237

Les principaux suffixes

- *powerful* = with power
- *regardless* = without regard
- *childless* = without child

Topic debrief

1. Choose the sentence which you think corresponds best to the main topic of the document.

a) Parent employees and non-parents are always two opposed groups.
b) Employers who have a paid time off policy have no conflicts to manage.
c) It is difficult to hire mothers and be satisfied.

2. Write an introduction to the document by using the word bank.

small business • *time off* • *children* • *elderly parents* • *discrimination* • *parent employees* • *non-parent employees* • *work done* • *employers* • *request*

Methods

1. Give a title to each paragraph or select a key sentence.

2. Which paragraph best sums up the article? Translate it.

Train for the exam

1. Make a **summary / account** of the document (60 words).

2. Express your personal opinion:
What do you think of flexible time off at work? Explain and illustrate your point of view (100 words / 3-5 minutes).

3. Role play: work in pairs
You are going to take part in a conversation.
Student A: you are a parent and you need some time off for your children's soccer games.
Student B: you are the HR manager and you have an equitable time-off policy. Prepare your arguments.

6 | Work

Train with an oral document

WARMING UP

► Do you believe that achieving success is possible for anybody in the business world? Why / why not?

CD n° 2
Track n° 26

From Pakistan to America and back

Lexical work

1. Choose the best equivalent for the following words.

a) Start from scratch:
– start from nothing
– start from something

b) Promised land:
– paradise
– hell

c) odd jobs:
– prestigious jobs
– simple jobs

d) make ends meet:
– make a living
– failure

2. Work on figures: write in full and read aloud.

40 years • 20 years old • jobs • 11-hour shift • 5 am

Pronunciation work

CD n° 2
Track n° 27

1. Listen and observe.

Pakistan → Pakistani: [ɪ]
America → American: [ən]

2. Listen and fill in the grid according to the pronunciation of their adjectives.

Israel • Africa • Arabia

Pakistani [ɪ]	American [ən]

3. Listen to these words that you may find difficult and repeat.

land of opportunity • an engineering student • quite tough • success • money

Work on the title

1. Look at the title of the document.

2. Try to imagine why an immigrant would like to go back to where he came from.

Check the facts

1. Listen to part 1.

a) What is the name given to America?
b) What does this name mean?
c) When did Abdul-Hadi come to America?
d) What is his country of origin?
e) How much money did he have in his pocket when he arrived in America?
f) Was he educated?

2. Listen to part 2.

a) In which sectors did AH work?
b) How many jobs did he have during the same day?
c) What did he do with the money?
d) What was his family situation at the time?
e) What happened during the first three years?
f) How many service stations does he own today?

3. Listen to part 3. Say if the following statements are true or false.

a) AH founded an association to help Pakistani immigrants.
b) AH thinks education and money are necessary to succeed.
c) Why did AH found an association?

Topic debrief

1. Choose the sentence which you think corresponds best to the main topic of the document.

a) The reporter is interviewing a man who recently emigrated from Pakistan to the U.S. and was able to become a successful entrepreneur; that's why he invites other Pakistanis to immigrate to the U.S.

b) The reporter is interviewing a Pakistani immigrant who came to the U.S. a long time ago, and who became a successful entrepreneur very easily and decided to go back to his home country.

c) The man being interviewed is a Pakistani immigrant who arrived in the U.S. in the 1970s and who, after enduring many hardships, succeeded in becoming a thriving entrepreneur and has decided to help his home country.

2. Rephrase the correct sentence in order to make a short introduction to the document.

Methods

1. Complete the sentences with the following words and phrases you have heard in the document.

odd jobs • engineering • openings • success • land of opportunity • hardworking • finish • obstinate • wealth• 40 years ago • entrepreneur street • anybody • degree

a) Good evening, ladies and gentlemen, and welcome to ... .

b) America is known as the ... . It's up to ... to start from scratch and find ... as long as they are ... and ... .

c) I believe you arrived from Pakistan nearly ... .

d) I was an ... student. I left Pakistan because at the time, I did not see any real ... in the near future. I knew my only chance for ... was to go to America.

e) But once there, I had to ... my engineering ..., and for that I did all sorts of ... .

2. Write down 4 key sentences on Abdul's life.

a) What he did before he came to America

b) When he arrived

c) How he achieved success

d) His plans for the future

Train for the exam

1. Use your notes to make an **oral presentation** about Abdul-Hadi's success story and record yourself (3-5 minutes).

2. Express your personal opinion:
Do you think the American Dream is still possible today? **Explain and illustrate your point of view (100 words / 3-5 minutes).**

3. Role play: work in pairs

You are going to take part in a conversation.
Student A: you are an immigrant from France living in the U.S.; you have started a business and it is now successful.
Student B: you are an American radio reporter interviewing student A.

TIPS

• *For student A:*
– Make up an identity (gender, age, education, date of birth).
– Choose a business sector (a relevant one if possible).
– Find reasons for emigrating to the U.S.
– Say where in the U.S.
– Explain how you adapted to the U.S. lifestyle.
– How you managed to set up your business.
• *For student B:*
– Find a name for your radio programme.
– Introduce your guest to the audience.
– Ask relevant questions inducing the answers above.
• You should use your notes in order to present a realistic conversation. Don't read them, look up.
You can:
– record the conversation (the recording should last between one and two minutes at most);
– videotape the scene and show it to the class;
– act out the scene in front of the class;
– listen to your classmates' recordings and write what you have understood in a short and structured paragraph.

Go online

• Find out about famous immigrant businessmen who succeeded in America.
• Get prepared to report to your group / class (a PowerPoint presentation is recommended).

WARMING UP

▸ What do you think of gender discrimination and gender abuses?

CD n° 2
Track n° 28

"Prison-like" conditions for Chinese workers making IBM, Dell, HP, Microsoft and Lenovo products

US organisation the National Labour Committee (NLC) found 2,000 workers at the Meitai factory working an average of 74 hours a week, for a base wage of 64 cents an hour. This drops to 41 cents an hour after room and board is removed. The workers, mostly young women aged from 18 to their mid-20s, are not allowed to talk, listen to music, look around them, put their hands in their pockets or go to the toilet unless it is an official break.

Workers are encouraged to monitor each other and are fined if they break rules. These include being one minute late for a shift or putting personal items on a work desk. On the assembly line, a keyboard passes each worker every 7.2 seconds. The worker has to snap six or seven keys into place in that time. The NLC visited the factory between June and September 2008 and in January this year. One worker said, "I feel like I am serving a prison sentence. We are really livestock and should not be called workers."

The Meitai Plastics and Electronics factory in Dongguan City, Guangdong Province, China, makes keyboards and other equipment for Dell, HP, IBM, Microsoft and Lenovo. The companies said they would investigate conditions at the factory but none said they would cancel contracts linked to the factory. Microsoft said the factory supplies one of its contracted manufacturers. A spokesperson said, "We are working closely with our industry partners and contracted supplier to conduct an investigation."

A spokesman for HP said, "The factory named in the report is not one of HP's direct suppliers, but is a supplier to two of our suppliers. HP will audit this facility through a validated industry audit. Based on the results of the audit, we will work together with our supplier to develop corrective actions where appropriate." Dell said it was "actively investigating" the issues in the report.

Charles Kernaghan, report author and director at the NLC, said, "The $200 personal computer and the $22.99 keyboard may be seen as a great bargain, but in the long run they come at a terrible cost."

Computerweekly.com UK, 17 Feb 2009

Lexical work

1. For each of the following words of the text (§ 1, 2), choose the appropriate meaning thanks to the context.

a) average: maximum / moyenne / minimum
b) wage: prix / coût / salaire
c) monitor: surveiller / aider / remplacer
d) fined: en bonne santé / verbalisé / mis à l'amende / trouvé

2. Find the English equivalents in the text.

a) salariés **§ 1**
b) usine **§ 1**
c) chaine de montage **§ 2**
d) annuler **§ 3**
e) porte parole **§ 4**
f) fournisseur **§ 4**

Pronunciation work

CD n° 2
Track n° 29

1. Listen and fill in the grid according to the pronunciation of the letter "a".

[ɑː]	[eə]	[e]	[əː]	[ə]	[æ]

2. Work on figures: write in full and read aloud.

a) 74 hours a week
b) 64 cents an hour
c) 18 to their mid-20s
d) 7.2 seconds
e) $22.99

Work on the title

1. Identify the source of the document (title, date, nature).

2. Look at the headline and paragraph 1 to give more details about the workers.

Check the facts

1. Read § 1.
a) What is the name of the factory?
b) What is the basic wage of a Chinese worker?
c) How many hours do they work a week?
d) What sex and what age group do most of the workers belong to?
e) What are the 3 things they are not allowed to do during their working hours?

2. Read § 2.
a) What happens if they break the rules?
b) How much time can they spend on each keyboard?
c) What sentence in the article shows that the workers suffer in this factory?

3. Read § 3, 4.
a) List 3 international companies working with the Meitai factory.
b) How did HP, Dell and Microsoft react to the NLC's report?
c) What was HP's response?

5. Read § 5.
What are the prices of the computers and keyboards manufactured in the Meitai factory?

Grammar

→ p. 237

L'expression de la fréquence

- *74 hours a week*
- *64 cents an hour*
- *every 7.2 seconds*

Go online

- Carry out a research on www.globallabourrights.org about other examples of difficult working conditions in the country of your choice.
- Get prepared to report to your group / class (a PowerPoint presentation is recommended).

Topic debrief

1. Choose the sentence which you think corresponds best to the main topic of the document.
a) American computer companies decided to relocate their production to China; that is why the U.S. workers are angry, because they are losing their jobs.
b) Global computer firms manufacture some of their products in a Chinese factory which does not respect basic human rights.
c) Chinese factories do not have the same way of treating their employees as U.S. companies, that's why Dell, HP and Lenovo are thinking about leaving China.

2. Rephrase the correct sentence in order to make a short introduction to the document.

Methods

1. Which paragraph best defines the problem?

2. Translate it.

3. Express the working conditions in your own terms.

Train for the exam

1. Make a **summary / account** of the document (60 words / 3-5 minutes).

2. Comment: find an answer to the following question. Discuss and give examples (150 words).
What does Charles Kernaghan mean when he says that the PCs and keyboards made in the Meitai factory come at "a terrible cost"?

3. Role play: work in groups
You are going to take part in a debate.
Think about this quotation in groups: "One worker said, 'I feel like I am serving a prison sentence. We are really livestock and should not be called workers' ".
You are a group of members from the NLC. What advice / proposals / suggestions could you give to these workers? Discuss your ideas in class.

6 | Work

Train with an oral document

WARMING UP

- Have you ever worked from home?
- Do you think you enjoyed the same working conditions?

CD n° 2
Track n° 30

Teleworking

Lexical work

1. Find the English equivalents in the document.

Part 1

a) en moyenne
b) envolée des prix de l'essence
c) prendre un moyen de transport pour se rendre au travail et en revenir (one word)
d) prendre une pause
e) empreinte carbone

Part 2

a) ordinateur portable
b) internet haut débit
c) sécurisé
d) diminuer
e) éviter
f) immobilier
g) climat extrême
h) valeur ajoutée
i) mener à bien

Pronunciation work

CD n° 2
Track n° 31

1. Listen and observe.

The pronunciation of "a"	
[eɪ] able	[ə] affect, among, avoid, amount

2. Listen to these words that you may find difficult and repeat.

skyrocketing • footprint • secure • permanent

Work on the title

1. Look at the title of the document.

2. Guess who might be interested in teleworking.

Check the facts

1. Listen to part 1.

a) Where is June Antbridge's company located?
b) What sort of company is it?
c) What is her job in the company?
d) Where does she work once or twice a week?
e) Why did she choose this solution?
f) What consumes the most energy?

2. Listen to part 2.

a) What do we learn about the company's history?
b) What does the company do for its employees?
c) What kind of equipment does she need?
d) What are the main elements encouraging employees to choose teleworking?
e) What percentage of employees work full-time from home?
f) What does hot desking consist of?
g) How much money does the company save? On what costs?
h) What is the consequence on productivity?
i) What are the advantages of teleworking in Canada?
j) Do employees working from home work less than those working in an office?

Topic debrief

1. Choose the sentence which you think corresponds best to the main topic of the document.

a) A woman employee from a high-tech firm in Canada works full-time from home; this choice was made for her by the company but she is satisfied with the arrangement.

b) A woman executive from a high-tech firm chose to work a couple of days a week from home to reduce her carbon footprint and to spend more time with her small children.
c) A woman working in a Canadian company explains the advantages and the drawbacks of working from home.

2. Write an introduction to the document by using the word bank.
work from home • gas prices • small children • carbon footprint • technology • extreme weather

Methods

1. Write down 5 reasons which might lead someone to telework.

2. Now rephrase two of them in 2 sentences.

Train for the exam

1. Use your notes to make an **oral presentation** of the document and record yourself (3-5 minutes).

2. Comment: find an answer to the following question. Discuss and give examples (100 words / 3-5 minutes).
Does teleworking mean emancipation or domination to women?

3. Role play: work in groups (3 people)
You are going to take part in a conversation between 2 employees and their boss.
Student A: you are the boss. You want to implement teleworking to your staff. You give the advantages for them and for the company.
Student B: you are an employee (1) and you are happy about it. Give your reasons.
Student C: you are an employee (2) and you refuse it and explain why.

PRACTICE • AUDIO • VIDEO

Train with a video

Social networking workforce dangers

→ http://www.youtube.com/watch?hl=en&v=eRaG9A9syHI&gl=US

28 January, 2010

Look at this video on the Internet about social networking

Check the facts	Methods
1. What is the main concern in this video?	• Which words / phrases / pictures are repeated most?
2. Which people might have problems?	• Do you think there is a generation gap in the network users?
3. How can they be involved in such dangers?	• Is there a lack of information when joining these networks?
4. When did you personally join a social network?	• Who invited you to join a social network or did you do it on your own?
5. Issues ... – Is privacy threatened by our new ways of life? – Are there positive developments due to social networking?	• Have you heard of people who have been in trouble due to their social network involvement? • What do you think of the "Arab Spring" as far as social networking is concerned?

WARMING UP

▸ How many women CEOs do you know? Who are they?

CD n° 2 Track n° 32

How women entrepreneurs are changing the world

Rio de Janeiro • Women entrepreneurs are changing the world. While they're at it, they're making a lot of money – sometimes a whole lot of money. It's inspirational to see some of the women who are becoming economic powerhouses internationally, often overcoming huge obstacles and discrimination. I've just met many of them at the second annual Dell Women's Entrepreneur Network global conference here.

The conference was an inspirational coming together of women from diverse nations who are building substantial businesses, creating jobs and solving problems.

"About five years ago, we saw some of the opportunities around women and technology. When we looked at emerging markets, we looked at women entrepreneurs, and we saw this amazing opportunity," said Karen Quintos, Dell's chief marketing officer. Rapidly developing countries are the fastest growing part of their business, and women entrepreneurs like Leila Velez are a substantial part of the growth in those markets.

Velez grew up in the infamous favelas, the slums, here. She got a job at McDonald's and eagerly learned everything she could. Taking some of her newfound skills, she started a beauty salon, serving some of the lowest-income women in Rio.

"We had no money or investors because no one believed in salons specializing in curly hair serving women at the bottom of the pyramid," Velez said. "I had to sell a very old, beat-up car to start." Now she has 11 salons, serving 1,000 customers a day. With 1,300 employees, she's doing more than just changing women's appearances; she's changing people's lives. "Seventy percent of our employees are ex-customers, most coming from the favelas," she said. But Velez has bigger plans. "I've already chosen the street in New York where I'm going to open my first store," she said. "I know I'm going to reach my dream." Having met Leila, I have no doubt she will.

But it's not just developing countries where women are building vibrant companies. Katherine Sampson, another conference attendee, mortgaged her house in 1992 to buy one small sandwich shop in Melbourne, Australia.

Sampson remodeled her store, renamed it Healthy Habits and focused in on healthy sandwiches. She worked like crazy to succeed, even while juggling her role as the single mother of a 2 year old. In 1999, she was able to open a second store and soon she had two more – all the time securing and paying back bank loans. For aspiring female entrepreneurs – and males, too – these women prove to all of us that women can overcome great obstacles to build great businesses.

USA Today, 10 June 2011

Lexical work

1. Find the English equivalents in the text.

§ 1 surmonter • énorme
§ 2 construire • résoudre • rassemblement
§ 3 marchés émergents
§ 5 au bas de l'échelle sociale
§ 6 vivace • hypothéquer • pays en voie de développement

Pronunciation work

CD n° 2 Track n° 33

1. Listen to these words that you may find difficult and repeat. inspirational • powerhouses • diverse • appearances

2. Listen to these "transparent" words and practice pronouncing them with the right stress. entrepreneur • obstacles • global • conference • diverse

Work on the title

1. Identify the source of the document (title, date, nature).

2. Pick up the words from the headline which appear several times in the article. How do you explain their repetition?

Check the facts

1. Read § 1.

a) Which problem do women have to solve when they start a business?

b) Which company organised the conference? When did it take place?

2. Read § 4, 5.

Who is Leila Velez? Give all the details you can about her and her business.

3. Read § 6, 7.

Who is Katherine Sampson? Give all the details you can about her and her business.

Grammar

→ p. 236

Les propositions infinitives (avec ou sans "to")

• *... mortgaged her house in 1992 to buy one small sandwich shop ...*

Topic debrief

1. Choose the sentence which you think corresponds best to the main topic of the document.

a) Women entrepreneurs in Brazil are opening an increasing number of businesses.

b) Women entrepreneurs around the world are hindered by many obstacles they can't overcome.

c) In spite of a huge amount of hundles, women entrepreneurs around the world are gaiming momentum.

2. Rephrase the correct sentence in order to make a short introduction to the document.

Methods

1. Rephrase the main idea in each paragraph with your own words like in the example given for § 1.

Business women from different countries choose to meet at this conference.

You can use the following starters:

a) Five years ago, Dell's chief marketing officer noticed ... . § 3

b) After working at McDonald's, Leila Velez ... . § 4

c) Today, L. Velez has opened ... . § 5
She employs ...; she has become an important ... .
Now she dreams of ... .

d) Katherine Sampson, a single Australian mother, managed to / succeeded in ... . § 6, 7

2. According to the article, what are the major qualities of women entrepreneurs? List them.

Train for the exam

1. Make a **summary / account** of the document (60 words / 3-5 minutes).

2. Express your personal opinion:

Do you think women entrepreneurs have to overcome more obstacles than men when they start a business? In which countries?

Explain and illustrate your point of view (100 words / 3-5 minutes).

3. Role play: work in groups (3 people)

You are going to take part in a conversation.

Imagine a short conversation between Leila Velez, Katherine Sampson and an antidiscrimination activist. They explain how the road is still long for women in the world after the Dell conference and how they would like to write a UN work regulation charter.

Student A: you are Leila Velez.
Student B: you are Katherine Sampson.
Student C: you are an antidiscrimination activist.

Go online

• Find information about women at work in two types of countries: developed and developing.
• Collect the data. You can log on to the UN and UNICEF websites, WOW (Work of Women), etc.
• Get prepared to report to your group / class (a PowerPoint presentation is recommended).

Working in the logistics department

1 • Situation

You have been recently hired in the logistics department of a company. You have been asking your line manager for new software and the appropriate training for the logistics department for over six months, to no avail.

2 • Process

a) Look at the following documents: the job offer letter you received a year ago (Document A), the advertisement you have found (Document B) and the document about the Work Worries department to fix an appointment to discuss the problem with them (Document C).
b) Get into pairs.
Students A: you are an unsatisfied employee. *Students B:* you work for the Work Worries department.
c) *Students A:* you call the Work Worries department / students B, outlining the problem and asking for an appointment. Suggest an appointment (date, time and place) to discuss the matter.
d) Now discuss the problem. Remember to speak in English only!
Students A: you present your arguments for purchasing the new software and benefitting from the training offered by the organisation.
Students B: you discuss the problem (arguments for and against), and decide upon what action is to be taken.

3 • Follow up

You work for the Work Worries department. Send an e-mail to Ms Brown's line manager explaining your discussion and the outcome. Start by saying: "Following my meeting with the Work Worries department on (date), I would like to ..."

TIPS

• **Start by saying**
Students A:
I don't want to complain, but ...
I know that I'm new here, but ...
I really think that the department could benefit from ...
Students B:
On the one hand... but on the other hand ...
I can see where you are coming from ...
Don't you think that ... ?

• **There are many useful expressions in English for making suggestions:**
How about + V-ing ...
What about + V-ing ...
If I were you I would + base verb ...
You could (always) + base verb ...
You should / I don't think you should / you shouldn't + base verb ...
You ought to / I don't think you ought to + base verb ...
Why don't you + base verb ... ?
I suggest + V-ing ... / I suggest that you + base verb ...
I advise you + infinitive ...
Have you considered + V-ing ...?
Would it be a good idea to + infinitive ... ?

Go online

Look on the Internet to find various supply chain software suppliers and compare their prices.

Doc • A

TLC Incorporated

August 2012-01-10

Dear Ms. Brown

TLC Incorporated is pleased to offer you the position of procurement officer in our logistics department. Should you accept this job offer you will be eligible to receive the following:
Annual gross starting salary: £23,000/annum.
Health, dental, life and disability insurance.
Annual stock options and profit sharing.
5 weeks paid leave.
Regular training to update and improve your efficiency as procurement officer.

Should you decide to accept this offer, please complete the attached form and return it to our office before 24th August 20- - .
We look forward to welcoming you aboard. Your line manager will be J. Meano.
Please do not hesitate to call us should you have any questions.

Sincerly,
TLC Incorporated

Doc • B

Learn how to manage your supply chain with our new APS (Applied Procurement Software) program in only 3 days!

- Streamlined and foolproof system for ordering, invoicing, tracking…
- Program installation included in the price.
- Free 2-year guarantee and monthly reviews of software efficiency and applicability.
- Costs partly covered by government training scheme.

IT expertise

Just call us on 0800 666 888

Doc • C

TLC Incorporated

WORK WORRIES DEPARTMENT

Over 5,000 people are employed by our company. Many of the day-to-day problems you may come across are caused by people. We have therefore created this special department to help you solve such problems before they get out of proportion.

Common problems you may need our help with:
Bad boss, bullying, career management, difficult co-workers, e-mail and Internet privacy, employee rights, harassment and discrimination, problem employees, wages and salaries, training…

Should you require any advice, please send us an e-mail on info@workworries.tlc

Any request for help or advice will be treated 100% confidentially.

6 | Work

Background

One of the first questions people ask each other is "What do you do?" One common factor which links people from all around the world is that most people have to work to earn a living. Work gives people a sense of identity and a purpose, and in most cases provides an income. However, half the families in the world are living on under $2 income a day, and unemployment figures remain high, especially for 15-24 year olds, and the over 50s. The face of the world of work is changing – globalisation is leading to labour migration (→ SEE CHAPTER "GLOBALISATION" PAGE 166) *and new technologies are changing our everyday way of work.* → SEE CHAPTER "NEW TECHNOLOGIES" PAGE 102.

1 What practical changes are taking place in the workplace?

Teleworking: New technology (ICT – information and communication technology) has led to more and more people working **full-time** or **part-time** away from the office. This includes: telecommuting, or working from home; mobile telework, when staff using ICTs can work "on the road"; and telecentres which are local offices open to everyone to save **commuting** time. Telework also includes functional relocation and outsourcing to places which are sometimes thousands of miles away. One advantage of this is being able to have 3 different teams working consistently throughout different time zones in a 24-hour day. → SEE CHAPTER "NEW TECHNOLOGIES" PAGE 102.

Hot desking: Means that there are more employees in a work space than there are desks, so employees take it in turns to use fully equipped work stations, or log in with their own laptop. The upside is the savings, as overhead costs are cut, however many say it is bad for team-building.

Flexibility: Another cost-saving trend is to do away with job stability, and employ staff on a JIT (just in time) basis – they only work when they are needed, either as **temps** (temporary workers) or by working annualised hours (which mean some weeks they work 48 hours, and others few or no hours at all). Employees are often given short-term contracts. Workers are encouraged to be multitaskers (able to do more than one job). The downside of this organisation is workers do not feel part of the company and lack motivation.

→ SEE CHAPTER "COMPANIES" PAGE 22.

Questions

- What are the current changes taking place in the workplace? Do you know any others?
- What are the main reasons for people losing their jobs?
- Would you like to work for a company like Google? What would motivate you otherwise?

2 What is happening in the job market?

There is a direct link between the job market and unemployment. When unemployment is high, employers can negotiate terms and lower **wages**, whereas when there is more demand than supply, the employees have the upper hand. There are various causes of **unemployment**:

Relocating the company to another country with lower labour costs and fewer work regulations.

Outsourcing certain activities to companies in low-cost countries. However, for economic reasons (national lack of jobs) and reasons of sustainable development, many companies are bringing their production sites back to the homeland. In 2011, President Sarkozy introduced the "Made in France" slogan to encourage citizens to "manufacture it in France".

→ SEE CHAPTER "COMPANIES" PAGE 22.

Laying off employees or short-time working because of financial difficulties (for example in a period of recession) or because of new technologies where a machine takes the place of one or more employees. Employees in these cases are entitled to **redundancy pay**.

→ SEE CHAPTER "NEW TECHNOLOGIES" PAGE 102.

Info

Increasingly popular is the **"work-life balance"** debate. Here are a few tips:

- Take time for downtime – moments spent with friends and family.
- Don't waste time or energy – put limits on the time you spend on social networks, surfing the Web and worrying.
- Organise your time – set priorities for work and personal tasks and fit things in together.
- Take some exercise – do some sport – even if you think you don't have time it boosts your energy levels.
- Chill out – find the time to relax on your own every day to recharge your batteries.

You cannot go **on the dole** (receive unemployment benefits) if you are fired, sacked or dismissed for professional misconduct.

Work culture: The former "job for life" attitude has changed. Inasmuch as 25 years ago, people expected to work for the same company throughout their working life, more than a quarter of younger (16-34) workers now expect to change jobs 8-10 times during their careers (with a maximum of 4 jobs for the over 35s). This has led to fears about job insecurity but is seen by some as a challenge. With retirement age being pushed back to 65 or 68 in many countries, it has been suggested that in the future most people will have at least two totally different careers in their lifetime.

The working poor are people who have a job (or who are looking for a job) but their incomes fall below the poverty line. In 2010 it was estimated that nearly 1 out of 3 families in the USA were "low income", as especially blue-collar workers' wages decreased. In Europe in the same year, "working poor" applied to about 6% of employees and 18% of the self-employed. It is therefore not only a phenomenon in developing countries, and the finger is often pointed at globalisation (competition from low-labour-cost countries) as one of the major causes.

→ SEE CHAPTER "GLOBALISATION" PAGE 166.

3 Do happy employees improve corporate performance?

Social motivation is said to be the future of innovative companies. If the "Google" example is anything to go by, with free gourmet meals, on-site doctors, gym facilities, etc., worker motivation might depend on **perks**. However, the employer's attitude towards the employees is equally important. Employees need to feel that:

They can show every day that they are doing their best (self-inspection, work autonomy...)

Their opinion counts (idea boxes, brainstorming meetings at every level ...).

Everyone is committed to quality and company excellence.

Their job is an important link in the chain, whatever their position in the company.

Trade unions (UK) / labor union (USA) are organisations that represent and defend paid workers. They fight for wage increases and better working conditions. Sometimes they need to take industrial action (for example, call the workers out on strike) to make their voice heard.

In a **works council** (or works committee), employees and employers work together at a company level to discuss and negotiate working conditions, and discuss grievances and other matters not covered by the trade union. They also organise staff benefits such as subsidised holidays and Christmas parties. Every company with over 50 employees has to have a works council and every employee contributes to the works council, which is subsidised by the company.

TIPS

Good ethics hand in hand with good business

To reinforce ethical behavior at work

Business ethics are the moral rules and regulations (or moral code of conduct) which guide the decision-making process in the strategic and operational management of a business.

1. Screen job applicants carefully for behavioural information.
2. Give new employees a solid grounding in the company's Code of Ethics.
3. Require compulsory annual "ethics updates" of all staff (training and workshops).
4. Have a completely confidential "ethics alert" system so staff members can alert the management to malpractice.
5. Managers are to set the example.
6. Set up a carrot and stick system to reward or punish ethical or unethical behaviour.
7. Treat all employees with fairness and respect.
8. Work towards sustainable development and improving the local community.
9. Get regular feedback from all concerned (stakeholders, employees ...).

http://ibmadison.com/employment?id=171

Questions

- What do you understand by "business ethics"?
- Should every company have a Code of Ethics?
- Should there be severe disciplinary measures for companies who do not respect a Code of Business Ethics?

Focus

The new workplace: open office versus digital nomads

The traditional workplace for white-collar workers has always been associated with office work. An office, in most people's minds, is a closed, hence private, space where one or two employees have their own desk. Mass production and the growing size of companies have increasingly transformed the working space and implemented what is referred to as open office plans, better known as open space. Today, thanks to the boom of new technologies, the concept of work space has shifted from bricks and mortar to virtual space: a new breed of workers has been on the rise for the past twenty years and is generally referred to as teleworkers, telecommuters or digital nomads. The question is to find out what type of work environment is the most suitable for individuals.

Open plan office, a new workplace?

Definition

- The open plan office is an open work space which accommodates over ten employees and offers little or no separation between each desk. It is now often referred to as open space.
- The open plan office concept has existed since the beginning of the 20th century, when skyscrapers began to adorn the urban landscape of America's big cities. Open space as we know it today has been developing since the 1950s, but it was from the 1990s onward that open space really gained momentum until it became the most frequent office layout. Open plan offices allow companies to save over 50% of their real estate cost.
- It is opposed to enclosed private offices occupied by one or two employees who can carry out their daily tasks behind closed doors.

Figures

- In France, 50% of all offices are open space.
- In the USA, 59% of all offices are open space.

Questions

- Why are open office plans interesting for companies? Give several reasons.
- What are the advantages for employees?
- What are the drawbacks?
- What consequences can they have on employees' lives?

Advantages

- Open plan offices are more economical: more work spaces and more employees in an office.
- Communication is easier between work stations and departments.
- There is no time wasted between offices because everyone is in the same area.
- Managers are in constant contact with the staff.
- Open space offices are more economical when it comes to operating costs, i.e. air-conditioning and electricity, real estate: the company saves money.
- The layout of the office can be changed quickly.

Drawbacks

- Noise and chaos: several conversations at a time, phone rings, printers, noise of keyboards.
- Employees can't focus properly.
- People passing to and fro can also distract employees.
- Security is reduced: employees can be robbed more easily of their personal belongings.
- Privacy is difficult to obtain with an open office plan. If family members call, or if a confidential call needs to be made, it can be difficult.
- Employees feel watched by their colleagues and supervisors.
- Sicknesses and infections can spread very fast (i.e. flu epidemics).
- Impossible to customise the light, heating, air-conditioning.
- May breed stress and anger and lead to "burn-out".

Digital nomads, the 21st century teleworkers

Definition

Teleworking, also known as telecommuting or digital nomads, has been made possible thanks to the IT revolution. Computers, mobile phones, faxes, broadband and WiFi Internet access enable an increasing number of employees to work outside the conventional brick and mortar open space or private office plan.
Today, digital nomads can work from any possible location provided they have the adequate equipment and Internet access. Could this new working trend become mainstream in the future?

Figures

- 18% of European employees are teleworkers.
- Teleworking is catching up in Europe; one exception: France, with only 9% .
- In the U.S. there has been a 74% increase in the number of digital nomads since 2005.
- 54 % of American employees say they would opt for teleworking if given the choice.
- 21% say they are not interested in working remotely.
- Several famous computer firms (Dell, HP, etc.) have a digital nomad website.

Advantages

Digital nomads have:
- no working hours: no need to clock in and out;
- complete freedom in the choice of their lifestyles;
- the ability to opt for their own workplace;
- no monitoring by supervisors or colleagues;
- no dress code, they can work in their swimming costumes or pyjamas;
- employers get a high-performing, happy and relaxed staff: a win-win situation.

Drawbacks

- They do not have an office, a private space.
- They don't know what the Internet connection will be like when they travel around the world.
- Their work is not taken seriously by traditional office workers.
- Some employers do not trust employees' productivity if they can't be monitored.
- They travel with digital equipment worth over $10,000, making them an ideal target for thieves.
- They do not really work in teams, and can lose contact with their colleagues.
- Their creativity and innovative spirit can eventually decline.
- The boundaries between work and leisure may disappear, leading to a dangerously unbalanced lifestyle.

Questions

- Why are teleworkers increasingly called "digital nomads"? Explain.
- What makes a growing number of people choose to be digital nomads? Explain the advantages in your own words.
- What job categories are the most liable to attract teleworkers? Explain.
- What difficulties can teleworkers be confronted with? Explain.
- Why are some employers reluctant to let their employees become digital nomads? Explain.

Express your point of view

- What do the different studies about the workplace reveal?
- What would be the ideal workplace for you?

Focus

When the workplace becomes hell: harassment at the workplace

Women in particular have been suffering for years from sexual harassment at work. Harassment can also occur when sex is not involved. When an employee undergoes constant pressure, negative comments about his / her tasks, contradictory orders or missions, is demeaned in public, when he / she is refused promotion for no reason, etc., the harassed employee may now file a complaint and eventually win his case.
Confronted with the mounting numbers of suicides committed by harassed staff members, human resources departments are now aware of the problem and one of their missions is to make sure their company is "harassment free".
Nevertheless, figures show that an increasing number of ailments and health hazards are directly related to stressful working conditions even when there is no harassment per se. The Anglo Saxons have coined the word "burn out" to refer to a nervous breakdown due to stressful working conditions.

The cost of burn out and harassment

- In 2009, the cost of stress In the EU amounted to 20 billion euros.
- In France, stress and burn out has cost 45 billion euros.
- In the EU, 10% of employees have been victims of harassment at the workplace.
- 20% of French women employees reported having been victims of sexual harassment.
- 10 to 15 % of suicides in Sweden are the direct consequence of harassment at work.
- 78% of UK employees have witnessed incidents involving harassment.

A few examples of workplace harassment

- **Verbal:** sexual innuendoes and other suggestive comments; racial or ethnic jokes or teasing about sex, race, age or religion; comments about a person's body or dress, excessive flattery or questioning of a personal nature; abusive language or insults; or threats.
- **Visual or non-verbal:** leering or staring in a sexual manner; whistling or hooting; suggestive or insulting looks; vulgar sounds or gestures, etc.
- **Physical:** inappropriate touching of the body such as brushing, patting, hugging, pinching or shoulder rubs; physically blocking another individual's movement, etc.

What is the obligation of the employer in preventing harassment in the work-place?

- The employer must take all reasonable steps to prevent discrimination and harassment from occurring.
- The employer must develop and implement a harassment prevention policy.
- The employer must also educate its employees as to the kind of behaviour that is to be avoided.
- Human resources managers should use positive reinforcement.

Questions

- How much do stress and harassment cost every year in the EU?
- What does the figure 20% represent?
- What is the situation In the UK?
- What are the different types of harassment that can occur at the workplace?

Express your point of view

- Does physical harassment necessarily imply violence?
- What should companies do to prevent harassment?
- What type of management is advised?

Test yourself

Try to use your memory – do not look at the vocabulary list!

1 BEWARE OF “FALSE FRIENDS”

Put in the right English word to replace the underlined word(s) which is (are) wrong.

training course • bonus • economic • overtime • relocated • hardworking • trained • shift • earns

a) The company has ~~delocalised~~ to Eastern Europe for ~~economical~~ reasons.

b) You will be sent on a ~~stage~~ to be ~~formed~~ to use our high-tech IT system.

c) He’s paid a fortune for his job – he ~~wins~~ at least €20,000 a month!

d) You will work on the night ~~team~~, and we offer a productivity ~~prime~~ at the end of each month.

e) We are looking for a ~~courageous~~ employee who isn’t afraid of working ~~supplementary hours~~.

2 A JOB OFFER

Look at the letter from a company offering you a job, and replace the French words by the correct English words.

Dear Ms Whitecollar,
Following your **1.** *entretien*, we are pleased to offer you the **2.** *temps* position of marketing assistant at BBRANDS Inc.
You will be paid a **3.** *salaire minimum* at the beginning, which will be increased according to the **4.** *competences* and **5.** *savoir faire* you acquire.
Your **6.** *horaires de travail* will be from 7am to 8pm, 5 days a week, and you will not be paid for any **7.** *heures supplémentaires*. You are entitled to 2 weeks **8.** *congé payé* and you may accrue **9.** *RTT* at 8 hours per pay period.
This employment offer is in effect for 7 business days. Should you wish to **10.** *decliner* this offer, please contact the personnel department.

3 MIND MAPPING

Put the words of the following list into the right column.

1) apply for (to)
2) be made redundant (to)
3) bonus
4) commute (to)
5) covering letter

6) day care
7) day off
8) dismiss (to)
9) economic redundancy
10) employ (to)

11) fire (to)
12) fixed-term contract
13) flexitime
14) heavy workload
15) hire (to)

16) hot desking
17) interview
18) lay off (to)
19) overworked
20) parental leave

21) part-time
22) pension
23) perks
24) recruit
25) resign

26. sack (to)
27. shift work
28. training course
29. teamwork
30. teleworking

A. Looking for a job	B. Working conditions	C. Leaving or losing a job

4 IT TAKES ALL KINDS TO MAKE A WORLD

Sort the word snake to find lots of different people you might meet at work.

workmateapplicantskilledlabourbluecollarworkeremployerninetofiverworkaholicoddjobmanself employedpersontempunskilledlabourcolleaguebreadwinneremployeefreelancerjobseekerwhite collarworker

6 | Work

Words

"The difference between a job and a career is the difference between forty and sixty hours a week." (Robert Frost)

Applicant: candidat
Apply for (to): poser sa candidature
Benefits: avantages sociaux
Be made redundant (to): être licencié
Blue-collar worker: ouvrier
Bonus: prime
Breadwinner: soutien de famille
Career: carrière
Child labour: travail des enfants
Commuting: faire le trajet aller-retour tous les jours
Covering letter, cover letter (USA): lettre de candidature
Day care / child care: crèche, garde d'enfants
Day labour: travail journalier
Day off: jour de congé
Dismiss (to): renvoyer
Dole (to be on the): être au chômage (UK)
Earn (to): gagner (par le travail)
Economic redundancy: licenciement économique
Employ (to): employer
Employee: employé(e)
Employer: employeur
Equal opportunities: chances égales
Fixed-term contract: contrat à durée déterminée
Flexitime: horaires à la carte
Freelance: indépendant
Full-time: temps complet
Hardworking: qui travaille dur / courageux
Hire (to) / take on (to): embaucher
Homeworking: travail à domicile
Hot desking: partage de bureaux
Interview: entretien
Job cuts: suppressions d'emplois
Job hopping: changement de boulot
Job security: sécurité de l'emploi
Jobless: sans emploi
Job-seeker: demandeur d'emploi
Know-how: savoir-faire
Labour force: main d'œuvre
Lay off (to): licencier
Letter of application: lettre de candidature
Lose a job (to): perdre son travail
Make someone redundant (to): licencier
Minimum wage: salaire minimum
Moonlight (to): « travailler au noir »
Night / day shift: equipe de nuit / jour
Nine-to-five job: emploi de bureau
Odd job: petit boulot
Opening: poste disponible
Outsourcing: externalisation
Overtime: heures supplémentaires
Overworked: surchargé de travail
Paid holidays: congé payé
Parental leave: congé parental
Part-time: temps partiel
Pension: retraite (revenus)
Perks: avantages en nature
Permanent job: CDI
Position: poste
Recruit (to): embaucher
Redundancy: licenciement
Redundancy pay: indemnités de licenciement
Relocate (to): délocaliser
Resign (to): démissionner
Restructuring: restructuration
Retire (to): prendre sa retraite
Retirement: retraite (condition)
RWD (reduction of work duration): RTT
Sack (to) / fire (to): virer (familier)
Salary: salaire (mensuel / annuel)
Self-employed person: travailleur indépendant
Senior: supérieur
Severance pay: prime de licenciement
Sick leave: congé maladie
Skill: compétence
Staff: personnel
Training course: stage de formation
Sweatshop: atelier de misère
Take-home pay: salaire net
Teamwork: travail d'équipe
Teleworking: télétravail
Temp (orary): intérimaire
Temping: faire de l'intérim
Time off: congé
Train (to): former
Trainee: stagiaire
Turn down an offer (to): décliner une offre
Union: syndicat
Unskilled: non qualifié
Voluntary redundancy: départ volontaire
Wage: salaire (horaire)
White-collar worker: employé de bureau
Work council: comité d'entreprise
Work off the books (to): travailler au noir
Work placement, internship (USA): stage en entreprise
Work station: poste de travail
Workaholic: accro du travail
Worker: travailleur, employé, salarié
Workforce: main d'œuvre
Working conditions: conditions de travail
Working hours: horaires de travail
Work-life balance: equilibre entre la vie et le travail
Workload: charge de travail
Workmate: collègue de travail (blue collar)
Workplace: lieu de travail

Europeans

For better and for worse

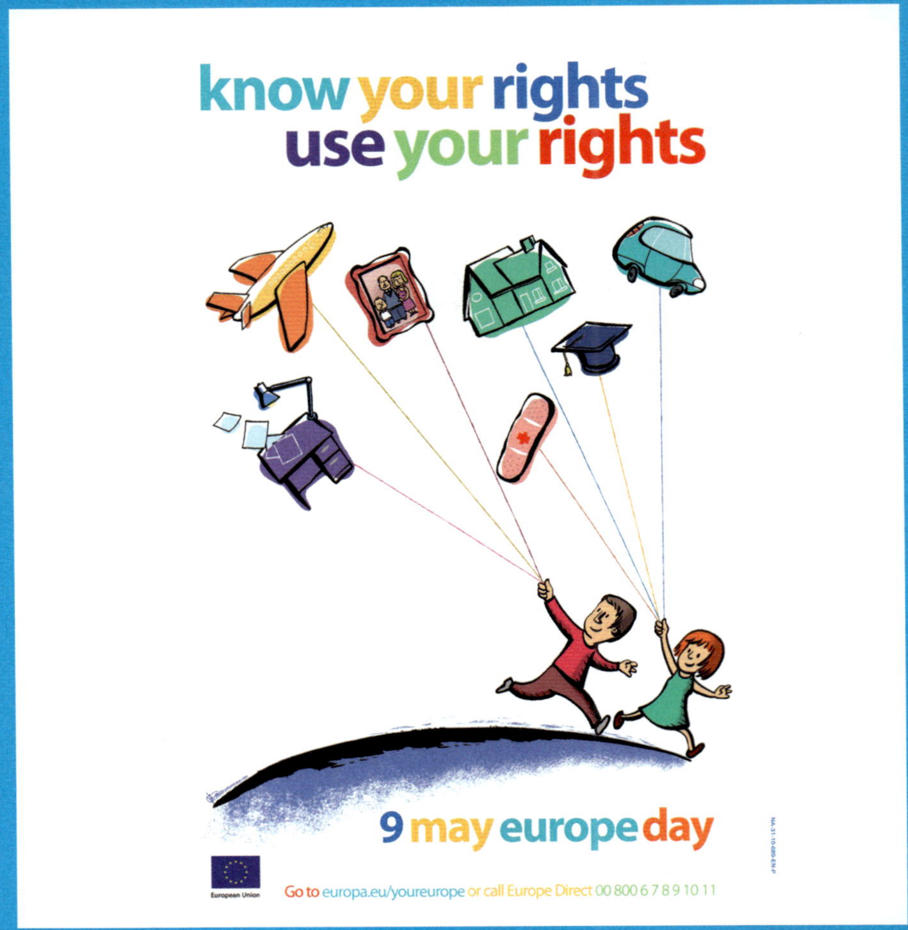

Question

What does the EU do for its citizens?

WORD BOX

Robert Schuman • 9th May 1950 • to grant rights • to protect citizens • a necessary institution • to suffer • from crises • a single currency • to avoid wars • peaceful relations • to hold very unusual kites • to symbolise • to travel • safely • to enjoy art • education • to promote • to encourage partnerships • exchanges • rights in the working world • parental leave • discrimination

7 Europeans

1 • Look and discuss

Look at the following documents. Answer the questions and discuss in class.

a) How many countries are in the European Community?
b) Associate the names of the countries to their flags.

2 • Read and understand

Match the question to the answer.

a) What does the EU do?
b) Why do countries join the EU?
c) What are the aims of the EU?
d) What actually is the EU?

1. It is a group of countries whose governments work together.

2. To benefit from the improvements and changes the EU makes.

3. – It reduces controls and taxes to make trade between EU countries easier.
– It removes controls which prevent people from moving around the EU freely.

4. – To promote economic and social progress.
– To represent the European Union on the international scene.
– To introduce European citizenship with 4 special rights*.
– To develop Europe as an area of freedom, security and justice.
– To maintain and build on established EU law to protect people's rights.

Info

*The 4 special rights:
– the freedom of movement and residence throughout the Union;
– the right to vote and stand as a candidate in municipal elections and in elections to the European Parliament in the state where he/she resides;
– the protection by the diplomatic and consular authorities of any Member State where the State of which the person is a national is not represented in a non-member country,
– the right to petition the European Parliament and apply to the Ombudsman.

3 • Look and understand

a) Look at these maps of what is now called the EU.

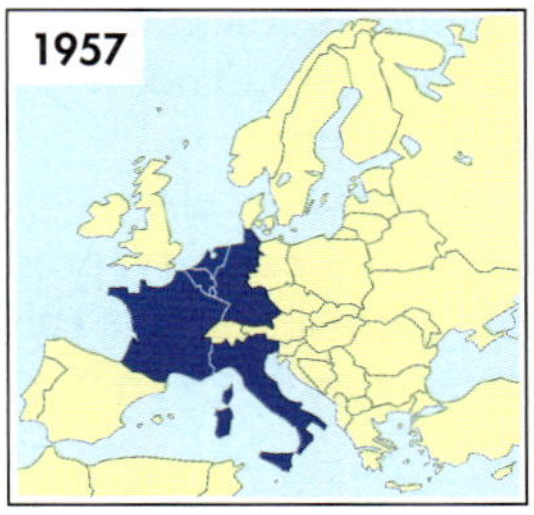

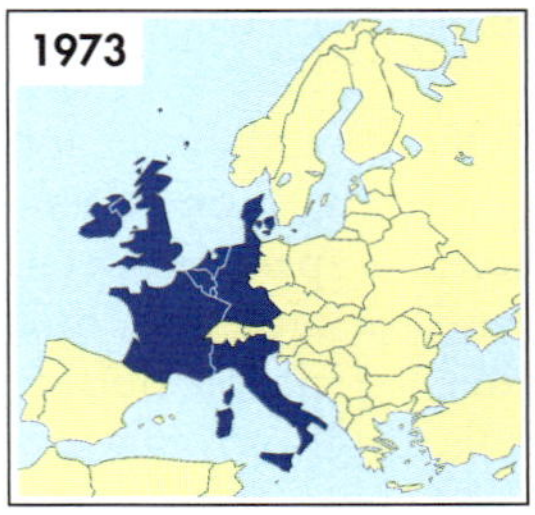

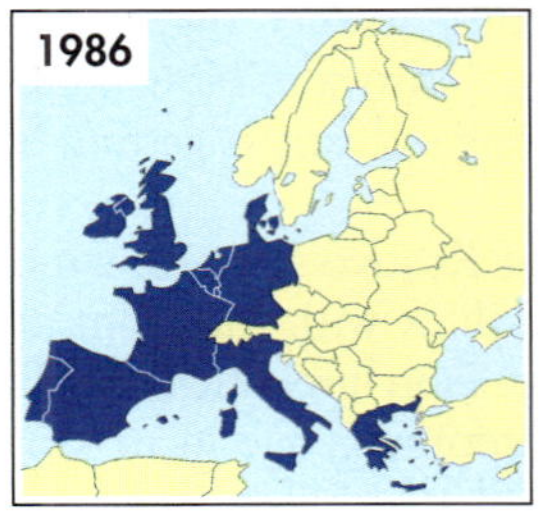

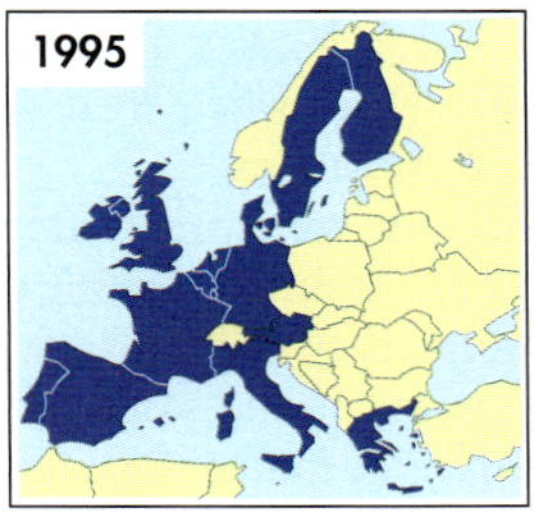

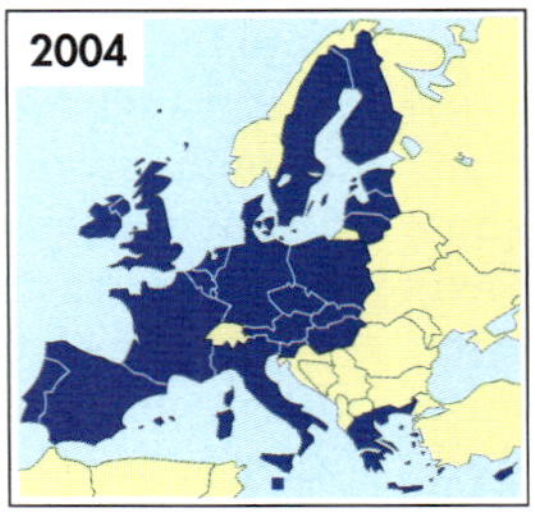

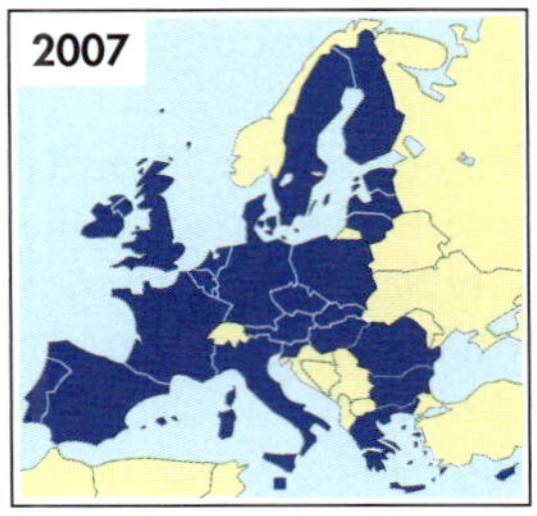

b) Answer the questions.

1. 12 countries were part of the single currency that introduced euro notes and coins in January 2002. Which are they?
2. 3 countries decided to remain outside. Which are they?
3. Now name the countries that joined the euro zone later. Which were they in 2007? In 2009? And in 2011?
4. Here is the list of the countries. Place them on the map to make sure you know where they are located.
Ireland • Portugal • Spain • France • Italy • Germany • The Netherlands • Belgium • Luxembourg • Greece • Austria • Finland • the United Kingdom • Denmark • Sweden • Slovakia • Estonia • Slovenia • Malta • Cyprus
5. There are other currencies in the 10 other European Union countries. Match the currency and the country.

a) Poland	**f)** Denmark	**1.** the pound	**6.** the zloty
b) Hungary	**g)** Romania	**2.** the lev	**7.** the forint
c) The United Kingdom	**h)** The Czech Republic	**3.** the leu	**8.** the lats
d) Sweden	**i)** Lithuania	**4.** the krone	**9.** the litas
e) Bulgaria	**j)** Latvia	**5.** the krona	**10.** the koruna

4 • Listen and understand

CD n° 3
Track n° 1

a) Does Jim regret the former different currencies such as the lira or the French franc?
b) Does it take a long time now for people and goods to get through customs?
c) Can European citizens get emergency medical treatment anywhere within the EU?

WARMING UP

▸ Which countries in Europe are most famous for their vineyards?

CD n° 3 Track n° 2

Kosovo's wines flowing again

Kosovo's wine industry was facing ruin in the 1990s, when the former Yugoslavia fell apart and it was plunged into war. Now there are signs that a once-thriving industry is getting back on its feet.

In the cellar of Kosovo's largest winery, Stone Castle, the air is thick with the scent of oak and wine. Some five million litres, including Pinot Noir, Merlot and Chardonnay, age in massive barrels. General manager Shani Mullabazi sips a glass of the 2010 Chardonnay. "It's fresh, has a really optimal acidity, is crispy, and very good in the mouth," he says proudly.

Stone Castle Winery is situated in Rahovec, an area in the southwest of Kosovo. Called Orahovac by the minority Serb population, it has been Kosovo's main winemaking area for centuries. Its table wines once flowed to the rest of communist Yugoslavia. "By the 1980s, Kosovo had long had a good reputation, especially for Pinot Noir," says Angela Muir, a wine consultant with expertise in the former Yugoslav region. "And by the 1990s, it had a well-established link with a very big volume brand in Germany."

Kosovo's wine industry collapsed as Yugoslavia disintegrated in the 1990s, and much of the infrastructure was destroyed by war. After the fighting subsided, a number of state-owned wineries, including Stone Castle, were privatised, and production began to recover. Now an optimistic air has returned to the Kosovan wine industry.

Economist-turned-wine-producer Miro Brkic, who lives in Rahovec, says with its average 270 days of sunshine each year, the area remains an ideal spot to make fine wine. Go south to Macedonia, he says, the grapes have too much sugar. Go north to Serbia, and they're too acidic, he claims.

Stone Castle's Shani Mullabazi claims his company is operating at near-full capacity, producing around 30 million litres per year. And he says more people outside Kosovo are getting a chance to try Kosovan wine.

The company is exporting table wines in bulk once again to Germany. And it's trying to break into the lucrative American market. This summer, it sent a shipment to New York, where there's a large community of Kosovar Albanians.

But if Kosovo's energetic winemakers are intent on selling to more countries and achieving greater international recognition, they still have a few hurdles to jump closer to home. In the past three years, they've been hindered by a de facto trade embargo with Serbia, which was imposed in retaliation for Kosovo's unilateral declaration of independence from Belgrade in 2008.

That hit the Kosovan wine industry hard, and at a time when it was just recovering from the wars of the 1990s. Stone Castle alone saw its exports to Serbia – two million litres per year – grind to a shuddering halt. Now agreements have been reached to open the way for trade to – and importantly through – Serbia, once more. For Kosovo's winemakers, the hope is that despite ongoing political quarrels, the day may soon come when they can truly brandish their wines on a bigger world stage.

BBC News, 29 October 2011

Lexical work

1. Find the English equivalents in the text.

a) florissant § 1
b) établissement viticole § 2
c) le parfum / fumet § 2
d) étatique § 4
e) se redresser § 4
f) en moyenne § 5

2. Find the French equivalents.

a) to claim § 6
b) in bulk § 7
c) a shipment § 7
d) hurdles § 8
e) retaliation § 8
f) quarrel § 9

Pronunciation work

CD n° 3 Track n° 3

1. Listen and fill in the grid according to the words' pronunciation.

achieving • reached • established • sunshine • brandish • shipment

fresh [ʃ]	much [tʃ]

2. Listen to these words that you may find difficult and repeat.

Kosovo • thriving • south • retaliation • agreements

Work on the title

1. Look at the title of the document.

2. What happened to Kosovo's wine industry?

Check the facts

1. Read § 1.
Which country was Kosovo located in before the 1990s?

2. Read § 2, 3.
a) Describe Stone Castle.
b) What is known about the winemaking area?

3. Read § 4.
What happened to the Kosovan wine industry in the 1990s?

4. Read § 5.
Why is it a good area for producing wine?

5. Read § 6.
How much is produced at Stone Castle per year?

6. Read § 7.
What would Stone Castle like to do?

7. Read § 8.
Why has there been a trade embargo?

8. Read § 9.
What were the consequences for Stone Castle?

Grammar → p. 237

Les temps des verbes (le passé)

- *Kosovo's wine industry was facing ruin in the 1990s ...*
- *And by the 1990s, it had a well-established link with a very big volume brand in Germany.*

Topic debrief

1. Choose the sentence which best corresponds to the main topic of the document.
a) Kosovan wines are now standing on their own two feet.
b) In Kosovo winemakers are pleased to be able to produce.
c) Kosovan winemakers have gone through a rough period but are now about to reach an international market.

2. Write down an introduction by using the following words (40 words).
to deal with • collapse • to recover • in the 1990s • to be published • wineries in Kosovo • to become known internationally • to tap new markets

Methods

1. Find a title for each paragraph.

2. Which paragraph best sums up the document? Translate it.

3. What are the problems Kosovo must solve?

Train for the exam

1. Make a summary / account of the document (60 words / 3-5 minutes).
Use the following sentences.
a) Although the Kosovan wine industry did not do well in the 1990s, it is now ....
b) At Stone Castle there are 5 million litres which ....
c) For centuries the main winemaking area ....
d) With the war in the 1990s, the wine industry ....
e) Now the wine industry in Kosovo would like to ....

2. Comment: find an answer to the following question. Discuss and give examples (100 words / 3-5 minutes).
How can the wine industry benefit or not from regional trade agreements? Use the examples from the text.

3. Role play: work in pairs

You are going to take part in a phone conversation.
Student A: you are the Sales Manager at Stone Castle and have received an e-mail from a large British distributor who is interested in getting to know your wines. Mr. or Mrs. Siri has asked you many questions about your wines and their prices.
Student B: you are Mr. or Mrs. Siri.

TIPS

Do not forget: greetings, what the British distributor sells, what price ranges/he is interested in.
Talk about: your Pinot Noir, Chardonnay and Merlot, the labels that have been recently changed and that are in English and Kosovan, the currency (£ or euros).
Conclude by: sending your website address and planning a visit to your cellar.

7 | Europeans

Train with an oral document

WARMING UP

- What do you know about the EU?
- What do you know about Serbia?

CD n° 3
Track n° 4

In Serbia, life is certainly not a bed of roses if you want to join the EU!

Lexical work

1. Match the following words to find their equivalents.

a) applied
b) negotiations
c) almost
d) the overthrow
e) achieved
f) granted
g) to abide by
h) manufacture
i) on the path

1. on the way
2. make
3. realised
4. not quite
5. the fall
6. talks
7. to submit to
8. provided
9. asked to join

2. Find the odd word out.

a) candidate – applicant – opponent
b) allow – permit – forbid
c) upgrade – renew – abandon
d) increase – grow – decline

3. Work on figures: write in full and read aloud.

by 2016 • before 2020 • €200m • € 190m • 250,000 vehicles • 20%

Pronunciation work

CD n° 3
Track n° 5

1. Fill in the grid with the following words, according to the pronunciation of "the".

the war • the end • the overthrow • the extradition • the Balkans

join the EU [ɪ]	Serbia and the Hague [ə]

2. Listen to these words that you may find difficult and repeat.

Serbia • infrastructures • financial aid

Work on the title

1. Look at the title of the document.

2. Explain the phrase "bed of roses" to understand the headline of the document.

Check the facts

1. Listen to part 1.
a) When will Serbia get the EU candidate status?
b) When will Serbia fully join the EU?
c) Why were the proceedings especially slow?
d) Why has Serbia been able to apply for EU membership?

2. Listen to part 2.
a) How many inhabitants are there in Serbia?
b) What did the EU demand Serbia to do?
c) What happened on 3 May 2006?

3. Listen to part 3.
a) How much money is Serbia given as aid?
b) What must Serbia renounce when joining?
c) What is the financial aid for?
d) What is the point of view of Deputy Prime Minister Delic?
e) How many vehicles will be manufactured?
f) What is the unemployment rate?

Topic debrief

1. Choose the sentence which you think corresponds best to the main topic of the document.
a) Serbia is almost an EU candidate after ten years of trials and tribulations.
b) Becoming an EU candidate takes time but it is feasible.
c) Serbia has not always been very motivated to obtain the EU candidacy.

2. Write down an introduction to the document by using the following words (40 words).
to join the EU • the entry into • to abide by rules • EU enlargement • to reform • to be granted

Methods

1. Here are the main issues of the document. Answer the following questions.
a) What is the democratisation process? (part 1)
b) What is at stake with joining the European Union? (part 2)
c) What is the importance of foreign investment in countries like Serbia? (part 3)

2. Now write 2 sentences for each part of the document, corresponding to the issues above, to get ready for your account.

Train for the exam

1. Use your notes to make an **oral presentation** about the document and record yourself (3-5 minutes).

2. Comment: find an answer to the following questions. Discuss and give examples (3-5 minutes / 100 words).
Why should it take so long for a country to join the EU? What has to be double-checked first? Why is it important to reform before you are granted membership?

3. Role play: work in pairs
You are going to take part in a conversation.
Student A: you are working with the Fiat company as a manager and have to establish a list of what needs to be known before opening a plant in Serbia. Write down the list of questions you need to ask before investing money there. Remember Serbia is not yet a EU member.
Student B: you are an official at the Serbian Embassy.

TIPS

You should use your notes in order to present a realistic conversation. Don't read them, look up.
You can:
– record the conversation (the recording should last between one and two minutes at most);
– videotape the scene and show it to the class;
– act out the scene in front of the class;
– listen to your classmates' recordings and write what you have understood in a short and structured paragraph.

7 | Europeans

WARMING UP

- What do you know about the Berlin Wall?
- Have you already watched TV programmes about families parted on each side of the wall?

CD n° 3 Track n° 6

Berlin Wall is gone, but mental barriers remain

Berlin • On Aug. 13, the 50th anniversary of the building of the Berlin Wall, the regional branch of Germany's Left party will gather. The delegates, many of them former East German Communists but also younger people, will debate an extraordinary motion put forward by some members: They want their party to declare that the building of the wall was an inescapable necessity.

That leaves no doubts about the Left party's nostalgia for a wall that imprisoned 17 million people for nearly 30 years. Support for the wall is not confined to the Left party. The poll from *The Berliner Zeitung* also showed that over all, a third of Berliners thought the 155-kilometer, or 96-mile, construction that curtained off West Berlin from its East German surroundings, not to mention the 1,400-kilometer, heavily guarded border between the two Germanys, was at least partly justified. Respondents said that the wall was necessary to stop the exodus of qualified people. Such support for the wall makes a mockery of the hundreds who were killed trying to escape.

This perpetuation of the wall in the mind is linked to economic insecurity, especially among women who were in their late 30s or early 40s when the wall collapsed in November 1989.

Women were in a particularly privileged position in Communist East Germany. There was an excellent child-care system, allowing mothers to return to flexible or full-time work. West German conservatives claim that such facilities gave the Communist regime a chance to indoctrinate the next generation. Yet these are opportunities West German women are seeking today.

When reunification did take place in 1990 and the huge, uncompetitive industrial companies in the former East Germany were shut, millions lost their jobs. Men and women who were then in their 40s now are not even on the unemployment register anymore. Instead, they live off state handouts, becoming invisible statistically, analysts say.

Many lost out. But the most troubling aspect of this anniversary is the imprint the wall has left on the younger generation, analysts say.

The International Herald Tribune, August 9, 2011

Lexical work

1. Find the English equivalents in the text.

a) se réunir **§ 1**
b) des anciens communistes **§ 1**
c) présenter **§ 1**
d) soutien **§ 2**
e) être confiné **§ 2**
f) un sondage **§ 2**
g) encercler / former un rideau de fer **§ 2**
h) l'exode **§ 2**

2. Work on figures: write in full and read aloud.

17 million people • 30 years • 155-kilometer • 96 mile • 1,400-kilometer

Pronunciation work

CD n° 3 Track n° 7

1. Listen and pronounce the following dates properly.

on Aug. 13: on August the thirteenth
the 50th: the fiftieth
the late 30s: the late thirties
Nov. 1989: November nineteen eighty-nine

2. Listen to these words that you may find difficult and repeat.

indoctrinate • flexible • privileged position

Work on the title

1. Look at the title of the document.

2. Explain the word "but" in the title and find the two words that are synonymous.

3. Explain the first paragraph and say in which way it exemplifies the title.

Check the facts

1. Read § 1.
a) Who will gather to celebrate the building of the Berlin Wall?
b) What idea do they want to defend?

2. Read § 2.
a) Who thinks the wall was a necessity?
b) How long was the wall?
c) What was it for?
d) What is the point of view of the journalist?

3. Read § 3.
According to the journalist, why do people wish the wall was still there?

4. Read § 4.
Who lost most with the collapse of the wall?

5. Read § 5.
What happened with reunification?

Grammar

→ p. 236

L'expression du contraste

- *Yet these are opportunities ...*
- *Instead, they live off state handouts ...*

Topic debrief

1. Choose the sentence which you think corresponds best to the main topic of the document.
a) The celebration of the 50th anniversary of the building of the Berlin Wall is a joyful event.
b) The reunification of Germany left a bitter taste.
c) Some former East Germans feel like second-class citizens today.

2. Write down an introduction to the document by using the following words (40 words).
to be entitled • to be published • to deal with or to tackle the issue • to be a topical issue • the title refers to • to imply that • to be nostalgic about • nostalgia • a sentimental longing for the past • liberty / freedom • to be left out • a better life

Methods

1. Give a title to each paragraph.

2. Which paragraph best sums up the document? Translate it.

Train for the exam

1. Make a **summary / account** of the document by using the following words (60 words / 3-5 minutes).
reunited • women in their 30s and 40s in 1989 • work • former Communist Party members • to lose out • east • unemployed • to provide • care • disappointed • shut down • jobless • handouts • child care

2. Comment: find an answer to the following question. Discuss and give examples (3-5 minutes / 100 words).
Think of the various goals of the EU. Would you say that they have been reached in the reunification of the two Germanys?

3. Role play: work in pairs
You are going to take part in a conversation.
Student A: you are an elderly customer. You complain about the present and regret the time when people used to buy at the counter and consume just to their needs.
Student B: you work in a big supermarket as a sales assistant. You are enchanted with the changes in your country. You argue that choice and freedom are essential.

Go online

- Find out more about East Germany.
- Then document the economic situation of former East Germans.
- Make a comparison between Germany as it was before the wall was destroyed and now.
- Get prepared to report to your group / class (a PowerPoint presentation is recommended).

Berlin Wall, 1989

7 | Europeans

Train with an oral document

WARMING UP

- Say what you know about Poland and shale gas.
- What is the problem with European energy?

CD n° 3 Track n° 8

Poland and shale gas*

* *gaz de schiste*

Lexical work

1. Match the following words to find their equivalents.

a) planned	**1.** scheduled
b) safe	**2.** secure
c) regulate	**3.** vote laws
d) stating	**4.** saying
e) ban	**5.** forbid
f) tighten	**6.** be stricter
g) outlawing	**7.** making illegal
h) amendement	**8.** addition to a law

2. Find the odd word out.

a) gas • petrol • water • oil
b) rock • stone • liquid • fossil
c) share • partake • keep
d) aware • conscious • ignorant

3. Work on figures: write in full and read aloud.

September 18, 2011 • 2014 • 2035 • 90 licences • 50%

Pronunciation work

CD n° 3 Track n° 9

1. Observe and underline the silent / mute letter. Then listen to check the right answer.

parliament • listen • controversial • could

2. Listen to these words that you may find difficult and repeat.

shale gas • Polish • environmentally • friendly

Work on the title

1. Look at the title of the document.

2. Anticipate the problems with shale gas.

Check the facts

1. Listen to part 1.
a) When will Poland start to produce shale gas?
b) Who should come up with regulations, according to environmentalists?
c) What is shale gas?
d) Why is Poland so keen on producing shale gas?
e) What did France decide to do?

2. Listen to part 2.
a) What effects shale-gas tapping have?
b) Who will exploit shale gas?
c) What will the sales of shale gas mean for Poland?
d) What did senators in France outlaw?
e) What are the two points of view?

3. Listen to part 3.
a) What are senators opposed to?
b) What is the main reason for banning exploitation?
c) What does the documentary film show?
d) What will Ukraine use to export shale gas?

Topic debrief

1. Choose the sentence which you think corresponds best to the main topic of the document.
a) Poland does not want its shale gas policy to be dictated by Europe.
b) Shale gas mining is dangerous for some, harmless for others.
c) European rows about shale gas are in the making.

2. Write down an introduction to the document by using the following words (40 words).
Poland • expert • shale gas • commercialisation • security • change global energy market • energy dependence

Methods

1. Translate the following sentences into French.
a) Environmental concerns were dismissed.
b) Poland has already granted shale gas exploitation licences.
c) Certain types of energy are detrimental to the environment.
d) Opposition has centred over potential pollution.
e) Shale-gas tapping is dangerous and costly.

2. Rewrite the sentences above with linking words.

Go online

Find out more about shale gas reserves in China and in the United States. Write down where the reserves are located, if it is costly to tap the mines, etc.

Train for the exam

1. Use your notes to make an **oral presentation** about the document and record yourself (3-5 minutes).

2. Comment: find an answer to these questions. Discuss and give examples (3-5 minutes / 100 words).
Should all members of the EU have exactly the same policy, whether environmental, financial or trade policy? Or should member states have some leeway in specific areas especially if it impacts their economy?

3. Role play: work in pairs
You are going to take part in a conversation.
Student A: you belong to a watchdog organisation for the protection of the planet. You want to be certain that shale gas production presents no danger for the planet.
Student B: you are a Polish manager in charge of commercialising shale gas in Europe. Be ready to answer.

PRACTICE • AUDIO • VIDEO

Train with a video

EU lifelong learning program

→ http://www.youtube.com/watch?v=r6pX06sOEdw&feature=related

13 November, 2009

Look at this video on the Internet about the EU

Check the facts	Methods
1. What is the main topic of this video?	• What is the main goal of the EU? Why is education essential for better cooperation between people?
2. What main skills contribute to European creativity?	• What is the interest of lifelong learning? • At which stages of life is it necessary?
3. Which different programs are part of these lifelong learning schemes?	• Who were Erasmus, Jean Monnet, Comenius and Leonardo Da Vinci?
4. When were these opportunities created?	• Have you benefited from one of these programs?
5. **Issues ...** – Who is targeted by this video? – Are you interested in lifelong learning?	• What are the everyday life opportunities which might make you feel you are a European citizen?

WARMING UP

- Have you heard of the "PIGS"?
- Who uses the acronym "PIGS"? Why?

CD n° 3 Track n° 10

Germany's economy, a case of the sniffles

Unlike some of its neighbours, Germany is slowing rather than melting down. Much of Europe has pneumonia. How is that affecting Germany, the Continent's biggest economy? Exports are surprisingly buoyant considering the European pandemonium; they rose by 0.9% in September. But industrial production dropped by 2.7% in September and new orders, a harbinger of future output, fell by 4.3%, the third monthly decline in a row.

Business is bracing for harder times. Expectations have been falling since February, according to the Info Business Survey. The biggest problem is the euro crisis, which is playing havoc with Germany's trading partners. Industrial orders from the euro zone plunged by 12.1% in September. Demand will also wane from Asia and Eastern Europe, which have been Germany's fastest-growing markets. Exports make up around half of the country's GDP, so a slowdown is inevitable. On November 9th the government's advisory council of economic "wise men" predicted that growth would shrink from 3% this year to 0.9% in 2012. Some pundits think the economy will shrink.

This may look like poetic justice to peripheral euro-zone countries, which are suffering partly because Germany demands austerity in return for aid. But there are no grounds for *schadenfreude*. First, German strength has helped them; they will fare worse if Germany falters. Second, Germany is still in pretty good shape. Germany's economy is often more volatile than that of its neighbours like France. Its specialisation in investment goods, cars and other expensive consumer products makes the upswings higher but downturns sharper. That pattern may now be broken. As Europe slides, Germany is likely to sink less than the others. But this rests on a hope: that European leaders – the German Chancellor, Angela Merkel, in particular – will stop mismanaging the euro crisis.

Germany's trump card is its labour market. Unemployment barely rose during the 2008-09 recession. With the recovery, it has dropped to a 20-year low. After years of sacrifice, wage-earners are starting to profit. Gross wages are expected to rise by nearly 5% this year and by about 3% in 2012. Disposable income, adjusted for consumer inflation, should increase by about 1% next year. Consumption is now contributing to growth, alongside exports. "German growth is much more balanced," says Holger Schmieding of Berenberg Bank.

Employment should remain resilient during the downturn. Earlier labour-market reforms continue to put pressure on the unemployed to find work, notes Eckard Tuchfeld of Commerzbank. As before the last recession, employers remain "extremely reluctant to let go of skilled staff", he says, in part because the labour force is shrinking. "Working time accounts" make it easier to avoid redundancies. These are credited when employees work extra hours and can be drawn down when activity is slack. During the last two busy years they have been replenished. The wise men expect the unemployment rate to drop from 7.1% in 2011 to 6.9% next year. The hope is that Germany's downturn will be short and shallow. But that depends on Europe's leaders coming to grips with the euro crisis.

The Economist, November 12th, 2011

Pronunciation work

CD n° 3 Track n° 11

1. Listen and underline the stressed syllable.

a) pandemonium • expectations • inevitable • specialisation
b) unemployment • mismanaging • replenished

2. Listen to these words that you may find difficult and repeat.

buoyant • harbinger • upswing • wage • earners • resilient • replenished

Lexical work

1. Find the English equivalents in the text.

a) un petit rhume titre
b) contrairement § 1
c) s'effondrer § 1
d) actif / soutenu § 1
e) chahut / charivari § 1
f) signe avant-coureur § 1
g) production § 1
h) rassembler ses forces § 2
i) bouleverser / être très mauvais pour § 2
j) s'estomper § 2
k) experts § 2

2. Find the French equivalents.

a) poetic justice § 3
b) to falter § 3
c) volatile § 3
d) upswings § 3
e) to slide § 3
f) a trump card § 4
g) wage § 4
h) earners § 4
i) resilient § 5
j) to be reluctant § 5

Work on the title

1. Look at the title of the document.

2. Look at the headline which mentions a benign disease.

Check the facts

1. Read § 1.
Which industry has been affected by the euro crisis?

2. Read § 2.
a) Which two markets for German products have been rapidly growing?
b) Where is German economic wealth generated?

3. Read § 3.
a) Why is Germany's economy more volatile?
b) Which word reflects the point of view of the journalist?

4. Read § 4.
What are the two areas that contribute to German growth?

5. Read § 5.
a) What do workers do when activity is slack?
b) What labour regulation has been introduced to avoid redundancies?

Grammar

→ p. 237

L'expression du conseil

- *Disposable income should increase by about 1%.*
- *Employment should remain resilient during the downturn.*

Topic debrief

1. Choose the sentence which you think corresponds best to the main topic of the document.
a) The German economy is not affected by the euro crisis and its labour market is not so bad.
b) The German economy cannot escape the euro crisis but won't be hit as harshly.
c) The euro crisis has brought about havoc and Germany is no exception.

2. Write down an introduction to the document by using the following words (40 words).
to deal with • be affected / impacted • exports • to sell • to manufacture • trading partners • the economic downturn • the economic slowdown • austerity measures • orders • to drop • consumption

Methods

1. Give a title to each paragraph.

2. Which paragraph best sums up the document? Translate it.

Train for the exam

1. Make an account / summary of the document (3-5 minutes / 150 words).
First focus on the German economy. Then describe the labour market. You can use the following words.
labour force / workforce • flexitime • flexible hours • to be jobless / unemployed • skilled staff • wage-earners • a raise in salary • a pay increase • purchasing power / buying power

2. Comment: find an answer to the following question. Discuss and give examples (3-5 minutes / 100 words).
Do austerity measures only have effects on the economy?

3. Role play: work in pairs
You are going to take part in a conversation.
Student A: you are a 30-year-old French manager and you think the new retirement measures are very good for the economy.
Student B: you are a 30-year-old German employee and you complain about the retirement age limit since you don't know if you will enjoy your retirement pension. Moreover, you believe the other European countries are responsible for such drastic measures.

Export department, French tableware company

1 • Situation

You work for Tabletrends and your company is based in France. Your turnover and margins are good, in fact, your company is growing nicely and the boss would like to expand outside the domestic market. For now, the idea is to try and enter other European markets, one at a time. The choice is between Sweden and Spain.

2 • Process

a) Look at the following documents.
b) Get into groups.
Students A: you represent the Tabletrends company. *Students B:* you are the distributor in Spain or observer of A and C. *Students C:* you are the distributor in Sweden or observer of A and B.
c) First, decide together whether you are going to export to Spain or Sweden.
d) *Students A:* one person of your group makes a telephone call to the distributor / students B in the country of your choice and fixes a date and time for a meeting.
e) You have to prepare the first meeting. Create your business card respecting the cultural norms of your distributor.
Students A: you might have to persuade the distributor that your product is worth selling! You could also include which stores your goods are to be shown in, how many items they will be ordering, etc.
Students B and C: you adopt the chosen country's cultural code.
f) Now discuss terms and prices during the meeting. Remember to speak English only!
g) Analyse the first contact, underline the positive points and what can be improved (presentation, needs, appraisal, objections, conclusions).

3 • Follow up

– Either prepare an invoice for the distributor;
– or write a draft contract for the distributor to confirm what you have agreed on.

Go online
For more useful information about other cultures in the world, visit this website: www.deborahswallow.com

TIPS

Remember...
To turn up on time for an appointment with an Anglophone or Northern European. If you are late, give a short excuse. Decide in advance on a selection of 2 or 3 possible dates and times so you do not waste time going through your diary. It is always wise to confirm an appointment made over the telephone by e-mail. Use full wording, especially because of misunderstandings about dates (6th July 2011 – USA: 07/06/11 – Europe: 06/07/11), and the time (16:00 will often be misunderstood as "6" by people not used to the 24-hour clock, and they may turn up 2 hours late!).

Doc • A

TABLE TRENDS

Fine china tableware for every occasion.
Made to the highest standards by French craftsmen, our range of classical and contemporary crockery, with coordinated glassware and cutlery, will be the pride of every housewife.

Doc • B

Culture …

The difference between the North and the South: There are many differences between the Southern and Northern countries of Europe. In the South, business moves along more slowly, and is less predictable. Take time to enjoy yourself and get to know your counterpart – relationships need to be forged and can influence the success or failure of your deal. The general pace of life still tends to be slower, and people may not always be on time. Southern Europeans do not tend to be bound by rules like those from the North, so you need to keep a bit of flexibility. Avoid August because most people are on holiday.

Nordic countries are driven by a strong work ethic, with high values. They do not tolerate bribery or corruption, and do not look kindly upon people who are not on time. They may be seen as being rather unfriendly and abrupt because of their straightforward and "down to business" approach. Holidays tend to be taken in July.

Doc • C

Documents needed to export to another European country

Trade of Goods Declaration (DEB) – (monthly) including your filing number.
(Your filing number is your VAT number (the letters FR, a two-digit computer code and your nine-digit SIREN number).
Your tax service will issue your filing number.

VAT: Exports are exempt from VAT as long as:

- The purchaser has provided his filing number (see above) – you must check that it is right.
- You can give proof that the goods have been physically moved from one member state to another.

The invoice must include:

- Date of invoice
- Name, address & filing number of buyer and seller
- Delivery date
- Exact description and quantity of the goods delivered
- Unit price (exclusive of tax) of the goods
- Applicable tax (VAT) rate and the amount (or legal reference in the case of tax exemption)
- Price reductions (discount / rebate)
- The total amount to be paid
- The reference currency
- The date and means of payment, discount method, late payment penalties

PRACTICAL INFORMATION:

- No trade barriers, border formalities or inspections. There could be a language barrier.
- Selling from France (Paris) to Spain (Madrid): Distance 1,260 km – road or rail transport only.
- Selling from France (Paris) to Sweden (Stockholm): Distance 3,163 km – road or rail transport + ship.

7 | Europeans

Background

Europe is an area of land which could almost be considered a continent, either as the western extremity of the Eurasian continent, or as one of the subparts of the Afro-Eurasian super-continent. It is sometimes called the "Old Continent" as compared to the "New World" (America).
Culturally speaking, Europe has had a multiplicity of influences throughout the ages, and is made up of many countries with a common heritage; language, religious and historical differences; as well as more recent contributions since globalisation (→ SEE CHAPTER "GLOBALISATION" PAGE 166). *Europe is a community of people building political union in the shape of the European Union, in an area with a shared civilisation partly forged by an age-old common history.*

1 How did the European Union come about?

1950s The Frenchman Jean Monnet (1888-1979) and his team dreamed up the idea of a European Community (following the trauma of World War 2 and renewed tensions worldwide). Among many of his famous quotes is: "To create Europe is to create peace".

1951 The European Coal and Steel Community (ECSC): between Belgium, West Germany, Luxembourg, France, Italy and the Netherlands (Treaty of Paris).

1957 The six countries signed the Treaty of Rome and created the EEC (European Economic Community) and the EAEC (European Atomic Energy Community).

1962 CAP (Common Agricultural Policy): at the outset to ensure enough high quality food for European consumers, and now also to preserve rural areas and set environmental and animal welfare standards.

1967 The ECSC, EEC and EAEC merged.

1979 The first European Parliament direct elections (in which citizens voted).

1992 The Maastricht Treaty (or TEU – Treaty on European Union) which led to the EU (European Union), European citizenship and the beginnings of monetary union (EMU).

1985-1995 The Schengen Agreement ensured free movement of European citizens within the Schengen zone (the UK and Ireland only cooperate in some aspects).

Questions

- What advantages has the Schengen agreement given to European citizens?
- What are the main pros and cons of the EU?
- Would you like to take a year studying or doing a work placement in another European country?

2001-2003 The Treaty of Nice: institutional reforms because of the increasing size of the EU.

2004 The EU Constitution submitted for ratification to the 25 member states and 3 candidate countries. To date, French and Dutch citizens have rejected the Constitutional Treaty and many other member states have not yet decided (some of them will hold referendums).

2009 The Treaty of Lisbon entered into force on 1st December 2009. For most member states, agreement was reached in national parliaments, although Ireland held a referendum.

2 What does an "Economic Union" really mean?

The eurosystem: is made up of the European Central Bank which is responsible for the **monetary policy** within the euro area / zone, and the national central banks of each country which uses the euro. Certain aspects of monetary policy, for example tax, labour, pensions, remain the responsibility of individual national governments.
The economy: The euro area economy is the world's second largest – just after the USA – and is used more and more in the international financial and monetary system. The euro is the second-most important **currency** worldwide, after the U.S. dollar.
→ SEE CHAPTER "GLOBALISATION" PAGE 166.
European products account for more than 45% of the world's exports. The main economic sectors are: investment and banking services (the City of London is the largest European financial centre); agriculture, forestry, fishing and mining (40% of the EU budget is spent on agriculture due to the CAP (SEE ABOVE) although it only accounts for 2.3% of GNP); manufacturing (25% of the labour force is employed in manufacturing); the service sector (for example IT → SEE CHAPTER "NEW TECHNOLOGIES" PAGE 102); passenger and freight transport (→ SEE CHAPTER " TRANSPORT" PAGE 186) and tourism (→ SEE CHAPTER "TOURISM" PAGE 206).

3 What are the benefits for EU citizens?

Free movement: There are no frontiers within the euro zone so European citizens can live and work anywhere in Europe. This has also had a positive impact on the **job market** and the tourist industry.
→ SEE CHAPTER "TOURISM" PAGE 206.
However, this causes fears of "cheap labour" moving from Eastern Europe to Western Europe.
Standardisation of university systems: is leading to equivalent rating of qualifications, and educational and cultural exchanges (i.e. Erasmus and many others).
Cultural exchanges: between European citizens. A better mutual understanding reduces the possibilities of war. However, some people fear losing their national identity.
The languages: There are 24 official languages in Europe. Europeans have become more and more aware of their neighbours.

Info

1999: The euro was introduced for banking and other financial operations.
1st January 2002: Euro banknotes and coins were launched in 12 EU countries (15 in 2011). Denmark and the UK chose not to use the euro and several other countries have not yet met the convergence criteria.
The countries which currently use the euro are: 1999 – Belgium, Germany, Ireland, Spain, France, Italy, Luxembourg, the Netherlands, Austria, Portugal, Finland; 2001 – Greece; 2007 – Slovenia; 2008 – Cyprus, Malta; 2009 – Slovakia; 2011 – Estonia – in other words, 330 million people.

Free trade zone: giving access to markets all over Europe; but loss of **national sovereignty** means laws governing one part of Europe may not be appropriate for another.
Financial difficulties in certain countries in the Euro zone can be a drain on the other **member states**.
Humanitarian aid: ECHO (European Commission Humanitarian Aid Organisation) is the world's biggest donor, and provides over 50% of humanitarian aid and civil protection through the world.

TIPS

Even within Europe there are cultural differences which could lead to offense being taken by someone you are doing business with. It is worth finding out the cultural values of the country you are going to visit to avoid problems. Here are a few examples:
Handshaking: In France and Belgium you shake hands every time you arrive at or leave work. In other countries, a handshake is used the first time you meet someone only.
Mealtimes: Dutch people tend to have dinner at around 6pm, the French at around 8pm and the Spanish one or two hours later (but they often have a siesta in the afternoon).
Personal Space: Northwestern Europeans are generally more reserved and need more personal space than Mediterranean and Eastern Europeans. Don't offend the latter by backing away if they get too close to you.
Movements: In Bulgaria, nodding your head (up and down) means "no" whereas shaking your head (side to side) means "yes".

European Parliament

Focus

The European Union: love it or loathe it? Opt in or opt out?

The economic crisis has brought forth numerous questions about Europe and its raison d'être and the euro zone's debt crisis is reviving old demons.
The heyday of the European Union seems to be over with the many debt-ridden euro zone countries that need bailing out. However is it just a few voices expressing temporary discontent or a more general outcry against an institution that has failed its member states?
We can focus on what is not working or needs reforming but we can also stress how the European Union has helped countries like Ireland and Portugal to reach a noticeable growth rate. Eurosceptics have always been around, even before the European Union existed. Their voice has become louder with the euro zone crisis. But what should prevail? A EU at 27? At 33, 34, 35 countries? Or, as Mr. Sarkozy said, a two-speed Europe or two Europes?

Here are the most often heard criticisms

- Too much power has been transferred to Europe or Brussels.
- There is not any benefit in trade or jobs from EU membership.
- EU rules should be ignored as well as fines for disobedience to Brussels masters.
- A great majority of the important decisions that affect our daily life are made by the EU, not by national parliaments, regional or local assemblies or councils.
- On Oct 6, 2011, a survey in Britain showed that 48% of the British think Britain would be more prosperous outside the EU.
- EU decision-making seems opaque and undemocratic: The European Union is often regarded as a slow machine not attuned to the European citizens' needs, run by technocrats not representative of the people.
- The EU has been developed in a distinctly undemocratic fashion.
- The EU is wasteful and corrupt.
- Countries outside the euro zone can devalue and control their interest rates.

Questions

- What are European citizens most afraid of?
- What can a country do if it does not belong to the single currency market?

Here are the reasons for staying in the EU or joining the European Union

- The existence of the EU promotes prosperity and competitiveness throughout Europe: One of its goals is the well-being of its people.
- Being part of the EU provides key benefits: consolidation of democracy, economic growth and prosperity. Today Germany is reluctant to bail out Greece, Italy or Spain but who buys Siemens products, BMWs or Esprit garments? The EU is its first buyer.
- Europe and the EU are not perfect but the alternatives are no better and are in fact worse.
- Europe has been the forum to lead coordinated policies on issues such as terrorism, environmental issues, GM food labeling, shark protection, etc. Today we are critical of GM food labeling but because there is a European regulation on nutrition and health, EU consumers are protected from false or misleading claims.
- Greater involvement in the European Union will bring about a more peaceful world.
- Removing oneself from the EU would cost jobs and major trade partners.

Questions

- What does the EU promote?
- What does the EU provide?

Express your point of view

- How would you describe yourself if you were asked? As a citizen of the world, as a European and / or as French?
- What characteristics would you use to identify yourself as French, as European or as a citizen of the "global village", as Hillary Clinton said? In other words, are national identity and sovereignty automatically at odds with being pro-European?

@-Go online

Find out what advantages there are of belonging to the euro zone and what disadvantages there are.

Perspectives

Despite the fact that the EU is going through a rough period, there are countries such as Serbia, Ukraine and Turkey which want to join the EU. A debate about Europe is a necessary evil and will enable the institution to be reformed and to work more smoothly.
It is true that it is an organisation with complex structures, the workings of which are not truly visible. The institution remains somewhat difficult to understand for the average European as the media tend to focus on problems and not on its daily work. Therefore the media should stress its work and engage the public with weighty issues. With 27 members, many languages, different historical backgrounds and different perceptions, coverage by the press is not easy. However, Europe should not be presented as a scapegoat and / or blamed for every mishap. Inaccuracy does not help democracy.
It is no easy job to have a 27 member-state institution work together and it demands effort and negotiation. But its merit is to envisage a common policy economically, socially and politically, and it tries to make it work as smoothly as possible.
The EU is one important institution which may prevent future possible wars but only if it has the clout to tie close relationships between countries and promise a better economic future so that nationalistic passions will die down. A united EU is better able to negotiate with China or other nations than a non-united EU.

Focus

The euro zone crisis

The new currency has been around since the first of January 2002 and started with 12 countries. Today, in 2012, 17 countries belong to the euro zone: Austria, Belgium, Cyprus, Estonia, Finland, France, Germany, Greece, Ireland, Italy, Luxembourg, Malta, The Netherlands, Portugal, Slovakia, Slovenia and Spain.
Some countries opted out, such as the United Kingdom and Denmark.
However, other non-euro members are legally bound to join the single currency.
In 2010, 329 million people shopped with the euro.

What did the euro bring?

- It made it possible to travel across a now 17-country zone without having to change money. It also put an end to fluctuating exchange rates between European currencies. It allowed interest rates to be lowered and so it incited people to borrow. People in countries like Spain, Greece, Portugal and Ireland took advantage of low interest rates to borrow money and buy houses and became indebted.
- To guarantee the stability of the new currency, the euro zone countries agreed to a budget deficit lower than 3% of their gross domestic product (GDP).
- However, the single currency was an experiment in monetary union that was not well thougth-out. For instance, David Boyle from the New Economics Institute in Massachusetts challenges conventional thinking and said that "it is wrong to believe that the euro and its common interest rates can bring equal benefits to all areas where it is used." Different policies on key economic questions were adopted: Spaniards were borrowing money from Spanish banks as the interest rate was low, at the same time prices of goods were a little higher than in Germany. So goods from Spain were less competitive than German goods. Why? For two decades real wage levels had not increased in Germany, which enabled Germany to become a top exporter.

What went wrong?

- First Lehman Brothers, an American bank, went bankrupt. This brought about a financial crisis worldwide including the euro zone. Indeed, European banks that had lent much money were hit by the financial crisis. Governments came to the rescue of their banks by taking on private bank debts. The clearest case is Ireland, which took responsibility for all that its banks owed. Consequently, what was a private debt became a public one. The current European debt crisis originated with the financial crisis and the rescue provided by governments.
- In addition, bailing out private banks means that ordinary people are paying for the financial crisis.
- At the end of 2009 Greece had to admit its deficit stood at 12.5% (some may come up with another figure) although it only represents a mere 2% of the European economy. This made it impossible for Greece to repay its debts or to find funds. Economists agree that this straightforward economic issue of indebtedness and default could have been resolved much earlier if the no bailout clause in the Maastricht Treaty (1992) had not been there. Later on, Greece, Ireland and then Portugal were helped to keep European banks from failing.

Questions

- In your eyes, why is it more difficult to fight a crisis in the euro zone than in the United States or Japan?
- Do you think we should expect the 17 countries of the euro zone to adopt the same economic guidelines?

Express your point of view

- What kind of Europe do you want?
- European governments should have one top priority, the well-being of its people, and not respond to the financial sector; otherwise, democracy is hard hit. Explain and illustrate your point of view.

Test yourself

Try to use your memory – do not look at the vocabulary list!

1 WHAT ABOUT THE PEOPLE IN EUROPE?

Use one of the following words (word groups) to complete what the people are saying.

aging • applicant • asylum seeker • birth rate • citizen • foreigner • haves and have nots • immigrant • inhabitant • interpreter • MEP • migrant • non-EU • refugee

a) "Did you know that 4 new M__________ have been elected to the European Parliament?"
b) "We must do more to integrate I__________ in our European schools."
c) "Applications to the university are welcome from N__________ and European students."
d) "Is it right that some European countries are now taking a hard line against A__________?"
e) "That man is not from this country – he's a F__________".
f) "We are worried about the A__________ population in Europe – what about retirement?"
g) "The influx of economic R__________ from certain countries is worrying."
h) "She is a European C__________ by birth".
i) "This person doesn't speak a word of French. We're going to need an __________."
j) "This new Certificate of Application will allow the A__________ to work in the UK."
k) "There is a widening gap between the H__________."
l) "Not one nation in Europe has a high enough B__________ to replace its native-born population".
m) "In the European Union in 2007, the average I__________ travelled 800 km by train."
n) "The question is: should the number of economic M__________ be limited by quotas?"

2 COMPOUND NOUNS

Join a word from column (1) to a word in column (2) and make a compound noun to suit the definition.

1	Monetary	**A**	line	Economic strategy and regulation chosen by a regulatory committee.
2	Free	**B**	policy	The right to travel.
3	Job	**C**	policy	The number of jobs available for those seeking work.
4	Living	**D**	principle	A level of material comfort, income and consumption.
5	Poverty	**E**	market	The minimum level of income required to have what you need.
6	Information	**F**	rate	Where information is only known by some people, not all.
7	Founding	**G**	state	The standard rules the EU was started with.
8	Foreign	**H**	standard	The policy which governs international relations.
9	Growth	**I**	movement	The rate of increase in size per unit of time.
10	Member	**J**	gap	A country which is party to the treaties of the EU.

→ SEE GRAMMAR PAGE 233.

VOCABULARY

7 Europeans

Words

"The European Union is the world's most effective invention for advancing peace." (John Bruton)

Austria / Austrian: Australie / Australien

Belgium / Belgian: Belgique / Belge

(Great) Britain / British / Briton (a): Grande-Bretagne / Britannique

Bulgaria / Bulgarian: Bulgarie / Bulgare

Cyprus / Cypriot: Chypre / Chypriote

Denmark / Danish: Danemark / Danois

Estonia / Estonian: Estonie / Estonien

Finland / Finnish: Finlande / Finlandais

France / French: France / Français

Germany / German: Allemagne / Allemand

Greece / Greek: Grèce / Grec

Hungary / Hungarian: Hongrie / Hongrois

Ireland / Irish: Irlande / Irlandais

Italy / Italian: Italie / Italien

Latvia / Latvian: Lettonie, Letton

Lithuania / Lithuanian: Lituanie / Lituanien

Luxembourg / from Luxembourg: Luxembourg / Luxembourgeois

Malta / Maltese: Malte / Maltais

Poland / Polish: Pologne / Polonais

Portugal / Portuguese: Portugal / Portugais

Romania / Romanian: Roumanie / Roumain

Slovakia / Slovakian: Slovaquie / Slovaque

Slovenia / Slovenian: Slovénie / Slovène

Spain / Spanish / Spaniard (a): Espagne / Espagnol

Sweden / Swedish: Suède / Suédois

The Czech Republic / Czech: République Tchèque / Tchèque

The Netherlands / Dutch: les Pays-Bas / Néerlandais

The United Kingdom (UK) / British: Royaume-Uni / Britannique

Ageing / aging: vieillissant

Agreement: accord

Applicant: candidat

Apply (to) for a job: poser sa candidature

Asylum seeker: demandeur d'asile

Barrier: barrière

Belong to (to): appartenir à

Birth rate: taux de natalité

Border: frontière

Breach (to): enfreindre

Channel (the British): la Manche

Citizen: citoyen

Common Agricultural Policy (CAP): politique agricole commune (PAC)

Common market: marché commun

Cost overrun: dépassement des coûts

Council: conseil

Crossing: une traversée / traversé par

Currency: devise

Directive: directive

Domestic: intérieur

Economic and Monetary Union (EMU): Union économique et monétaire

EEC (the): CEE

Enlargement: élargissement

Entitled to (to be): avoir droit à

Eurocentric: Eurocentrique

European Commission: Commission européenne

European Union (EU): Union européenne (UE)

Eurosceptic: eurosceptique

Euro zone: zone euro / euroland

Foreign (adj): étranger

Foreign policy: politique étrangère

Foreigner: étranger (n)

Former: ancien / précédent

Founding principle: principe fondateur

Free movement: libre circulation

Fund (to): financer

GDP (gross domestic product): PIB (produit intérieur brut)

Gender: genre / sexe

Grant: bourse

Growth rate: taux de croissance

Haves and have nots (the): les riches et les pauvres

Immigrant: immigré

Information gap: déficit d'information

Inhabitant: habitant

Interpreter: interprète

Job market: marché de l'emploi

Join (to): adhérer à

Legislate: légiférer

Living standard: niveau de vie

Member state: État membre

Membership: appartenance

MEP (Member of the European Parliament): député européen

Migrant: immigré

Monetary policy: politique monétaire

National sovereignty: souveraineté nationale

Non-EU: n'appartenant pas à l'UE

Official language: langue officiel

Parliament: parlement

Policy: politique

Poverty line: seuil de pauvreté

Red tape: bureaucratie, paperasserie

Refugee: réfugié

Regulation: réglementation

Scheme: projet, dispositif

Shuttle: navette

Social gap: écart social

Statement: déclaration

Streamline (to): rationaliser

Translation: traduction

Treaty: traité

8

Globalisation

A new world in the making?

30 ITEMS NO LONGER MADE IN THE U.S.A.

Barbie dolls
Bazooka bubblegum
cameras
canned sardines
cell phones
clothespins
Converse All Star basketball shoes
flatware
Gerber baby food
gumball machines
harmonicas
hepatitis vaccine
Hummers
incandescent lightbulbs
Levi's jeans
minivans
movie projectors
Mr. Coffee coffeemakers
Nike shoes
Oldsmobiles
photographic paper
plastic pink flamingos
Pontiacs
rabies vaccine
RCA radios
Schwinn bicycles
Spalding basketballs (official NBA ball)
television sets
Vice-Grips
Wurlitzer jukeboxes

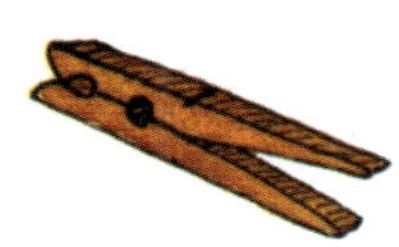

Question

Where are the factories that produce all these goods?

WORD BOX

to relocate • low-cost countries • cheap labour • lower operating costs • to streamline • unemployment rate • type of goods • low added value goods • to manufacture • working conditions • impact on the environment • shipping costs

8 | Globalisation

1 • Look and discuss

a) Look at the map which shows where the different parts a pair of jeans are made. Did you think jeans came from the USA? Are you surprised at their origins? Discuss in class.

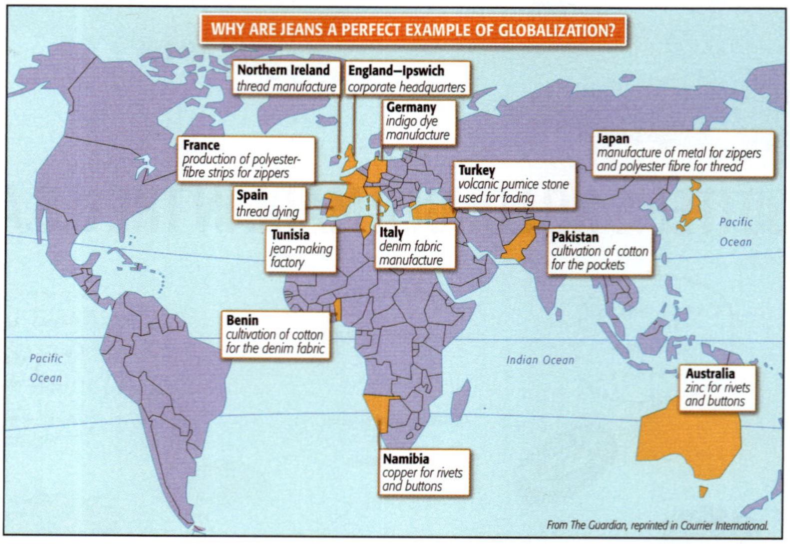

@ Go online

Look on the Internet and see if you can find globalised sourcing information for other products.

b) Read the following text. What are the advantages and disadvantages of a global marketplace? Discuss in class.

Free trade is the interchange of goods and services (but not labour and capital) without high tariffs (such as customs duties) or barriers (such as quotas or government regulation). A free trade area is a group of countries who have decided to work together on this basis – for example NAFTA (North American Free Trade Agreement), EFTA (European Free Trade Association), EEA (European Economic Area) and AFTA (Asian Free Trade Area).

2 • Read and understand

World Trade Organization (WTO)

→ Who we are

There are a number of ways of looking at the World Trade Organization. It is an organization for trade opening. It is a forum for governments to negotiate trade agreements. It is a place for them to settle trade disputes. It operates a system of trade rules. Essentially, the WTO is a place where member governments try to sort out the trade problems they face with each other.

→ What we do

The WTO is run by its member governments. All major decisions are made by the membership as a whole, either by ministers (who usually meet at least once every two years) or by their ambassadors or delegates (who meet regularly in Geneva).

1. The WTO is basically a place where member governments ... trade problems.
a) organise b) categorise c) find solutions to

2. In the text, "bulk" means:
a) a large size b) a big volume c) the main part

3. WTO negotiations are ... to open the markets for free trade.
a) not only b) only c) just

4. The governments' ... purpose is to help trade flow as freely as possible.
a) subordinate b) predominant c) secondary

5. The agreements negotiated in the WTO system are ... negotiated.
a) fastidiously b) painfully c) easily

3 • Read and write

a) Read the short text and answer the questions.

BRIC is an acronym that refers to Brazil, Russia, India and China. The term was coined by economist Jim O'Neill from Goldman Sachs. On December 24, 2010, South Africa officially became a member nation. So the group has been renamed BRICS. And it now has five members.

- **Locate each country on a map.**
- **Write down its capital, the number of inhabitants and its size.**
- **Explain by writing a few sentences, its economic and political power.**

b) Read the short text and complete the sentences with the right words.

MIST is another acronym that refers to Mexico, Indonesia, South Korea and Turkey. The term was coined by the same economist from Goldman Sachs, Jim O'Neill. The MIST countries are the successors to the BRICS countries in terms of the next big economies for investors to watch. It is not a household name yet but could become one. Goldman Sachs says that the next eleven countries to watch are Bangladesh, Egypt, Indonesia, Iran, Korea, Mexico, Nigeria, Pakistan, Philippines, Turkey and Vietnam.

most populated • per capita • markets • poverty rate

1. South Korea has a much higher ... GDP than the others ($27,000).
2. Indonesia, with over 245 million people, is the ... country of the four.
3.Turkey's asset is its proximity to ... in the region such as the Middle East, Russia, the Balkans, Central Asia and Europe.
4. Mexico, with over 113 million people, has an increasing middle class and a declining ....

4 • Listen and understand

CD n° 3
Track n° 12

a) How many countries are mentioned in the dialogue?
b) How would you define "food miles"?
c) Should we make an effort to "eat locally" and help sustainable development by reducing food miles, or is this a natural consequence of globalisation?

WARMING UP

► Are you happy when you find a home retailer abroad?

CD n° 3 Track n° 13

Marks & Spencer turns to India and China following better-than-expected profit rise

In his first set of results for the UK retailer, chief executive Marc Bolland increased market share in food and clothing as advertising costs jumped by more than 16%.

Mr Bolland, who joined from supermarket chain WM Morrisons in May 2010, said: "Marks & Spencer had a good year, with sales and profits ahead of last year. We traded well in a challenging environment, growing our market share in both clothing and food. We did this by offering customers great quality and value, and more choice through innovation."

Carrying out his plan of "evolution not revolution", Mr Bolland increased M&S's share of the clothing market to 11.7%, while its food sector increased to 3.9%. The retailer plans to increase the latter's range from 7,000 to 8,000 lines.

With solid growth in key areas, M&S is turning its attention to emerging markets, with India and China at the top of its list. In the past year Mr Bolland has poached Jan Heere from Spanish fashion group Inditex to lead its push for business overseas. He also hired Laura Wade-Gery from supermarket group Tesco to head M&S's online business.

There are plans to open 10 new stores in India over the next year, bringing the total in the country to 29. In China, M&S is looking to unveil a further six stores in addition to the three opened in 2010 / 11.

"In November we set out our plan to grow M&S into a truly international, multi-channel retailer," added Mr Bolland. Mr Bolland is also looking to return to the French market, following the disastrous decision to pull out of the country in 2001. A new flagship store will be unveiled in November on the Champs-Elysées in Paris.

Despite the retailer remaining cautious on future trading, as a result of austerity cuts and tighter consumer spending, analysts at Investec were more confident. "Customers have proved to be less price-resistant than feared and have bought into fashion stores, which is good for average selling prices," Investec said. "We continue to believe that the scope for self-help at M&S will allow it to out-perform its peers over a period when we see continuing pressure on sector earnings."

The Telegraph Friday, June 10th, 2011

Lexical work

1. Find the English equivalents in the text.

a) part de marché § 1
b) la confection § 1
c) difficile § 2
d) mener un projet § 3
e) le secteur alimentaire § 3
f) la gamme § 3
g) les secteurs clés § 4
h) débaucher § 4
i) embaucher § 4

2. Find the French equivalents.

a) to unveil § 5
b) further § 5
c) multi-channel § 6
d) to pull out § 6
e) a flagship store § 6
f) to remain § 7
g) cautious § 7
h) the scope § 7
i) to out-perform § 7

Pronunciation work

CD n° 3 Track n° 14

1. Listen to the sound "th" and fill in the grid with the following words according to the pronunciation.

clothes • both • clothing • cloth • three

Thirty [θ]	Then [ð]

2. Listen, underline the stressed syllable and pronounce the words properly.

a) push • business
b) clothes • clothing
c) fashion • revolution • innovation • evolution

Info
Retail (noun): the sale of goods to the public in relatively small quantities for use or consumption rather than for resale: [as modifier] the retail trade.
(From the Oxford Dictionary of English)

Work on the title

1. Look at the title of the document.

2. Focus on the headline and the 2nd paragraph then explain the title of the document.

Check the facts

1. Read § 1.
Which markets have increased at M&S?

2. Read § 2.
a) Who is Marc Bolland? Where was he before? When did he start at M&S?
b) How does Marc Bolland explain the increase in the food and clothing markets?

3. Read § 3.
Quote the two percentages and what they correspond to.

4. Read § 4.
a) Who will be developing M&S's market shares overseas?
b) What are Laura Wade-Gery's responsibilities?

5. Read § 5.
How many stores will open in China and in India?

6. Read § 6.
What will happen in November?

7. Read § 7.
Why is the retailer cautious about the market?

Grammar

→ p. 238

Les propositions relatives
• *Customers have proved to be less price-resistant than feared ..., which is good ...*

Topic debrief

1. Choose the sentence which you think corresponds best to the main topic of the document.
a) M&S's unexpected profit will be reinvested in China and India.
b) M&S is certainly moving in different directions: emerging countries and online retailing as well as business overseas.
c) After an unexpected profit rise, M&S is becoming an even more international retailer by investing in China and India.

2. Write an introduction to the document by using the word bank.
to be published • to deal with • to be entitled • straightforward • retailer • British • chief executive • emerging countries • on the domestic market

Methods

Write a presentation of the company when in recession by using the word bank.
tough trading conditions • challenging • a sharp increase in advertising • a belt-tightening policy • market shares • to expect

Train for the exam

1. Make a **summary / account** of the document (60 words / 3-5 minutes).

2. **Comment:** find an answer to the following question. Discuss and give examples (100 words / 3-5 minutes).
What are the difficulties companies may have when tapping a foreign market?

3. **Role play: work in pairs**
You are going to take part in a presentation.
Student A: you are a trainee at a consultant firm conducting market research for M&S to find out where and how you could open up stores in India. You must report to your manager and propose new ideas. The middle class that should count 335 million people by 2015 is M&S's likely customer base.
Student B: you are the manager. You have given the following information to your trainee.

TIPS
For student A: remember that M&S has already got 19 stores. So find out where they are located, how big the stores are, how M&S has met the Indian demand: if it advertises its goods differently, if the Indian prices are not too high.
M&S has a joint venture with Reliance who knows the Indian market. Indian prices had to be lower by 30% because of complaints from Indian customers. It does not sell food but it will sell products sourced locally.

8 | Globalisation

Train with an oral document

WARMING UP

- What is a startup?
- Have you ever worked in a fast delivery system company?

CD n° 3 Track n° 15

Go-Jek

Info

Go-Jek is a new social enterprise whose founders believe that business and social impact can go hand in hand. Go-Jek was built upon the belief that the ojek industry is an increasingly relevant transport mode amid Jakarta's increasingly untenable traffic conditions. We believe that by professionalising ojeks in Jakarta, we can improve the welfare and status of ojek drivers while providing Jakartans a practical and fast convenience service.

Lexical work

1. Find the nouns corresponding to the adjectives and their meanings.

Adjectives	Nouns	Meanings
available		
reliable		
safe		
secure		
difficult		
transparent		

2. Work on figures: write in full and read aloud.

a U.S. $10,000 prize • 200 • 80 • 50-60 • 2011

Pronunciation work

CD n° 3 Track n° 16

1. Underline the stressed syllable of the words below. Then listen to check the right answer.

Indonesia • motorcycle • unlicensed • depending • location

2. Listen to these words that you may find difficult.

business • leisure • professionalisation • competitors

Work on the title

1. Look at the title of the document.

2. The title is very short so use the info box giving information on the company to find its meaning.

Check the facts

1. Listen to part 1.

a) When did Go-Jek start?
b) Who started it?
c) What service does it provide?
d) Why is it doing well?
e) What is Jakarta famous for?
f) How are motorcycle drivers described?
g) In which way is Go-Jek different from the other motorcycle businesses in Jakarta?

2. Listen to part 2.

a) Describe the step-by-step procedure to have a package dispatched to a business district:
Step 1: What does the customer do?
Step 2: What is specified?
Step 3: What does the customer receive?
Step 4: Where does the driver arrive from?
Step 5: What does the driver do?
Step 6: What does the driver get once he or she has dropped the package?
b) Describe Go-Jek's drivers (2 elements).
c) Who invested in Go-Jek?
d) What is an angel investor?
e) What is lying in the future for Go-Jek?

Topic debrief

1. Choose the sentence which you think corresponds best to the main topic of the document.

a) The startup Go-Jek offers a motorcycle service in the city of Jakarta.

b) Go-Jek is a new Indonesian startup based in Jakarta that offers a reliable, professional delivery service.

c) Go-Jek delivers packages in Jakarta very efficiently.

2. Rephrase the correct sentence in order to make a short introduction to the document.

Methods

Complete the following sentences with your own words in order to give more details about the company.

a) Go-Jek does not offer a new service, however it ….

b) A Go-Jek driver is somebody who ….

c) A Go-Jek driver is more likely to offer a better service because ….

d) The motorcycle service won ….

Train for the exam

1. Use your notes to make an **oral presentation** about the document in which you describe this new startup and say why it is successful and record yourself (3-5 minutes).

2. Comment: find an answer to the following question. Discuss and give examples (100 words / 3-5 minutes).

What are the advantages and disadvantages of setting a delivery service company in an emerging country such as Indonesia?

Go online

- Find information about the Dabbawallas in India.
- Get prepared to report to your group / class (a PowerPoint presentation is recommended).

3. Role play: work in groups

You are going to take part in a phone conversation.

Group A: you are a Go-Jek client, and you want an important document to be brought to the airport to UPS. Imagine the conversation. Work with partners on this phone conversation.

Group B: you represent the Go-Jek company.

TIPS

- For Group B: before you start, you need to find out about the Indonesian currency, where the airport is from where you are yourself (so it means you need to look at a map) and how much a similar service is charged. Do not forget the usual greetings when telephoning.
- Here are a few phrases you can use: *Good morning, Go-Jek, can I help you? / Hold on a second / Sorry to keep you waiting / Let me write it down / Let me check who is available now, etc.*
- You should use your notes in order to present a realistic conversation. Don't read them, look up. You can:
  - record the conversation (at the multimedia lab or with your own MP4 recorder; the recording should last between one and two minutes at most);
  - videotape the scene and show it to the class;
  - act out the scene in front of the class;
  - listen to your classmates' recordings and write what you have understood in a short and structured paragraph.

Info

The Global Entrepreneurship Program Indonesia (GEPI) aims to catalyse Indonesia's entrepreneurship strategies by working in partnership with existing programs and linking aspiring Indonesian entrepreneurs to global developments and investment prospects.

- **Indonesia**, officially the **Republic of Indonesia** (Indonesian: Republik Indonesia), is a country in Southeast Asia and Oceania. Indonesia is an archipelago comprising approximately 13,000 islands.

8 | Globalisation

WARMING UP

- What is "Chindia"?
- Find out three assets in relocating to India or China.

CD n° 3 Track n° 17

India starts trade talks with African countries in effort to rival China

India's prime minister, Manmohan Singh, and dozens of business leaders began trade talks in Ethiopia on Monday as the Asian giant strives to catch up with China in what has been dubbed "the new scramble for Africa".

Manmohan Singh received a red-carpet welcome as he led a delegation to the India-Africa summit in Addis Ababa, aiming to trumpet historical and cultural links with the continent in an effort to emerge from Beijing's shadow.

"The India-Africa partnership rests on three pillars of capacity building and skill transfer, trade and infrastructure development," said Singh at the start of the six-day trip to Ethiopia and Tanzania. "Africa is emerging as a new growth pole of the world, while India is on a path of sustained and rapid economic development." The trade meeting is to be attended by 15 African leaders.

Bilateral India-Africa trade has grown from about £620m in 2001 to £28.5bn in 2010. India's Commerce and Industry Minister, Anand Sharma, hopes it will reach £43bn by 2012. Some 250 Indian companies have invested, mainly in telecommunications and chemical and mining companies.

But India remains about a decade behind its Asian rival. China says its two-way trade stands at £75bn, a 43.5% increase over the previous year, and up from just £620m in 1992. It has built roads, bridges, railways and power stations in return for access to markets and resources.

The fierce competition between China and India for resources, minerals and food to fuel their turbo-charged economies has been likened by commentators to the so-called scramble for Africa among European countries in the 19th century.

India is especially focused on energy. The country imports 70% of its oil and has turned to new suppliers such as Nigeria, Sudan and Angola to reduce its dependence on the Middle East. It also needs uranium for its ambitious civil nuclear programme. India is also looking to Africa to expand its diplomatic influence.

India's wooing of Africa includes aid, technology and education, such as a new centre in Uganda to train businesses about global markets, a diamond processing facility in Botswana, and assistance to cotton farmers in four of the continent's poorest countries. Officials in New Delhi stress that India's links with Africa are centuries old, bolstered by trade across the Indian Ocean and a million-strong Indian diaspora across Africa.

The Guardian, Monday, 23 May 2011

Lexical work

1. Find the English equivalents in the text.

a) négociations § 1
b) rattraper § 1
c) surnommer § 1
d) transfert de connaissances § 3
e) chemin § 3
f) durable § 3
g) la pétrochimie § 4
h) des usines hydroélectriques § 5

2. Find the French equivalents.

a) fierce § 6
b) competition § 6
c) turbo-charged § 6
d) to be likened § 6
e) the scramble for Africa § 6
f) to woo § 8
g) a facility § 8
h) to bolster § 8

Pronunciation work

CD n° 3 Track n° 18

1. Listen and observe.

Canada → Canadian • Japan → Japanese
The stressed accent changes when the noun of nationality becomes an adjective.

2. Listen to these words and underline the stressed syllable.

Ethiopia • Nigeria • Sudan • Angola • Tanzania

Work on the title

1. Look at the title of the document.

2. Read the first paragraph to understand who the trade talks involve.

Check the facts

1. Read §1.
a) What does India want to do?
b) The Addis Ababa summit is a part of what international trend?

2. Read §2.
Why was there so much talk about historical and cultural links between India and Africa?

3. Read §3.
What does the African-Indian relationship rest on?

4. Read §4.
a) How many companies have invested in Africa?
b) What does Mr Sharma want to achieve?

5. Read §5.
Make a comparison between China and India.

6. Read §6.
What are China and India compared to?

7. Read §7.
Which natural resources is India keen on importing from Africa?

8. Read §8.
How will India help African countries?

Grammar

→ p. 238

to be to

• *The trade meeting is to be attended by 15 African leaders.*

Topic debrief

1. Choose the sentence which you think corresponds best to the main topic of the document.
a) India's Prime Minister is meeting with African leaders to develop economic partnerships.
b) The India-Africa summit at Addis Ababa aims at strengthening ties between India and Africa.

2. Write an introduction to the document by using the following words.
23 May 2011 • competitive • India • trade • website • rival • guardian.co.uk • countries • same

Methods

1. Prepare your account of the document by collecting figures.

Bilateral trade between India & Africa	2001	2010	2012
Bilateral trade between China & Africa	1992	2010	2011

2. Complete the sentences with your own words.
a) The figures for Chinese trade with Africa and the figures for Indian trade cannot be ....
b) China has been tapping the African natural resources for ....
c) India is a decade ....
d) China has spent more time and more resources in Africa. For example, China has built ....
e) India will have to invest a lot in African countries if it wants to ....
f) India has as many ... as China to trade ....

Train for the exam

1. Make a summary / account of the document by using the word bank (60 words / 3-5 minutes).
to compete with • to compete for • minerals • food • emerging countries • natural resources • to import • to offer • technical assistance • to have access to • to operate • sustainable growth • construction projects • to benefit • to meet the needs of African businesses • to develop infrastructures • to hire people

2. Comment: find an answer to the following question. Discuss and give examples (100 words / 3-5 minutes).
After colonisation by the Western countries, is Africa undergoing a new form of colonisation with China and India?

3. Role play: work in pairs
You are going to take part in a conversation.
Student A: you are a young Chinese manager newly arrived in Angola and you want to adapt to the population.
Student B: you are an elderly African supplier who complains about Chinese companies and their lack of interest for the local population.

8 | Globalisation

WARMING UP

- Do you like Chinese food?
- When eating Chinese food
- Where do you place your bowl?
- Can you eat with chopsticks?

Train with an oral document

CD n° 3 Track n° 19

Chopsticks made in America

Info

Chopsticks are small, often tapered, sticks used in pairs of equal length as the traditional eating utensils of China and its diaspora, Japan, Korea, Vietnam and the northern provinces of Laos, Thailand and Burma.

Lexical work

1. Match the opposite words.

a) wood
b) flexible
c) increase
d) demand

1) decrease
2) supply
3) plastic
4) tough

2. Work on figures: write in full and read aloud.

63bn • 2m • 23bn • 57

Pronunciation work

CD n° 3 Track n° 20

1. Listen to the sounds [ju] and [ʌ] and fill in the grid according to the words' pronunciation.

Sue • used • us • produce • product • due

[ju]	[ʌ]

2. Find the appropriate article. Then listen to check the right pronunciation.

underclothed • undelivered • unique • uncommon • uncooked • unusual • usurpations • unity • unitary • university

Work on the title

1. Look at the title of the document and the info box.

2. Explain what chopsticks are.

Check the facts

1. Listen to part 1.

a) Who founded the company?
b) How many pairs of chopsticks are made by Chinese companies per year?
c) What are they made of?
d) Why are there chopsticks made in the USA?

2. Listen to part 2.

a) How many people use chopsticks worldwide?
b) How much does it cost to make one pair?
c) How does the company ship the goods?
d) How many people work for Georgia Chopsticks?
e) Where are the goods sold?

Topic debrief

1. Choose the sentence which best corresponds to the main topic of the document.

a) Georgia Chopsticks is a Chinese company which produces wood, especially poplar trees, to export to America.
b) Georgia Chopsticks is making chopsticks to export to China since China does not have enough wood to meet the demand.
c) Georgia Chopsticks are made in China and sold in the U.S. like so many manufactured goods.

2. Rephrase the correct sentence in order to make a short introduction to the document.

Methods

1. Reorder the following sentences to prepare your account of the document.
a) Georgia has a lot of wood.
b) Making chopsticks requires a lot of flexible and tough wood.
c) Most chopsticks are made in China.
d) Georgia Chopsticks understood there was a demand.
e) The Georgia-based company is producing 2m pairs.

2. List the important words you need.

3. What linking words can you use to make your account clearer?

Train for the exam

1. Use your notes to make an **oral presentation** about the document by using the following linking words (60 words / 3-5 minutes).
actually • first • however • once • finally

Say everything you know about the company Georgia Chopsticks. Say who the Chief Executive is, why the company is located in Georgia, how many chopsticks are made, the workforce, the plans for the future, etc.

2. Write an e-mail to Jae Lee's sales department (100 words).
You are Ms / Mr Ming, the owner of a Hotel group located in Danang. One of your American clients has told you about Georgia Chopsticks. You are interested in finding out more about the company, the type of wood used, the shipping cost, the price, etc.

3. Role play: work in groups
You are going to take part in a negotiation with three people.
Student A: you are Ms / Mr Ming of the Vietnamese hotel group located in Danang. You now know for a fact that Georgia Chopsticks are environmentally friendly. You have decided to order 100,000 pairs of chopsticks. *Student B:* you are in Jae Lee's sales department.
You want to place an order for 100,000 pairs of chopsticks. *Student C:* you are a public relations manager or communications manager.

Train with a video

Chinese exports fall to two-year low

→ http://www.youtube.com/watch?v=IfQGDTTDfqY

14 January, 2012

Look at this video on the Internet about globalisation

Check the facts	Methods
1. What is the main topic of this video?	• What is the state of Chinese overseas exports?
2. Why is the export amount very challenging?	• What would the consequences be of raising the value of the Chinese currency?
3. Who do Americans want to target?	• How do Americans want to boost exports? • What is a free trade agreement?
4. Why is there a trade gap in America?	• What spending impacted Americans' purchasing power?
5. Issues ... How does the economic crisis affect the global market, in China and in America?	• As China has joined the WTO, will the situation be economically easier?

8 | Globalisation

WARMING UP

▸ Find the reasons why clothes are made in China.

CD n° 3 Track n° 21

Good darning, Vietnam

"Fashion is a form of ugliness so intolerable that we have to alter it every six months." Oscar Wilde's quip now sounds hopelessly out of date. Fashions change more often than twice a year. And the rag trade is as footloose as its customers are fickle. It goes wherever clothes can be made cheaply and reliably. Until recently, it meant China. But as Chinese wages soar, buyers are looking elsewhere. Southeast Asia could be the next best thing.

China still dominates the business. It supplies nearly half of the European Union's garment imports and 41% of America's. But more orders are shifting to lower-wage economies such as Cambodia and Vietnam, where garment factories are mushrooming. Vietnam is already the second-largest supplier of clothes to America.

The new tigers are still cubs. They often have to import fabrics from China to stitch into clothes, so their transport costs are high. For buyers in a hurry, it is hard to beat China's mix of scale, speed and flexibility. Suppliers in Southeast Asia are all clearly behind China.

One way to catch up would be to knit together textile and garment producers in the Association of Southeast Asian Nations (ASEAN) to create a regional supply chain. Vietnam does not produce denim, but Indonesia does, and its denim can be exported tariff-free within ASEAN to sew jeans. This sort of partnership, promoted by USAID, America's aid agency, is attractive to fashion buyers who prefer an integrated, one-stop service. It is also a step towards the single market that ASEAN is supposed to turn into by 2015 [...].

ASEAN manufacturers are forming alliances. For example, Phongsak Assakul, who owns a textile mill in Bangkok, ships his pre-dyed fabrics by road to neighbouring Cambodia, where another factory cuts and sews them into summer blouses for Benetton, an Italian brand.

To compete with China, ASEAN needs to make it easier to move goods around. New roads and railways, plus faster customs clearance, all help. But infrastructure bottlenecks can delay shipments. This is a no-no for fast fashion. Winter frocks delivered in the spring are worthless.

China still has plenty of cheap labour in northern and inland cities, far from the overheated coastal boomtowns. But as it grows richer, wages will rise in the hinterland, too. Its factories will continue to churn out clothes, but they will increasingly churn out simple items, such as polo shirts.

Even the Chinese are starting to outsource low-end clothes manufacturing to Vietnam and Cambodia, observes Peter Hevicon, a Hong-Kong-based buyer for Debenhams, a British retailer. And when wages rise in Southeast Asia, the rag trade will move again.

The Economist, June 4th, 2011

Lexical work

1. Find the English equivalents in the text.

a) la confection § 1
b) démodé § 1
c) correctement § 1
d) s'envoler § 1
e) l'importation de textile § 2
f) pousser comme des champignons § 2
g) être à la traîne / être derrière § 3

2. Find the French equivalents.

a) a supply chain § 4
b) a textile mill § 5
c) pre-dyed fabrics § 5
d) summer blouses § 5
e) customs clearance § 6
f) to delay shipment § 6
g) frocks § 6
h) to churn out § 7

Pronunciation work

CD n° 3 Track n° 22

1. Listen to the sounds [ʃ] and [tʃ]. Then fill in the grid according to the words' pronunciation.

fashion • cheap • shifting • Chinese • partnership • China • shipment • chain

Shanghai [ʃ]	chat [tʃ]

2. Practise pronouncing these words then listen to check the right pronunciation.

chip / ship • cheap / sheep

Work on the title

1. Look at the title of the document.

2. The headline is a play on words. Explain the pun used here.

Check the facts

1. Read § 1.
Where are clothes made at the lowest price now?

2. Read § 2.
Who is competing with China now?

3. Read § 3.
Why is China still the best for buyers?

4. Read § 4.
a) What should garment producers in ASEAN create in order to become more attractive for buyers?
b) What will the ASEAN single market provide buyers with by 2015?

5. Read § 5.
Explain what is meant by "alliances".

6. Read § 6.
What is needed to overcome infrastructure problems?

7. Read § 7.
Which parts of China can still compete with Southeast Asia? Why?

8. Read § 8.
What is expected to happen when wages rise in Southeast Asia?

Grammar

→ p. 238

Le présent (simple et continu)

• *It goes wherever clothes can be made cheaply and reliably.* • *China still dominates the business.*
• *They often have to import fabrics...*
• *But more orders are shifting to lower-range...*

Topic debrief

1. Choose the sentence which you think corresponds best to the main topic of the document.
a) Vietnam is about to become the N°1 garment factory of the world.
b) China is almost being outranked as the leader in the textile industry but not quite.
c) Southeast Asia, with more flexible ASEAN rules, will soon offer very attractive prices to European and American clothes retailers and fashion designers.

2. Write an introduction to the document by using the word bank.
to be published • to be entitled • to tackle the issue • a play on words • to refer to • to convey the meaning that

Methods

1. List the 5 Asian countries, the 2 organisations and the name of the writer mentioned in the article.
• For the 5 countries, find out their size, the population and the capital.
• For the 2 organisations, find out when they were founded and their role.
• For the writer, find out who he was and what he was known for.

2. Now write down the main idea of this article by using the following word bank.
China vs Vietnam • used to be • labour cost • wages / salaries • to skyrocket • the garment industry • to relocate • cheap and reliable

Train for the exam

1. Make a **summary / account** of the document (60 words / 3-5 minutes).

2. Comment: find an answer to the following questions. Discuss and give examples (100 words / 3-5 minutes). There is a play on the word "darning". Can you think of the word that has been replaced by the journalist?

3. Role play: work in pairs
You are going to take part in a conversation.
Student A: you are the purchasing manager for Europe at Debenhams, a British retailer, and you want to have your garments manufactured in Vietnam.
Student B: you are a Vietnamese textile business woman, Ms. N'Guyen.

TIPS

For student A:
Ask questions about colour, time, price, material, working conditions.

For student B:
you are interested in this deal but you will have to compromise.

PRACTICE • TEXT

Custom-Comp

1 • Situation

You work in the procurement team of Custom-Comp, and you receive an e-mail from your General Manager.

2 • Process

a) Read the e-mail (Document B) and look at the other documents which should help your discussion.
b) Get into groups.
Students A: you are purchasers. *Students B:* you are component suppliers.
c) *Students:* you decide which country you are going to source your components from (China, India ...), and which component(s) and quantities you would like to order.
d) *Students B:* you call the purchasers to fix an appointment to discuss the purchase of components.
e) Now discuss all / some of the points listed in "Seven Tips on Managing Low-Cost Country Sourcing". Remember to speak in English only!
Students A / purchasers: you discuss the offers you have received and choose which supplier you are going to source your components from. Negotiate prices, quantities, delivery times, shipping conditions, etc.
Students B / suppliers: you discuss the advantages and disadvantages of your different offers during this time.

→ FOR MORE INFORMATION ON PREPARING A NEGOTIATION, SEE "TOOLS" PAGE 248.

3 • Follow up

- Purchasers: write an e-mail to the General Manager summarising your meeting with the suppliers, and the conclusions you reached.
- Suppliers: write a commercial proposal for the purchasers.

→ FOR MORE INFORMATION ON HOW TO WRITE A LETTER / COMMERCIAL PROPOSAL, SEE "TOOLS" PAGE 246.

@ Go online

Look up different international logistics companies on the Internet and see what they offer.

TIPS

Start by saying
May I suggest that we begin by ... and then we can discuss ...

Purchasers:	**Suppliers:**
Our position is this ...	*Our proposal would be ...*
Our main worry is that ...	*We would be willing to ...*
What we are looking for is ...	*We can offer you a (quantity) discount of ...*
We hope to achieve ...	*That is our final offer!*
Could you quote me for ...?	
Could you guarantee ...?	
What's your best offer for ...?	
Would you be able to ...?	

Doc • A

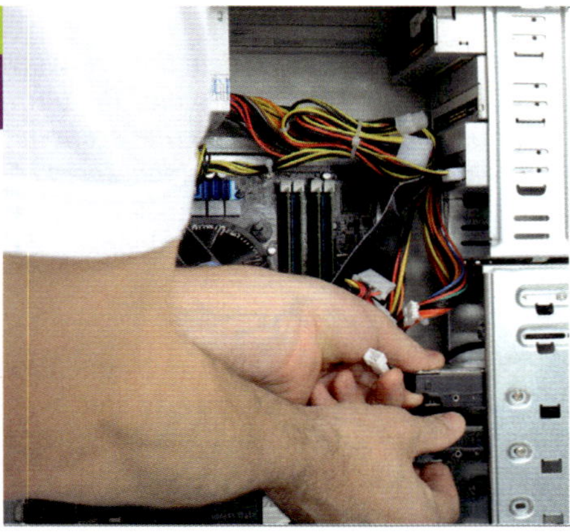

CUSTOM-COMP

WE OFFER THE BEST CUSTOM-MADE COMPUTERS ON THE MARKET.

Check out our website for more details:
www. custom-build-computers.com

Doc • B

CUSTOM-COMP • E-mail

Answer | Forward | Delete | Print

From: General Manager
To: Procurement manager and team
Subject: Parts sourcing for motherboards

It has come to my notice that although we shall certainly continue to make our motherboards in England, we should be able to get many of the small components from low-cost countries. I would be grateful if you could look into the matter and get back to me within the next 2 weeks.
Deadline 4th March 2012

Doc • C

Seven Tips on Managing Low-Cost Country Sourcing

Low-cost country sourcing or LCCS is the process in which supplies are moved from a low-cost country by a business located in some other country where the costs are comparatively higher. […]
For example, when a firm located in the United States gets its raw materials from a Central American company instead of a costlier U.S. company, then the U.S. firm would be said to be doing low-cost country sourcing. There are 7 critical tips to ensuring low-cost country sourcing is truly low-cost.
1. Understand the tariff and tax structures involved. They may be expensive.
2. Do a real transportation cost analysis. Ship transport can be economical but the overall cost may be high.
3. Consider the Economic Ordering Quantity delta based on potentially longer lead time. Longer lead times or bigger safety stocks may create zero-sum gain.
4. Determine the importance of quality control to business outcomes. It might be a lower quality product, or you may have to invest in costly inspection on product receipt.
5. Calculate potential cost if supplier fails to meet the Level of Service timeline. If you use JIT (just in time) you may have expensive production stoppages if the goods arrive late.
6. Research risk of political instability in the region. This could play havoc with your supply chain.
7. Project cost of having to directly or indirectly monitor suppliers. Evaluate the cost carefully.
As a general rule, this form of sourcing is used for simple components or cheap consumer goods. If the stitching is poor on textiles, it is less critical than even a minor error on a printed circuit.
Education and skill level of the workers will dictate the type of products and services sourced from lower wage or weak currency countries.

8 | Globalisation

Background

Globalisation means the expansion and harmonisation of interdependent links between nations, human activities and the political systems on a worldwide scale. The term, particular to the human environment, is often used nowadays to describe economic globalisation, and the changes which have been brought about by the global spread of digital information, for example via the Internet. → SEE CHAPTER "NEW TECHNOLOGIES" PAGE 102.
Globalisation is also closely associated with the stakes of sustainable development.
→ SEE CHAPTER "ENVIRONMENT" PAGE 226.

1 Does globalisation only concern the economy?

Not at all. Globalisation has an effect on many other factors as well.
International **trade** dates back to ancient civilisations. Globalisation, however, involves more than just trade: the flow of products, services, labour, finance, information and ideas.
Products: Many Western companies manufacture their products in countries outside the Western world. → SEE CHAPTER "COMPANIES" PAGE 22.
Services: Technological advances are speeding up globalisation of the tertiary sector, which includes off-shoring services in the education, health, legal, accounting and R&D fields.
Labour: Political changes, economic reforms, developments in technology and fewer restrictions to cross-border trade have led to increasing flows of labour around the world. The aging population in developed countries will lead to labour migration from the developing countries, while MNCs (multinational companies) seek labour in **low-wage countries**.
→ SEE CHAPTER "WORK" PAGE 122.
Finance: Greater freedom of capital movements and innovations which have changed the way capital circulates **worldwide** has economic advantages, but has also placed the world economy in a vulnerable position and led to the 2008 financial crisis.
Information: The globalisation of ICT has led to many cost reductions for companies. All around the world people have access to the same information, in real time. → SEE CHAPTER "NEW TECHNOLOGIES" PAGE 102.
Ideas: Cultural and geographical boundaries are no longer a **barrier**, except for certain people. The 2011 uprisings – also known as the Arab Spring – which spread all around the world are just one example.

2 Which institutions are involved in globalisation?

The World Trade Organization (WTO):
→ SEE "STARTERS" PAGE 152.
The World Social Forum (WSF): Brings together many political / social movements around the world to discuss and promote people-centred and self-reliant progress as alternatives to a market-driven approach.
The World Bank: A development bank whose mission it is to fight **poverty** and improve the living conditions of people in **developing countries** by practical help such as low-interest loans, advice, technical assistance, etc. It is currently involved in over 1,800 projects in developing countries around the globe.
International Monetary Fund (IMF): The IMF is a group of 187 countries who work towards the same goal of raising living standards in its member countries as the World Bank, but within the United Nations system. A Frenchwoman, Christine Lagarde, is currently Managing Director of the IMF.

3 What is fair trade?

Fair trade is a movement which seeks greater equity on a global marketplace. This means helping farmers in developing countries to get direct access to international markets, as well as helping them to develop their business so they can compete on the global marketplace. Fair trade organisations help them learn to market their own harvests and receive a fair price for their goods. The better trading conditions lead to higher living standards and more sustainable farming practices, thus contributing to sustainable development. There are two main international organisations: FLO (Fairtrade Labelling Organisation) and WFTO (World Fair Trade Organisation).
→ SEE "STARTERS" PAGE 152.

Info

Anti-globalisation: An umbrella term for many organisations who are against globalisation because they believe it leads to exploitation of the world's poorest workers, and has a negative impact on the environment. They also fear the "steam-roller" effect of Americanisation. Protests are usually non-violent and often take place on May Day.

Questions

- What has been affected by globalisation?
- Could you explain what free trade and fair trade are?
- What do you know about organisations which are not followers of globalisation?

Focus

China and India in Africa: for better or for worse?

China and India have always had strong links with Africa but now India and China are especially keen on developing stronger commercial relationships with African countries, although China has been accused of replacing old colonial powers in Africa. And some Africans are asking "whether China is making their lunch or eating it". But aren't the two emerging countries true investors involved in African development? Are they not drivers of change? If some see them as cut-throat competitors, others congratulate them on their high-octane engagement. Maybe there is a bit of both, and if Chinese and Indian investments are a blessing, it is still a mixed blessing.

Where is China in Africa?

Figures

With a population of 1.3 billion and a booming economy, China needs natural resources to manufacture goods that are then exported abroad or sold on its domestic market. But China is also eager to invest and produce abroad and gain international recognition. If there are still Chinese people living on just a few dollars a day, there is also a burgeoning middle class who is now travelling abroad and wants to have access to Western goods and improve its standard of living. China clearly needs African resources and its $126bn ties to the continent have been mostly in commercial and infrastructure investment. One should keep in mind that China is way ahead of India in Africa and that most Chinese investors in Africa are state-owned enterprises with access to extremely low-cost capital from state-owned banks.

Trade has risen between China and Africa by an average of 28% a year between 2001 and 2010 for three main reasons:

– to have access to natural resources for China's own growth;
– to nurture a market for its products;
– to invest in new markets.

Natural resources

- Oil resources: Algeria, Nigeria, Sudan, Gabon, Niger, Angola, Chad.
- Mines: iron ore in Gabon; copper in Zambia; cobalt in Congo; manganese in South Africa; uranium pits in Nigeria as well as tantalum and diamonds.

Examples:

- China is now the world's biggest consumer of copper. For example, in copper-rich, Zambia (13 million people) there are more than 300 Chinese companies, most of them privately-owned, employing 25,000 locals.
- China buys more than one-third of its oil from Africa. For example, in Angola (18 million people), Africa's largest oil producer before Nigeria: a hospital was built in Luanda by the Chinese, who buy Angola's oil.

Chinese investments

- Chinese investment in roads, railways, schools, computer networks, telecom systems as well as agriculture in Congo, Zambia and Sudan have been increased, in exchange for natural resources.
- Relocating jobs in Africa: some manufacturing jobs are to be outsourced from China. Assembly plants are established as manufacturing locally avoids an import tax and manpower is cheap.

Questions

- What is China mostly interested in when investing, creating joint ventures or building roads, hospitals or schools?
- Mr. Hu Jintao has already visited Africa 4 times since he became president in 2003. How do you understand these visits (his last visit was in 2009)?
- What is the point of creating free trade zones in Nigeria?

ACTIVE BUSINESS CULTURE

Focus → Where are Indian investments in Africa?

Figures

With a population of 1.2 billion and a fast-growing economy, India and Indian companies are interested in investing in Africa to import oil, to develop commercial relationships, and some say to rival China's huge presence on the continent. If India is focused on Africa's development, it is also looking for the support of African states to secure a seat at the UN Security Council. India exports 20% of its goods to South Africa, 14% to Nigeria, 8% to Kenya. Oil-refined goods, medicine and cars are among export goods. India imports from South Africa (28%), Morocco (17%) and Egypt (8%). Crude oil (66% of imported goods in 2006) as well as gold (10%) comes from African countries. Imports have increased.

Trade between India and African countries has been increasing, as many Indian companies are investing in India in many economic sectors ranging from energy to consumer goods as well as in the cement and textile industries. Unlike China, Indian multinationals and private companies arrived before the Indian government. There have now been two India-Africa summits, one in 2008 in New Delhi and the other in 2011 in Addis-Ababa (Ethiopia), but India's relationship is driven by the private sector and focused heavily on investing and creating jobs in Africa.

Indian acquisitions

- Bharti Airtel is the second-largest mobile operator in Africa and has successfully transferred its frugal innovation model from India to Africa. It has acquired mobile phone operations in 15 African countries.
- Godrej has acquired Nigerian personal care product maker Tura.
- Essar Steel, India's second biggest private sector steel-maker, is investing in businesses ranging from power, steel and mining to telecommunications and construction.

Producing in Africa

- Tata Hispano, a subsidiary of the giant Tata Motors, invested in an assembly line to increase its production and exports to Sub-Saharan Africa.
- Indian companies have already set up ventures to export flowers, medicinal plants, etc. in Togo.
- A multi-facility economic zone is being developed for Indian companies to set up manufacturing and services industries in Zambia.
- Alok Industry opened a spinning mill in Burkina Faso to transform cotton production.

Tapping natural resources

- ArcelorMittal, the world's largest steel-maker, started exporting iron ore from West African nations.
- Indian companies have contracts to work in the timber industry and on social housing projects in Gabon; Ramky Infrastructure is working on road construction to connect Libreville and Franceville.
- Indian companies have a contract to engage in mining exploration in Congo.

Questions

- ▶ What does India want to achieve in Africa?
- ▶ Why is India so keen on developing partnerships based on skill transfer, trade and infrastructure development?
- ▶ Why is it an asset for African countries to be trading not only among themselves but also with China and India?

Express your point of view

- After reading this short presentation, do you think that Chinese and Indian investments will modernise Africa and introduce new business models that will benefit Africans?
- Or do you believe that China and India only see their own interests?

Test yourself

Try to use your memory – do not look at the vocabulary list!

1 MCQ (MULTIPLE CHOICE QUESTIONS)

Choose the right answer.

1. A country beyond the boundaries of your home country is:
a) strange
b) abroad
c) foreigner

2. Agricultural products, especially fresh fruit and vegetables:
a) agricults
b) produce
c) produce

3. To move (a company) to a different place:
a) dislocate
b) relocate
c) delocate

4. A sum of money given by a government to help an industry, business, country, etc.:
a) subsidy
b) subvention
c) subfunding

5. The difference between a country's imports and exports:
a) balance of commerce
b) balance of trade
c) commercial balance

6. Something picked manually is:
a) hand-picked
b) hand-collected
c) manual-picked

7. Customs duties settled so the goods can be made available:
a) duty spent
b) duty done
c) duty paid

8. A group of people with a special interest who conduct a campaign to change opinions:
a) snobby
b) hobby
c) lobby

9. A legal prohibition:
a) ban
b) band
c) bond

10. The level of material comfort shown by the ability of individuals to buy goods and services:
a) live standards
b) living standards
c) life standards

2 ODD MAN OUT

Choose the word which does not fit in the list, and explain why.

a) premium price / low-wage country / underpay / child labour / unfair competition

b) embargo / erect barriers / free trade / protectionism / trade sanctions

c) seize / threaten / support / crackdown (on) / liberalise / impose

d) import / export / currency / home market / customs duties / duty free

e) developing countries / monopolistic / aid / recipient / donor

f) crop / farmer / foodstuff / GMO / goods / soya beans

3 TRADE

Using the definition for help, fill in the missing letters.

a) When the cost of imports exceed the value of exports:
Trade D _ _ _ _ _ T

b) Countries using tariffs or barriers to damage each other's trade:
Trade W _ R

c) Complete or partial prohibition of trade with a particular country:
Trade E _ _ _ _ _ O

d) Trading penalties to punish a particular country:
Trade S _ _ _ _ _ _ _ S

e) An agreement between countries to reduce trade barriers:
Trade B _ _ C

f) When the value of exports exceeds the cost of imports:
Trade S _ _ _ _ _ S

g) A regulation or activity which restricts international trade:
Trade B _ _ _ _ _ R

h) Another word for "e":
F _ _ E Trade A _ _ A

8 | Globalisation

Words

"We must ensure that the global market is embedded in broadly shared values and practices that reflect global social needs, and that all the world's people share the benefits of globalisation." (Kofi Annan)

Abroad: à l'étranger
Aid: aide / soutien
Balance of trade: balance commerciale
Ban: interdiction
Barrier: barrière
Chamber of commerce: chambre de commerce
Child labour: travail des enfants
Controversial: sujet à controverses
Controversy: polémique
Currency: devise
Customs: douane
Customs duties: droits de douane
Deregulate (to): déréguler
Developing: en voie de développement
Donor country: pays donataire
Duty free: détaxé / hors taxe
Duty paid: dédouané
Economies of scale: économies d'échelle
Erect barriers (to): ériger les barrières
Exchange: échange
Export / export (to): exportation / exporter
Exporter: exportateur
Fair trade: commerce équitable
Farmer: agriculteur
Fast-growing countries: pays émergents, à forte croissance
Foodstuff: produits alimentaires
Foreign: étranger
Free circulation: libre circulation
Free trade: libre échange
Free trade agreement (FTA): accord de libre échange
Free trade area (FTA): zone de libre échange
Global: mondial
Go global (to): se mondialiser
Goods: marchandises
Guideline: directive
Hand-picked: cueilli à la main
Home market: marché intérieur
Import / import (to): importation / importer
Importer: importateur
Impose an embargo (to): imposer un embargo
Incentive: incitation
Interdependence: interdépendance
International Monetary Fund (IMF): FMI
Joint venture: coentreprise, partenariat
Lax: souple / laxiste
Liberalize (to): libéraliser
Lift an embargo (to): lever un embargo
Living standards: niveau de vie
Lobby: groupe de pression
Located: situé
Location: emplacement / lieu
Low-wage country: pays à bas salaire
Lower trade barriers (to): abaisser les barrières douanières
Managed trade: protectionnisme
Monopolistic market: marché monopoliste
Parity: parité
Poverty: pauvreté
Premium price: prix fort
Price conscious: attentif aux prix
Produce: produits agricoles
Product: produit
Protectionism: protectionnisme
Question (to): remettre en question
Quota system: système de quota
Raise (funds) (to): rassembler (des fonds)
Recipient country: pays bénéficiaire
Regulate (to): réguler
Relocate (to): délocaliser
Retaliation: représailles
Seize (to): saisir
Shift production (to): transférer la production
Smuggler: contrebandier
Subsidy: subvention
Support (to): soutenir / aider
Tariff / tariff barrier: droits de douane
Threaten (to): menacer
Trade: échanges commerciaux
Trade barrier: barrière douanière
Trade block: communauté économique
Trade deficit: déficit commercial
Trade embargo: embargo commercial
Trade sanctions: sanctions économiques
Trade surplus: excédent commercial
Trade war: guerre commerciale
Underpay (to): sous-payer
Unfair: inéquitable
Unfair competition: concurrence déloyale
Untapped: inexploité
World bank: banque mondiale
World Health Organization (WHO): Organisation mondiale de la santé (OMS)
World Social Forum (WSF): Forum social mondial
World Trade Organization (WTO): Organisation mondiale du commerce (OMC)
Worldwide: dans le monde entier

9

Transport and logistics

Towards cleaner and more efficient means of transport

Question

Are electric cars our near future?

WORD BOX

shuttle • railways • timetable • transportation • lorry (GB), truck (USA) • delivery • carriage • carrier • aircraft • airline • airport

9 | Transport and logistics

1 • Look and discuss

a) Look at the following picture. Please do some research about the topic in advance to give you some ideas and facts for the discussion that will follow.

Infrastructure EU

EU INFRASTRUCTURE

The Future of Public Transport?

With fossil-fuels swiftly running out, the drive to find more eco-friendly forms of transport is on.

Driverless Pods
A four seater vehicle that runs automatically along a guideway. There will be not timetable, so it is anticipated to run more like a taxi service than a bus service, with the advantage of bypassing current traffic congestion and travelling at speeds of up to 32 km/h.
Leading Example: Heathrow Airport, London
Positives: Uses 1/4 energy per passenger per mile of a car

SkyTran
Computer controlled, personal sized vehicles that ride on "guideways" built above ground. They will run like a non-stop freeway with designed exits and entrances to SkyTran stations.
Speed: 160 km/h in cities
Negatives: It will cost approx $10 million per 1 mile of track

Zeppelins
Zeppelins are making a comeback 70 years after the Hindenburg disaster. Environmentalists are favouring this alternative to airplanes due to their low usage of fuel and the low altitudes at which they fly.
Leading Example: Zeppelin NT, Germany
Positives: Do not need a runway to take off

Electric Bicycles
In an attempt to solve the problem of increasingly congested streets the electric bikes combine the convenience and simplicity of riding a bike with electric power thereby increasing the speed and ease at which you can get from A to B.
Leading Example: YikeBike ($3,500)

Backpack Helicopter
A backpack helicopter consists of strapping a helicopter motor and rotor to an individual's back. It has been suggested that it will function significantly better than a jet-pack, which has had very few successful flights.
Negatives: Significant training will be required to use

MagLev Trains
Using magnetic-levitation, trains are propelled forwards at higher speeds than wheeled mass transit systems, with the potential to even reach speeds of 640 km/h. Not only being significantly faster than conventional trains, they will emit less CO_2 and will be much quieter.
Leading Example: Transport, Shangai, China
Negatives: Incompatible with existing tracks

Segway
A 2-wheeled mode of transport running from electricity which allow the user to travel as speeds of up to 20 km/h along a pavement.
Negatives: Is not classified as a bike and is not often allowed on the roads limiting how fast the user will potentially be able to travel

SlideWalks
Similar to the travelators you find in airports, slidewalks will replace a high percentage of conventional pavements in major cities, allowing passengers to travel at higher speeds than walking whist also reducing pedestrian congestion.
Leading Example: Trottoir roulant rapide, Paris - Top Speed: 9 km/h during tests
Negatives: Cost of implementation

Info

Incoterms are international commercial terms, which are published by the International Chamber of Commerce, and have an impact on the contract of carriage of goods. Incoterms identify at what moment the seller or the buyer is responsible for the movement of the goods, the insurance, and when this responsibility is transferred to the other party. Common incoterms include: ex-Work, FOB (free on board), CIP (carriage and insurance paid to)...

b) Discuss in class.

1. With the ever-increasing demand for "green" means of transport, what do you think the future holds?

2. How would this tie in with sustainable development?

SEE CHAPTER "ENVIRONMENT" PAGE 211.

2 • Read and write

a) Work in pairs or small groups.
How many means of transportation do you know?
Fill in the table, and then write a sentence to describe each of them.
Give the French translation. Brainstorm all the words in a group.

Transport	Description	French	Transport	Description	French
Hovercraft	A vehicle that travels on land or water on a cushion of air	*Aéroglisseur*	Freight train	A train for transporting goods	*Train de marchandises*

b) To follow up, each team can prepare a word puzzle for another team, using the vocabulary.

3 • Read and understand

a) Read the short text.

The issue of transportation is on the front burner and many cities and states are heading toward bettering infrastructures. Atlanta, Ga., has a long list of projects to keep Georgia competitive and offers Atlantans better public transport. But Atlanta is one city among others to be willing to spend more per head on transport. There are many more in the United States.

b) Complete each sentence with words from the following list.

streetcar systems • *rail network* • *the longest average rush-hour commute* • *tram lines* • *worst traffic* • *high-speed rail* • *shorten travel*

1. It is estimated that Atlantans have ... in America: 127 minutes.
2. Atlanta has the ... as half the state's population lives in the Atlanta metropolitan area.
3. Creating a ... would ease traffic and reduce pollution at the same time.
4. Building railway and ... is also part of the greening of cities.
5. However, even if Mr. Obama allotted $8 billion for ... projects, many estimate that it is a slow-moving progress of the rail infrastructure in the United States.
6. 22 cities are exploring new ... . Streetcars were deprioritised under the Bush Administration because they don't ... times.

4 • Listen and understand

CD n° 3
Track n° 23

a) What business activities are mentioned?
b) Which pair of words is a synonym for the most important part of something?
d) Would you like to work in logistics? Can you explain why, or why not?

9 | Transport and logistics

WARMING UP

► What problems are raised by airport extensions?

CD n° 3 Track n° 24

Beijing set to become biggest aviation hub

Beijing is moving to overtake London as the world's busiest aviation hub with construction of a third airport that could have nine runways. The mega-project – part of a huge expansion of China's airline industry – has alarmed environmental groups, who warn aircraft will increasingly contribute to the country's already dire pollution problems and high greenhouse gas emissions.

The government has yet to announce details, but there are signs of construction in the rural district of Daxing, about 50 km south-west of the city centre.

It was only four years ago that the existing airport in the north of the city opened a huge third terminal ahead of the Beijing Olympics. Designed by the British architect Norman Foster, it was then the world's biggest airport building, with more floor space than all five Heathrow terminals combined. But it has filled faster than expected due to China's rapid economic growth. Last year the airport handled 73.9 million passengers. By 2015 this is likely to rise to 90 million – 12 million more than it was designed for.

Beijing authorities have said they will start work this year on land acquisition and demolition for a new airport. In addition to a semi-military airport in Nanyuan, this first phase – due for completion in 2015 – will give the city the capacity to handle 120 million passengers a year. Depending on growth, this would see Beijing overtake London and Tokyo, which each had about 100 million in 2010. Even by Chinese standards, the proposals for the later stages of construction are staggering. Once completed, the airport will be connected to a new expressway and high-speed train line that will speed travelers to the centre of the city in 30 minutes.

Many others hope for economic benefits, and not just in Beijing. China's aviation industry is already booming. Last year it reported a profit of 43bn yuan ($6.7bn), triple the figure of the previous year. In the next 20 years, China is forecast to buy 4,300 jet aircraft.

The Guardian Weekly, 16 September 2011

Lexical work

1. Find the English equivalents in the text.

a) une plate-forme de correspondances § 1
b) dépasser § 1
c) piste d'atterrissage § 1
d) désastreux § 1
e) aérogare § 3
f) desservir § 3

2. Find the French equivalents.

a) due for completion § 4
b) to handle § 4
c) staggering § 4
d) to speed § 4
e) to be booming § 5

3. Work on figures: write in full and read aloud.

73.9m • 2015 • 90m • 120m • 43bn • 4,300

Pronunciation work

CD n° 3 Track n° 25

1. Listen and observe.

aviation • alarmed • announce (2) • acquisition

"a" can be pronounced either [ɑː]: dark or [æ]: black or [ə]: alone.

2. Listen and fill in the grid according to the "a" in the following words.

aviation • have • part • China • alarmed • warm • gas • ahead • faster • last • passengers • start • about

[ɑ]: dark	[æ]: black	[ə]: alone

Info

Beijing Capital International Airport is the main international airport that serves the capital city of Beijing, People's Republic of China. It had become the busiest airport in Asia in terms of passenger traffic and total traffic movements by 2009.

Work on the title

1. Identify the source of the document (title, date, nature).
2. Look at the headline and explain it in your own words with the help of the info box.

Check the facts

1. Read §1.
a) What is the world's busiest aviation hub?
b) How many runways will the new airport have?
c) What term does the journalist use to qualify the project?
d) What do environmental groups think of the project?

2. Read §2.
Where will it be built?

3. Read §3.
a) What happened for the 2008 Olympic Games?
b) How many passengers were there in 2010?
c) How many are expected by 2015?

4. Read §4.
a) How many passengers did London and Tokyo handle in 2010?
b) What will be built once the airport is completed?

5. Read §5.
Who is in favour of this project?

Grammar

→ p. 238

Les propositions relatives

• *The mega-project ... has alarmed environmental groups, who warn aircraft ...*

Topic debrief

1. Choose the sentence which best corresponds to the main topic of the document.
a) Beijing is only interested in overtaking London.
b) Beijing is about to build its third airport as there are more and more passengers.
c) Beijing is so ambitious that it will build a third airport that is not necessary.

2. Write a short introduction with the help of the word bank.
to be entitled • to tackle a topical issue • to be published • to be related to • country • reasons for building • growth rate • Chinese population • Beijing

Methods

Write about the two different points of view by completing the sentences.
a) Some Chinese workers are quite happy to ... .
b) Environmental groups see the building of a third airport ... .
c) The airline industry is all in favour of ... .
d) Building a new airport in a rural area will turn the area into ... .
e) The government is eager to project a prestigious image so ... .

Train for the exam

1. Make a summary / account of the document (60 words / 3-5 minutes).
Use the sentences written for "Methods" and the following expressions: On the one hand ... / On the other hand ...

2. Comment: find an answer to the following question. Discuss and give examples (100 words / 3-5 minutes).
Why has China been accused of having invested in gigantic projects that have not always been built according to rules? Find arguments against building such a huge airport.

3. Role play: work in pairs
You are going to take part in a conversation.
Student A: you are a passenger going to Beijing and you ask your travel agency about the Beijing airport (Where will you land? How can you go from the airport to the city centre? Taxi? Public transport? Hotels?).
Student B: you represent the travel agency.

TIPS
Some examples of arguments: to resettle farmers; to be relocated; to be misconceived; to build on farmland; to be shoddily constructed; human migrations; to be forced to move; to be offered poor compensation; to have no consultation with the people whose land will be taken away; to undervalue the farmers' plots of land; etc.

9 | Transport and logistics

Train with an oral document

WARMING UP
- Are you a collectible car person?
- Which cars have become legends?

CD n° 3 Track n° 26

The Jeep is jumpin'

A 2012 Jeep Wrangler is shown next to the assembly line at Chrysler Group's Toledo Assembly complex, in Toledo, Ohio.

Lexical work

Match the words to find their equivalents.

a) issued	**1.** made
b) purpose	**2.** aim
c) vehicle	**3.** published
d) manufactured	**4.** injured
e) hand-built	**5.** arms
f) wounded	**6.** car
g) weapons	**7.** a little
h) slightly	**8.** handmade

Pronunciation work

CD n° 3 Track n° 27

1. Listen and observe.

Jeep • vehicle • believe • reason • grease • received • appearance

The sound [i :] may come from the combination of different vowels.

2. Listen to these words that you may find difficult and repeat.

1940 • the wounded • Popeye • World War Two • luxury

Work on the title

1. Look at the title of the document.

2. What do you know about the Jeep? Try to explain the title of the document.

Check the facts

1. Listen to part 1.

a) When was it manufactured?
b) Where was it manufactured?
c) How long did it take to create this new all-terrain vehicle?
d) Who requested the automobile industry to come up with a new model?
e) What was its use during WWII?

2. Listen to part 2.

a) What was the Jeep named after?
b) What happened at the end of the war?
c) What needed to be improved for it to be bought by civilians?
d) Is there a difference between the American market and international markets?
e) What has been improved with the newest Jeep?

Topic debrief

1. Choose the sentence which best corresponds to the main topic of the document.

a) A Jeep is an old-fashioned car everybody has forgotten.
b) The Jeep was one of the famous American military cars and now it has gained a place among American consumers.
c) The Jeep is a war vehicle so it does not appeal to people anymore since it reminds them of dark periods in the American story.

2. Write an introduction to the document by using the word bank (40 words).

during the Second World War • the city of Butler • a combat vehicle • to transport the wounded • to lay telephone communications • a powerful weapon • the civilian market • safety • comfort • a Jeep pickup • the international market

Methods

1. Rephrase the correct sentence (from "Topic debrief") and add info heard in the document to write two sentences on each part of the document.

2. There are famous inventions in war times. Use the Jeep (and the Internet) to explain why they were created and what their advantages and drawbacks are.

Train for the exam

1. Use your notes to make an **oral presentation** about the Jeep from its early beginning to what it has become today and record yourself (3-5 minutes).

2. Comment: find an answer to the following questions. Discuss and give examples (100 words / 3-5 minutes).
a) What are the advantages of public transport?
b) What do you think of the use of women in car ads? Describe a recent car and express your opinion.

3. Role play: work in groups

You are going to take part in a debate.
Group A: you are a Jeep aficionado, however you strongly believe that public transport should be developed in the U.S. List arguments in favour of public transport.
Group B: you are against public transport and in favour of individual cars.

TIPS

• Here are phrases to help you respond:
I strongly believe / I think you are wrong in thinking that / I must say that I do not quite agree with you / you might be partly right but ...
• You should use your notes in order to present a realistic conversation. Don't read them, look up.
You can:
– record the conversation (the recording should last between one and two minutes at most);
– videotape the scene and show it to the class;
– act out the scene in front of the class;
– listen to your classmates' recordings and write what you have understood in a short and structured paragraph.

Go online

• Find out more about the place of Detroit in the American car industry.
• Get prepared to report to your group / class (a PowerPoint presentation is recommended).

PRACTICE • AUDIO

WARMING UP

- Have you ever been in an electric car?
- What are the main debatable characteristics of electric cars?

CD n° 3 Track n° 28

Electric cars highly charged

China has lots of people, not much oil and rulers who love big projects. Small wonder that makers of electric cars see it as the market of the future. The Chinese government wants to have 500,000 electric cars, lorries and buses on the country's roads by 2015 and 5m by 2020. It is providing customers with subsidies worth up to 60,000 yuan ($9,250) and other incentives, too. If it carries on doing so, electric cars and plug-in hybrids could account for 7% of new-car sales in China by 2020, assuming an oil price of $130 a barrel, says a forthcoming report by the Boston Consulting Group. That would make China the biggest market for electric vehicles, by volume, in the world.

Foreign firms are salivating. But they are also nervous. The price for market access has gone up as foreign producers are being told about new "draft" rules which mean they must share more intellectual property and branding rights with their Chinese joint-venture partners.

On June 27th Carlos Ghosn, the boss of Nissan – which with its partner Renault is taking the biggest electric car bet by launching a range of plug-in models – said he would wait to learn more about the new policy before deciding how many electric cars Nissan will make in China (including the new Nissan Leaf). "We will adapt our strategy to the rules," he added.

As a new generation of electric cars, such as the Nissan Leaf, arrive in showrooms worldwide, China's home-grown contender is absent. BYD, a battery-maker turned car-maker, is struggling to get its new e6 electric car to market. It is now being tested by taxi fleets in Shenzhen, where BYD is based.

The Chinese government could juice up the market for the e6 and its foreign rivals by insisting that more taxis and government vehicles switch to electric. But persuading Chinese consumers may be harder. Electric car-makers typically claim that their vehicles can travel a long way without recharging, but that range can fall by a third or more if you turn on the air-conditioning, accelerate hard or otherwise drive normally. BYD claims that the e6 has a range of 300 km (186 miles), which is about twice that of Nissan's Leaf. Motoring hacks have yet to put that claim to a good road test.

The Economist, June 30th, 2011

Lexical work

1. Find their English equivalents in the text.

§1, 2

a) dirigeants **b)** camions **c)** fournir **d)** subventions **e)** incitations **f)** des voitures hybrides à brancher **g)** un baril

§ 4, 5

a) les salles d'exposition **b)** flotte de taxis **c)** la climatisation

2. Match the words to find their equivalents.

a) intellectual property **b)** branding rights **c)** draft

1. une première mouture de réglementation

2. propriété intellectuelle

3. droits / lois relatives à l'utilisation de la marque

Pronunciation work

CD n° 3 Track n° 29

1. Listen and observe.

China • Boston • Carlos Ghosn • Nissan • Shenzhen

Family names and places may be difficult to pronounce, all the more so as they are often not pronounced like in French! Practise repeating these words aloud.

2. Key words of "Transport".

a) Look at the following words. All of them contain the sound [ɪ], except for one word which contains the sound [ai] and one word which contains the sound [i:]. Identify these words.

subsidies • incentives • hybrids • electric vehicles • taxi fleets • switch

b) Practise repeating these words aloud.

Info

Joint venture (joint ventures, plural): a business or project in which two or more companies or individuals have invested, with the intention of working together.
It will be sold to a joint venture created by Dow Jones and Westinghouse Broadcasting.

Work on the title

1. Identify the source of the document (title, date, nature).

2. Look at the headline. There is a pun on the word "charged". Find it and explain the title.

Check the facts

1. Read §1.
a) What are the three reasons to move to electric cars?
b) How many vehicles are expected to be on the road by 2015?
c) What will the Chinese government do to incite customers to buy electric cars?

2. Read §2.
a) What are the reactions from foreign car-makers?
b) What are the new "draft" rules?

3. Read §3.
a) What does Mr. Ghosn want to do?
b) What does Nissan want to launch?

4. Read §4.
What is BYD? What are they testing? Where?

5. Read §5.
a) What could the government do to increase the number of electric cars?
b) Why will Chinese customers be hard to convince?

Grammar

→ p. 239

Les subordonnées introduites par *if*
- *If it carries on doing so ...*

Topic debrief

1. Choose the sentence which you think corresponds best to the main topic of the document.
a) China is about to launch its first electric car.
b) China is thinking of introducing electric cars on a large scale.
c) China's government has planned to have 500,000 electric vehicles by 2015.

2. Write an introduction to the document by using the word bank.
to be entitled • to be published • to deal with or to tackle the issue • to be a topical issue • a play on the word • to have several meanings • the title refers to ... • to imply that • to apply the word "charged" to cars and emotions

Methods

Fill in the blanks in the following summary.

The ... government wants to boost the number of ... vehicles in the country to reach ... by 2015 and ... by 2020. However electric ... are expensive so the government will provide ...with ... to make them buy ....
The reason for boosting the manufacturing of electric cars is that oil can cost up to ... a barrel. So it is better to introduce ... vehicles and ... hybrids so China will not have to rely so much on oil imports.

Train for the exam

1. Make a summary / account of the document (60 words / 3-5 minutes).

2. Comment: find an answer to the following question. Discuss and give examples (100 words / 3-5 minutes).
What are the disadvantages of "highly charged" cars in the last §?

3. Role play: work in pairs
You are going to take part in a conversation.
Student A: you would like to buy a new car. You meet a car dealer who suggests you try the Nissan Leaf and the BYD e6. You are not totally convinced.
Student B: you are a car dealer. You show A the advantages of an electric car and you come up with the drawbacks. Use the last § to find arguments. Think of the price.

Go online
Here is a site to help you out: http://www.electric-cars-are-for-girls.com/electric-car-advantages.html

9 | Transport and logistics

Train with an oral document

CD n° 3
Track n° 30

Smaller cars scale the U.S.

WARMING UP

- Is everything bigger in America: flats, houses, cars ...?
- Why are the American cars bigger?
- Do you think they can change their buying habits?

Lexical work

1. Match the following words to find their equivalents.

a) shift	**1.** recognise
b) thriving	**2.** slowdown
c) downsizing	**3.** taking
d) downturn	**4.** change
e) acquiring	**5.** shrinking
f) acknowledge	**6.** booming

2. Find the odd word out.

a) closeness – far away– proximity
b) ingredients – components – amount
c) gained – lost – obtained
d) explained by – accounted to – ignored

3. Work on figures: write in full and read aloud.

$100 • 4th season • the Big 3 • 10 years • 2013

Pronunciation work

CD n° 3
Track n° 31

1. Observe and understand.

automobile • vehicle • retirement • acquiring

2. Listen and fill in the grid according to the words' pronunciation.

thriving • type • examined • high • impact • styling

retirement – acquiring [aɪ]	automobile – vehicle [ɪ]

3. Listen to these words that you may find difficult and repeat.

gas • diesel • German • engineered • acknowledge • economic downturn • sustainability

Work on the title

1. Look at the title of the document.

2. What do you think "scale" means in the context.

Check the facts

1. Listen to part 1.

a) Who is it about?
b) In which country?
c) What is the new trend on the car market?
d) What are the reasons for this move? (4)

2. Listen to part 2.

a) Who are the car manufacturers mentioned?
b) Why is it difficult to make a distinction between German and American cars?
c) Are the words in the slogan in English?
d) Who is responsible for this new love for European cars, according to Sheryl Connelly?
e) What have Ford and General Motors in common?
f) What about diesel cars? Who makes them and for which market?

Info

The **Big Three**, when used in relation to the automotive industry, most generally refers to the three major American automotive companies: Ford, General Motors and Chrysler.

Topic debrief

1. Choose the sentence which you think corresponds best to the main topic of the document.
a) North Americans are getting a taste for more European-style vehicles.
b) American consumers like big cars, especially baby boomers.
c) More and more Americans live in cities so there is no need for big cars.

2. Rephrase the correct sentence in order to make a short introduction to the document.

Methods

1. Complete the following sentences with your own words.
a) It is a well-known fact that Americans … .
b) American consumers are gradually turning away from the notion that … .
c) Baby boomers are … .

2. What are the four reasons explaining this new trend?

Train for the exam

1. Use your notes to make an **oral presentation** about the document and record yourself (3-5 minutes).

2. Comment: find an answer to the following question. Discuss and give examples (100 words/3-5 minutes).
Why has the car market become global?

3. Role play: work in pairs
You are going to take part in a sales pitch.
Student A: you are a car seller. Prepare your sales pitch to convince your customer.
Student B: you are a customer. You are interested in new types of vehicles.

TIPS
Keep in mind where car manufacturers operate, if they offer the same model on international markets, how the same model could be slightly modified to appeal to another type of customer. Do not forget to mention the Japanese car industry in the U.S.

PRACTICE • AUDIO • VIDEO

Train with a video

International transportation and export management

→ http://www.youtube.com/watch?v=qDbnx6nLrQo

31 August, 2008

Look at this video on the Internet about logistics

Check the facts	Methods
1. What activities are dealt with in this video?	• What are the first four images shown in the video? • Why are they important?
2. What is the importance of such activities? Who are the people in charge of logistics?	• What is said about the bicycle? • Which jobs are mentioned?
3. What are the various steps shown in the video?	• What does the "pipeline" explain?
4. What is said about the logistics system?	• Why is "the right time" repeated?
5. **Issues …** What are the problems raised by goods transport?	• Do you think that the transport of goods is necessary? • Which alternatives can you imagine?

CD n° 3 Track n° 32

Looking east

WARMING UP

► Do you mind flying with low-cost companies?

In Africa, the skies are busier than ever before and the airlines more efficient. The best African carriers can compete with the old colonial giants, British Airways and Air France. New routes open monthly.

Several companies stand out for being profitable, international and growing. Of these the largest are EgyptAir, South African Airways (SAA) and Royal Air Maroc (RAM). All three operate from corners of the continent: RAM in the north-west, EgyptAir in the north-east and SAA in the south. But the future may lie with the slightly smaller but fast-growing airlines in the middle: Kenya Airways ("The Pride of Africa") flies to 42 non-domestic African cities, up from 16 in 2000; Ethiopian Airlines ("The Next Spirit of Africa") serves 35 African cities outside Ethiopia, up from 22.

Ethiopian is state-owned and some analysts doubt it is profitable as it claims. Last year the airline says it earned a $118m profit on revenue of $1.3 billion. Its passenger numbers, which no one doubts, have grown by 20% a year for the past decade. Its bosses predict that its revenues and passenger numbers will increase six-fold by 2025. It has ordered three dozen new Boeing and Airbus airplanes.

Kenya Airways is 23%-owned by the Kenyan government; KLM, a Dutch airline, has 26%. Its strategy is to spread its wings throughout Africa, with a new fleet of Brazilian Embraer jets. This month it announced a 74% increase in after-tax profits: $45m on revenue of $1.1 billion. It was a tough year, the airline says, thanks to political unrest in Côte d'Ivoire and elsewhere. Most of the profit came from successfully hedging fuel costs. The firm expects to do better this year.

Plenty of challenges remain. Safety has improved a lot, but not enough. Too many planes are old and tired. The EU has banned some smaller African airlines from European airspace.

IATA says African airports are among the costliest in the world, and offer shoddy service. Nairobi has iffy security and few comforts. A lack of competition on many routes has led to inflated prices. Flying from Addis to Nairobi is nearly as costly as flying to Europe. Between Uganda's Entebbe airport and Nairobi, by contrast, competition is fiercer and prices reasonable. Fliers hope that spunky new budget airlines, such as Arik Air in Nigeria, Fly540 in Kenya and 1Time in South Africa, will keep Africa's elephants on their toes.

The Economist, June 18th 2011

Info

IATA: the International Air Transport Association (IATA) represents, leads and serves the airline industry. Its members comprise all major passenger and cargo airlines. IATA is an international trade body, created over 60 years ago. Today, IATA represents some 230 airlines.

Lexical work

1. Find the English equivalents in the text.

a) les longs courriers § 1
b) des destinations § 1
c) à forte croissance § 2
d) international § 2
e) desservir § 2
f) public / appartenir au secteur public § 3
g) prétendre / affirmer § 3
h) se multiplier par six § 3

2. Find their French equivalents.

a) to spread its wings § 4 **b)** a fleet § 4
c) to hedge § 4 **d)** to ban § 5 **e)** shoddy § 6
f) iffy § 6 **g)** spunky § 6

Pronunciation work

CD n° 3 Track n° 33

1. Listen to these words that you may find difficult and repeat.

throughout • enough • south • Ethiopian • hedging • European airspace

2. Work on figures: write in full and read aloud.

42 • 16 • 2000 • $1.3 billion • 74%

Work on the title

1. Identify the source of the document (title, date, nature).
2. Look at the headline and the 1st paragraph. Explain the title of the document.

Check the facts

1. Read §1.
What has improved a lot?

2. Read §2.
a) Which airlines are profitable, international and growing?
b) Which airlines are considered the future?

3. Read §3. Let's focus on Ethiopian Airlines.
a) Who owns it?
b) What will happen by 2025?

4. Read §4. About Kenya Airways ...
a) Who owns Kenya Airways?
b) What type of aircraft did they buy?
c) How was most of the profit made?

5. Read §5.
What challenges do the two airlines face?

6. Read §6.
a) What is the point of view of IATA?
b) What do fliers expect low-cost airlines will do?

Grammar

→ p. 233, 239

Les adjectifs composés

• *fast-growing airlines* = airlines that are growing fast
• *state-owned* = owned by the state

Les pronoms personnels

• *Ethiopian is state-owned and some analysts doubt it profitable as it claims.*

Topic debrief

1. Choose the sentence which best corresponds to the main topic of the document.
a) African airlines are competing with the old colonial giants.
b) African airlines are expanding thanks to trade from the east.
c) African Airlines have become fierce competitors in their own right.

2. Write an introduction of the document by using the following words.
to be entitled • to be published • to deal with / to be about • misleading (trompeur) *• airline companies • Africa • colonial carriers • to be replaced • on the rise*

Methods

1. Make a presentation of the various African companies quoted in the document with the help of the following word box.
to be on the rise • to expand • to have more passengers • to grow fast • non-domestic flights • to serve • state-owned vs private • profits

2. Complete the following sentences with your own words.
a) Although some African airlines are growing rapidly ....
b) Ethiopian Airlines has seen the number of ....
c) IATA is very critical of some African airlines because ....
d) Passengers believe that the coming of budget airlines will ....
e) Airlines offer tickets at very high prices because ....

Train for the exam

1. Make a **summary / account** of the document (60 words / 3-5 minutes).

2. Comment: find an answer to the following question. Discuss and give examples (100 words / 3-5 minutes).
Which are the most high performing: regular or low-cost airlines?

3. **Role play: work in pairs**
You are going to take part in a business appointment.
Student A: you are an IATA agent. You have an appointment with an African airline director at his office. You want to build an airport with a successful African company. Create your business card for the first contact.
Student B: you are a Managing Director at Kenya Airways. You introduce yourself then your company, its growth, your expectations.

Dealing with logistics problems

1 • Situation

You work for the procurement department at Yarwell Yacht Club. The company has a very busy summer season coming up and would like to renew their stock of sails, ropes, kitbags and other equipment for their boats.

2 • Process

a) Look at the following documents (on the next page).
b) Get into pairs.
Students A: you work for Yarwell Yacht Club.
Students B: you work for Speedy Sails Ltd.
c) *Students A:* using the example, you write up a purchase order to send to Speedy Sails Ltd / students B.
d) Now discuss the purchase order sent. Remember to speak in English only!
Students B: you receive the purchase order (Document B) from Yarwell Yacht Club / students A. You cannot meet the delivery time on the purchase order. You call Yarwell Yacht Club / students A and negotiate another delivery deadline.

→ FOR MORE INFORMATION ON PREPARING A NEGOTIATION, SEE "TOOLS" PAGE 248.

e) A few days later...
Students B: using the examples, you make out a delivery note and an invoice for Yarwell Yacht Club / students A. There must be some discrepancies between the delivery note and the invoice (for example, quantities, unit price, you forget to add the usual quantity discount or a discount for loyal customers...).
f) *Students A:* you receive the invoice from Speedy Sails Ltd / students B. There is a difference between what you received (and signed for on the delivery note) and the invoice. You call Speedy Sails / students B to complain.

3 • Follow up

– *Students A:* send an e-mail to Speedy Sails confirming what you have agreed on the telephone.
– *Students B:* send an e-mail to Yarwell Yacht Club apologizing for the mistake and the inconvenience and offering a special discount on their next order as compensation.

@ Go online

Use the search engine to find other examples of purchase orders, delivery notes and invoices.

TIPS

Start by saying
Students B: *I am afraid ... / I am sorry but ... Would you accept delivery on ...? /Would the 15th be convenient?*
Students A: *I'm sorry to bother you but there would seem to be a mistake ... / Unless I am wrong, there is a difference between ... / Could you just double-check the invoice, do you think?*

Doc • A

Doc • B

SPEEDY SAILS Ltd — PURCHASE ORDER

Your company name: (+ address / phone number / e-mail address)			**Date:**
Account number:		**P.O. Number:**	
Vendor:	**Ship to:**		**Delivery date:**
Name:	**Name:**		
Address		**Address**	
REQUISITIONER	**SHIP VIA**	**F.O.B. Point**	**SHIPPING TERMS**

QTY (Quantity)	**UNIT**	**DESCRIPTION**	**UNIT PRICE**	**TOTAL**

Authorised by:	Sub total	
Date: _ _ / _ _ / _ _	Sales Tax	
(The P.O. number must appear on all retail correspondence, shipping papers and invoices)	Shipping & handling	
	TOTAL	

SPEEDY SAILS Ltd — DELIVERY NOTE

Your company name: (+ address / phone number / e-mail address)	**Page**...... **of**......
	P.O. Number:
Delivery address:	**Date:**
	Customer N°:

Stock code	**Description**	**Unit**	**Quantity**

Payment: 30 days	**Delivery accepted**
Ref:	**Name:** ....
Company registration N°:	**Date:** ....
	Signature: ....

SPEEDY SAILS Ltd — INVOICE

Your company name: (+ address / phone number / e-mail address)	**Invoice N°:**
BILL TO:	**SHIP TO:**
Name:	**Name:**
Adress:	**Address:**

Purchase Order N°	**Sales Rep. Name**	**Ship Date**	**Ship Via**	**Terms**	**Due Date**

Ref N°	**Description**	**Qty**	**Unit Price**	**Line Total**

Sub Total	
Sales Tax	
Shipping & handling	
TOTAL	
Less Paid	
TOTAL DUE	

ROLE PLAY

9 | Transport and logistics

Background *Almost everything (people, food, petrol, etc.) needs to be moved from one place to another at one time. For this, we need different means of transport either overland (using road or rail), through the air or across the water (rivers, canals and the sea). Transport means more than just trains, planes and lorries,* (→ SEE "STARTERS" PAGE 172) *because huge infrastructures (motorways, railway lines, airports, etc.) are also required.*

1 What are the main means of transport?

Rail transport: Rail freight is the most fuel-efficient and environmentally friendly way of transporting goods overland, and often the cheapest, but the drawback is that goods trains cannot deliver to the door, so it is not flexible enough for many companies and has led to a decline in rail freight. A combination of road and rail freight services is usually on offer from **freight forwarders**.

Road transport: The advantage of the national highway systems is that trucks can transport freight door-to-door and in their own time, meeting JIT requirements. However, there are many lobbies against road haulage – environmentalists because of the environmental impact, and the general public as truck-related casualties are on the increase, with bigger and bigger trucks and higher demands on **lorry drivers** who can drive for too long without stopping. In 2010, just over 2/3 of total freight transport in Europe was on the roads.

Air transport: 14.2 million tonnes of national and international freight was handled by EU airports in 2009. Although air freight is fast and practical for the mail and urgent or perishable goods, it is expensive and not adapted for bulky or heavy freight.

Water transport: Compared to other means of transport, water transport is relatively slow, but more economical and leaves less of a carbon footprint.

Segway

Questions

- What different kinds of freight transport are there?
- What do you think of the recent developments in rail and road transport?
- What can be done about the environmental impact of transporting goods?

2 What recent developments have there been?

Environmental concern has led to the creation of TOFC (trailer on flatcar) or "piggy-backing". The trailer of the lorry becomes a special wagon, called "EuroSpine", which is just re-attached to the cab for local delivery.

High-speed train (or "bullet train") networks are expanding throughout the world. The fastest is a Chinese train which travels at average speeds of up to 350 kph!

Driverless commuter trains are the cause of many debates for employment and safety reasons.

New IT tools for road haulage firms will allow progress in terms of **traceability**, performance and route calculations, leading to greater safety and reductions in fuel consumption.

Growing demands for JIT delivery, "make-to-order" and small IT components from low-cost countries have led to growth in world air freight traffic (6% predicted over the next 15 years).

3 What safety and ecological measures are being taken?

Higher technical standards and rail corridor requirements to eliminate bottlenecks or weak links and establish best practice standards throughout Europe should help meet increasing demand. The electrification of railway lines not only reduces the impact on the environment, but electric trains are easier and cheaper to maintain.

As **freight flow** increases, the European Commission (→ SEE CHAPTER "EUROPE" PAGE 144) has launched several measures to reduce the number of road traffic accidents by half. Added to this are 3 road safety requirements for hauliers: good repute, a certain financial standing and CPC (Certificate of Professional Competence).

Info

Keeping the goods off the roads: according to the *Guinness Book of Records*, the heaviest freight train ever weighed over 90.5 million kilos and was more than 7.3 km long. That is the equivalent of roughly 537 lorries.

Focus

Competing for the Indian compact car market: Tata's Nano versus Ford's Figo

Emerging countries such as India are attracting many companies eager to do business. The car industry is one area where much money can be made. We may assume that a domestic car-maker such as Tata Motors should be better able to figure out the type of cars Indians might be interested in buying as their first purchase. However, it is not so simple. Let's have a look at Tata's Nano and Ford's Figo.

The Nano

Tata, Nano

Info

Tata Motors is part of India's biggest business conglomerate, the Tata Group. It started as a locomotive and truck maker and gradually built market share in the car business over the last 20 years on the strength of modestly priced cars and sport utility vehicles. Its chairman, Ratan Tata, will be replaced by Cyprus Mistry in December 2012 at its Mumbai headquarters. It manufactures different types of vehicles: compact, mid-size, commercial and trucks. In 2008 it bought the luxury car brand Jaguar Land Rover.

Description

- Introduced on the Indian market in early 2009.
- Nicknamed the "wonder car". It is a symbol of frugal innovation.
- Is the world's cheapest car at one "lakh" (100,000 rupees, roughly $2,500, before tax when introduced in 2009).
- It is simple, small and fuel-efficient: it can seat up to five people; it is a four-door model; its air-cooled engine is in the back, like the original Volkswagen Beetle.
- Attracted orders for more than 200,000 Nanos in 2010 in India.

Questions

- What might be likely reasons for not buying the cheapest car?
- Has the Nano long-term potential?
- What would a first-time small-car buyer expect from a small car? Safety? Availability? Allure?
- Can a small car and a cheap car satisfy every type of consumer?

Strategy

- First, the Nano targets the Indian market: 13 million cars are expected to sell in the short term.
- Then the Nano goes global – first in other developing countries and then Europe and possibly even the United States.

Reasons for a modern-day people's car

- To bring greater mobility to the masses of India.
- Its likely buyers are aspiring families who will swap their overloaded motorbikes for compact, air-conditioned four-wheelers.
- Car sales are likely to shoot up in India because the economy is growing at nearly 9 percent annually. And in 2011 the car market was booming in India.
- Some Nano owners – there are now more than 71,000 – praise the car's performance, its fuel efficiency and its surprisingly spacious interior.

Tata's Nano: a failed strategy in its home market. Why?

- The Nano faced strong social unrest when farmers were displaced to allow the building of the manufacturing plant, which led to disruption in the supply chain: Tata had to relocate the factory to another state, Gujarat.
- A wave of safety scares; reports of fires have hurt the sales.
- Pricing was higher than predicted because of a lack of volume.
- A misunderstanding of the Indian emerging middle-class aspiration, a steady decrease of its sales by the end of 2010.
- A failed marketing campaign which didn't reach the targeted audience.
- The necessity to export the Nano to other developing countries (i.e. Sri Lanka).

9 | Transport and logistics

Focus → The Figo

Figo, Ford

Ford's Figo: a successful strategy overseas. Why?

- Indians are more likely to buy smaller cars.
- It invested $500 million to double the plant's production capacity.
- Production techniques are eco-friendly: fewer carbon dioxide emissions.
- Major advances in high-quality automation are used.
- It has two engine options: petrol and diesel.
- It is presented as a luxury small car.
- The car design is bold and muscular with spacious interiors.

Info

Ford Motor Company is one of the "Big Three" in the USA with General Motors and Chrysler. It was founded by Henry Ford in 1903. It is the second largest automaker in the U.S. and the fifth in the world. It manufactures almost 6 million cars per year and employs over 213,000 employees. It has 90 plants and units worldwide. Its domestic market is saturated and so Ford has expanded abroad, especially in China and India. Its CEO Alan Mulally said that Ford is developing small compact cars as 60% of the vehicles worldwide are smaller cars.

Description

- Introduced in early 2010 and means "cool" in Italian.
- Will be priced in the range of 3.5-4 lakh rupees.
- Manufactured in its plant near Chennai.
- Is designed to compete in India's small car segment.
- Has a very distinct and aggressive look.
- Can deal with congested urban driving conditions.
- Will be exported to South Africa and Asia.
- Won the Indian Car of the Year Award in 2011.
- Is selling so well that in February 2010, 28 sales and service facilities were opened.

Questions

- How can you explain that Tata Motors, an Indian car company, has been overtaken by its rivals?
- How can you account for such a success?
- What does winning awards bring to the company?
- Isn't the market big enough to have more than one automaker?

Express your point of view

- Reflecting on the small car market in India, should we not expect the domestic car-maker, Tata Motors, to be in a more comfortable position to launch a new product?
- Or are car-makers such as Ford or Suzuki more likely to understand the Indian car market as they are specialised in manufacturing and selling cars and have been doing it for much longer?

@ Go online

Tata Motors is one car-maker among others. Find out about the Maruti Suzuki Alto and other car competitors in India.

Test yourself

Try to use your memory – do not look at the vocabulary list!

1 SHIPPING

Find the word to match the definition.

a) Pick-up truck
b) Lead time
c) Tanker
d) Container
e) JIT
f) Deadline
g) Dispatch
h) Harbour
i) Procurement
j) Delay
k) Articulated lorry
l) Freight
m) Load
n) Trailer
o) Ship
p) Delivery
q) Haulier
r) Bulk

1	The time by which something must be completed		**10**	A smaller lorry, uncovered at the back, with low sides	
2	Goods carried by a commercial carrier		**11**	Dropping off goods at a designated destination	
3	The part of the lorry the goods go in		**12**	Ordering and obtaining goods	
4	In large volume		**13**	Sending goods somewhere	
5	A large 2-part lorry		**14**	Put the consignment on the vessel	
6	A standardised 10 / 20 / 40 ft. box which can be loaded from one means of transport to another		**15**	The time from order to the reception of the goods	
7	A large ocean-going vessel		**16**	A large vessel containing liquids	
8	Lateness		**17**	A firm that transports goods	
9	Goods available just when needed		**18**	A safe haven for ships – a natural port	

2 WHAT MEANS OF TRANSPORT?

Identify the means of transport.

a) Used for passengers and transporting lightweight goods, it travels at speeds of up to 950 kph and needs a lot of space to take off and land.

b) With between 4 and 22 wheels, these are used for transporting goods of any weight or size, and the occasional passenger (a hitchhiker*).

c) For both goods and passengers (who can choose between first and second class, or even a sleeper), this form of transport takes the weight off the road networks and is seen as more eco-friendly.

d) A short trip takes place on this regular service, usually by bus or train, which takes you for example from one part of an airport to another, or from one part of a city to another. There is even one under the English Channel!

e) Using the waterways, this slower way of transporting goods is also a way of life. It has become a very popular way of taking a holiday, travelling along canals.

f) Otherwise known as "inter-city" because they travel from one major city to another; on the ground, this form of transport competes against air and road travel.

* hitchhiker: *autostoppeur*

VOCABULARY

9 | Transport and logistics

Words

"Basically all the world's computer parts come from the same supply chain that runs from Korea, down through coastal China, over to Taiwan, and down to Malaysia." (Thomas Friedman)

Aeroplane / plane: avion
Aircraft: avion, appareil
Airline: compagnie aérienne
Airliner: avion de ligne
Airport: aéroport
Articulated lorry: semi-remorque
Barge: péniche
Behind schedule (to be): être en retard
Bulk (in): en gros / en vrac
Cancel (to): annuler
Car park: parking
Car pooling: co-voiturage
Cargo: cargaison
Carriage: transport
Carrier: transporteur
Container: conteneur
Container ship: porte conteneur
Cost & time efficiency: qui permet d'économiser de l'argent et du temps
Crew: équipage
Customs: douane
Customs clearance: dédouanement
Deadline: date ou heure limite
Delay: retard
Delivery: livraison
Dispatch: expédition
Distribution: distribution
Downtime: durée d'indisponibilité
Driver (lorry / truck): camionneur
Flight: vol
Flow: circulation
Freeway (US) / motorway (GB): autoroute
Freight: fret
Freight forwarder: transporteur
Global network: réseau mondial
Handle (to): manutentionner
Handling: manutention
Harbour: port
Haulier: transporteur (routier)
High-speed train: train à grande vitesse
Highway: route nationale
Hub: aéroport international
Just in time (JIT): juste à temps
Lead time: délai entre commande et livraison
Link (to): relier
Load: charge
Load (to): charger
Lorry (GB), truck (USA): camion
Lorry / truck driver: camionneur
Low-cost airlines: compagnies aériennes bon marché
Maiden flight / voyage: vol / voyage inaugural
Means of transport: moyen de transport
Metric ton: tonne (1,000 kg)
Network: réseau
Pick-up truck: camionnette
Platform: quai
Port: port
Procurement: approvisionnement
Purchase order: bon de commande
Railway network: réseau ferroviaire
Railway track / line: voie de chemin de fer
Railways: chemin de fer
Reroute (to): dérouter
Risk: risque
Road blockade: barrage routier
Route: trajet
Run / be on time (to): être à l'heure (train)
Safety standards: normes de sécurité
Security program: programme de sécurité
Ship: navire
Shipper: expéditeur
Shipment: cargaison, fret, expédition
Shipping: transport maritime / acheminement
Shuttle: navette
Sourcing: approvisionnement
Station: gare
Storage: stockage
Supply chain: chaîne logistique
Supply system: système d'appros
Tanker / supertanker: pétrolier (géant)
Terms: conditions
Time difference: décalage horaire
Timetable: horaire (bus, trains)
Traceability: traçabilité
Tracking: suivi
Trailer: remorque
Transportation: transport
Turnpike (USA): autoroute à péage
Van: utilitaire / camionnette
Vehicle: véhicule

10

Tourism

What are the trendy destinations for tourists?

Question

What do modern travelers look for?

WORD BOX

abroad • book (to) • booking • board (to) • delay • guide book • jet lag • low-cost company • luggage • tour operator • Paradise island • trip • relaxation

10 | Tourism

1 • Look and discuss

a) Look at the following pictures.

b) Discuss in class.

1. What kind of holidays are these and where do they take place?
2. What kind of holiday do you prefer and do you prefer travelling by plane, boat, train or car?
3. What do you think is the most popular kind of tourism at the moment for the British? What about the French?
4. Can you tell your classmates about a holiday experience you have had?

@ Go online
Look on the Internet and try to find out what kind of tourism the French prefer.

2 • Read and understand

Put the missing words into the text.

impacts • field • geared • know-how • agency • authorities • implementation • membership • policy • regional • promoting • destinations

The World Tourism Organization (UNWTO / OMT) is a specialised ... of the United Nations and the leading international organization in the ... of tourism. It serves as a global forum for tourism ... issues and a practical source of tourism ... .
UNWTO plays a central and decisive role in ... the development of responsible, sustainable and universally accessible tourism, paying particular attention to the interests of developing countries.
The Organization encourages the ... of the Global Code of Ethics for Tourism, with a view to ensuring that member countries, tourist ... and businesses maximise the positive economic, social and cultural effects of tourism and fully reap its benefits, while minimising its negative social and environmental ... .
Its ... includes 154 countries, 7 territories and over 400 Affiliate Members representing the private sector, educational institutions, tourism associations and local tourism ... .
Direct actions that strengthen and support the efforts of National Tourism Administrations are carried out by UNWTO's ... representatives (Africa, the Americas, East Asia and the Pacific, Europe, the Middle East and South Asia), based at the headquarters in Madrid.
UNWTO is committed to the United Nations Millennium Development Goals, ... toward reducing poverty and fostering sustainable development.

3 • Read and write

a) Read the following text.

An examination of information services and smartphone applications

The information services provided by smartphone applications identified in this study facilitate tourists' experience in many ways. First, the twelve categories of smartphone apps demonstrate that the range of mobile information services goes beyond the destination guides [...]. The smartphone apps can not only support tourists' information-processing activities such as connection and navigation in the tourism consumption stage, but also the activities in the pre-consumption and post-consumption stages. For example, the online travel agency apps can help tourists plan trips and complete online transactions as desktop or laptop computers do. The integration of experience-sharing functions in most apps enables tourists to share and document their experiences anytime and anywhere. Second, the information services of smartphone apps are personalised so that they can support many micro-moments in the travel process. For example, smartphone apps can help tourists find dog parks, restrooms and the cheapest gas stations. Such kinds of information services are minor but considerate, so that tourists can have a better travel experience. With the personalised services of smartphone apps, tourists feel like they are staying with a "perfect concierge" (from one customer review).

b) Answer by true or false.

1. Smartphones are only used by tourists to plan their holidays before they go.
2. Smartphone apps can give tourists lots of little but useful information.
3. It is possible that smartphone apps have an influence and even alter tourists' behaviour.
4. Smartphone apps are unable to give tourists made-to-measure information.
5. Smartphone apps make it easy for travellers to change their travel plans.
6. The information in the text is irrelevant to professionals in the tourist industry.

c) Answer the question by writing a few sentences.

1. In what ways can smartphones revolutionize tourism?
2. Imagine the ideal smartphone apps which could help you enjoy your weekend. What would it be able to tell you? You can imagine its logo.
3. Imagine an ideal smartphone app which would help you during your next summer holidays. What would it be able to tell you? You can imagine its logo.

4 • Listen and understand

CD n° 4
Track n° 1

a) Why does the man want an aisle seat and not a window seat?
b) Is the reference number 1558369 / AB78?
c) Have you ever missed a plane or train? If so, what happened?

10 | Tourism

WARMING UP

- Have you been to China?
- Have you noticed an increase in the number of Chinese tourists in Europe?

CD n° 4 Track n° 2

Spain aims to welcome one million Chinese tourists in 2020

Spain, Europe's second-most visited country after France, aims to welcome one million Chinese tourists in 2020, the government said Tuesday. The country received 89,523 Chinese tourists in 2009, the last year for which figures are available, and Tourism Minister Miguel Sebastian said this figure should rise to 300,000 in 2012.

To increase the number of visitors from China, Spain plans to ease visa requirements for Chinese nationals, encourage more direct flights between the two countries and open more tourist offices in the Asian giant, he added. The government also plans to publish guides about Spain in Mandarin and encourage restaurants and hotels to offer foods and opening hours that are suited to Chinese tastes. "This increase in the flow of tourists will increase knowledge about Spain in China and knowledge of China in Spain," Sebastian said at a China-Spain business forum in Barcelona.

Spain has just two tourist offices in China, in Beijing and Guangzhoo, and Air China, China's only national flag carrier, is currently the sole airline to offer direct flights between the two nations. The minister will present the government's plan to boost tourist arrivals from China, the world's most populous country, in Beijing on July 27. "We want to attract Chinese tourists, since Spain is a great country that has much to offer and where everyone can feel at home," Foreign Minister Trinidad Jimenez told the gathering.

While most of China's 1.3 billion people live on just a few dollars a day, the country is producing a burgeoning middle class that can dwarf the populations of many other countries, and who are eager to travel abroad. The UN World Tourism Organisation estimated that the number of Chinese tourists visiting foreign destinations will number 100 million by 2020, up from 31 million in 2005 when it was the seventh biggest spender on foreign travel.

Most overseas trips by Chinese are to other Asian destinations, but they are increasingly heading to Europe and the United States as restrictions on travel to these regions ease.

Spain tipped from third to fourth place among the world's most visited countries in 2010, behind France, the United States and China, according to figures from the UN World Tourism Organisation. It received 52.6 million foreign visitors last year, up slightly from 52.5m in 2009.

Independent.co.uk, Saturday, 9 July 2011

Lexical work

1. Find the English equivalents in the text.

§ 1 **a)** viser **b)** les données **c)** être disponible

§ 2 **a)** faciliter **b)** les exigences en matière de visa **c)** convenir **d)** le goût **e)** le flux

§ 3 **a)** compagnie nationale **b)** unique / seul

§ 4 **a)** les gens **b)** naissante **c)** éclipser

§ 6 **e)** glisser / passer de

2. Work on figures: write in full.

89,533 Chinese tourists • 300,000 in 2012 • July 27 • 1.3bn people • 52.6m foreign visitors

Pronunciation work

CD n° 4 Track n° 3

1. Listen and observe.

[əʊ]: know, home, most, told, open
[ʌ]: country, government, other
[ɒ]: knowledge, offer, populous, foreign

2. Listen to these words that you may find difficult and repeat with the right stress.

visitors • restaurants • requirements • hotel • guides • foreign

Work on the title

1. Identify the source of the document (title, date, nature).

2. Read the headline. Now look at the figures in the 1st paragraph and give more details about the document.

Check the facts

1. Read § 1.
Where does Spain rank as a tourist destination?

2. Read § 2.
What will Spain do to attract more Chinese visitors?

3. Read § 3.
Where will the minister go to present his plan?

4. Read § 4.
a) What has the booming economy in China engendered?
b) How many Chinese are expected to travel by 2020?

5. Read § 5.
What are the Chinese's favourite destinations?

Grammar

→ p. 240

Les noms indénombrables

- *knowledge*

Topic debrief

1. Choose the sentence which you think corresponds best to the main topic of the document.
a) Spain does not want to lose out on tourism.
b) Spain is doing its utmost to attract Chinese tourists.
c) Spain is planning to attract more Chinese tourists as greater numbers travel abroad.

2. Write down an introduction to the document by using the word bank.
to be published • to deal with or to tackle the issue • a fast-growing Chinese middle class • to improve facilities and infrastructures • to publish books in Chinese • a new market to tap

Methods

1. Find a title for each paragraph.

2. Which paragraph best sums up the document?

3. Translate it.

Train for the exam

1. Make a **summary / account** of the document (60 words / 3-5 minutes).

2. Make a **questionnaire** in order to understand better tourists' expectations when they go abroad.
Follow these guidelines:
a) Languages that hotel managers, restaurant owners, waiters, tourist offices should speak
b) Transport: cars to rent, public transport available, underground
c) Price: special pass for a few days, pass that you can buy before leaving
d) Museums: opening hours, audio-phone, brochures, leaflets
e) Airport transfer: by taxi, by metro
f) Places of interest with guided tours
g) Restaurants: type of food
h) Cultural expectations; a special breakfast if you are Chinese
i) Currency

3. Role play: work in pairs
You are going to take part in a telephone conversation.
Student A: you represent a travel agency. You call a restaurant owner to tell him about a Chinese tourist group (how many people, how many singles / couples, meals to be proposed ...) coming to Spain.
Student B: you are a restaurant owner in Barcelona. You are asked to accommodate a group of 20 Chinese tourists for a week.

Go online

- Find out information from the UN World Tourism Organisation: the number of Chinese tourists visiting the UK in 2010, 2011. Which city do they mostly come from?
- Get prepared to report to your group / class (a PowerPoint presentation is recommended).

Train with an oral document

WARMING UP

► Say what you know about business travel.

CD n° 4 Track n° 4

Carlson Wagonlit Travel

Info
Carlson Wagonlit Travel (CWT) is a global leader specialising in business travel management. CWT is dedicated to helping companies of all sizes, as well as government institutions and non-governmental organisations, optimise their travel programmes and provide best-in-class service and assistance to travelers.

Lexical work

1. Match the following words to find their equivalents.

a) provided	**1.** grow
b) corporate	**2.** ignore
c) increase	**3.** supplied
d) address	**4.** company
e) safety	**5.** security
f) overlooked	**6.** target

2. Work on figures: write in full and read aloud.

95% • 150 • 19,000 • 3rd • 2011

Pronunciation work

CD n° 4 Track n° 5

1. Listen and observe.

business [s] → businesses [ɪz]
organise [aiz] → organises [ɪz]
encourage [dʒ] → encourages [ɪz]
At the 3rd person singular you pronounce [iz].

2. Listen and fill in the grid according to the pronunciation of the letter "a" in the following words.

changed • save • safety • travel • manage • programme

[æ]	[ei]

3. Listen and fill in the grid according to the pronunciation of the letter "e" in the following words.

specialised • employees • corporate • developing

[e]	[i:]	[ɪ]	ø

Work on the title

1. Look at the title of the document.

2. Which field is this company specialised in?

Check the facts

1. Listen to part 1.
a) What is CWT specialised in?
b) Where does it operate?
c) How many employees has it got?
d) Who are its clients?

2. Listen to part 2.
a) How has its business model changed?
b) What part does online technology play?
c) What does CWT organise?
d) Why does it try to concentrate on a limited number of suppliers?
e) What percentage of the total cost does ground transportation represent?
f) What about corporate social responsibility?

3. Listen to part 3.
a) What happened on Nov. 3rd, 2011?
b) What will happen in Latin America and Asia?
c) What about North America and Europe?

Topic debrief

1. Choose the sentence which you think corresponds best to the main topic of the document.
a) The business travel industry is a growing industry that has suffered from recession.
b) Carlson Wagonlit Travel is a business travel company that has changed much over the last 15 years.
c) Carlson Wagonlit Travel is located in 140 countries.

2. Write an introduction to the document by using the word bank.
to meet the needs • to be tailored to the needs • to meet expectations • an increase in oil prices • airline fares

Methods

1. Write 2 sentences for each part of the document.

2. Present the companies.
– Thomas Cook: ...
– Carlson Wagonlit Travel: ...

Train for the exam

1. Use your notes to make an **oral presentation** about the document and record yourself (3-5 minutes).

2. Comment: find an answer to the following question. Discuss and give examples (100 words / 3-5 minutes).
Business trips are important for firms. In a recession, how can companies cope with their costs?

3. Role play: work in pairs
You are going to take part in a meeting.
Student A: you have to prepare a business trip for your company. Twenty executives and their boss will meet with potential clients in Mumbai. Imagine a meeting with CWT in which you give the dates of the trip, the number of people involved, the number of days you are staying there, the hotel accommodation you require. You need an estimate as you have been given a budget.
Student B: you are a CWT representative.

TIPS

You should use your notes in order to present a realistic conversation. Don't read them, look up.
You can:
– record the conversation (at the multimedia lab or with your own MP4 recorder; the recording should last between one and two minutes at most);
– videotape the scene and show it to the class;
– act out the scene in front of the class;
– listen to your classmates' recordings and write what you have understood in a short and structured paragraph.

Go online

• Find information on five-star hotels for equipment business trips. Get info on CWT's website.
• Get prepared to report to your group / class (a PowerPoint presentation is recommended).

WARMING UP

▶ Have you ever spent some time on a farm as a tourist?

CD n° 4 Track n° 6

Small U.S. farms find profit in tourism

Santa Margarita, Calif. • For all the talk about sustainable agriculture, most small farms are not self-sustaining in a very basic sense: they can't make ends meet financially without relying on income from jobs off the farm.

But increasingly farmers are eking more money out of the land in ways beyond the traditional route of planting crops and raising livestock. Some have opened bed-and-breakfasts, often known as farm stays, that draw guests eager to get a taste of rural living. Others operate corn mazes that often turn into seasonal amusements. Ranchers open their land to hunters or bring in guests to ride horses. Known as agritourism, such activities are becoming an important economic boost for many farmers.

Early each morning, Jim Maguire milks the sheep and goats and feeds the pigs on his small dairy farm here before heading off to his day job as a public defender in San Luis Obispo County. His wife, Christine, makes cheese and tends the animals. But in recent years, Ms. Maguire has added some new chores: changing linens and serving food to the guests who stay at Rinconada Dairy's two bed-and-breakfast units. Money from the paying guests is now enough to pay for the animals' feed, one of the farm's biggest expenditures.

"The whole idea is to get the farm in a productive state so that it pays its own way," Ms. Maguire said early on a recent morning as she watched sheep file onto the raised stainless steel platform of an automatic milking machine. "The farm stay is an important economic portion of that."

The United States Department of Agriculture predicts that this year the average farm household will get only about 13 percent of its income from farm sources. Agritourism is appealing because it increases the family's income from the farm, potentially reducing the need for off-farm jobs. The U.S.D.A.'s census of agriculture, which is conducted every five years, estimated that 23,000 farms offered agritourism activities in 2007, bringing in an average of $24,300 each in additional income. California, the nation's largest farm state, was among the leaders in agritourism, with nearly 700 farms averaging more than $50,000 in agritourism income. The agritourism movement is fueled by city dwellers who want to understand where their food comes from or who feel an urge to embrace the country life.

Still, there are hurdles. For example, many farmers complained about insurance costs, which rise with the number of farm visitors. Some states have acted to make it easier for farmers and to limit the liability of farmers when someone is injured on their property while participating in agritourism activities. Although many farmers said they enjoyed the city-country interaction at the heart of agritourism, it takes a particular type to pull it off. A lot of people just want that rural farm experience. But it is a lot of work for the farmers.

The New York Times, June 9, 2011

Lexical work

1. Find the English equivalents in the text.

§1 **a)** agriculture viable **b)** indépendant / autonome

§2 **a)** arrondir ses revenus / augmenter ses revenus **b)** au-delà

§3 s'occuper

2. Find the French equivalents.

§4 **a)** to pay its own way **b)** a milking machine

§5 **a)** appealing **b)** off-farm jobs **c)** to be fueled

§6 liability

Pronunciation work

CD n° 4 Track n° 7

1. Observe and underline the stressed syllable. Then listen to check the right answer.

sustain → sustainable tradition → traditional
finance → financial season → seasonal

2. Listen to these liaisons between the following words.

make ends meet • relying on income • known as • to get a taste of

Info
A public defender is a criminal defense lawyer appointed to represent people charged with a crime but who cannot afford to hire an attorney.

Work on the title

1. Identify the source of the document (title, date, nature).

2. Look at the headline and read the first paragraph and find out which farms are concerned.

Check the facts

1. Read §1.
What must small farmers do to make ends meet?

2. Read §2.
a) What do farmers rely on to increase their income? **b)** What is it called?

3. Read §3.
What are Jim Maguire's two jobs? What about his wife?

4. Read §4.
According to Ms. Maguire, how can farms remain productive?

5. Read §5.
a) What are the advantages of agritourism according to the USDA?
b) How much money does agritourism bring on average? What about in California?

6. Read §6.
a) Why are city dwellers interested in agritourism?
b) What are the problems encountered by farmers?

Grammar → p. 239

Les adverbes

- *They can't make ends meet financially without ...*
- *But increasingly farmers are eking more money out of the land ...*
- *... corn mazes that often turn into seasonal amusements.*

Topic debrief

Choose the sentence which you think corresponds best to the main topic of the document.
a) Working on a farm is not enough to make a living.
b) American farmers have found new ways to make ends meet: opening their farms to tourists.
c) By attracting paying tourists to their farm, American small farmers are able to make ends meet.

Methods

1. Give a title to §3 and to §4, then answer in your own words.
– Why do the Maguires accommodate agritourists?
– What are the additional tasks Ms. Maguire has to perform?

2. Describe Jim Maguire's first job on the farm and his second job.

3. Describe Ms. Maguire's opinion on agritourism and traditional farming.

Train for the exam

1. Make a summary / account of the document (60 words / 3-5 minutes).

2. Role play: work in pairs
You are going to take part in a phone conversation.
Student A: you are visiting the area and want to spend three nights at the Rinconada Dairy. You call Ms. Maguire, the manager. Her phone number is (805) 438-5667.
Ask her if some rooms are available, the rate, breakfast, check in and out time, directions to the coastal hills of San Luis Obispo County.
Student B: you are Ms. Maguire and you answer the phone.

3. Write a letter to Ms. Maguire, 4680 W. Pozo Road, Santa Margarita, CA 93453.
You mention your phone call. You give the dates of your visit and the time of your arrival. You mention your interest in cheese-making. You ask about events that are currently scheduled.

10 | Tourism

Train with an oral document

WARMING UP

- Say what you know about "copycat destinations".
- Have you seen the Eiffel Tower replica in Las Vegas?

CD n° 4 Track n° 8

Copycat destinations

Lexical work

Match the following words to find their equivalents.

a) featuring	**1.** copied
b) release	**2.** disagree
c) experts	**3.** best one
d) eager to	**4.** wanting to
e) counterpart	**5.** moreover
f) disapprove	**6.** launch
g) furthermore	**7.** representing
h) masterpiece	**8.** specialists

Pronunciation work

CD n° 4 Track n° 9

1. Listen and observe.

Manhattan • unhoped • heritage • hotel • inhabitants • humble

"h" is pronounced in most of the words in English.

Watch out! Two exceptions: hour [aʊə] • heir [eə].

Practise repeating these words.

2. Key words of "Tourism".

copycat • a spokesman • to attract • authentic • to approve (of) • counterfeit

a) Listen and focus on words stressed on the second syllable.

b) Practise repeating these words aloud.

Work on the title

1. Look at the title of the document.

2. Try to imagine how a place could be copied.

Check the facts

1. Listen to part 1.

a) What is the programme devoted to today?

b) Where is the village located?

c) Which company has started to build a copy of the village?

d) Who is Mrs Strommer? What about Mr Wang?

2. Listen to part 2.

a) Why did Mr Wang's company decide to build a copy of this village in China?

b) Does Mrs Strommer feel it is fine to copy Hallstatt?

c) Why did a lot of experts come to the village?

d) Why is Mrs Strommer still upset about the project?

e) What does Mr Wang acknowledge about the fact that Hallstatt's inhabitants have not been informed?

f) Why will it be a success both in Austria and in China?

3. Listen to part 3.

a) What does the mayor think of the project?

b) Does Mrs Strommer agree with the mayor?

c) Does Mr Wang feel the same way?

d) When will the building of the Chinese Hallstatt be completed?

Topic debrief

1. Choose the sentence which you think corresponds best to the main topic of the document.

a) Chinese entrepreneurs are bringing European wonders to China.

b) A famous village in Austria will have its twin in China thanks to a Chinese real estate agency.

c) The Chinese are on the look-out for money-making schemes.

2. Write down an introduction to the document by using the word bank (40 words).
travel destination • copy • village • China • Austrian • China Minemetals Land • attract • tourists

Methods

1. Write five sentences to describe this project by using the following linking words.
first • then • after • as a consequence • eventually

2. Write the two sides' opinions on the project in two sentences. Use the phrases "on the one hand" and "on the other hand" to express their views.

Train for the exam

1. Use your notes to make an **oral presentation** about the document and record yourself (3-5 minutes).

2. Write a **letter of complaint** to the UNESCO World Heritage Center to let them know how unhappy you are.
Do not forget it is a letter, so make sure you use the correct layout, and the usual greetings at the beginning and end of a letter (80 words).

3. Role play: work in groups
You are going to take part in a debate between two opposed groups.
Group A: you present the globalisation trend in which cultures are disappearing in favour of a world model. You praise traditions and originality. You don't like the idea of "copying" a village.
Group B: you know the excesses of tradition and you think that good ideas should be exploited to the full. It is giving an opportunity to all.

Go online
- Find information on the official Las Vegas site (number of visitors, money invested ...).
- Get prepared to report to your group / class (a PowerPoint presentation is recommended).

Train with a video

Climate change, tourism and the Maldives

→ http://www.youtube.com/watch?v=OkJEBUoBNKA

March 2011

Look at this video on the Internet about the Maldives

Check the facts	Methods
1. What is the main subject of this video?	• What does the word "change" qualify? The climate or tourism?
2. Who might be targeted to spend holidays there?	• Can you describe the landscape?
3. Where are the Maldives situated?	• Use a map. Which continent do you situate them in?
4. When has tourism become an important issue in this area? But what are the dangers?	• What do you think of when you imagine "paradise islands"? • Which tsunami is described at the beginning of the video, with what consequences?
5. Issues ... Has tourism got only individual consequences?	• What are the final pictures of the video? Why?

WARMING UP

► How do you organise your holidays? On the Internet or with a travel agency?

CD n° 4 Track n° 10

Tour operators: horrible holidays

Europe's travel industry has had four terrible years: a recession, an Icelandic volcano, unrest in the Middle East, costly oil, a weak dollar and a widespread sense of malaise. People want to get away from it all, but worry that they can't afford to.

Airlines, hotels and cruise ships have all suffered, but the worst-hit are the tour operators. To survive, they have merged and cut costs. In 2007 Thomas Cook, a German-owned travel firm, took over MyTravel, a British rival, to create Europe's second-biggest package-tour firm. A couple of months later Hanover-based TUI, Europe's biggest travel company, merged its travel business with First Choice, another British package-holiday company, to create TUI Travel, a company based in London and listed on the London Stock Exchange. Both package-holiday giants cut capacity by as much as 25% in the following years.

Yet mergers and downsizing have provided only temporary relief. On August 3rd, Holidays 4 UK, a tour operator specialising in trips to Turkey, went bankrupt, leaving 12,800 holidaymakers stranded.

TUI Travel has several advantages. It is less centralised than Thomas Cook, more flexible and better managed. It sells fewer holidays in the turbulent Middle East. And its margins are buoyed by its focus on fancy holidays rather than bargain booze-ups on beery beaches.

Even so, a spokeswoman for TUI Travel admits that the high oil price is a worry. TUI Travel owns 143 aircraft. The company was fully hedged for oil-price volatility this year but next year it is expecting a 30% increase in its fuel bill.

The traditional tour operators' business model is out of date, says Jamie Rollo of Morgan Stanley, a bank. Their fixed costs are high. They book flights and rooms months in advance, and still have to pay for them even if a volcano or terrorist forces travelers to cancel. And although they now do a lot of business online, they struggle to compete with cheaper online-only firms such as Expedia, Travelocity and Orbitz. So further consolidation is likely. TUI Travel and Thomas Cook might even merge or marry a low-cost airline. Holidays are supposed to be relaxing, but for the firms that provide them, they are anything but.

The Economist, August 13th, 2011

Info

A merger is a combination of two or more independent business corporations into a single enterprise, usually the absorption of one or more firms by a dominant one.

Lexical work

1. Find the English equivalents in the text.

a) avoir les moyens § 1
b) racheter § 2
c) fusionner § 2
d) être côté en bourse § 2
e) réduire les effectifs / dégraisser § 3
f) des vacances de luxe § 4

2. Find the French equivalents.

§ 6 **a)** to be out of date **b)** fixed costs **c)** to book **d)** to cancel **e)** to be likely

Pronunciation work

CD n° 4 Track n° 11

1. Listen and observe.

[i:]: relief • weak • Turkey
[ɪ]: hit • trip • ships

2. Fill in the grid with the following words.

worry • ships • company • bill • compete • cheaper

[i:]	[ɪ]

3. Practise pronouncing these words with the right stress.

hotels • cruises • package • tour

Work on the title

1. Identify the source of the document (title, date, nature).

2. Imagine why the holidays are so horrible.

Check the facts

1. Read §1.
Why do people want to go on holiday even more today?

2. Read §2.
a) What have tour operators done to cut costs?
b) What are the two tour operators that are mentioned?

3. Read §3.
What happened to Holidays 4 UK's clients in August?

4. Read §4.
Why is TUI Travel better off than Thomas Cook?

5. Read §5, 6.
a) What is the impact of oil increases on package holidays?
b) Why are traditional tour operators not competitive? What will happen soon?

Grammar

→ p. 240

Les particules adverbiales

• *get away (from)* • *took over MyTravel*

Topic debrief

1. Choose the sentence which you think corresponds best to the main topic of the document.
a) Europe's travel industry has suffered from many ills that have led to restructuring.
b) The travel industry and especially its tour operators have been forced to rethink their strategies.
c) Tour operators in Europe have had to merge so as to avoid losing money.

2. Write down an introduction to the document by using the word bank.
to be published • *to tackle the issue* • *to explain the lower sales* • *to be entitled*

Methods

1. Give a short title to each paragraph.

2. Which paragraph best corresponds to the title of the document?

Train for the exam

1. Make a **summary / account** of the document (60 words / 3-5 minutes).

2. Comment: find an answer to the following question. Discuss and give examples (100 words / 3-5 minutes).
What are the major threats to in the tourism industry?

3. Role play: work in pairs
You are going to take part in a conversation.
Student A: you are Jamie Rollo and you believe that a new business model should be introduced to reduce fixed costs. Come up with at least 5 arguments that would allow tour operators to better face problems related to natural catastrophes or political conflicts. Think in terms of destinations, costs, flexibility, transportation means, etc. Report to your team and the managing director.
Student B: you are the managing director of a traval firm.

TIPS

You should use your notes in order to present a realistic conversation. Don't read them, look up. You can:
– record the conversation (the recording should last between one and two minutes at most);
– videotape the scene and show it to the class;
– act out the scene in front of the class;
– listen to your classmates' recordings and write what you have understood in a short and structured paragraph.

Go online

• TUI Travel and Thomas Cook are two European tour operators. Find out which destinations they offer and which country is the most successful.
• Look at their online competitors and make a comparison.
• First list the arguments in favour of each: which clients they target, which countries they work with, what type of holidays they offer, etc.
• Get prepared to report to your group / class (a PowerPoint presentation is recommended).

Organising a team-building weekend

1 • Situation

You work for Tiptop Travel, in the business travel department. You do a lot of business with International Assets, a company with European subsidiaries. Your customers are very demanding but very loyal, so you always want to do your best for them.

2 • Process

a) Look at the following documents. You receive the following e-mail (Document C) from the HR department of International Assets.
b) Get pairs or small groups. Create a really dynamic proposal for International Assets. Each pair/group will then present their commercial proposal to the class.

→ FOR MORE INFORMATION ON HOW TO WRITE A LETTER / COMMERCIAL PROPOSAL, SEE "TOOLS" PAGE 246.

c) Now discuss. Remember to speak in English only!
Each pair/group presents their proposal to the class, who will then choose the best proposal by secret ballot.

3 • Follow up

Write up a summary of the proposal and send it to International Assets attached to an e-mail.

Go online

Use the Internet to research flight times and prices, a suitable hotel, etc. Look on the Internet for other ideas for team-building weekends.

TIPS

Start by saying
First we will talk about ...
Then we'll move on to ... .
We'll finish by / finally / lastly .... / finally we shall see in the conclusion ... .
This is called "sign-posting" and is used to explain the aims of your presentation.
In other words: Tell them what you will tell them (introduction); tell them (development); tell them what you have told them (conclusion)!
Also: *If you look at the graph / picture / chart ...*
This ... highlights / underlines the ...
This is due to / because of / will lead to ... .
If you are organising a team-building or any other kind of event, remember to keep in mind your customers' culture (see "Role play", chapter "Europeans", p. 142).

Doc • A

CORPORATE EVENTS

Creative Events and Quality Experiences for your Clients and Colleagues

Happy workers make good companies great. Whether you want to motivate, entertain or innovate, our events offer outstanding outcomes to take your organisation forward. Chillisauce are event experts and our speciality is offering a truly personalised service that combines fun with faultless planning.

Whether you need exciting ideas for an amazing activity day, a quality conference venue, a party planner or a combination of all three, we are brimming with great ideas and offer the most competitive rates. Please note our events are arranged for groups of 14 people or more.

What are you looking for?

Team Building and Corporate Events

Events in Fixed Locations

Evening Events

New RECORD BREAKING Event

Training and Development

Hotels Venues and Conferences

Doc • B

TIPTOP TRAVEL

Business and pleasure travel

Specialists in travel to all European destinations, let us take care of your travel and hotel reservations. Our customised service ensures your safety and comfort at every step of your journey.

Doc • C

Answer ▾ Delete Print

From: Mr. Bill Smith - Tiptop Travel
To: John Pelly - International Assets

We would like to organise a "team building" weekend for all our exhausted auditors. There will be 20 people who will be needing both rest and comfort, as well as stimulating and team-building activities. The program is attached. We would like you to make us an all-inclusive proposal for the two days.
Yours sincerely

PS: We have of course sent this proposal to other travel agencies so we can choose the best option.

"Team Building weekend" • Programme

- **"Welcome cocktail and dinner"** on Friday evening at 8pm.
- **Conferences** Saturday and Sunday mornings from 9-12 followed by a light lunch.
- **A challenging "adventure" outing** organised for Saturday afternoon.
- **A cultural visit** organised for Sunday afternoon.

We will need the following facilities:

- Conference room with data projector & screen for Saturday and Sunday mornings.
- Single and twin bedrooms (list to be provided at a later date).
- Air / train travel to and from each person's place of residence (list attached).

10 | Tourism

Background *The UNWTO'S (United World Tourism Organization) definition of tourism is: "Tourism comprises the activities of persons traveling to and staying in places outside their usual environment for not more than one consecutive year for leisure, business and other purposes."* → SEE "STARTERS" PAGE 192.

1 What were the origins of tourism? What kinds of tourism are there now?

Tourism developed from a quest for education, and then for health reasons. Dating back to the Babylonian and Egyptian empires, it saw rapid growth in the 17th century (the "Grand Tour" and the development of spas), and again after the industrial revolution when many people who had moved to towns travelled to the seaside or the countryside for a break. The advent of railways and then air travel, social progress and the entitlement to paid holidays and increased leisure time further increased the numbers of tourists.

The first **all-inclusive holidays** began with "Thomas Cook", a British tour operator who started in 1841 and is still predominant in the market now.

Recent ICT developments have led to changes in tourism marketing and management, causing the closure of a certain number of **tour operators** unable to compete with the online tourist market. Tourism products are one of the most traded products on the Internet. → SEE "STARTERS" PAGE 192 AND CHAPTER "NEW TECHNOLOGIES" PAGE 102. Changes have also been brought about by low-cost airlines, making travelling more accessible to a greater number of people, and an upmarket trend with tourists seeking better quality products in distant destinations.

Types of tourism:

Apart from the traditional forms of leisure travel and health tourism, winter tourism and international mass tourism which are often organised as **package holidays** to seaside or ski **resorts**, and cultural tours to foreign countries, there are now many forms of "alternative tourism" such as adventure, space, sustainable or even "armchair" tourism.

Info

A 2008 poll showed that the world's best tourists were (from best to worst): Japanese, English, Canadian, German, Swiss ... and last for the third year running, the French. The criteria included: spending, leaving a tip, speaking the language of the host country, politeness and behaviour (second to last, just ahead of the Americans for the last two criteria). France however came in 4th in the "most quiet" section and 3rd in the "best dressed" section (behind the Italians and the British). → SEE CHAPTER "CONSUMERS": WRITING A SURVEY, PAGE 40.

2 Which countries are the most popular and what are the statistics linked to tourism?

Despite the continuing recession in 2011, tourism statistics continued their positive curve. According to the UNWTO (→ SEE "STARTERS" PAGE 192), the number of international tourist arrivals increased by 4.5% in the first 8 months of 2011, to a total of 671 million. The highest growth rate was in Europe (+ 6%). This growth is expected to continue in 2012. France is currently at the top of the world's ranking for international tourism, in terms of the number of people arriving, closely followed by the USA. China ranks third. However, in terms of receipts, the USA is the leader, with France coming in third place after Spain. The biggest spenders are the Germans, followed by the Americans, the British and then the fast-growing numbers of Chinese tourists. The most popular tourist attraction in the world is said to be Times Square (New York), with the Eiffel Tower in 18th position.

3 What are the social, cultural and environmental impacts of tourism?

Tourism is a key component of economic activity, providing about 10% of the world's income and employing about 10% of the world's workforce. There are positive and negative social, cultural and ecological impacts of tourism.

↑ Income from tourism can help the local community. ↓ Only about 20% of the income from a **package tour** goes to local business and workers.

↑ Employment can be created locally. ↓ Most of the senior management positions in hotels are not filled by local staff.

↑ Mass tourism can be a source of ecological destruction and pollution.

→ SEE CHAPTER "ENVIRONMENT" PAGE 226.

Questions

- What changes and developments have there been in tourism?
- What different kinds of tourism do you know of and can you describe them?
- What are the pros and cons of setting up a holiday hotel in a small remote village?
- How do you think the ideal tourist should behave?

Focus

Chinese and Indian tourists: a new breed of visitors to cater to

With the spectacular opening and growth of China, an increasing number of Chinese tourists come every year to visit the world's most famous countries and sites. Likewise thanks to growing disposable incomes, more Indians are travelling abroad for leisure. The necessity to answer to the needs of these new travelers and leisure-seekers has become a number one priority for all the professionals whose jobs are to cater to foreign visitors. Whether it is through its hoteliers, restaurant owners, luxury shop keepers or tour operators, Europe has a tough time competing with other parts of the world.

Indian tourists visit Buckingham Palace, in London.

Indian tourists in London

Facts about the Indian travelers

- India's outbound tourism is rising significantly.
- It has increased by 15% since 2008.
- Nature and the environment, culture and art, safety and hygiene are the main incentives.
- Singapore is the number one travel destination for Indians.
- Dubai, Australia and Malaysia are close behind.
- Indian visitors are at the origin of Malaysia's thriving tourism sector.
- Indians spend on average $1,789 per person per leisure trip, while 75% of the Indian population lives with less than 2 dollars a day.
- Most Indian tourists spend on shopping for accessories, electronics, local souvenirs, perfumes and fashion.
- Indian tourists travelling to mainland Europe are expected to increase by 100% in the near future.
- Indians love travelling to the UK but the visa hassle and the rising airport taxes are still obstacles.

Express your point of view

- What do European tourists look for when they travel abroad?
- What would be your favourite destination and why?

Questions

- Why are Indians able to travel abroad today?
- What are their favourite destinations?
- What are the main criteria for choosing a country?
- What is the situation of Indian tourism in Europe?
- What is the average spending of an Indian tourist abroad?
- What do they spend their money on?

ACTIVE BUSINESS CULTURE

10 | Tourism

Focus

Chinese tourists visit the British Museum, in London.

A much coveted tourist: the Chinese tourists

Facts about the Chinese tourists

- Over 50 million Chinese travelled abroad in 2010.
- Their top ten destinations were Bali, Australia, Cape Town, Endinburgh, Hawaii, Madrid, Egypt, Niagara Falls, Paris and Switzerland.
- The number of Chinese tourists visiting Europe is expected to grow from 3 million in 2010 to 4.5 million by 2015 and around 8.6 million by 2020.
- Italy, France and Germany attract between 500,000 and 700,000 Chinese each per year.
- France is one of their favourite destinations with over 550,000 visitors in 2011.
- Paris, the French Riviera, the castles of the Loire, the Mont St Michel and the Alps are the main attractions.
- They come mostly on organised two-week tours starting in Germany, with stops in Switzerland, Italy or the Netherlands.
- They almost always end in Paris, and it is in Paris that most do their shopping.
- A Chinese tourist in Europe spends more than an American.
- The UK not being part of the Schengen area makes it much harder for the Chinese to travel to the UK; they need a special visa. In 2010, only 127,000 Chinese visited the UK.
- Yet the number of Chinese tourists in London has increased by 450% since 2008.
- Chinese tourists in London go to the luxury stores where they spend an average of £800 for each purchase, whereas the average income for a Chinese worker is $100 a month.
- Harrods introduced Chinese bank card terminals in February 2011: its sales to Chinese consumers have risen significantly.

Questions

- How many Chinese travel abroad each year?
- What are their top destinations?
- Why do they end their European tours in Paris?
- Why are there fewer Chinese tourists in the UK?
- What shows that London is becoming increasingly attractive for Chinese tourists?
- How much do they spend on average?
- On what type of goods or services?

Perspectives

Although Chinese and Indian tourist numbers have been increasing drastically for the past decade, there are fears that the trend might slow down because of the difficult economic context which has settled in since 2008.
On the other hand, the toll of mass tourism from every part of the planet poses a real threat to the environment. This leads to the conclusion that sustainable tourism is the only viable form of leisure travel today.

@ Go online

- Log on to the Internet and find out more about Asian tourists in Europe.
- Log on to the Internet and explain with examples why increasing mass tourism is bad for the environment.

Test yourself — Try to use your memory – do not look at the vocabulary list!

1 TAKING THE PLANE – WHICH WORD DOES NOT BELONG, AND WHY?

Choose the odd word.

a) overbooking / jet lag / domestic flight / lack of legroom

b) board the plane / make a booking / check in / flight

c) runway / hand luggage / hold luggage / baggage allowance

d) fasten your seatbelt sign / flight attendant / window seat /non-stop / aisle seat

e) taxi on the runway / time difference / get clearance / take off / land / fly

f) low-cost / no-frills / business class / reduced rate

2 RENTING A CAR

Complete the story about why Joe is late, using the vocabulary you have learnt.

I'm sorry I'm late, Bob, but my car broke down[1] so I had to rent a car, which took me ages. First of all, I showed my clean d _ _ _ _ _ _ l _ _ _ _ _ _ and then I paid for the car, including the drop-off charge[2] and unlimited m _ _ _ _ _ _ because I didn't know how far it was, and d _ _ _ _ off. I stopped at the p _ _ _ _ _ s _ _ _ _ _ _ to fill up the car, and checked my r _ _ _ _ on the map. I got lost of course, but found a m _ _ _ r _ _ _ which took me to the m _ _ _ _ _ _ _ and I could get up some speed at last. There are no t _ _ _ _ in the UK, so you travel for free. Then I hit the M25 and the most dreadful t _ _ _ _ _ _ j _ _. I got off on the first s _ _ _ r _ _ _ and wriggled round some b _ _ _ r _ _ _ _. I stopped and asked my way several times and at last found the c _ _ p _ _ _ you had told me about, parked, and here I am. Shall we start the meeting?

---

1. break down (to): *tomber en panne* 2. drop-off *charge*: *supplément si vous déposez votre voiture à un autre endroit*

3 LET THE TRAIN TAKE THE STRAIN

Choose the right answer.

a) He waited for the train on the *track / platform / station*.

b) It's wonderful, for once the trains are *running on time / behind schedule!*

c) I think you should take the *shuttle / level crossing / high-speed train* from Edinburgh to London.

d) What's the fare for a *link / single / return* to Portsmouth? Just one way, I'm not coming back.

e) The train is delayed I'm afraid. Could you wait in the *waiting room / reclining seat / timetable*?

4 MAKING A HOTEL BOOKING

Fill in the blanks in the text below with the following words.

a) half-board
b) double
c) meal
d) inclusive
e) twin
f) arrangements
g) destinations
h) rates

Dear Sir / Madame
I am writing to book a ... room (one king-size bed) and an adjoining ... room (two single beds) for the nights of 7th to 9th November 20– ... (3 nights), in the name of Peter and Joan Lewis. We require ... (continental breakfast and dinner only). Could you please let me know your low-season ... (the tariff for the high season being the summer months I suppose)?
We would also like information about tourist ... in the area, and where you suggest we could take our midday ... (we shall no doubt be hungry after our visits).
We would be grateful for an answer by return of post as we wish to confirm our travel ... as soon as possible.
Yours faithfully ...

VOCABULARY

10 | Tourism

Words

"If you reject the food, ignore the customs, fear the religion and avoid the people, you might better stay at home." (James Michener)

Abroad: à l'étranger
Accommodation: logement
All-inclusive: tout compris
Back road: route secondaire
Baggage allowance: franchise de bagages
Baggage claim: retrait des bagages
Board (to): embarquer
Boarding: embarquement
Boarding pass: carte d'embarquement
Book (to): réserver
Booking: réservation
Brochure: brochure
Business class: classe affaires
Car park: parking
Car rental / hire: location de voitures
Catering: restauration
Check-in: enregistrement
Clearance: autorisation de décoller
Climate: climat
Coach: car
Coast: côte
Conference facilities: salle de conférence
Connecting flight: vol de correspondance
Cruise: croisière
Delay: retard
Deposit: acompte
Desert: désert
Domestic flight: vol intérieur
Driver's license (USA), driving licence (GB): permis de conduire
Entertain (to): distraire
Entertainement: distraction
Facilities: équipements / installations
Fare: tarif
Fasten your seatbelt (to): attacher la ceinture de sécurité
Flight: vol
Flight attendant: membre de l'équipage
Fly (to): voler
Full board: pension complète
Fully booked: complet
Gas station (USA), petrol station (GB): pompe à essence, station service
Guide book: guide de voyage
Half board: demi-pension
Hand luggage: bagages à main
Highway code: code de la route
Hold luggage: bagages en soute
Holdall: fourre-tout
Hold a room (to): garder la chambre
Holiday (GB) / vacation (USA): vacances
Holidaymaker: vacancier
Jet lag: fatigue due au décalage horaire
Land (to): atterrir
Landscape: paysage
Legroom: place pour les jambes
Leisure: loisir
Level crossing: passage à niveau
Low-cost company: compagnie à bas prix
Luggage: bagages
Main road: route principale
Make a stopover (to): faire une escale
Mileage: kilométrage
Miss (to): manquer / rater
No frills: avec service minimum
Non-stop flight: vol sans escale
On board: à bord
One-way (USA), single (GB): aller simple
Outing: sortie, excursion
Overbooking: surréservation
Overseas: outre-mer
Package holiday / tour: voyage organisé
Passenger: passager
Platform: quai
Reclining seat: siège inclinable
Reduced rate: tarif réduit
Remote: lointain
Return flight: vol aller-retour
Round trip (USA), return (GB): aller-retour
Runway: piste d'atterrissage / décollage
Seaside resort: station balnéaire
Seat: siège
Sightseeing: visites
Single / double / twin room: chambre simple / double / à deux lits
Ski resort: station de ski
Sliproad: bretelle d'accès
Station: gare
Steward(ess): steward / hôtesse de l'air
Stopover: escale
Take off (to): décoller
Tip: pourboire, tuyau, astuce
Toll: péage
Tour operator: voyagiste
Tourist trap: piège à touriste
Traffic: circulation
Traffic jam: embouteillage
Vacancies: chambres libres
Waiting room / lounge: salle d'attente
Window / aisle seat: siège hublot / allée

11

The environment

The planet is our future

Questions

What can we personally do to save our planet? Which species are in danger in your area?

WORD BOX

tiger • elephant • rainforest • poachers • solidarity • charity • sustainable development

11 | The environment

1 • Look and discuss

a) Look at these pictures showing environmental problems.

b) Discuss in class.

1. What kind of problems do the pictures show?
2. Do you know of other problems which affect the environment?

c) Of course, we can all do something (even a small something) to help reduce these problems. In groups, make a poster or a flier which lists as many "ways to save the planet" as you can, both on a small and large scale. Remember, "every little bit helps". Here are some ideas.

2 • Read and understand

a) Read the text and look at the diagram.

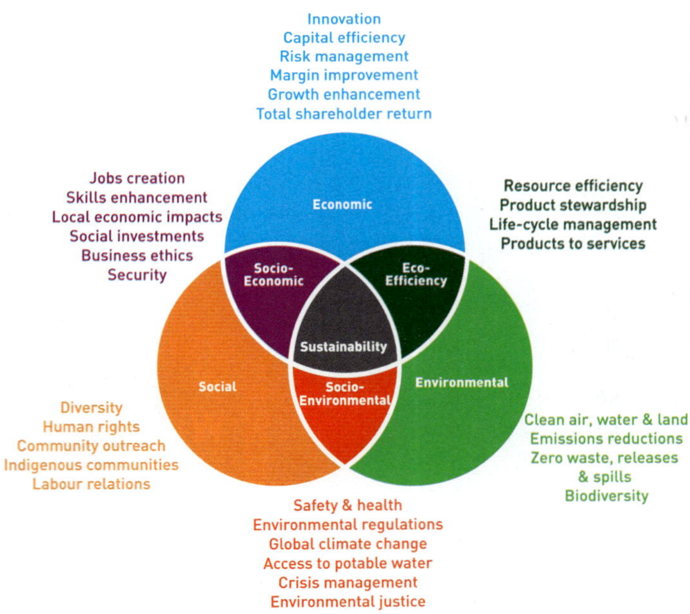

The diagram explains the 3 main factors involved: economic, social and environmental.

What is sustainable development?
When people talk about "sustainable development", they tend to think in terms of the environment, but nothing else. Contrary to common belief, sustainable development is not just environment. The first definition to appear was probably this one: "Development that meets the needs of the present without compromising the ability of future generations to meet their own needs." (World Commission on Environment and Development's report *Our Common Future* (OUP, 1987).

b) Match a word from the list to a definition.

a) Life-cycle management
b) Safety and health
c) Risk management
d) Business ethics
e) Resource efficiency
f) Zero waste
g) Product stewardship
h) Skills enhancement
i) Community outreach
j) Local economic impact

1. Means using natural resources in the most efficient way.
2. Involves assessing and quantifying, then controlling or reducing business risks.
3. Requires efforts and procedures to identify hazards and reduce accidents and illness.
4. Strong local partnerships can have a positive effect on finances.
5. This can promote graduate employability.
6. This concerns the whole chain of a product from beginning to end.
7. Implementing this idea will mean all discarded materials can be recycled or re-used.
8. These programs aim at providing information and services to those in need.
9. These are the written and unwritten codes of conduct a company should follow.
10. This calls on everyone, from manufacturer to disposer, to be responsible for a product and reduce its environmental impact.

@ Go online
If you would like more information on the environment, visit: www.sciencedaily.com

3 • Read and write

a) Answer the following questions about your carbon footprint.

1. When you brush your teeth, do you let the water run?
2. Do you recycle and / or compost ...?
☐ Paper ☐ Food ☐ Tin cans ☐ Plastic ☐ Glass ☐ Clothes
3. Do you regularly turn off lights and appliances?
4. Do you buy locally grown fruits and vegetables?
5. How do you do your grocery shopping? By car? On foot?
6. How often do you travel by air?
7. How do you commute to work?
8. Is your home energy efficient? Has it got double glazing? Do you use energy saving light bulbs? Is your home insulated?
9. How warm do you keep your home?
10. How much water do you use daily? Shower? Bath? Doing the dishes? Doing the washing?
11. Do you buy a lot of disposable goods such as tissues, ready-made meals, etc.?
12. Do you go shopping with your shopping bag or do you use plastic bags?

b) Once you have answered all the questions, figure out if you need to reduce your carbon footprint.

c) Now see what you could do to make your country greener. You could have a more sustainable lifestyle and have a lower impact on the planet. Write a few sentences.

@ Go online
To calculate your carbon footprint: http://www.carbonfootprint.com/

4 • Listen and understand

CD n° 4 Track n° 12

a) What is particular about the food items the woman has bought?
b) What is the point of the man's last remark?
c) Do you make any "green" choices when you shop? Explain why/ why not.

WARMING UP

- Are you involved in any NGO?
- Do you think that protesting / demonstrating can be difficult?

CD n° 4
Track n° 13

Poison protests

These are worrisome times for China's rulers. The Communist Party's credibility was already damaged by a collision of two high-speed trains on July 23rd that left 40 people dead and prompted even the state-supervised media to indulge in a rare outcry about official disregard for public safety. Now comes a demonstration in the north-eastern city of Dalian: on August 8th a storm smashed through the protecting wall of a paraxylene (PX) factory in the city. To Chinese environmentalists, PX, a chemical used to make polyester, is synonymous with toxicity. Around 12,000 people joined the protest demanding the plant's closure. Demonstrations of this size are exceptional in China's boomtowns.

So too are immediate capitulations. The protest was generally orderly. But its mobilisation without clear leadership, with the help only of mobile phones and the Internet, must have unnerved officials made jumpy by fears that China might copy the Arab Spring.

Later in the day, officials announced that they would close the factory. Chinese media say that 9.5 billion yuan ($2.5 billion) has been invested in the factory, a joint venture between a private developer and a state-owned chemical company. The siting of the factory so near the centre of Dalian was remarkable given an outcry in 2007 over plants for a similar project in the southern city of Xiamen. The Xiamen demonstrations are often cited as one of the first and most dramatic displays of a growing willingness of urban Chinese to confront officials over environmental issues.

Since the high-speed train crash, there has been much debate about the power of Internet social-networking services to wrong-foot the government. True to form, the authorities have clamped down. Searches for the terms PX have been blocked. In a country choked with polluting factories, the authorities do not want to encourage copycats.

The Economist, August 20th, 2011

Info

The Kyoto Protocol: the five-year compliance period stipulated in the Kyoto Protocol commenced on Jan. 1, 2008. During this period participating countries needed to meet targeted reductions in greenhouse gas emissions but could also trade emissions credits with each other.
Countries were expected to make most of their emissions reductions within their own borders, but they could buy leftover credits from other countries and earn supplementary credits through projects to reduce emissions in other developed countries and in less-developed countries (LDCs).

Lexical work

1. Find the English equivalents in the text.

a) préoccupant § 1
b) un tollé § 1
c) la fermeture de l'usine § 1
d) en ordre § 2
e) nerveux / instable § 2
f) le Printemps Arabe § 2

2. Find the French equivalents.

a) display § 3
b) to wrong-foot § 4
c) true to form § 4
d) to clamp down § 4
e) to choke § 4

Pronunciation work

CD n° 4
Track n° 14

1. Listen, observe and pronounce.

south → southern • north → northern

2. Underline the stressed syllable. Then listen to check the right answer.

west → western
east → eastern
Middle East • Far East

3. Listen to these words that you may find difficult and repeat.

dead • indulge • smashed • joined • developer • chemical

Work on the title

1. Identify the source of the document (title, date, nature).

2. Poison is used to qualify the protests. Find a synonym in the first paragraph in order to explain the title of the document.

Check the facts

1. Read § 1.
a) Which event damaged the leadership's reputation?
b) What was the protest in Dalian about?

2. Read § 2.
How was this protest organised?

3. Read § 3.
a) Who has invested in this chemical plant?
b) What had happened in Xiamen?

4. Read § 4.
What does the government fear?

Grammar → p. 240

L'auxiliaire modal *must*

- *It must have unnerved officials.*

Topic debrief

1. Choose the sentence which you think corresponds best to the main topic of the document.
a) The Chinese government is unwilling to deal with protests.
b) Protests against poisonous chemical plants are threatening the Chinese government.
c) Protests against a polluting plant make the Chinese government capitulate.

2. Write an introduction to the document by using the word bank.
to be entitled • to tackle the topic • environmentalists • China • chemical factory

Methods

1. Complete the following sentences with your own words to describe the emerging environmental movement.
a) Environmentalists believe that a chemical factory located in the centre of Dalian would ... .
b) It is exceptional to see ... .
c) In 2007 there had been demonstrations in ... because ... .
d) For the first time ever Chinese people had demonstrated en masse to ... .
e) Demonstrators were able to organise much more rapidly ... .

2. Connect the sentences above by using linking words.

Train for the exam

1. Make a summary / account of the document (60 words / 3-5 minutes).

2. Comment: find an answer to the following question. Discuss and give examples (100 words / 3-5 minutes).
Why do "made in China" products remain so controversial?

3. Role play: work in pairs
You are going to take part in a conversation.
Student A: you are an environmentalist and try to list ideas so as to have China subscribe to a world environment Agreement.
Student B: you are an expert in economics convinced that signing the Kyoto Protocol will slow down growth. Make two lists of arguments for protecting the environment and against.

Go online

- Go online and find out more about China and riots: www.greenpeace.org/international/en/campaigns/toxic/water/detox/
- Get prepared to report to your group / class (a PowerPoint presentation is recommended).

Train with an oral document

WARNING UP

- Who or what could need land?
- What do you know about India and its environment?

CD n° 4 Track n° 15

Getting hungry for land

Lexical work

1. Match the following words to find their equivalents.

a) get into conflict	**1.** expelled brutally
b) farmers	**2.** in cities
c) insatiable	**3.** never satisfied
d) urban	**4.** fight
e) seizing	**5.** expressing
f) voicing	**6.** schemes
g) projects	**7.** catching
h) postponed	**8.** factory
i) plant	**9.** delayed
j) bullied out	**10.** in agriculture business
k) populated	**11.** inhabited

2. Find the odd word out.

a) urban housing • city dwellers • country house
b) infrastructure • communication means • weather
c) tribe • ethnic group • a trade union
d) bauxite • gold • oil
e) wheat • rice • sugar cane

3. Work on figures: write in full and read aloud.

545m rupees • $12 billion • 17,000 jobs

CD n° 4 Track n° 16

Pronunciation work

1. Listen and observe the sound t → [ʃ].

insatiable • insatiate • negotiate • negotiation • negotiable

2. Listen to these words that you may find difficult and repeat.

industrialisation • seizing • steel giant • poorish • Bengal

Work on the title

1. Look at the title of the document.

2. What can you infer from it about the content of the article?

Check the facts

1. Listen to part 1.

a) Who are the main protagonists?
b) What does the government do to boost industrialisation?
c) How did the government use to expel farmers from their land in the past?
d) Which people have opposed the government?

2. Listen to part 2.

a) What is the name of the first company evoked?
b) Where is it from? What type of company is it?

Info

Watchdog organisations are usually non-profit groups that view their role as critically monitoring the activities of governments, industry or other organisations and alerting the public when they detect actions that go against the public interest.

c) What will happen in Orissa if the plant is built, according to activists?

3. Listen to part 3.

a) Who wanted to open a factory in West Bengal?
b) What is the second reason for opposing expulsion?
c) What did the British firm, Vedanta, do in the forested hills of Orissa?
d) Who is Pawan Kumar?

Topic debrief

1. Choose the sentence which you think corresponds best to the main topic of the document.

a) Due to colonisation, Indian people are very submissive to government and accept all the new projects.

b) The process of industrialisation in India is done at the expense of farmers who voice their opposition.

c) Many projects have been postponed in India because of their foreign investors.

2. Write an introduction to the document by using the word bank.

farmers • to grow • crops • Orissa • industrialisation • water supplies • to pay compensation • foreign investment • multinationals • to expel • activists • to postpone projects • democracy

Methods

1. Write 2 sentences for each part of the document.

2. Which European power dominated India? How long? With what consequences?

3. List the characteristics of POSCO and Vedenta.

Train for the exam

1. Use your notes to make an **oral presentation** about the document and record yourself (3-5 minutes).

2. Comment: find an answer to the following question. Discuss and give examples (100 words / 3-5 minutes).

Is democracy improving in India as far as buying land is concerned?

3. Role play: work in pairs

You are going to take part in a conversation opposing two points of view.

Student A: you are an Indian farmer and you strongly believe that you should not be expelled from your land. You meet a watchdog organisation activist to tell him / her about what is going on in India, especially in West Bengal and in Orissa. You mention the environmental damage that building plants will have. You explain why the government's compensation will not provide your family with a living.

Student B: you represent a watchdog organisation.

TIPS

You should use your notes in order to present a realistic conversation. Don't read them, look up.

You can:

- do the same with shoppers in your supermarket;
- record the conversation (the recording should last between one and two minutes at most);
- videotape the scene and show it to the class;
- act out the scene in front of the class;
- listen to your classmates' recordings and write what you have understood in a short and structured paragraph.

Go online

- Find out more about Orissa's farmers. Look up the name of an Indian artist who made video films of people who were harassed.
- Get prepared to report to your group / class (a PowerPoint presentation is recommended).

Indian women stand near the stems of trees chopped for the proposed $12 billion steel plant by South Korean conglomerate Posco at Noliashai in Jagatsinghpur district of Orissa state, India, Monday, July 25, 2011.

11 | The environment

WARMING UP

- What is done in your local municipality to stop pollution?
- What do you do personally?

CD n° 4
Track n° 17

Local authorities may be forced to ban heavily polluting traffic to avoid EU fines

The government may act to force local authorities to ban heavily polluting traffic in most British cities to try to control deadly nitrogen dioxide (NO_2) emissions and avoid unlimited fines from Europe. But even setting up dozens of low-emission zones, reducing emissions from power stations and getting a four-year time extension from Europe will not enable Britain to meet its statutory EU air quality target in some places until 2025, the government admitted on Thursday in a consultation document.

According to the document, Britain has reduced its nitrogen dioxide emissions by 39% between 2000 and 2009, and 95% of UK roads assessed are currently expected to meet the NO_2 limits by 2015. The official admission of failure to control the pollution was dismissed as "cynical" by environmental groups who warned that Britain now faced legal action from the European Commission in the months leading up to the London 2012 Olympics. Europe has the power to impose an unlimited lump sum and daily fines. "Funding must be prioritised for measures to help people walk, cycle and use public transport more. Schemes that increase the amount of traffic must be abandoned," said Jenny Bates, Friends of the Earth's London campaigner.

Britain's air quality record is among the worst in Europe and is already breaking European law for particulate, or PM10, pollution and nitrogen dioxide. According to a Mayor of London-commissioned study, poor air quality causes around 4,300 premature deaths in London every year and studies show that poor air quality increases risks of heart attacks, asthma attacks and respiratory illness. Government estimates say that the costs of air pollution in the UK are equivalent to between £9bn and £19bn a year.

"This is a continuing public health crisis that remains, to a large extent, invisible. The government's response is a patchwork solution designed to avoid fines imposed by the European Commission, rather than a mechanism for delivery of real public health benefits", said Ed Dearnley, policy officer with Environmental Protection UK.

The Guardian, Friday 10 June 2011

Lexical work

1. Match the English word with its French equivalent.

a) deadly	**1.** permettre
b) power stations	**2.** évaluer
c) to enable	**3.** un projet
d) statutory	**4.** un montant forfaitaire
e) target	**5.** mortel
f) to assess	**6.** centrales hydrauliques
g) to be dismissed	**7.** statutaire
h) to face legal action	**8.** être rejeté, écarté
i) a lump sum	**9.** risquer des poursuites en justice
j) scheme	**10**. cible, objectif

2. Work on figures: write in full and read aloud.

the year 2025 • 95% • 4,300 • £19bn a year

Pronunciation work

CD n° 4
Track n° 18

1. Find the mute letter(s) in the following words. Then listen to check the right answer.

schemes • walk • campaign • asthma

2. Listen to these words that you may find difficult and repeat.

local authorities • nitrogen dioxide • Olympics • asthma

Work on the title

1. Identify the source of the document (title, date, nature).

2. Pick up the key words and infer what the content of the article may be.

Check the facts

1. Read §1.
a) Why could the British government force local authorities to ban polluting vehicles?
b) Will Britain meet its statutory EU air quality target?

2. Read §2.
a) Whose points of view do we have? What are they?
b) What should be encouraged to reduce pollution?

3. Read §3.
a) What is air pollution responsible for?
b) How much does air pollution cost?

4. Read §4.
What is qualified as "a patchwork solution"? Why?

Grammar → p. 240

Le cas possessif

• *air quality* • *the government's response* • *official admission of failure*

Topic debrief

1. Choose the sentence which you think corresponds best to the main topic of the document.
a) Britain will have to reduce pollution drastically if it does not want to be fined by the EU.
b) Even if polluting vehicles are banned, Britain will not avoid EU fines.
c) Air pollution costs not only people's lives but also EU fines, so Britain should fund other means of transport.

2. Write an introduction to the text by using the word bank.
to be entitled • *to tackle a topical issue* • *to be published* • *to be related to* • *Britain* • *heavy traffic* • *to reduce* • *public transportation versus individual cars*

Methods

1. Complete the following sentences with elements from the text.
a) High NO_2 emissions need reducing if Britain wants ….
b) Pollution is so high that even if Britain sets up …, it won't be able to ….
c) Although Britain has …, it won't meet ….
d) The EU is entitled to ….
e) According to Jenny Bates, the government should fund ….
f) Poor air quality is responsible for ….
g) Air pollution costs the country between ….

2. Rewrite the sentences above by using linking words.

Train for the exam

1. Make a summary / account of the document (60 words / 3-5 minutes).

2. Comment: find an answer to the following questions. Discuss and give examples (3-5 minutes / 100 words).
What measures have been taken to reduce pollution in major cities? Think of Paris, London or Athens. Have these measures been efficient?

3. Role play: work in pairs
You are going to have a discussion. Choose between the two scenarios below.
1. *Student A:* you work in the transport department at the Oxford Town Hall. You meet the mayor and discuss what has been done to reduce air and noise pollution and what remains to be done to improve the quality of life.
Student B: you are the mayor of Oxford.
2. *Student A:* you are Jenny Bates, a friend of the Earth's London campaigner, and you meet with Mrs Johnson from the government. Imagine a dialogue in which you will try to convince Mrs Johnson that pollution must be reduced. Come up with arguments that support your point of view. Use the arguments from the texts.
Student B: you are Mrs Johnson.

Go online

• Find out how many vehicles there are in Britain, its carbon emissions.
• Get prepared to report to your group / class (a PowerPoint presentation is recommended).
• Go to *The Economist* website on its video programme entitled UK Motoring Costs, Dec. 2008.

Train with an oral document

WARMING UP

- Say what you know about fish farms.
- Why do we resort to fish farms?

CD n° 4 Track n° 19

Fish farms

Info
WWF is well-known for their pioneering work to save and protect iconic wildlife like pandas, tigers, whales and rhinos – and they have had some great achievements in those areas since they started in 1961.

Lexical work

1. Match the following words to find their equivalents.

a) running	**1.** disorderly
b) factory	**2.** price
c) increased	**3.** distance
d) short supply	**4.** little quantity
e) cost	**5.** plant
f) disease	**6.** managing
g) no denying	**7.** no doubt
h) messy	**8.** illness
i) gap	**9.** grew

2. Find the odd word out.

a) fish • barramundi • meat
b) engineered • genetically modified • natural
c) salmon • trout • sheep
d) food security • safe diet • sick

3. Work on figures: write in full and read aloud.

50 years • 47.3 million tons • the year 2008 • 7 billion

Pronunciation work

CD n° 4 Track n° 20

1. Listen and observe.

[u:]	[ʊ]
food • choose	look • good

2. Underline the stressed syllable. Then listen to check the right answer.

environmental • production • oceans

3. Listen to these words that you may find difficult and repeat.

environmental • wide variety • human health • aquaculture

Work on the title

1. Look at the title of the document.

2. Think of the consequences of overpopulation in order to explain it.

Check the facts

1. Listen to part 1.
a) What is fish farming?
b) What was fish farming production in 2008?
c) Where do fish that we consume come from?
d) Why will fish farming keep increasing?

2. Listen to part 2.
a) Why can we say that fishing the ocean has a cost?
b) What is China responsible for?
c) What are the reasons for fish farming if it is messy and polluting?
d) What is fish compared to?
e) Why is fish farming still a good tool?

3. Listen to part 3.
a) Why is the barramundi just perfect for aquaculture?
b) What do environmental groups call genetically modified salmon?
c) Is farmed fish a no-risk solution?

Topic debrief

1. Choose the sentence which you think corresponds best to the main topic of the document.
a) Fish farming is increasing as oceans are becoming more and more depleted.

b) Consuming more fish will be done at an environmental cost.
c) Fish farming has an environmental impact.

2. Write an introduction to the text by using the word bank.
fish farming • oceans • scarce • environmental • overpopulation • flexible diets • land animals • pollution

Methods

1. Write 2 key words for each part of the document.

2. Write 2 sentences for each part of the document. Use the following word bank.
salmon • pollution • genetically modified food • food shortage • food security • ocean • pollution • fish waste • meat production • the wild • consumers • barramundi

Train for the exam

1. Use your notes to make an **oral presentation** about the document and record yourself (3-5 minutes).

2. Comment: find an answer to the following question. Discuss and give examples (3-5 minutes / 100 words).
Should we be in favour or against aquaculture?

3. Role play: work in pairs
You are going to take part in a conversation.
Student A: you want to set up a fish farm in China. You have contacted your Chinese counterparts and your plan is to start as soon as possible.
Student B: you are a vegetarian restaurant owner. You advise and warn *A* about all possible excesses the food industry generates.
You meet at an organic food fair in your area.

PRACTICE • AUDIO • VIDEO

Train with a video

Sustainable development

→ http://www.youtube.com/watch?v=pT4eTpw8-Cw
→ http://www.dailymotion.com/video/x36zii_sustainable-development_news

15 October 2007

Look at these videos on the Internet about an experiment in Kenya

Check the facts	Methods
1. What is the main topic of these videos?	• Which continent is concerned in these videos? • Who do you see working in fields?
2. Who are the people involved in this project?	• Why is the word "community" repeated? • Who do these people work for?
3. Where does this scheme take place?	• Which continent is concerned in these videos?
4. What is the impact of such involvements?	• Which "virtuous circle" is described?
5. Issues ... Helping Africa has always been a burning issue. What are the implications of working together at a local level for a common future?	• Explain the word "harvest". What can be done now? • Can you imagine the consequences for this village?

WARMING UP

- What do you do personally to protect the planet?
- At home? During the holidays?

CD n° 4 Track n° 21

A clean-tech oasis deep in the Mojave Desert

Nipton, Calif. • Gerald Freeman was prospecting for gold in the Mojave Desert when he stumbled on Nipton. In 1984, it had become a virtual ghost town. But where most saw desolation, Freeman saw "a little place to make a home" and maybe some money too. The Caltech*-trained geologist shelled out $200,000 to buy the tiny, tattered outpost.

For a quarter-century, Freeman struggled to make something of the place, spending roughly $1 million on restoration costs. About 20 people eventually moved into town, most living in recreational vehicles and trailers.

But now Freeman thinks he's finally figured out a way to turn Nipton into a boomtown. He put up rows of gleaming solar panels, and recently began selling hats emblazoned with the hamlet's new motto: "Nipton, powered by the sun." It's part of a major push to make Nipton a sustainable wonderland, a green hospitality center for nature lovers headed into the neighboring Mojave National Preserve.

The 80-kilowatt solar installation – enough to power most of the town – is 10 miles from Interstate 15 and two miles from the Nevada border. Freeman has also erected five "eco-cabins" based on designs by Frank Lloyd Wright. In the next decade, Freeman envisions energy-efficient buildings, an organic farm, electric vehicle charging stations and even more solar installations. If the local winds weren't so weak, he'd erect wind turbines too.

Nipton isn't the only U.S. town hopping on the environmental bandwagon. Turbines are going up in Greensburg, Kan., where a tornado tore through in 2007; Soldiers Grove, Wis., moved its downtown out of a flood-prone area and equipped the new buildings with solar energy. But Nipton has one advantage: Freeman owns the town and can do whatever he wants with it.

Nipton is already experiencing a mini-boom. The panels made by Skyline Solar Inc. of Mountain View, Calif., are attracting out-of-state visitors curious about doing something similar in their communities. And since January, the population has more than doubled to 60 residents as clean-tech job seekers flood into the area. In the nearby hills, Molycorp Inc. is expanding its rare earths mine, digging up minerals used in wind turbines and smartphones. A 15-minute drive away in the Ivanpah Valley, BrightSource Energy Inc. is building a solar farm. So Freeman is really slowly giving the town a modern makeover, although some residents feel solar panels encroached on their view of the desert.

The Los Angeles Times, June 2011

* Caltech: California Institute of Technology

Lexical work

Match the French word with its English equivalent.

a) a ghost town §1	**1.** débourser
b) to shell out §1	**2.** minuscule
c) tiny §1	**3.** en lambeaux
d) tattered §1	**4.** à peu près
e) roughly §2	**5.** camping-car
f) recreational vehicles §2	**6.** étincelant
g) emblazoned §3	**7.** hameau
h) gleaming §3	**8.** ville fantôme
i) hamlet §3	**9.** marqué de
j) to head into §3	**10.** entrer dans

Pronunciation work

CD n° 4 Track n° 22

1. Listen and observe.

power • tower: you write "o" but you pronounce [aʊə].

2. Listen to these words that you may find difficult and repeat.

tattered • sustainability • shelled out • roughly • turbines • solar panel

Work on the title

1. Identity the source of the document (title, date, nature).

2. Look up the word "Mojave" in the title. Read the first paragraph and find what it is referring to and where it is located.

Check the facts

1. Read §1.
What did Gerald Freeman do in 1984?

2. Read §2.
In 2009, how many people were living there?

3. Read §3.
What did Freeman do to turn the town into a boomtown?

4. Read §4.
What does he want to do with this town?

5. Read §5, 6.
a) What are the two examples given? And what type of energy do they use?
b) What is happening in the Mojave Desert?
c) Is everybody pleased with Nipton's solar panels? Why? Why not?

Grammar → p. 240

Whatever / whoever / whichever...

- *Freeman owns the town and can do whatever he wants with it.*

Topic debrief

1. Choose the sentence which best corresponds to the main topic of the document.
a) A ghost town has been turned into a sustainably developed town.
b) Nipton has been able to develop thanks to solar panels.
c) Small towns investing in solar panels and sustainable development are attracting job seekers.

2. Rephrase the correct sentence in order to make a short introduction to the document.

Methods

1. Find a title for each paragraph.
2. Which paragraph best sums up the topic of the document? Translate it.

Info

The Los Angeles Times is a morning daily newspaper published in Los Angeles. In the 1960s, it began to develop from a regional daily into one of the world's great newspapers. The *Times* was established in 1881. The *Los Angeles Times* was long dominated by the Chandler family, beginning when Harry Chandler succeeded his father-in-law, Otis, as publisher in 1917.

Train for the exam

1. Make an **account / summary** of the document (60 words / 3-5 minutes).

2. Comment: find an answer to the following question. Discuss and give examples (3-5 minutes / 100 words).
What are the limits of alternative energies (in terms of aesthetics, comfort, costs)?

3. Role play: work in groups
You are going to take part in a debate.
Group A: you think people should have specific places to enjoy nature and a clean environment.
Group B: you think there is no "clean oasis" on earth. You find arguments against the idea of "paradise islands".

TIPS

You should use your notes in order to present a realistic conversation. Don't read them, look up.
You can:
– record the conversation (at the multimedia lab or with your own MP4 recorder; the recording should last between one and two minutes at most);
– videotape the scene and show it to the class;
– act out the scene in front of the class;
– listen to your classmates' recordings and write what you have understood in a short and structured paragraph.

Go online

- Look at the following link: www.bwea.com.
- Report on the article dated 21.11.11: "Renewable industry defends wind energy".
- Get prepared to report to your group / class (a PowerPoint presentation is recommended).

11 | The environment

An Industrial company which makes shelving

1 • Situation

You work in a factory which makes shelving for supermarkets in a small town. The company was taken over by an American group five years ago, and many changes are meant to be implemented to follow the group's corporate policies.

2 • Process

a) The CEO, who does not think you are applying the recommendations as you should, sent an e-mail to your General Manager. Read this e-mail (Document A).
b) Your General Manager needs some help to answer him within two weeks! Read the e-mail that you and your colleagues received from him (Document B).
c) Go through all the points on the CEO's list. Make sure you understand each of the points in the CEO's e-mail. Write a list.
d) Get into pairs.
Students A: you are the General Manager. *Students B:* you are the team.
e) Now discuss. *Students B:* you explain to students A what is being done about all the points. You use the KPI charts to help you where appropriate (Document C).

3 • Follow up

Write an e-mail to your General Manager (for the CEO) summarising the results of your meeting. In the e-mail, include a graph to show the KPI on one of the charts.

Go online
Look on the Internet to find other examples of KPI.

TIPS

Start by saying
Now, if we take point 1 ...
What are you doing about point 3?
Could you just explain why ... rose / fell between 2007 and 2008?
If you look at the health and safety KIP you'll see that ...
The figures in the chart show ...
Of course, that is because ....

Doc • A

Answer ▾ Forward Delete Print

From: CEO Corporate development
To: General Manager, PBC Industries

It has come to my notice that the factory you are responsible for is not complying with the group's sustainable development recommendations. Could you please read the following list and implement the necessary changes before the end of the year. I shall expect a report on activities within 2 weeks.
Please pay attention to the following guidelines:
1. Implement and maintain ethical business practices and solid management systems.
2. Include sustainable development in any decision-making process.
3. Never forget human rights and the respect of other people's cultures, customs and values.
4. Base risk management strategies on fact not fiction.
5. Improve health and safety performance.
6. Improve environmental performance.
7. Be part of biodiversity conservation and land use planning projects.
8. Apply responsible product design: use, re-use, recycle and dispose.
9. Contribute to the social, economic and institutional development of your local town.
10. Implement new direct communication and reporting arrangements for all concerned.
Kind regards

Doc • B

Answer ▾ Forward Delete Print ⬆ ⬇

From: General Manager
To: EH&S Manager and team

Hi – Look, I need your help with this e-mail I got from the top! Can we meet to discuss the answer to this one? Could you call me and fix a meeting? The statistics are attached to this e-mail.
After the meeting, I'll need you to do a couple of graphs for me, and a little presentation for when he comes in a fortnight. Many thanks for your help – I owe you one!

DOCUMENTS ATTACHED

1. Health and safety performance KPI (key performance indicators: *indicateurs clés de performance*)

Doc • C

Year	2004	2005	2006	2007	2008	2009	2010
Number of employees	110	120	160	90	80	50	52
Man-hours worked	286	312	416	235	208	130	135,20
Fatalities	0	0	0	0	0	0	0
Lost time accidents	1	1	2	1	2	1	1
Absenteeism	0	0	0	0	0	0	0
Number of days lost	0	3	6	3	2	0	0
First aid treatment only	0	10	4	3	4	1	2
Accident frequency rate	0.35	0.32	0.48	0.43	0.96	0.77	0.74

2. Environmental performance KPI

Healthy Planet	Unit	2007	2008	2009	2010
Accidental releases	Number of events	9	15	16	10
Environmental non-compliances	Number of individual findings	13	21	50	54
ISO certifications	% facilities with certification	100	100	100	100
Energy use	Billion BTU	13,131	13,362	12,821	13,005
Water use	Million m^3	11.9	11.5	10.9	11.3
Recycled water use	Million m^3	–	–	0.08	0.75
Non-hazardous waste	Million kg	54.4	56.3	42.7	55.9
Hazardous waste	Million kg	34.5	29.3	24.6	22.8

ROLE PLAY

11 | The environment

Background

The meaning of the word "natural environment" (or simply "environment") has changed over recent years and now stands for all of the natural components of the planet – the animate and the inanimate – everything which surrounds man and human activities. However, the central position of man on the planet leads to the debate about the environment.

The consequences of human activities have an effect on the environment, with a backlash on the individuals themselves. Sustainable development (→ SEE "STARTERS" PAGE 212)*, is a relatively new concept of public interest, applied to economic growth on a worldwide scale to take into account the environmental and social aspects of a globalised planet.* → SEE CHAPTER "GLOBALISATION" PAGE 166.

1 What are the impacts of man on the environment?

Acid rain: One of the most serious problems. Invisible and airborne, it spreads insidiously. The acidic pollutants mostly come from motor vehicles and coal-burning power plants and industrialisation.
Air pollution: Air contaminants in the form of gas or particles have both natural but mostly human causes. Towns with high numbers of vehicles often have high levels of air pollution.
Water pollution: Every year, about 6.5 billion kilos of sewage and waste, and 71 trillion litres of liquid waste (industrial waste included) are dumped into the world's oceans.
Hazardous waste: High-consumer humans and industries produce a lot of waste which can be hazardous, toxic or non-biodegradable. Nuclear waste is either dumped in the sea or buried, risking radioactive pollution.
Intensive farming: Overuse of pesticides and fertilisers damages the soil and seeps into the water supplies. Many trees are also cut down to make more room for intensive farming.
Overpopulation: The world's population (which reached 7 billion in 2011) is threatening to reach a level where there are too many people for the planet to support.

Ozone depletion: The earth is protected from the sun's ultraviolet rays by the **ozone layer**. A hole in the ozone layer above Antarctica has already been detected and contributes to global warming.
Desertification: Fertile land becomes a desert owing to drought, deforestation or over-farming.
Deforestation: Whole areas of forest are cleared to make way for farmland, urban developments, etc.
Water shortages: Millions of cubic litres of water are wasted in developed countries, while in developing countries increasing numbers of people have no access to clean water.
Food shortages: Leading to malnourishment and even starvation in certain parts of the world.
Urban sprawl: Because of the 4 last points, many people are driven to towns; which in turn causes increases in urban populations and the consequential effects on pollution and the local environment.
Smog: Millions of inhabitants in towns around the world are threatened by smog (= smoke + fog).
Extinction and loss of biodiversity: Some animal and plant species are already extinct. Many others are on the WWF list of endangered species.
→ SEE "STARTERS" PAGE 212.

2 What are the consequences?

Global warming: (or the greenhouse effect) means that gases trap heat near the surface of the earth, and the global temperature is gradually increasing.

Questions

- What kind of ecological problems are being caused by man?
- Do you belong to or know of any green movement or organisation?
- What are businesses doing to move towards sustainable development?

Info

A GMO (genetically modified organism) is an organism or micro-organism whose genetic characteristics have been changed by genetic engineering. The debate is whether the advantages of higher crop yields and a potential answer to starvation in parts of the world are enough to compensate for the questions about their safety in the food and biotechnology industries. In 1996, when GM crops were first commercially cultivated (mainly soybean, cotton, maize and rapeseed), there were about 2.8 million hectares worldwide. By 2009 this had grown to about 134 million hectares, with 64 million in the USA alone.

3 What are some practical sustainable solutions?

Sustainable development includes 3 main factors: economic, social and environmental, which need to be tackled. → SEE "STARTERS" PAGE 212.

Awareness: Education and training, leading to public awareness and reactivity are keys to sustainable development. Many NGOs, non-profit organisations and political parties work to this end.

Laws: International and national laws (e.g. carbon tax, green taxes) and agreements have been passed to reduce the effects on the environment.

New technologies: Innovation and implementation of renewable energy sources, recycling techniques, energy-efficient use, etc.

Fair trade: The fair trade movement seeks greater equity for farmers and craftsmen in developing countries. → SEE CHAPTER "GLOBALISATION" PAGE...

Microcredit: Very small loans are granted to impoverished people to help them set up their own business. The aim is to encourage entrepreneurship.

Renewable energy: Energy which comes from natural resources: hydropower (water, wave and tidal energy), solar power (from the sun), wind power (using wind turbines) and geothermal energy (using heat trapped underground). Bioenergy uses biological sources to provide energy, for example biofuels such as methane from plant biomass.

International summits on climate change include the Kyoto Protocol (an international agreement between UNFCCC[1] countries) which entered into force in 2007 (although it was approved in 1997). At the Climate Change Conference in Copenhagen in 2009, the main countries agreed to keep temperature increases below 2°C. More international decisions, especially to take action to make the global response quicker, were taken at the Cancun Agreements in 2010. COP17 [2] in Durban in 2011 brought together world leaders once again to advance the implementation of the Kyoto Protocol and other action plans which had been agreed on.

1. UNFCCC: United Nations Framework Convention on Climate Change 2. COP: Conference of the Parties

Info

- Businesses are under a lot of pressure to act ethically and respect sustainable development requirements. **Corporate** (or business) **ethics** cover a wide range of issues such as the abolition of child or forced labour and work in sweatshops, respecting the basic rights of workers, and applying the required health, safety and environmental standards.
- **The WBCSD** (World Business Council for Sustainable Development) is a CEO-led organisation of over 200 international companies (Coca-Cola, Sony, BP) working together for cooperation between businesses and governments to get a balance between economic and environmental needs.
→ SEE CHAPTER "WORK" PAGE 122.
- **Food miles** are a term used to calculate the number of miles FMCGs travel before they reach the consumer. Increasing "green lobbying" to choose local food which is in season should reduce the impact on the environment. (Food travels 30 billion kilometres a year in England, releasing 19 million tons of carbon dioxide into the atmosphere).

Focus

Is producing goods sustainably incompatible with economic growth?

Sustainable development can be defined in many ways, but it always involves preserving natural resources and ecosystems on the one hand and improving lifestyles and the feeling of well-being on the other hand, without compromising future generations. It also implies economic growth. So the question is: how to keep on producing goods and respond to a demand for happiness without polluting and endangering species? Are human beings capable of creating a stable balance between human activities and the natural world?

Some players are developing renewable energy

Solar and wind energy

One thing goes without saying: fossil energy must be got rid of and replaced by solar or wind energy. Oil, shale gas and coal pollute a lot. Others are eager to reap the fruits of shale gas mining although it pollutes. Governments as well as private companies should all work to develop less polluting or CO_2-free energy. Reducing our dependency on fossil fuels and heavy metals is one key principle to be sustainable. However, green growth is not seen as the engine of growth, especially when the economy is not picking up.

Here are a few examples

- China's government is frenetically building bullet trains, transmission lines and wind and solar plants.
- In Palo Alto solar-powered buildings sold very quickly. Solar business is a $15 billion business that has grown by 40% each year in the U.S.
- 100 schools across Britain will be fitted with solar technology.
- Wind green power reduces our dependency on fossil fuel, i.e. wind farms in Sweden.

- Renewable energy will have a growing share as we move forward: 40% of the UK's power should come from wind, wave and tide sources by 2030. This in turn will stimulate new industries: develop tidal power plants, wave generators, carbon capture and storage technology.
- Megacities with over 25 million people will require a greater amount of energy: 300,000 jobs related to renewable energy have been created in Germany.

Questions

- What type of energy should be used to become sustainable?
- Why is wind power called green power?

Express your point of view

- Do you think that the 197 countries that met in Durban, South Africa, should reverse the current rise in global carbon emissions, agree on a legally binding protocol to tackle climate change on a global scale and address the key challenges to achieving progress?
- Or do you agree with Prime Minister Stephen Harper's Conservative government in Canada that the Kyoto's goal is unworkable because the United States and China – the world's two largest sources of carbon emissions – never agreed to Kyoto?

Other players are inventing new ways to reduce global warming and deal with its consequences

Stop destroying nature

The second point is that we should stop destroying nature. Fresh air, clean water and producing food that allows us to have a high quality of life make up the second principle to attain sustainability. Global warming is responsible for extreme weather events that alter rain volumes.

Here are a few examples

... of what is done to reduce pollution, to conserve energy and avoid droughts and floods.

- With the Mississippi flooding, water management must be especially geared towards offering a system that addresses all the needs. Whether there is too much water or not enough water, systems must respond to local demand with pumping plants, new reservoirs, etc.
- In California, green farmers offer local produce so fruits and vegetables are not shipped from halfway across the world. Locally grown produce is part of sustainable agriculture.
- In semi-arid Kenya, sand dams are built to lessen the impact of the climate and conserve soil and water which in turn allows the planting of trees.

Questions

- How can water management prevent major disasters?
- Why should consumers buy locally grown food?

@ Go online

Oxfam, a famous charity, is also an expert on global warming and always has observers at the UN Climate Change Summit. In 2011 Oxfam was in Durban, South Africa. Find out online how a charity can become a major player in lobbying for an international agreement to tackle climate change. Write down what Oxfam says about green jobs, low-emission economies, etc.

Perspectives

There are many initiatives to fight global warming, to reduce pollution, to use $C0_2$-free energy, to avoid expanding recklessly – but new technology is what will help create more efficient models, and smart systems will reduce energy waste. Smart systems will focus on technology to deal with the problem on hand: "Why build billion-dollar lock expansions to relieve barge congestion on the Mississippi River when better scheduling and peak-hour pricing could solve most of the problem at virtually no cost?" said Michael Grunwald in *Time* magazine. Computerised traffic management that already exists in London is a good way to avoid jams and encourage mass transit to take cars off the road. Soon there will be rain gardens to absorb rain, green streets to avoid floods and green roofs to put less pressure on sewage, so-called rainwater harvesting. Leaving wetlands in Louisiana instead of having flood walls, recycling sewage water and seawater desalination are all small moves to protect the earth and at the same time to conserve natural resources.

But not everything is that rosy. Chinese firms will ignore basic legal, environmental and labour standards in their rush to secure resources. Having a double-digit growth rate has an environmental cost. The BP oil catastrophe in the Gulf of Mexico has also provoked an environmental disaster and has destroyed jobs. The nuclear catastrophe in Fukushima has taken its toll and has made quite a few rethink their nuclear energy policy. Extreme weather endangers the life of many as well as food security.

Focus

Are the international summits on climate effective? The example of the Durban Climate Change Summit

It took place from 28 November to 9 December 2011 in Durban, South Africa. It was the 17th session of the Conference of the Parties (COP17) organised by the United Nations that met for the first time in 1995. In 2010 it was in Cancun, Mexico, and the year before it was in Copenhagen (Denmark). UN negotiations are considered to be the most legitimate form for reaching agreements. 197 countries participated in them, as well as observers such as environmental groups, businesses, local governments and organisations, indigenous people.

The key issues

- The Kyoto Protocol that expires at the end of 2012.
- The reduction of greenhouse gas emissions and the targets.
- China and the United States are the world's largest greenhouse gas emitters and India is currently the world's third largest greenhouse gas emitter.

What was achieved

- Developed and developing countries will for the first time work on an agreement that should be legally binding on all parties. However, many are convinced that it will not be easy to reach an agreement with China, India, Europe and America by 2015 to come into force after 2020. It is called the Durban Platform.
- Europe will keep on reducing its emissions whereas developing countries which are defined as not responsible for 58% of global emissions will not have this burden imposed on them. Moreover, as the Kyoto Protocol cannot impose penalties, countries like Canada, a signatory, which has missed its target, will go "unpunished".

What still needs to be discussed

- Money is a key issue: developing countries have been promised $100 billion to help them develop a green economy. However, the Green Climate Fund has not yet the massive funds required that should be made available by 2020.
- Historic emissions are another bone of contention. Industrialised countries started burning fossil fuels much earlier and therefore are responsible for the CO_2 already in the atmosphere.
- Some countries have different capabilities: some have large forests, some have large populations, some have made efforts to use low-carbon power. Much remains to be discussed.

In conclusion...

- The Durban Climate Summit has led the way in the right direction as developing and developed countries will bear equal responsibility for the successor to the Kyoto Protocol.

Questions

- Some point out that Climate change is such a large topic that it will not be solved at the UN yearly conference. But instead, there should be more smaller conferences to deal with specific issues. What do you think?
- Global warming has an impact on food security. Can you think of recent weather events that have left many people stranded?

Express your point of view

Fewer and fewer people have shown an interest in the latest Climate Summit.
Do you think that at a time of an economic crisis, jobs should be the priority? Or can a green economy create jobs?

Test yourself

Try to use your memory – do not look at the vocabulary list!

1 WHAT ARE THE EFFECTS OF UPSETTING NATURE'S BALANCE?

Match the word to the definition on the right.

SET A:

1. Water table	**a)** Not enough water for farming and quenching people's thirst.
2. Water supplies	**b)** The top surface of groundwater.
3. Raise sea levels	**c)** The covering of ice over a large area starts to become water.
4. Floods	**d)** The (drinkable) water available to a community.
5. Drought	**e)** Too much water – rivers overflow their banks.
6. Melt polar cap / ice cap	**f)** The level of the sea's surface goes up.

SET B:

1. Rainforests	**a)** A class of animal which no longer exists.
2. Wildlife	**b)** The destruction or ruin of the variety of life in the world.
3. Extinction of species	**c)** Forests with heavy annual rainfall.
4. Natural habitat	**d)** Wild animals (and sometimes plants).
5. Loss of biodiversity	**e)** An area in which animals, people or plants naturally live.

SET C:

1. Food shortage	**a)** Too many people.
2. Hunger bouts / famines	**b)** When there is not enough food.
3. Overpopulation	**c)** Caused by the extreme scarcity of food.

SET D:

1. Global warming	**a)** The upper atmosphere (15-30 km away) with a high level of ozone.
2. Greenhouse effect	**b)** Rain made acid by atmospheric pollution (harmful to nature).
3. Ozone layer	**c)** The gradual increase in temperature of the earth's atmosphere.
4. Heat wave	**d)** Fog mixed with atmospheric pollutants.
5. Smog	**e)** Solar radiation trapped by the earth's atmosphere.
6. Acid rain	**f)** A long period of extremely hot weather.

2 CORPORATE AND PUBLIC COMMITMENT

Complete the text with one of the following words. (The number of letters gives you a clue).

corporate ethics • daunting task • awareness campaigns • mobilise public opinion • investments • print out • polluter pays principle • green taxes • tackle • commitment • offset • innovative • at stake • carbon trading • carbon tax • CSR

a) Do companies realise these days what is really 2 + 5?

b) Will the arrival of 6 + 3 get a firm 10 out of them, or will they find ways around the laws by 6 + 7?

c) The 8 + 3 + 9 was created in order to 6 the carbon footprint left by certain industries – however heavy 11 are required for industries to reduce their toxic emissions.

d) The increasing popularity of 9 + 6 and 3 is a move in the right direction.

e) What about the public? Despite many 9 + 9, some people continue to 5 + 3 every e-mail they receive, and 10 developments (hybrid cars for example) tend to be very expensive.

f) 5 + 5 on electrical and electronic goods make a small contribution but we need to 8 + 6 + 7 so that we can really 6 the "unsustainable" issue.

g) It's a 8 + 4!

3 WHAT CAN YOU DO?

Add a vowel to find the verb.

a) D_n_t_ money
b) R_cycl_ or re-use
c) S_v_ and don't waste
d) S_rt rubbish
e) Sw_tch to energy-saving devices

11 | The environment

Words

"Modern technology / Owes Ecology / An apology." (Alan M. Eddison)

Acid rain: pluie acide
Alternative energy: les énergies alternatives
At stake (to be): être en jeu
Aware (to be): être conscient
Awareness campaign: campagne de sensibilisation
Biodiversity: biodiversité
Biofuel / biogas: biocarburants / biogaz
Bottle redemption centre: point vert
Bury (to): enterrer
Campaigner: militant
Carbon dioxide: gaz carbonique
Carbon footprint: empreinte carbone
Carbon tax: taxe sur le CO_2
Carbon trading: le commerce de CO_2
Climate change: changement climatique
Commitment: engagement
Conserve energy (to): économiser l'énergie
Corporate ethics: éthique de l'entreprise
Corporate social responsiblity (CSR): responsabilité sociétale
Cut carbon emissions (to): réduire les émissions carbone
Dam: barrage
Damage (to): endommager
Deforestation: déforestation
Desertification: désertification
Destroy (to): détruire
Donate (to): faire un don
Drought: sécheresse
Dump / dump (to): décharge / décharger
Eco- / environment-friendly: bon pour l'environnement
Emerging countries: les pays émergents
Energy-efficient: à faible consommation d'énergie
Environmental standards: normes environnementales
Extinction of species: extinction des espèces
Fertiliser: engrais, fertilisant
Flood: inondation
Fuel / fossil fuel: carburant / combustible fossile
Genetically modified: génétiquement modifié
GMO (genetically modified organism): OGM (organisme génétiquement modifié)
Global warming: réchauffement de la planète
Green tax: taxe écologique
Greenhouse effect: effet de serre
Harm: endommager
Harmful: nuisible, dangereux
Harmless: sans danger
Hazard: risque, danger
Heat wave: vague de chaleur, canicule
Hunger bout / famine: famine
Industrialisation: industrialisation
Innovative: innovant, novateur
Intensive farming: agriculture intensive
Investment: investissement
Lack / lack (to): manque, manquer de
Landfill: décharge
Low-energy / consumption: basse-consommation
Melt polar ice cap (to): faire fondre la calotte glacière
Mobilise public opinion (to): sensibiliser l'opinion
Natural gas: gaz naturel
Natural habitat: habitat naturel
Nuclear waste: déchets nucléaires
Offset (to): compenser
Oil spill / slick: nappe de pétrole, marée noire
Organic fuel: carburant vert
Overpopulation: surpopulation
Ozone layer: couche d'ozone
Pest: animal nuisible
Pollute (to): polluer
Polluting: polluant
Print out (to): imprimer
Rainforest: forêt tropicale
Raise sea levels: augmenter le niveau de la mer
Recycle (to): recycler
Renewable: renouvelable
Reusable: réutilisable
Save (to): economiser
Sea level: niveau de la mer
Shale gas: gaz de schiste
Shortage: pénurie
Smog: nuage de pollution
Solar energy / power: énergie solaire
Sort (to): trier
Species: espèces
Sustainability: durabilité
Switch (to): passer à
Tackle (to): s'attaquer à / aborder
Tidal energy: l'énergie marine
Vehicle emissions: gaz d'échappement
Waste (to): gâcher
Waste / rubbish: déchets
Waste disposal: traitement des déchets
Water (to): arroser
Water supplies: réserves d'eau
Wildlife: faune et flore
Wind farm: parc éolien
Wind turbine: éolienne

1 • Le superlatif

a) **Le superlatif de supériorité = le plus**
• ***The* + adjectif court + *-est* ou *The* + adjectif terminaison en *y* + *iest***
Coca-Cola is the largest company in the world. New York is the busiest city in the U.S.
• ***The* + *most* + adjectif long**
One of the most successful entrepreneurs of our age.
• **Les adjectifs irréguliers (à connaître)**
good / well → the best; bad → the worst; far → the farthest / the furthest
GM had the best results of the year. The worst is yet to come. This is the furthest / farthest we can go.

b) **Le superlatif d'infériorité = le moins**
***The least* + adj**
The product was abandoned by the brand because it was the least successful.
→ *Le produit a été abandonné par la marque car c'était le moins réussi.*

c) **Le superlatif avec *ever* + present perfect**
He's the best manager the company has ever had.
→ *C'est le meilleur dirigeant que l'entreprise n'ait jamais eu.*

2 • Le pluperfect (ou past perfect)

• **Construction :** sujet + *had* + participe passé
• **Emploi :**

a) Le pluperfect s'emploie dans un contexte passé. Il sert à marquer une antériorité par rapport à une action exprimée au prétérit.

b) Le pluperfect + *-ing* est l'équivalent du présent perfect en *-ing*, mais dans un contexte passé. Il sert à mettre l'accent sur l'activité décrite.

c) Au style indirect, le prétérit comme le present perfect, sont transformés en pluperfect au style indirect passé.

3 • Le discours rapporté

• **Emploi :** le discours rapporté s'emploie pour rapporter les propos d'un tiers.
• **Construction :**

a) Lors du passage du discours direct au discours rapporté il faut faire attention **aux pronoms susceptibles de changer et à la concordance des temps**.
Discours direct : *S.O. said "We don't see it as necessary to be the largest automaker in the world".*
Discours rapporté : *S.O. said they didn't see it as necessary to be the largest automaker in the world.*

b) Pour les phrases interrogatives, l'ordre des mots n'est pas celui de la question directe : le point d'interrogation disparaît.
"When will Toyota recover from the earthquake?", experts asked.
→ *Experts asked when Toyota would recover from the earthquake.*

4 • Les noms et les adjectifs composés

a) Les noms composés sont très fréquents en anglais. Ils se construisent de plusieurs façons : **nom + nom** (*air fresheners*), **adjectif + nom** (*bottled water*), **verbe + nom** (*cooking oil*), mais aussi **nom + particule adverbiale** (*a take-off*), **participe passé + particule adverbiale** ou **verbe + particule adverbiale**.

b) Ils prennent parfois un tiret entre les deux termes (*name-brand*). La marque du pluriel se porte sur le dernier élément, quelle que soit sa nature grammaticale.

c) Le dernier élément est celui qui porte le sens principal, le premier ayant valeur d'adjectif. Il est d'ailleurs invariable (*a ten-dollar-bill*) → pas de « s » de pluriel à *dollar*, car il a valeur d'adjectif.

d) Les adjectifs composés se forment sur le schéma suivant : **nom / adv + V-ing** (*an air conditioning device*), **nom / adv + V-ed** (*ready-made*), ou **nom + adj**.

5 • Les comparatifs

a) **Les comparatifs dits de « supériorité » = plus ... que**
• **Les adjectifs courts + *-er... than***
Europe is smaller than America.
• **Les adjectifs en *y* + *-ier ... than***
London is rainier than Paris.
• **Les adjectifs longs : *more* + adjectifs longs ... *than***
Cars are more expensive in France than in Germany.
• **Les adjectifs irréguliers (à connaître) :**
good / well → better... than; bad → worse....than far → further / farther...than
Roads are better now than 50 years ago. Los Angeles is farther / further than Chicago.
Pollution is worse today than in the last century.

Remarques :
Pour indiquer un accroissement progressif, on utilise :
Prices are higher and higher / goods are more and more expensive.
→ *Les prix sont de plus en plus élevés / les produits sont de plus en plus chers.*
Ces formes peuvent être remplacées par l'adverbe *increasingly* :

GRAMMAR

Prices are increasingly high / goods are increasingly expensive.
Pour indiquer un accroissement parallèle :
Some consumers think that the more expensive an item is, the better it is.
→ *Certains consommateurs pensent que plus un article est cher, meilleur il est.*
Attention à l'ordre des mots qui diffère dans les deux langues.

b) **Les comparatifs dits d'infériorité = moins ... que *less* + adjectif... *than*** : quelle que soit la longueur de l'adjectif. C'est la même construction pour les adjectifs irréguliers : *Silver is less expensive than gold.*

Remarque :
Le comparatif d'infériorité est moins utilisé en anglais qu'en français. On préfère en anglais dire *smaller* (plus petit) que *less tall* (moins grand).

c) **Les comparatifs dits d'égalité = aussi ... que *as* + adjectif ... *as*** : la forme est identique pour tous les adjectifs, irréguliers compris.
Par contre, ***as*** se substitue à ***than***: *India will soon become as rich as China.*

Remarque :
*Prices are **the same** (as before)* → *Les prix sont **les mêmes** (qu'auparavant).*

6 • Le gérondif (la forme en -ing)

On utilise la forme en -ing (gérondif) :

a) **Pour remplacer une subordonnée relative ou traduire un participe présent (français).**
The biggest factor deterring customers from refill is cost.
→ *Le facteur le plus important qui dissuade / dissuadant les clients de réutiliser les emballages, est le côut.*

b) **Après les verbes indiquant un début, une fin, une continuité :** *start, begin, stop, continue, keep on, go on*, etc.
Twelve years after one supermarket chain first began testing ways to encourage shoppers to refill detergent bottles.

c) **Après les verbes dits d'appréciation :** *like, love, enjoy, prefer, hate, dislike, can't bear, can't stand*, etc.
Before, customers didn't like refilling their empty ink cartridges. They preferred buying new ones.

d) **Après les prépositions :** *in, by, with, without, after, before*, etc.
... the challenge we have in reducing packaging...
... Dairy Crest has cut down on its packaging by selling some of its milk in pouches...

e) **Pour transformer un verbe en nom :**
Paying a premium for recyclable packaging has become necessary.
→ *Payer un supplément / un surcoût pour un packaging recyclable est devenu nécessaire.*

Remarque :
– Certains noms se terminent par -ing : *packaging, advertising, marketing*, etc.
– Un grand nombre d'adjectifs également : *tiring, surprising, shocking, interesting*, etc. On notera qu'ils se traduisent en français par la terminaison *-ant*
→ *fatigant, surprenant, choquant, intéressant*, etc.

7 • Le passif

a) La voix passive permet de mettre en valeur les actions subies par le sujet alors que la forme active sert à mettre en valeur ce qui est à l'origine de l'action.
The new look was inspired by global research. (forme passive)
Global research inspired the new look. (forme active)

b) La forme passive est reconnaissable en anglais par la présence de ***be*** suivi du participe passé du verbe.
Attention : il n'existe aucune exception à cette règle.

c) Le complément d'agent, quand il est exprimé, est introduit par la préposition *by*. Le passif est rarement suivi d'un complément d'agent, car lorsqu'il s'agit de préciser qui fait l'action, on a recours à la voix active.

d) La forme passive s'utilise à tous les temps : présent passé, futur, etc. C'est *be* et lui seul qui marque le temps.
Coffee is exported / will be exported / was exported / has been exported / had been exported / would be exported, etc. → *Le café est exporté / sera exporté / a été exporté*, etc.

Rappel : le passif n'est pas un temps, c'est une forme, une manière d'exprimer une action (comme en français).

e) L'anglais ne possédant pas de pronom indéfini *on* à proprement parler, les tournures impersonnelles en anglais sont exprimées par le passif.
I was given a day off to take my driving licence.
→ *On m'a donné un jour de congé pour passer mon permis de conduire.*
They will be asked to give their names at the reception desk. → *On leur demandera de donner leur nom à la réception.*

8 • L'expression du futur

a) Le futur se construit en général avec l'auxiliaire ***will*** : sujet + *will* + base verbale.
Britain's Internet grocery market will double to £9.9bn by 2015.
Il peut aussi se construire avec ***be going to*** (le locuteur est sûr que quelque chose va arriver).

b) Plusieurs expressions sont utilisées dans un contexte futur : *in the next year, in the years to come, in the long run... when, as soon as, as long as, until / till, unless...* (conjonctions subordonnées de temps)

Attention : à la concordance des temps dans les propositions subordonnées temporelles : *when* + présent simple (proposition subordonnée) → *will* (proposition principale)

9 • Le prétérit

• **Construction :**

a) Le prétérit des verbes réguliers se forme an ajoutant *-ed* à la base verbale.
The store opened 7 years ago.

b) Beaucoup de verbes ont un prétérit irrégulier. Il faut les apprendre.

c) Une phrase négative se construit sur le type : *did* + *not* + base verbale.
The store did not open in January. They did not break the record.
En anglais écrit, on n'utilise pas de formes contractées. Elles sont réservées à l'anglais oral.

d) Pour poser une question, utilisez soit : auxiliaire + sujet + BV (pour les yes / no questions), soit : wh... + word + *did* + sujet + BV? (pour les wh- questions).

• **Emploi :**
Le prétérit (ou *simple past*) est utilisé pour quelque chose qui est complètement terminé et sans lien avec le présent. De ce fait le prétérit est toujours associé (soit dans la phrase même, soit dans le contexte sans que cela ne soit exprimé), à une expression qui ramène à un moment précis du passé : *5 years ago, yesterday, last year, on 22nd January 1957, when I was at school...*

10 • L'auxiliaire modal *may*

• **Construction :**
May obéit aux particularités de tous les auxiliaires modaux : pas de *to* à l'infinitif, pas de -s à la 3e personne du présent simple, prend la marque de la négation et se place à la 1re place dans une phrase interrogative.

• **Emploi :**
Comme de nombreux autres modaux, comme *must* (→ *must*, p. 240) *may* peut être utilisé de deux façons différentes:

a) Quand le locuteur veut faire pression sur celui dont il parle. Avec *may*, on marque l'autorisation, dans une langue soutenue. On peut également utiliser le modal *can* pour la permission ou la possibilité.

b) Pour parler des chances de réalisation d'une action. Avec *may*, la probabilité est moyenne. Dans ce type d'utilisation, on peut marquer que l'action a des chances de se réaliser (*may* + BV), qu'elle est peut-être en train de se réaliser (*may* + verbe + *-ing*), ou bien qu'elle s'est probablement réalisée dans le passé (*may* + *have* + participe passé). Si l'action n'a que peu de chances de se réaliser, on utilisera l'auxiliaire modal *might*.
Kate may have boosted clothes sales / may be boosting clothes sales / may boost clothes sales.

Remarque : *may* + BV peut se remplacer par : *is likely* + *to* + verbe. *That's likely to be good news for Zara.*

11 • L'article défini: *the* ou ø ?

Quand on emploie un nom dans son sens général, on n'utilise pas d'article en anglais (ø), au singulier comme au pluriel. Par contre, si on veut parler d'une notion en particulier, ou si l'on connaît précisément la personne ou l'objet dont il est question, on utilise *the*.
ø People work more today than a decade ago.
≠ all the people I saw in this company work a lot.

Remarques :
– Certains noms sont presque toujours employés avec *the* car ils sont uniques : *the Sun, the Earth...*
– Les noms de pays ne prennent pas d'article, à quelques exceptions près : *the Lebanon*.
– Pour les titres, si l'on donne le nom de la personne, on supprime le *the* : *the President of the United States / ø President Obama.*

12 • Le present perfect

• **Le present perfect simple (*have / has* + participe passé) s'emploie pour :**

a) Se référer à un évènement, fait ou action qui n'est pas daté, et qui n'a pas d'occurrence précise dans le passé.
The lights have reflected momentous events.
→ *Les lumières ont reflété des moments importants et peuvent en refléter d'autres ultérieurement.*

Attention : s'il y avait eu un repère temporel : *two years ago, during the Royal Wedding*, etc. le prétérit aurait été obligatoire.

b) Se référer à une action / un fait commencé dans le passé et qui perdure jusqu'à maintenant.
...which has flashed its name since 1978
→ *dont le nom brille depuis 1978*

Attention : ce cas précis d'emploi du present perfect se traduit par du présent de l'indicatif en français.

• **La différence entre *for* et *since* dans les phrases au present perfect :**
The brand has flashed its name since 1978.
The brand has flashed its name for 30 years.

GRAMMAR

On utilise ***since*** devant une date, un point de départ précis dans le passé.
On utilise ***for*** devant l'expression d'une durée.

• **Le present perfect progressif (*have* + *been* + BV *-ing*) est utilisé pour :** donner plus de relief à la phrase.
Avec le present perfect progressif, l'intention / l'implication du locuteur (celui qui parle / écrit) change.
Coca-Cola has been adding life to the lights since 1955.
→ *Cela fait depuis 1955 que Coca-Cola ajoute de la vie aux enseignes lumineuses.*
Coca-Cola has added life to the lights since 1955.
→ *Coca Cola ajoute de la vie aux enseignes lumineuses depuis 1955.*

13 • Les quantifieurs

a) Différencier *much* et *many* = beaucoup
Les noms indénombrables (au singulier) sont précédés de *much* → *much money*.
En anglais les noms dénombrables (au pluriel) sont précédés de *many* → *many employees*.

b) Différencier *a little* et *a few* = peu
Les noms indénombrables (au singulier) sont précédés de *a little* → *a little money*.
Les noms dénombrables (au pluriel) sont précédés de *a few* → *a few employees*.

c) D'autres adverbes et expressions adverbiales sont utilisés pour : exprimer une grande quantité et sont utilisés indifféremment avec les noms dénombrables et indénombrables : *a lot of / lots of / plenty of*.

d) Comparer des quantités
Plus de : *more* + nom... *More companies are involved in sustainable development today.*
De plus en plus : *more and more*
Moins de : *less* ou *fewer*
less + nom indénombrable (singulier) → *less know-how*
fewer + nom dénombrable (pluriel) → *fewer applications*
De moins en moins : *less and less / fewer and fewer*
Autant de : *as much as* ou *as many as*
You can have as many friends as you want on Facebook, but will you get as much real friendship?

Remarque : *too much / too many* = trop
too much money → trop d'argent
too many people → trop de gens

14 • Les propositions infinitives (avec et sans *to*)

a) Construction du verbe *want (vouloir)*
– *Want* lorsqu'il précède un verbe est toujours suivi de *to*. *Mr Hunt wants to crack down on piracy.*
→ *M. Hunt veut réprimer le piratage.*
– *Want* + CO + *to* + verbe : *Jeremy Hunt wants Net firms to do more to prevent access to pirate sites.*
– Contrairement au français qui utilise une subordonnée complétive (*M.Hunt veut que les entreprises du net en fassent davantage pour empêcher l'accès aux sites pirates.*), l'anglais utilise une proposition infinitive.

Remarque : la 2e partie de la phrase *: to prevent access to pirate sites* est aussi une proposition infinitive exprimant un but. Le français le traduit par : *pour empêcher l'accès aux sites pirates.*
Ne pas traduire le *pour* français par *for* en anglais.
Le *to* suffit à exprimer le but.

b) Construction avec *would like (voudrait / aimerait)*
Would like est une formule atténuée de *want* qui se construit de façon identique :
Ideally the government would like to see Google remove pirate sites from its search engine completely.

c) Construction du verbe *allow (autoriser)*
– *Allow* se construit toujours avec *to*, comme *want* : *allow* + CO + *to* + verbe.
We do not allow certain products to be sold in the shops on the High Street.
– *Allow* se construit fréquemment au passif.
People are not allowed to download music and films on their PCs.

d) Construction particulière du verbe *make (faire)*
Make + CO + verbe signifie *faire faire quelque chose à quelqu'un*.
The aim of Hadopi is to make people stop illegal downloadings.

e) Construction du verbe *let (laisser, permettre)*
Let se construit sans *to : let* + CO + verbe.
Google shouldn't let people have access to illegal sites.

15 • L'expression du contraste

a) Pour marquer le contraste entre deux notions, on utilise une proposition subordonnée introduite par des prépositions spécifiques comme ***while*** (*tandis que*), ***whereas*** (*alors que*, anglais formel), ***although***, ***though*** (*bien que, quoique*) et ***even though*** ou ***even if*** (*même si*).

b) On peut également marquer une différence, un contraste ou une concession en utilisant les adverbes suivants : ***still*** *(pourtant)*, ***however*** *(cependant, toutefois, en revanche)*, ***yet*** *(cependant)* ou ***nevertheless / nonetheless*** *(néanmoins)*.

c) *Instead* peut se construire soit seul en début ou en fin de phrase, ou bien avec la structure ***instead of*** + V -ing.

16 • Les principaux suffixes

On peut ajouter un suffixe à un nom, un verbe ou un adjectif, de façon à créer un mot dérivé.

Les principaux suffixes sont les suivants :
-ful (plein de, caractérisé par) : *powerful* → *puissant*. Ce suffixe s'écrit avec un seul l à la fin !
-less (sans, dénué de) : *childless* → *sans enfant*.
-y ou ***-ly*** (pour marquer une qualité) : *wealthy* → *riche*, *friendly* → *amical*.
-ish (pour marquer quelques chose de négatif) : *selfish* → *égoïste*.

17 • L'expression de la fréquence

a) Pour connaître la fréquence à laquelle un tiers pratique une activité, l'anglais utilise *how often* :
How often do you visit your family?
How often do you watch tv / do you entertain your friends / go to the doctor's?

b) Les réponses à ce type de questions vont exprimer la fréquence à laquelle l'activité est pratiquée.
Once / twice / three times / a year / a week / a month...
→ *une fois / deux fois / trois fois / par an / par semaine / par mois...*

c) Pour donner plus de détails sur la durée de cette activité, on utilisera des expressions telles que :
one hour a week / two hours a month...
→ *une heure par semaine / deux heures par mois...*

d) Pour exprimer une action qui se répète à intervalle régulier, on utilise *every* :
Every 7.2 seconds they have to snap six or seven keys into place. → *Toutes les 7,2 secondes, ils doivent placer 6 ou 7 touches.*
Every second, a new child is born. → *Un enfant naît toutes les secondes / chaque seconde.*

Rappel :
Pour dire ***tous les jours / mois / ans***, etc., on emploie ***every : everyday / every Christmas / every evening.***
Pour dire **à chaque fois**, on utilise ***every time*** : *Every time someone is one minute late, he's fined.*
→ *Chaque fois que quelqu'un est en retard d'une minute, il est mis à l'amende.*
Pour dire ***n'importe quand***, on emploie ***whenever***.
→ Voir p. 240.

18 • Les temps des verbes : présent et passé

Il n'y a pas d'exacte équivalence entre les temps des verbes en anglais et en français.

a) Le présent
– Activité en cours → présent : *be* + *-ing*
– Activité récurrente, vérité intemporelle → présent simple
– Bilan au moment présent d'une activité commencée avant mais toujours valable → present perfect

b) Le passé
– La notion d'imparfait ou de passé composé n'existe pas en anglais. La question à se poser est : l'action est-elle finie (pétérit) ou bien a-t-elle des répercussions dans le présent (present perfect) ?
– Il faut faire attention aux marqueurs temporels, certains ne sont possibles qu'avec le prétérit (*ago*) et d'autres qu'avec le present perfect (*in the past three years*).

Remarques :
– Pour traduire ***depuis*** : verbe au present perfect + ***for*** avec une durée (*he's been there for three hours*) et *since* avec une date (*I've lived here since 1990*).
– ***During*** ne s'emploie qu'avec un événement spécifique et signifie *au cours de*.
During the week, I start working at 9.00 a.m. / I work for eight hours per day.
– Pour parler d'un événement antérieur à un fait déjà exprimé au prétérit, on utilisera le pluperfect : sujet + *had* + participe passé.

c) La forme en *-ing*
Quel que soit le temps auquel elle est associée, cette forme appelée « aspect du verbe », met l'accent dans la plupart des cas sur l'activité dont on parle. Au passé, elle insiste sur le temps pris par une activité, avec une interruption marquée par *when* + verbe au prétérit.

19 • L'expression du conseil

a) *Should* + verbe
Le modal *should* s'utilise pour donner un conseil, pour exprimer une projection probable dans le futur qui n'engage que la personne qui le donne ou qui l'exprime.
– Employment should remain resilient.
– Disposable should increase downturn by about 10%.
Should est comme les autres modaux : il est suivi du verbe sans *to*. Il se traduit en français par la forme conditionnelle du verbe *devoir* : *devrais (-ait, -ions, -iez, -aient).*

b) *Ought to* + verbe
Ought to permet d'exprimer un conseil davantage fondé sur un usage général, admis, qu'il convient de respecter. C'est en cela qu'il se distingue dans l'usage de *should*.
Citizens ought to respect their countries' institutions : c'est la bienséance, la morale qui le prescrit.

c) *Had better* + verbe / *'d better* + verbe
Une autre manière de donner un conseil :
They had better find a way to repay their debt.
→ *Ils feraient mieux de trouver un moyen de rembourser leur dette.*

d) *Advise* + COD + *to* + verbe
Pour conseiller à quelqu'un de faire quelque chose.

GRAMMAR

Governments advise people to get ready for further sacrifices.

Remarque : changement d'orthographe entre le nom *advice* (→ « LES INDÉNOMBRABLES », P. 240) et le verbe *advise* (conseiller).

20 • Les propositions relatives

• **Emploi :** les propositions relatives peuvent être ou non encadrées par des virgules. Il existe deux types de propositions relatives : certaines sont déterminatives, c'est-à-dire essentielles à la phrases, les autres sont dites non-déterminatives (ou appositives), car elles ne sont pas essentielles, mais donnent une information complémentaire.
Mr Bolland, who joined from supermarket chain WM Morrisons in May 2010, said...

• **Construction:** la proposition relative est introduite par un pronom relatif. Pour choisir le bon, il faut prendre en compte deux paramètres concernant l'antécédent : la nature (humain ou objet / idée) et la fonction (sujet / complément). → Voir le tableau ci-dessous.

Remarques :
– Quand on annonce quelque chose, la proposition relative en début de phrase commence par *what*.
– Quand on veut reprendre tout ce qui a été dit dans la proposition précédant la virgule, on utilise *which*.
What I mean is that more sales are expected.
More sales are expected, which means that...
– Pour les relatives exprimant la possession (*dont*), on utilise le pronom relatif *whose*.
– Il y a aussi les adverbes relatifs (utilisés comme pronoms) : *where, when, why.*
The place where I was born.

21 • *To be to*

a) L'expression *to be to* peut exprimer :
– Ce qui est déjà prévu : *the plane is to take off at 6:00.*
– L'obligation : *you' re not to leave until I say so.*
– L'hypothèse, au prétérit modal: *if the authorities were to do that, the UN would react immediately.*

b) D'autres expressions assez proches permettent de parler de ce qui est imminent (*to be about to*), de ce qui va inévitablement arriver *(to be bound to)*, de ce qui est susceptible d'arriver *(to be (quite) likely to)*.
→ « L'EXPRESSION DU FUTUR », P. 234

22 • Le présent (simple et continu)

a) Le présent simple (*the simple present*)
Il s'utilise pour exprimer: une vérité générale, une caractéristique, une action habituelle, itérative (répétée).
China still dominates the business → *La Chine domine toujours le commerce* (comme par le passé et comme vraisemblablement dans le futur).
It supplies nearly half of the European Union's garment imports → *La Chine fournit presque la moitié des imports de vêtements dans l'Union Européenne* (comme par le passé et comme dans le futur).

Rappels :
– Seule la 3e personne du singulier modifie le verbe avec l'ajout du -s ou du -*es* suivant la terminaison du verbe :
China supplies half of the European garment imports.
La forme négative et la forme interrogative se caractérisent par la présence de l'auxiliaire *do* pour toutes les personnes, sauf à la 3e personne du singulier pour laquelle on emploie *does*.
– Attention à l'ordre des mots dans les questions :
How much of the European garment imports does China supply?
– **Attention aux formes contractées à la forme négative :** *China doesn't supply 100% of the European garment imports.*

b) Le présent continu : *be* + *-ing*
Le présent en *be* + *-ing* peut être utilisé pour décrire un évènement qui continue au moment présent.
But more orders are shifting to lower-wage economies such as Cambodia and Vietnam where garment factories are mushrooming. → *Les commandes se tournent en ce moment même (are shifting) vers des pays aux salaires plus bas, d'où les usines de textiles qui poussent comme des champignons en ce moment même (are mushrooming).*

Rappel : le présent en *be* + *-ing* se forme avec les trois formes du présent du verbe *be* : *am / is / are* + BV *-ing*.

antécédent	fonction du pronom relatif			
	sujet	COD	COS	Complément de nom
humain	who, that	who(m), that, ø	who ... to, ø ... to	whose
non-humain	which, that	which, that, ø	which ... to, ø ... to	whose, of which

23 • Les subordonnées introduites par « if »

a) *If* + présent simple exprime une condition réalisable
Ici, le *could* de la proposition principale exprimant une possibilité pourrait être remplacé par : *will / may / might*, tous indiquant une projection future avec une éventualité plus ou moins forte, et précédent le verbe *account*.
If it carries on doing so, electric cars and plug-in hybrids could account for 7% of new car sales in China by 2020.
Si la tendance actuelle persiste, les voitures électriques et hybrides pourraient totaliser 7 % des ventes de voitures neuves enChine.

b) *If* + prétérit exprime ce qu'il est convenu d'appeler « l'irréel du présent »
If electric cars were not too expensive, more people would buy them. Ce qui ce traduit en français par le mode conditionnel :
→ *Si les voitures électriques étaient moins chères, plus de gens en achèteraient.*
Le sous-entendu étant que les voitures électriques sont trop chères dans l'état actuel des choses.

c) *If* + past perfect exprime ce qu'il est convenu d'appeler « l'irréel du passé » (regret)
En effet, l'action ne peut plus être réalisée, c'est trop tard, il n'y a aucun retour en arrière possible.
If Toyota had not sold faulty hybrid cars a few years ago, they would have kept their leadership.
→ *Si Toyota n'avait pas vendu de voitures hybrides défectueuses il y a quelques années, l'entreprise aurait conservé sa position de leader.*

Remarque : on notera la formation du conditionnel passé avec modal + *have* + participe-passé.

24 • Les pronoms personnels

a) Les pronoms personnels sujets *I, she / he / it, you, we, they*
He et ***she*** ne peuvent être utilisés que pour se référer à des êtres humains, hommes ou femmes, voire des animaux familiers. Le pronom personnel sujet ***it*** se réfère au non-humain.
Ethiopian is state-owned and some analysts doubt it is profitable as it claims.
Dans l'exemple, les deux ***it*** se réfèrent à la compagnie aérienne *Ethiopian*.

b) Les pronoms personnels compléments *me, you, him, her, it, us, them*
Ils n'ont qu'une seule forme. Lorsque qu'ils sont compléments d'objet, les pronoms sont toujours placés après le verbe.

c) Les déterminants possessifs *my, your, his, her, its, our, their* : ils n'ont qu'une seule forme.

Attention :
His → possesseur masculin :
his company → son entreprise (à lui)
Her → possesseur féminin :
her company → son entreprise (à elle)
Its → possesseur non humain : *its passenger numbers* → son nombre de passagers (à l'entreprise)

d) Les pronoms possessifs *mine, yours, hers, his, ours, theirs*
The responsibility is theirs, not ours.
→ La responsabilité est la leur, pas la nôtre.

e) Les pronoms réfléchis *myself, yourself, himself, herself, itself, ourselves, yourselves, themselves*
Big brands consider themselves to be everlasting.
→ *Les grandes marques se considèrent éternelles.*
À ne pas confondre avec les pronoms réciproques : *each other / one another*.
As soon as they met, they started arguing with each other. → *Dès leur rencontre, ils ont commence à se disputer (l'un avec l'autre).*
Air companies compete with one another in order to increase their market shares. → *Les compagnies aériennes se concurrencent (les unes les autres) dans le but d'augmenter leurs parts de marché.*

25 • Les adverbes

a) Les adverbes sont des mots invariables qui sont utilisés pour modifier le sens d'un verbe, d'un adjectif, d'un autre verbe; ils peuvent également servir à nuancer une phrases entière. Il existe une grande variété d'adverbes : de manière, de temps, de lieu, de degré, etc. Leur place peut varier suivant leur nature.

b) Certains adverbes sont formés à partir de l'adjectif auquel on rajoute la terminaison *-ly* : *financial – financially; increasing – increasingly; angry – angrily.*
– They can't make ends meet financially...
Attention aux adjectifs en -ly qui eux ne sont pas des adverbes : *lovely*.

Rappel : les adverbes dits de fréquence (*often, sometimes, always, never*) sont toujours placés entre le sujet et le verbe ou entre l'auxiliaire et le verbe.
Les adverbes de temps (*yesterday, tomorrow*...) sont généralement placés en fin ou début de phrase.

Attention aux faux amis : *actually* → *en réalité* ; *hardly* → à peine ; *eventually* → *pour finir, finalement*.

26 • Les noms indénombrables

a) Les noms indénombrables sont généralement les mots que l'on ne peut pas compter : liquides (*water, milk...*), aliments, matières (*iron, air...*), certains noms abstraits (*love, happiness...*) ou concrets

GRAMMAR

(equipment, fruit...). Ils ne prennent jamais de *s*, ni d'article *a / an*, et le verbe est toujours au singulier. *This soft drink is delicious. What brand is it?*

Retenez bien : voici quelques noms indénombrables usuels à bien connaître : *abuse, advice, business, equipment, furniture, garbage, hair, information, luggage, news, progress, weather...*

b) **L'article utilisé est :** *some* (phrases positives), *any* (phrases négatives / interrogatives) or "no". They don't do any publicity. He wants no advertising for his product. Have you got any news about the teaser campaign?

c) **Vous pouvez rendre dénombrable un nom indénombrable en lui donnant une quantité :** *The market information is interesting. → He's got a new piece of information.* **Ou en utilisant un nom composé :** *The product placement software is efficient. → Can we buy a new software program?*
Dénombreurs usuels : *a piece of (advice), a glass of (water), a pair of (jeans, scissors)...*

27 • Les particules adverbiales

a) **Les particules adverbiales modifient le sens du verbe.** Il ne faut pas les confondre avec les prépositions qui servent à introduire le complément.
Thomas Cook, a German-owned travel firm, took over.
to take = prendre, mais *to take off = décoller / enlever*

b) **Le verbe à particule adverbiale, lui, peut se construire sans complément.** Si le complément est un pronom, il se place avant la particule adverbiale (le plus souvent, mais il existe des verbes à particules qui ne peuvent pas être séparés).

c) **À l'impératif, la particule adverbiale reste** (*Take it off!*), alors qu'une préposition n'est présente que lorsque le complément intervient (*He listened to me / Listen!*).

28 • L'auxiliaire modal *must*

• **Construction :** *must* obéit aux particularités de tous les auxiliaires modaux : pas de *to* à l'infinitif, pas de *s* à la 3e personne du présent simple, prend la marque de la négation et se place à la 1re place dans une phrase interrogative.

• **Emploi :** comme de nombreux autres modaux, comme *may* (→ *"may"*, p. 235), *must* peut être utilisé de deux façons différentes :

a) Quand le locuteur veut faire pression sur celui dont il parle. Avec *must*, on marque une obligation.

Attention :
– *Mustn't* marque l'interdiction. Pour dire que *Je ne suis pas obligé de...*, on utilisera l'expression *I don't have to...*
– *Must* n'existe pas au prétérit (on utilise alors *had to*) ni au futur (on utilise alors *will have to*).

b) Pour parler des chances de réalisation d'une action. Avec *must*, la probabilité est très forte.
(The) mobilisation (...) must have unnerved officials.
Dans ce type d'utilisation, on peut marquer que l'action a de grandes chances de se réaliser (*must* + BV), qu'elle est certainement en train de se réaliser (*must* + verbe *-ing*), ou bien qu'elle s'est certainement réalisée dans le passé (*must* + *have* + participe passé).

29 • Le cas possessif

a) **Le cas possessif ou génitif**
the government's response → la réponse du gouvernement
Cette forme de complément du nom, appelé génitif ou cas possessif, marque ce qu'il est convenu d'appeler la possession. Le « possesseur » peut être un nom propre ou un nom commun. **Attention à la place des mots dans cette structure.** Au pluriel, le **s** disparaît, seule l'apostrophe demeure. *Governements' difficult choices* → les choix difficiles des gouvernements

b) **Nom + *of* + nom**
On évite le cas possessif lorsque le nom du possesseur est trop long ou quand on veut créer un effet (insistance, suspens...) : *and the name of the winner is... → et le nom du gagnant est...*

Remarque : le 's du génitif disparaît parfois avec l'usage en formant des noms composés. Le premier nom jouant alors un rôle de déterminant par rapport au second : *air quality → la qualité de l'air ; unemployment rate → taux de chômage ; staff turnover → rotation du personnel ; football match → match de football.*

30 • Whatever, whoever, whichever

Les pronoms composés en *-ever* se construisent à partir des mots en *wh* et siginifient *peu importe, qui que / quoi que...* Un équivalent en anglais moins formel serait : *no matter what / who / where...*
whoever *: peu importe qui, qui que ce soit,* ***whatever / whichever*** *: quoi que ce soit,* ***whenever*** *: n'importe quand,* ***wherever*** *: n'importe où, quel que soit l'endroit,* ***however*** *: quelle que soit la façon dont...*
Freeman owns the town and can do whatever he wants with it.

Remarque : ne pas confondre *however* + adjectif ou *however* + proposition avec l'adverbe *however* qui signifie *cependant*.

Tools for the exam

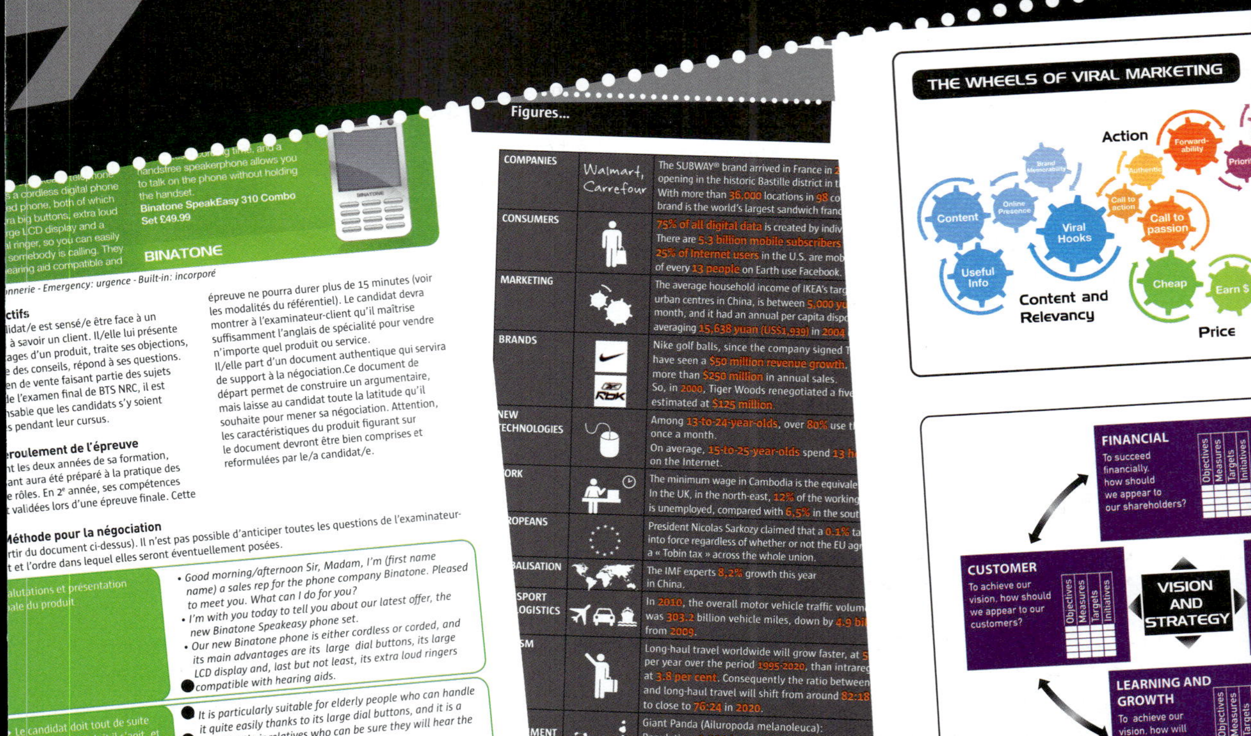

Faire un compte rendu oral à partir d'un document écrit en anglais

Compréhension écrite et production orale en continu et en interaction (CE ➤ POC / POI)

Objectifs

Le/a candidat/e devra faire valoir qu'il/elle possède une bonne maîtrise de la langue anglaise et qu'il/elle a acquis un vocabulaire de spécialité professionnelle. Sa présentation orale mettra en valeur ses capacités à organiser son discours dans une langue correcte et claire. Le candidat doit se rappeler qu'il s'agit aussi d'une épreuve de communication.

Déroulement de l'épreuve

Pour de nombreux BTS, cette partie de l'épreuve orale comporte deux volets : une préparation de 15 ou 20 minutes, suivie d'une présentation de 15 ou 20 minutes.

Comprendre un document

➤ *Voir le texte annoté p. 243.*

1• Observez le titre et le sous-titre : ils orientent la lecture. **2 •** Lisez le document une 1re fois. D'emblée, car le temps vous est compté, prenez des notes qui vous serviront à rédiger l'introduction de votre document (pour le début de l'épreuve : voir ci-dessous). Ces notes vous donneront de l'assurance et vous permettront de canaliser votre stress. **3 •** Listez les informations fournies dans le texte : faite une lecture détaillée du document pour bien cerner l'idée principale de chaque paragraphe et repérer les exemples donnés.

Méthode pour la présentation orale

Vous devez construire et suivre un plan en prenant appui sur des définitions et des exemples si nécessaire.

1• Introduction : source, idée(s) principale(s) *The article I have just read is dated 31st December 2011 from The Economist, a British reliable magazine. It deals more precisely with strategic choices some big companies have made in the USA.*

2• Développement en trois parties (ici car le texte s'y prête) : *First, I shall define what the word advertising means. Then, I shall examine the term "ethnic advertising" and see which advertising agencies support this approach as well as why a multinational might want to target a specific group. Finally, I shall see what the term "cross-cultural" advertising is all about.*

3• Conclusion : *I shall give my point of view and a conclusion.*

Les expressions utiles

Pour assurer des transitions d'une idée à l'autre : les **mots de liaison** démontrent que vous savez contraster votre propos, opposer des idées, nuancer les points de vue exprimés.

As I mentioned in my introduction, the document tackles the issue of advertising. Let's define advertising. First of all... Secondly, we can also say that... Finally, every company will advertise its product to expand its market share.

For instance, Nestlé favours ethnic ... In other words, to attract a specific group Nestlé uses ads that target Hispanics. In brief, some see that ethnic ... Others might be more willing to invest money... Let me quote the text. On line 16 we can see that...

To conclude / As a conclusion, we can say that companies promoting items can use both ethnic or cross-cultural advertising. However, when there is a crisis, ethnic advertising is no longer considered. To my eyes, France does not seem to target .... I strongly believe that race relations would be better if there were more ads with Blacks or Asians or Hispanics.

Conseils

- Montrez que vous savez organiser votre discours : *First, Then, Finally*.
- Citez les lignes du texte pour montrer que vous vous appuyez sur le texte : *On line 12, we can see that...*
- Si vous n'êtes pas sûr, utilisez ce type de phrase : *If I understood correctly, the journalist says that ethnic advertising is no longer used by McDonald's.*
- Si vous avez un « blanc », que vous ne trouvez pas le mot adéquat, faites une périphrase. Ainsi, si vous avez oublié le mot *consumer*, dites *clients* ou *customers*.
- En conclusion, n'hésitez pas à faire appel à votre expérience personnelle pour comparer : *McDonald's in France versus McDonald's in the USA.*

À partir du titre et du sous-titre : il s'agit d'une campagne publicitaire (*advertising*) associée au mot *ethnic*, déclinée en plusieurs publicités (*ads:* contraction de *advertisements*). Le pays est donné (§2) : *America*. Deux démarches publicitaires sont décrites : *ethnic* et *cross cultural* (cette dernière est déclinée en *integrated ads*).

§1 In the 60s, a character in a TV show declared that ads would improve sales if they were targeting Blacks as well as White. Only one ad for Blacks and Whites.

§2 Targeting everybody at the same time is the rule today as the minorities will soon be the majority. One ad = one message.

§3 Ad agency Ogilvy&Mather as well as companies such as Burger King use cross-cultural ads. One ad = one message (title).

§4 Burrell from Chicago believes ethnic ads should prevail. Example: cream for black skin. Many ads = many messages.

§5 Nestlé targets Hispanics as they spend a lot on food. As for McDonald's, it introduces products that are favorites among Afro-Americans and Hispanics to mainstream America. Example: caramel mocha smoothies and mango ice-cream. Many ads for Nestlé. One ad for McDonald's.

§6 Very small budget for ethnic ads. Cross-cultural ads are favoured over ethnic ads.

§7 Ethnic ads can displease a minority. Indeed, Asians can be of Chinese, Korean, Vietnamese, etc. origin.

Ethnic advertising One message, or many?

The uses and limitations of ethnic ads

In the television series "Mad Men", a 1960s adman makes a pitch to a television-maker whose sales are flat. "Among Negroes sales are actually growing," he chirps. He proposes making "integrated" ads that appeal to both black and white consumers.

Things have changed since. America's minorities will eventually be a majority of the population: by 2045, according to the most recent census. Many advertisers now favour cross-cultural ads that emphasise what Black, Hispanic and Asian-American consumers have in common. This approach is thought to work well with the young.

Ogilvy & Mather, a big ad agency, formed Ogilvy Culture in 2010 as a unit specializing in cross-cultural marketing. It was the census data that made Ogilvy change its model. In 2010 Burger King stopped employing ethnic agencies to address its consumers as a whole rather than taking a segmented approach.

Yet some admen feel ethnicity remains relevant. McGhee Williams Osse, co-chief executive of Burrell, a Chicago-based agency specialising in the African-American market, argues that ethnic origin is the key to people's identity, much more than education, income, religion, sex and sexual orientation. Maurice Lévy, the boss of Publicis Group, the French ad giant that owns 49% of Burrell, says that ethnic advertising makes sense for advertisers that are very big (and so can afford multiple ad campaigns), or very specialised. A maker of cream for black skin, for example, will probably not bother marketing it to Asians.

Nestlé, a huge food firm, aims some ads at Hispanics, America's largest minority. Hispanics are younger than other Americans, have more children and spend more on food. McDonald's has been a pioneer of ethnic advertising since the 1960s. Minorities represent about 40% of its customers in America. In 2010 McDonald's learned that African-Americans liked sweeter, weaker caramel mocha, so it started offering such blends everywhere, with great success. A similar thing happened with its mango and pineapple smoothies, a big hit with Hispanics. McDonald's featured the drinks in restaurants nationwide.

David Burgos, co-author of a book on marketing to the "new majority", says that in spite of the increasing importance of minority consumers, advertisers tend to cut its budget first when the economy goes sour. Only 7% of marketing dollars are spent on targeted ethnic campaigns, although nearly half of Americans belong to ethnic minorities.

Getting the right ethnic perspective is tricky. Hispanics are a varied lot. An ad that delights Cuban-Americans may irritate immigrants from Venezuela. Asians are hardly monolithic, either. Even the wittiest Korean catchphrases will provoke only bafflement in Chinatown.

Many advertisers count on the Internet to get a better knowledge of their audiences and propose them customized ads although it will cost a lot.

The Economist, January 5th, 2012

§8 Conclusion: the Internet will unable admen to adapt their ads to every single group. Solution rests on the net.

TOOLS FOR THE EXAM

Faire un compte rendu à l'écrit en français
(en nombre de mots limités à partir d'un document écrit en anglais)

Objectifs
Le/a candidat/e devra dans son compte rendu en français, en nombre de mots limités, rendre compte des idées principales du texte.
Il/elle organisera ses idées selon un plan : une introduction, un développement en deux parties ou trois et une conclusion.

Déroulement de l'épreuve
- Lisez bien la consigne : le compte rendu doit être fait en français.
- Le/a candidat/e a le droit d'utiliser un dictionnaire unilingue.

Comprendre un document
Voir le texte annoté p.245 et les indications données pour « Faire un compte rendu oral » p.242-243.

1• Observez le titre et le sous-titre : ils orientent la lecture.
2 • Lisez le document une 1re fois.
3 • Listez les informations fournies dans le texte (paragraphe par paragraphe).

Méthode de rédaction
Rédigez votre compte rendu en ayant élaboré au préalable un plan.

1• Introduction: elle comportera toujours la source, la date. Le titre n'est pas nécessaire. Vous aurez aussi le thème ou l'idée principale du texte à donner. Vous n'aurez pas d'annonce de plan à faire.
C'est un article qui traite de ... paru dans le magazine..... le 26 novembre. Il parle de la place de l'automatisation dans les entreprises françaises.

2• Développement : il aura deux ou trois parties que physiquement vous ferez apparaître dans deux ou trois paragraphes distincts.
- 1re partie: l'automatisation en particulier avec l'exemple du métro parisien ;
- 2e partie: l'automatisation en général et les raisons.

3• Conclusion : vous pouvez **ou non** poser une question d'ouverture, sachant qu'il s'agit bien d'un compte-rendu. *Qu'en est-il du chômage ? Le chômage à 10 % en France...*

Exemple de corrigé

Compréhension de l'écrit
Vous rédigerez en français un compte rendu du texte.
Vous indiquerez le nombre de mots utilisés. (160 mots maximum)

« Driveless, workless » est un article du magazine The Economist *du 26 novembre 2011 dont le thème central est l'automatisation. Le/a journaliste s'empare de la mise en route de la ligne 1 du métro parisien pour élargir son propos.*
En effet, la plus vieille ligne du métro parisien est désormais sans conducteur. Une révolution qui offre plusieurs avantages : élimination de l'erreur humaine, les rames sont plus sûres – il y a moins d'accidents, une plus grande fréquence des rames est possible si affluence, et les grèves n'affecteront plus la ligne.
Néanmoins, l'automatisation a aussi d'autres avantages : éviter des charges salariales élevées en France (39%) et contourner une législation du travail complexe. Cette automatisation s'est étendue à d'autres domaines. Ainsi, les supermarchés ont des caisses sans caissier(e)s, McDonald's permet aux clients de passer commande grâce à un écran, les stations d'essence fonctionnent sans pompistes. Alors faut-il s'étonner si le taux de chômage s'élève à 10% ? (160 mots)

Conseils
- Prenez le temps de vous relire. Vérifiez l'orthographe (utilisez bien les mots français : *une entreprise, une société* et non *une compagnie*) et la conjugaison : des points sont attribués pour une copie bien écrite.
- Faites bien vos quatre paragraphes : le correcteur doit voir rapidement comment vous avez organisé vos idées.

Le titre et sous-titre indiquent le pays concerné *(France)*, le thème - ici l'automatisation *(automation)* et les trains sans conducteur *(driverless)* et le nombre moins important d'emplois *(workless)* indique aussi les progrès de la technologie, mais évoque aussi une législation du travail rigide.

France and automation

Driverless, workless

Driverless trains reflect not just new technology but also rigid labour laws

§1 **Le métro parisien :** la ligne 1 : Défense / Château de Vincennes - un train automatique

The bold fuchsia-pink and tangerine-orange stripes of the upholstery are shocking enough, but the really unsettling feature of the new trains on the Paris metro is the lack of a driver. Sit in front and you get a picture-window forward view as the train tears through a dark tunnel. This month, the first automatic trains went into service on line one, the capital's busiest, running from La Défense to the Château de Vincennes. With trains guided remotely from a control room and protective platform-edge barriers, the new trains seem to operate entirely on their own.

§2 **Le métro parisien :** la ligne 14: 725 000 usagers par jour. La construction n'a pas entraîné de mouvement de grève (ici *shutdown*).

At a launch ceremony all the talk was of engineering and operational prowess. Paris already has driverless trains on line 14, the world's first fully automatic underground line. But that was built from scratch. Never before has such an old line, this one dating to 1900, been re-equipped with reconfigured platforms and new electronics, for driverless trains. On a line that carries 725,000 passengers a day, and despite difficult talks with trade unions, all the work took place without a shutdown.

§3 **Les avantages :** un meilleur service *(better service)* sans erreur humaine. Les trains sont plus sûrs *(safer)* et ils ne se mettent pas en grève *(cannot go on strike)*.

The main aim is better service. By eliminating human error, driverless trains are "incomparably" safer, says Gérard Churchill, in charge of installing the automatic line. Since opening in 1998, line 14 has had no accidents. Trains can run closer together. Extra services can be laid on at the last minute during unexpectedly busy times. But could there be another unspoken benefit? Driverless trains cannot go on strike. "It was not an objective," insists Mr Churchill. "But it is true that, during industrial unrest, automatic trains are much more reliable."

§4 **Les raisons de l'automatisation :** une législation stricte *(strict labour laws)*, des charges patronales élevées *(costly payroll charges)* et des grèves *(strikes)*. L'automatisation dans d'autres secteurs d'activités: les supermarchés.

Strict labour laws, costly payroll charges and erratic strikes seem to make French firms especially keen on technology. Supermarkets, for instance, have enthusiastically adopted self-checkout tills. "All French hypermarkets have adopted this strategy over the past few years," says Alexis Lecanuet at Accenture, a consultancy. The idea is to speed up queues at peak times for impatient non-technophobes carrying light baskets. But it also cuts costs. "Self-checkout has worked better in countries where labour is expensive," says Serguei Netessine, a professor at INSEAD, a business school.

§5 **L'automatisation un peu partout en France :** station services, la restauration rapide avec écran tactile, des stations de lavage de voiture. Pourtant le code du travail a plus de 3300 pages et les charges patronales représentent une moyenne de 39% des coûts.

France excels at high-tech services: credit-card-operated petrol stations, touchscreen fast food counters, automatic car-washing. Two years ago, McDonald's pioneered the use of touch screen, credit-card-based ordering in its French fast food restaurants. Eléphant Bleu, a self-service high-pressure car-washing chain, has 472 outlets in France, and is expanding. All this in a country where the labour code runs to over 3,300 pages, an employer pays an average of 39% in payroll taxes, and unemployment is at 10%. Spot the connection.

The Economist, November 26th, 2011

Rédiger une lettre commerciale

Expression écrite

Objectifs

Vous devez montrer que vous savez rédiger et mettre en forme une lettre commerciale à l'usage des pays anglo-saxons à partir d'informations précises.

Déroulement de l'épreuve

- Lisez bien la consigne : la lettre doit être rédigée en anglais.
- Le/la candidat/e a le droit d'utiliser un dictionnaire unilingue.

Méthode de rédaction

1 • Vous aurez pris soin de lire le sujet de l'épreuve avec attention pour déterminer :

- l'expéditeur, le destinataire, les pays d'où les entreprises écrivent, la date, l'objet ;
- s'il s'agit d'un premier courrier ou s'il y a déjà eu des courriers échangés entre les deux entreprises ;
- le contenu de la lettre et l'ordre des idées pour faire plusieurs paragraphes avec des mots de liaison si nécessaire. Attention, il ne faut pas faire de la traduction mot à mot.

2 • Les types de lettres commerciales : il existe plusieurs types de lettres à caractère commercial : pour accuser réception d'une commande, pour demander des informations au sujet d'une commande passée ou d'un produit avant l'achat, pour formuler une plainte au sujet d'un produit acheté, pour faire une proposition commerciale, pour demander un devis... Dans tous les cas, vous pouvez être amené à prendre la position du consommateur ou du vendeur / de l'entreprise.

3 • La mise en forme

Dans le cadre professionnel, vous préparerez votre lettre commerciale à partir d'un logiciel de traitement de texte (Word). Le jour de l'examen, votre lettre sera manuscrite.
Pour un courriel ou un mémo : *Subject* (objet) : doit être renseigné clairement pour que le destinataire sache rapidement pourquoi on lui écrit. *Attached*: si pièces jointes. *Copy to*: si d'autres destinataires (visibles ou invisibles).
Veillez à bien relire votre lettre pour ne pas laisser de fautes d'orthographe avant de l'envoyer.

➲ *Voir l'exemple de lettre annotée p. 247 pour ne pas oublier de mentions.*

Les expressions utiles

Utilisez des formules de politesse comme: *I would like to book..., I would be grateful...., Should you be interested in...., Please, do not hesitate to contact... etc.*

- N'utilisez pas de forme contractée.
- Si vous ne connaissez pas votre interlocuteur, commencez par : *Dear Sir / Dear Madam* et finissez par : *Yours faithfully.*
- Si vous avez déjà écrit à votre interlocuteur, utilisez son nom de famille : *Dear Mrs Smith, Dear Ms Jones, et finissez par : Yours sincerely.*
- Faites des paragraphes et aérez votre lettre: il faut qu'elle soit facile à lire et que l'on en comprenne rapidement les points importants.
- Les formes passives sont très fréquemment utilisées : *The goods will be shipped within ten days, a double room has been booked in the name of Mrs Silicon.*

Exemple de sujet donné

Lettre à élaborer et à rédiger en anglais selon l'usage commercial courant.

Expéditeur : Directeur des ventes de THE POTTERIES, Cardigan Street, Manchester
Destinataire : Directeur des achats, TOUKADO, 9, rue de Tournelle, 91000 Evry
Date : 20 mai 2002
Objet : commande n°28900/1
Corps de la lettre :
- commande du 16 mai reçue et enregistrée: 15 services à café ref. 28900, 300 assiettes à dessert ref. 280901
- commande expédiée par avion sur le vol B.A.341, départ aéroport de Manchester le 24 mai à 13h35, arrivée Orly à 15h40
- emballage : 5 caisses en bois contenant chacune 3 cartons résistant aux chocs
- marquage : Toukado, caisses numérotées de 1 à 5
- documents de transport (lettre de transport aérien sans réserve, facture pro forma, certificat d'assurance et note de colisage en triple exemplaires) remis à la Westminster Bank, puis transmis à la Banque Parisienne de Commerce International
- traite à trente jours tirée sur la Westminster Bank pour la somme de 1943 €
- formules d'usage

Exemple de lettre commerciale

Nom et adresse de l'expéditeur

THE POTTERIES Ltd, Sales Director
27, Cardigan Street
Manchester UK
+ 44 131 247 5312
thepotteriesco@gmail.uk

La date

May 20, 2010

Nom et adresse du destinataire

TOUKADO
9, rue de Tournelle
9100 - Evry France

Formule de salutation

Dear Mr Dupont

Références du document / objet de la lettre

ORDER N° 28900/1

Corps de la lettre

We have taken and received your order of May 16:
- 15 coffee sets ref. 28900
- 300 dessert plates ref. 28901

Your order is to be airfreighted on flight B.A 341, departing from Manchester airport on May 24 at 1.35 pm and arriving at Orly airport at 3.40 pm.

The packing will be five wooden crates – each containing three shock-resistant cardboard boxes. The crates will be marked TOUKADO and numbered from 1 to 5.

All the transport documents – **air waybill with no exception, pro forma invoice,** insurance certificate and **packing note in triplicate** – have been handed over to Westminster Bank and then forwarded to the Banque Parisienne de Commerce International.

We **have drawn a draft** on Westminster Bank at 30 days for the sum of €1,945.

We trust **these arrangements are to your liking** and we look forward to doing further business with you.

Formule de politesse

Yours sincerely

Signature, nom et position de la personne qui signe

X

Mr John Smith
Sales Manager

Words

Airway bill (AWB) is a non negotiable shipping document proof of the contract between shipper and air carrier for transportation and delivery of cargo. (autres mots: airbill / waybill / air consignent note / consignent note).

Paking note: is a shipping document that accompanies delivery packages.

Pro forma invoice: is a document that states a commitment from the seller to provide specified goods to the buyer.

A draft: une traite / lettre de change.

To make a draft on a bank: tirer sur une banque.

Préparer la négociation en commerce international (CI)

Objectifs

Le/a candidat/e devra démontrer qu'il/elle a bien acquis les différentes phases de la négociation et qu'il/elle sait les mettre en œuvre dans la langue étrangère qu'il/elle a choisie.

Déroulement de l'épreuve

Pendant les deux années de sa formation, l'étudiant aura été préparé à la pratique des jeux de rôles.

En fin de 2e année, ses compétences seront validées lors d'une épreuve organisée par le professeur de commerce international et le professeur de langues.

Cette épreuve ne pourra durer plus de 25 minutes (voir les modalités du référentiel).

À l'issue du jeu de rôle en anglais suivra un entretien pendant lequel le candidat expliquera sa démarche en tant que vendeur et désignera le profile « SONCASE » du prospect (joué par le professeur).

Méthode pour la négociation

1• L'étude des documents

• L'étudiant/e aura un document qui lui indiquera quelle entreprise il/elle représente. Il/elle devra faire une recherche sur son entreprise, les produits qu'elle vend, les caractéristiques des produits, les marchés où elle est implantée.

• Puis une 2e recherche sur l'entreprise potentiellement acheteuse devra être effectuée afin de déterminer ses besoins, sa clientèle, ses concurrents, ses fournisseurs, etc.

2 • La situation de communication

- Si vous rencontrez le prospect pour la 1re fois, vous procéderez en trois temps :
  - Prise de contact
  - « Small talk »
  - Découverte des besoins
- Si vous avez déjà rencontré votre prospect et si vous êtes en 2e partie de la négociation, vous procéderez en deux ou trois temps :
  - Récapitulation des besoins et vérification
  - Traitement des objections
  - Conclusion avec commande, et les modalités de paiement, devises, et modalités de transport et incoterms
  - Prise de congé

Le profil "SONCASE"

S	SÉCURITÉ / SECURITY	S	Takes time to think, hesitates, is faithful to providers.
O	ORGUEIL / PRIDE	P	Dominant, vain, egocentric and difficult to lead.
N	NOUVEAU / NOVELTY	N	Interested in originality, curious, keen on changes.
C	CONFORT / COMFORT	C	Appreciates well-being, likes what is convenient and refuses complications.
A	ARGENT / MONEY	M	Interested in savings, gains, compares prices and is difficult to lead.
S	SYMPATHIE / SYMPATHY	S	Friendly, makes others feel comfortable and happy, enjoys life and is chatty.
E	ENVIRONNEMENT / ENVIRONMENT	E	Respects nature, ecology, involved in sustainable development.

Exemple de négociation

1re rencontre avec le prospect...

- **Prise de contact (présentation et raison de votre présence)**

Good afternoon. I am Mrs Smith, Sales Assistant at the French Poilâne Company and I have an appointment with Mrs Surrey, Sales Manager at the Hilton Hotel in London. She is expecting me at 2. Please let her know that I have arrived.

- **Small talk: the weather, the trip...**

How was your trip? Did you have nice flight over? How have you been since we last met?
> Vous devez instaurer une relation « personnelle » amicale, adpatée à l'origine culturelle du prospect, avant d'entrer dans le vif du sujet.

- **Découverte des besoins (needs appraisal)**

We met at the Food Fair last September and you were keen on getting to know our products. Could I ask you a few questions to find out what your needs are?
> Vous devez cerner les besoins de votre prospect afin de mieux répondre à sa demande. À la fin de la négociation, n'oubliez pas de récapituler ce que vous avez appris afin de vérifier auprès de votre prospect que vous avez bien compris.

2e rencontre avec le prospect...

- **Récapitulation des besoins**

Last time we met, you told me that you were interested in ....
Have you made up your mind on the colour / number / fragrance / ... you would like to have? / If I understand you correctly...
> Vous devez à nouveau vérifier que les besoins du prospect n'ont pas évolué, revenir sur les points restés en suspens.

- **Traitement des objections**

But does it stay fresh and crusty? And the slices would certainly be too big to handle, wouldn't they?
Are you sure you will be able to deliver the bread before 6 every day?
> Vous devez avoir prévu les objections du prospect et avoir anticipé une réponse car vous voulez conclure la vente. Au cas où vous n'avez pas de réponse ou vous ne pouvez prendre la décision, vous vous devez de le signaler au prospect et lui indiquer que vous le contacterez d'ici un jour ou deux (ou plus si nécessaire) pour apporter une réponse à sa demande.

- **Les modalités de paiement et transport**

A rye loaf is about £XX and a walnut is £XX. I assume that you would want to pay in pounds and by bank transfer. Here is the order form that I have filled in. You just need to sign here.
> La devise et les incoterms doivent avoir été discutés. Si c'est une grosse commande, le vendeur fera des concessions pour emporter la vente soit sur la devise, soit sur les incoterms. N'oubliez pas que pour que la relation commerciale perdure, il faut qu'aucune des deux parties ne se sente lésée et il faut pouvoir aboutir à une situation « gagnant-gagnant ».

- **Conclusion de la vente et prise de congé**

Thank you. It was a pleasure doing business with you. If you need to contact me, do not hesitate. You have my business card. Good bye, Mrs Surrey.

Conseils

- Vous êtes le vendeur, vous êtes donc à l'écoute de votre prospect.
- Vous le regardez, vous prenez des notes, vous reformulez ce qu'il dit pour vous assurer que vous avez bien compris.
- Vous êtes d'une courtoisie absolue : vous ne vous asseyez que si on vous en a prié, vous demandez toujours la permission, vous n'utilisez pas un langage familier, vous vous tenez correctement, vous n'interrompez pas, etc., mais cela va sans dire. Good Luck !

Préparer l'entretien de vente en négociation relation clients (NRC) : *sales pitch*

A great value: Big button Binatone cordless and corded telephone set with extra loud ringers*.
Our Binatone Speakeasy telephone set includes a cordless digital phone and a corded phone, both of which feature extra big buttons, extra loud ringer, a large LCD display and a large visual ringer, so you can easily see when somebody is calling. They are also hearing aid compatible and feature an emergency* call button. The built-in* answering machine has 14 minutes recording time, and a handsfree speakerphone allows you to talk on the phone without holding the handset.
Binatone SpeakEasy 310 Combo Set £49.99

BINATONE

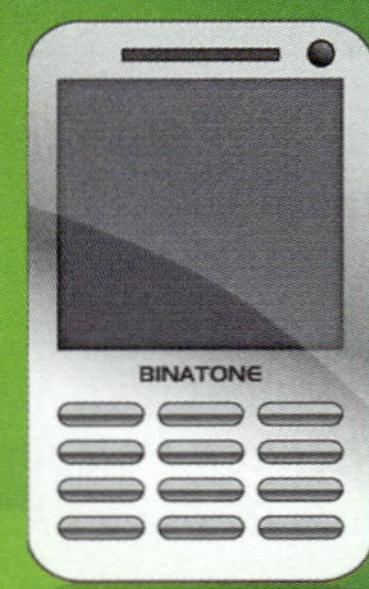

**Ringer: sonnerie - Emergency: urgence - Built-in: incorporé*

Objectifs

Le/a candidat/e est sensé/e être face à un prospect, à savoir un client. Il/elle lui présente les avantages d'un produit, traite ses objections, lui donne des conseils, répond à ses questions. L'entretien de vente faisant partie des sujets à l'oral de l'examen final de BTS NRC, il est indispensable que les candidats s'y soient préparés pendant leur cursus.

Déroulement de l'épreuve

Pendant les deux années de sa formation, l'étudiant aura été préparé à la pratique des jeux de rôles. En 2e année, ses compétences seront validées lors d'une épreuve finale.

Cette épreuve ne pourra durer plus de 15 minutes (voir les modalités du référentiel). Le candidat devra montrer à l'examinateur-client qu'il maîtrise suffisamment l'anglais de spécialité pour vendre n'importe quel produit ou service.
Il/elle part d'un document authentique qui servira de support à la négociation. Ce document de départ permet de construire un argumentaire, mais laisse au candidat toute la latitude qu'il souhaite pour mener sa négociation. Attention, les caractéristiques du produit figurant sur le document devront être bien comprises et reformulées par le/a candidat/e.

Méthode pour la négociation (à partir du document ci-dessus).

Il n'est pas possible d'anticiper toutes les questions de l'examinateur-client et l'ordre dans lequel elles seront éventuellement posées.

→ Salutations et présentation globale du produit	• *Good morning/afternoon Sir, Madam, I'm (first name name) a sales rep for the phone company Binatone. Pleased to meet you. What can I do for you?* • *I'm with you today to tell you about our latest offer, the new Binatone Speakeasy phone set.* • *Our new Binatone phone is either cordless or corded, and its main advantages are its large dial buttons, its large LCD display and, last but not least, its extra loud ringers compatible with hearing aids.*
→ Le candidat doit tout de suite repérer de quel produit il s'agit, et quelle entreprise le commercialise. Il doit également repérer le plus vite possible les avantages comparatifs du produit qu'il doit vendre : ici c'est indiscutablement sa convivialité.	• *It is particularly suitable for elderly people who can handle it quite easily thanks to its large dial buttons, and it is a relief for their relatives who can be sure they will hear the phone ring.* • *Moreover, the big screen display allows the user to avoid dialing errors, as well as to see the number on call.*

Exemple de négociation-vente

→ Mais également sa facilité d'utilisation pour des personnes âgées, en particulier, qui en font ses atouts principaux : grosses touches, grand écran, sonneries fortes.	• *If you have / your mother has / your grandmother has / serious hearing problems, our phone is compatible with your / her hearing aids.* • *The emergency button is also a huge advantage and can be a life-saving feature.* • *This telephone is on offer today for less than £50. You should be aware that the recommended retail price is at least 20 pounds higher in a store.*
→ Le candidat peut également décider si cette offre est une offre promotionnelle, en dessous du prix en magasin. Pour inciter son client à se décider, il pourra ajouter que l'offre est limitée dans le temps.	• *If you are interested in our offer, you shouldn't wait too long before you make up your mind; this product sells like hot cakes, and it's a limited offer.*
→ Le candidat doit également donner des informations ne figurant pas nécessairement sur le document de départ. Exemples : la garantie, les délais et coûts de livraison, ainsi que tout autre renseignement inhérent au produit, devis, SAV, condition de remboursement, conditions de paiement...	• *The phone is guaranteed one year / the delivery is free of charge* (gratuite/sans frais) */ our price includes the delivery / the product will be delivered within one week:* le produit sera livré dans la semaine *(within* indiquant l'intervalle pendant lequel la livraison aura lieu, ici dans une semaine maximum*).* • *If you are not satisfied after 15 days you'll get a full refund.* • *As for the terms of payment you can pay with the order* (à la commande) *or on delivery* (à la livraison).
→ Pour conclure, le client doit être rassuré et convaincu qu'il a fait un bon achat. La qualité de la prestation ne dépend pas de la conclusion de la vente et le client-examinateur peut revenir sur sa decision d'achat. Cela ne veut pas dire que l'anglais du candidat n'était pas à la hauteur.	• *I think you have taken the right decision, our product won't disappoint you, believe me.* • *if any problem should occur, please don't hesitate to call me at this number, I'll do my best to make sure your demands are met.*

Conseils

- Il faut adapter l'entretien au type de produit ou de service proposé (généralement un voyage).
- S'il s'agit d'un produit cher (*a big ticket item*), le candidat peut proposer à son clients de payer en plusieurs fois : *you can pay in several installments.*
- S'il s'agit d'un voyage, un minimum de vocabulaire lié à l'industrie du tourisme devra avoir été travaillé en amont (➲ *Voir p. 210, lexique chapitre « Tourism »*).
- Présentez-vous à l'examen de préférence en tenue professionnelle, regardez l'examinateur-client quand il s'adresse à vous, ne lisez pas trop vos notes, mesurez votre débit (ne parlez pas trop vite, articulez), demandez poliment à l'examinateur-client de répéter quand vous ne comprenez pas : *I'm sorry, I didn't understand what you've just said, would you mind repeating, please?*
- Évitez le « euh » qui marque l'hésitation, utilisez des « gap-fillers » tels que : *well, actually, you know, I think...* L'hésitation est normale dans un dialogue) et gardez un visage agréable et souriant si possible.
- La réactivité du candidat est très importante dans cette épreuve et pourra éventuellement compenser quelques éventuels manques linguistiques.

Préparer la négociation dans d'autres BTS (Management des unités Commerciales / MUC)

Objectifs

Le/a candidat/e devra montrer qu'il/elle connaît les 4 différentes phases de la négociation et qu'il/elle est capable de les mettre en œuvre.

- Prise de contact
- Recherche des besoins
- Argumentation
- Conclusion de la vente / demande et prise de congé

Déroulement de l'épreuve

Pendant les deux années de sa formation, l'étudiant aura été préparé à la pratique des jeux de rôles.

En 2e année, ses compétences seront validées lors d'une épreuve finale.

Cette épreuve ne pourra durer plus de 20 minutes (voir les modalités du référentiel).

Méthode pour la négociation

1 • L'étude des documents

Un document sera remis au candidat lui indiquant pour quelle entreprise il/elle travaille et quel poste il/elle occupe, ainsi que le jeu de rôle qu'il/elle devra mettre en œuvre selon deux situations possibles : soit une situation professionnelle (entretien d'évaluation par exemple), soit une situation de vente.

2 • La situation de communication

(exemple de négociation-vente)

- Si vous rencontrez le prospect pour la 1re fois, vous procéderez en trois temps :
  - Demande de rendez-vous
  - Découverte de la demande
  - Raisons pour soutenir la demande
- Si vous avez déjà eu un 1er rendez-vous et si vous souhaitez renforcer votre demande, vous procéderez en trois temps :
  - Récapitulation de votre demande et argumentation
  - Traitement des objections
  - Conclusion avec acceptation ou refus
  - Prise de congé

Conseils

- Arrivez à l'heure à votre rendez-vous, voire en avance.
- Soyez toujours poli.
- Habillez-vous d'une manière classique.
- Apportez des échantillons.
- Soyez positif et confiant.
  How about tomorrow morning?
  I can give you half an hour.
  Représentant: That sounds fine.
  Would (10 o'clock) suit you?
- Ayez une très bonne connaissance de votre produit, ainsi que de votre prospect.
- Avant le rendez-vous, mettez-vous dans la position de l'acheteur.
- Écoutez bien votre client et répondez clairement à ces questions.
- Si vous n'avez pas de réponse à lui apporter, n'hésitez pas à dire *I'll get back to you* plutôt que de donner une réponse fausse. La fidélité du client est basée sur la confiance.
- Gardez toujours quelques arguments de plus pour la 2e étape – convaincre.
- Anticipez les questions « pièges » que le prospect pourrait vous poser.

1re rencontre avec le prospect…

- **Demande de rendez-vous et raison de votre demande**

Sales representative: *Good morning, Mr Blake. I am …. from …. (name of company). I would like to come and see you to discuss putting our Fair Trade products in your store. Could you spare me a moment this week? / Could we meet up (tomorrow morning) to discuss…?*

- **Découverte de la demande**

Sales representative: *Thank you for giving me some of your time.*
I would like to show you our product range. Would you like to try a sample of our coffee / tea…?
Departement Manager: *Could you tell me more about your product?*
Sales representative: *Our products are well-known for their quality. We guarantee the source of our products.*

- **Raisons pour soutenir la demande**

Departement Manager: *We have a very good turnover with our ordinary products. We don't have a lot of room in the store. Why should we buy your product?*
Sales representative: *The average consumer is more aware of sustainable development nowadays. A supermarket which does not sell Fair Trade goods these days is less competitive.*
Departement Manager: *What gives you an edge over your competitors?*
Sales representative: *The Fair Trade label which is a guarantee of quality and/or our highly competitive prices. All our products are carefully selected by experts who actually visit the farmers.*
Departement Manager: *So what price range are we talking about?*
Sales representative: *Let me give you our price list. You will see that we cater for the mass market as well as for niche market sales. You won't be disappointed in your choice.*
Departement Manager: *I'll have to talk to my manager about this. I'll get back to you within a week.*

2e rencontre avec le prospect…

- **Récapitulation de votre demande et argumentation**

Sales representative: *It's nice to see you again.*
Departement Manager: *I've looked through your proposal and I still have a few questions.*
Sales representative: *I shall be pleased to give you all the answers you need.*
Departement Manager: *We must discuss the prices and delivery terms in more detail. I've looked at the competition and your prices are too high. We also need to have shorter delivery times – two weeks after a firm order is too long for us.*

- **Traitement des objections**

Sales representative: *I'm sure we can come to an agreement on those points.*
Departement Manager: *Could you quote me for 400 boxes?*
Sales representative: *Our proposal would be £1.50 per packet of 12 for 400 boxes.*
Departement Manager: *I'm afraid we could never accept that.*
Sales representative: *Well, we would be willing to give you a 5% quantity discount on any orders over 500 boxes. On top of which, for any repeat orders there is a loyalty discount of 2%.*
Departement Manager: *I think we could agree to that. What about delivery times?*
Sales representative: *If you guarantee a MOQ (minimum order quantity) per year, we would be able to give you a 10-day lead time for delivery.*

- **Conclusion avec acceptation ou refus**

Departement Manager: *There are still a few loose ends we should tie up. Could you provide us with some special promotional tools, someone to give out free samples for example?*
Sales representative: *I would have to discuss that with the marketing department. Perhaps we could give you a special display unit to promote the product in the store.*
Departement Manager: *Well, if you can see your way to helping us promote the product, we are willing to give you a try. Could you please send me a written proposal within the next couple of days?*
Sales representative: *It's a deal then. We agree on a first order of 500 boxes at a 5% quantity discount with a further 2% loyalty discount for any repeat orders. As a commercial gesture, I will guarantee a 10-day lead time for your first order as well.*
Departement Manager: *Thank you for coming to see me.*
Sales representative: *I am pleased to be doing business with you. Please keep those free samples for your staff.*

Parler de son expérience professionnelle

Déroulement de l'épreuve

Lors de l'épreuve orale, vous aurez 20 minutes de préparation pour présenter votre stage et la situation de communication : 10 minutes seront consacrées au stage et les autres 10 minutes à la situation de communication.

1 • LE RAPPORT DE STAGE

Objectifs

Vous devez rédiger un rapport de stage en anglais sur votre dernier stage (pour certains BTS) pour le présenter à l'oral lors de votre épreuve.

Méthode de rédaction

1 • Introduction : your internship...

- Where the company is located, when you carried out your intership, name of the company.
- A few details about the company.

2 • Développement

- *Type of company and the services it offers*

The hotel was founded by ... It is part of the famous Warwick International group. It offers many services, among them the banquet department.
Its customers are banks, etc.
It organises conferences, seminars and workshops for companies as well as private clients.

- *The tasks I had to carry out:*

I was in charge of redesigning the brochure that is sent to clients.
I was responsible for getting in touch with clients I had sent a brochure to.
I was also busy with finalising the booking of rooms with the number of guests, the menu, the number of tables, etc.
Of course, I also had to answer the phone to answer clients' requests and give them as many details as needed.
I was able to meet with customers and complete a customer file.

- *What I learned about these assignments*

First, I needed to be very organised to do the client follow-up.
Second, before contacting clients, I had to make sure I knew who they were and what they were looking for, and if the information was not there, I had to let the client know that I was new and that I needed to find out more about their request. So you must not be shy and you should take the initiative. It also means that you need to get to know your co-workers to ask them questions. Third, there are tasks that were new to me. You must not hesitate to ask questions. In many instances, people are very happy to help you. The employees were extremely helpful. My supervisor was really good and made me feel at ease.

3 • Conclusion : your point of view

- *To carry out a work placement / a 6-week intership / the personal assistant to the Sales Manager / to introduce the company / to describe the tasks / to analyse what I did...*
- *To be pleased / to get to know how / to be polite / to have helpful colleagues / to be on time / to enable sb to be more assertive / to be more outgoing / less shy / to be more self-confident / to learn from one's mistakes...*

Conseils

- Ne confondez pas les deux phases liées au rapport de stage :
  - la rédaction du rapport de stage,
  - la présentation à l'oral du stage.
- La rédaction est le fruit d'un travail que vous avez remanié et corrigé sur les conseils de votre professeur pour qu'il soit le plus pertinent et le plus complet possible.
- La présentation orale n'est pas une simple « récitation » du contenu du rapport de stage. Il vous faudra vérifier que l'examinateur vous suit. Vous ajouterez des mots de liaisons, des connecteurs logiques (first, then, finally). Vous aurez aussi besoin d'utiliser des *gap fillers* ou mots qui effacent le silence (*well, after that, let me say that again / differently, indeed...*). Vous pourrez revenir en arrière s'il vous semble pertinent d'insister sur un aspect du stage qui montre des qualités que vous avez acquises.

2 • LA SITUATION DE COMMUNICATION

Objectifs

Certains étudiants doivent rédiger une fiche qui décrit une situation de communication qui a souvent eu lieu lors du stage. Cette situation de communication sera rédigée de préférence en anglais sur une fiche, fiche qui sera l'objet de l'épreuve orale à l'examen final, en même temps que le rapport de stage.

Méthode de rédaction

Cette fiche devra évoquer un problème rencontré lors du stage qui a donné lieu à une situation de communication. Il peut s'agir d'une conversation téléphonique avec un client mécontent, au sujet d'une facture impayée, ou d'un entretien concernant la répartition des vacances d'été.

Elle est constituée de trois parties :

1. **La situation de communication :** *A telephone reminder: I have sent a brochure to a client who wishes to book a banquet room for 20 people. The company has not called back since.*
2. **L'organisation concernée :** *Hôtel Westminster, located rue de la Paix in Paris. The banquet department is the department in charge.*
3. **Le contexte de la situation :** *Reason for calling is to turn an estimate into an order.*

Les expressions utiles

I introduced myself and gave the reason for my call / I called the company... to find out if it had received our invoice / estimate / I asked to speak to Mr / Mrs... / The accountant told me that the company... / I had the documents in front of me / I let them know there was a mistake / I made an appointment with / the person I needed to talk to was not...

Conseils

Vérifiez que votre prononciation est juste. Enregistrez-vous, cela peut vous permettre de vous rendre compte de ce qui peut être amélioré. Vous regarderez l'examinateur/trice et vérifierez que votre explication est claire.

TOOLS FOR THE EXAM

Exemple de fiche de situation de communication

Context of the Situation

Setting: The directory of the Turkish professionals in France includes businesses from all sectors, in particular the construction industry.
Location: at the office
Duration: a one-hour meeting
Communication tools and technique implemented: face to face meeting with a potential customer

Protagonists

Presentation of the Protagonists: a Turkish business listed in our directory has been contacted to offer the company an advertising offer.
Relationship between the protagonists : they have known each other for some time and have renewed their contact with this special offer

Problem/Issues

For the PA: She had to welcome her customer and convince the customer that s/he would benefit from advertising her/his firm in the Turkish Directory. The purpose of the PA was to reach an agreement and have the company sign an advertising contract. She needed to have good selling arguments such as the number of companies that subscribes to the Directory.
For the customer: s/he had to be convinced that her/his company would gain clients with an advertisement in the Turkish Directory.

Resolution/Outcome

The contract was signed. It is a one-year contract that can be renewed a year from now.

Rédiger une lettre de motivation *(covering letter)*

Notez :

- Il est toujours mieux d'adresser votre lettre à une personne précise. Prenez le temps de téléphoner à l'entreprise afin de connaître le nom de la personne concernée.
- La *cover letter* (USA) / *covering letter* (UK) n'est pas manuscrite, elle doit être saisie sur ordinateur.
- *Resume* (USA) / *CV* (UK): pour le *curriculum vitae*
- Restez simple et précis (1 page maximum), et vérifiez bien la grammaire et l'orthographe.
- Dans une lettre de motivation en anglais, vous pouvez parler de vous à la 1re personne du singulier : « I ».
- Si vous répondez à une annonce, relevez les points clés de l'annonce et assurez-vous que ces points se retrouvent dans votre lettre.
- Il y a 3 parties à faire figurer dans votre lettre :

1. qui vous êtes et le poste qui vous intéresse ;
2. ce que vous savez sur l'entreprise ;
3. en quoi votre embauche sera bénéfique pour vous et l'entreprise.

Sarah Jones
54 Early Street
Cobham, Kent

Tel: 01631 774 345
Mob: 0277 841 912
sarah.jones@jones.com

May 20, 2010

NOM DE L'ENTREPRISE
ADRESSE DE L'ENTREPRISE

Dear Mrs. Pettyworth / Dear Sir or Madam

I am writing to apply for the position of salesperson which was advertised on GreatJobs.com. As you can see from the enclosed CV, I have the skills and training that you are looking for.

BUYRIGHT Department Stores is a young and dynamic chain of stores, with new sales techniques and customer-friendly priorities. The environmental interest and ethical standpoint of the company are exemplary and the beginning of a new kind of commercial approach.

The experience I have gained from my work placements means I have learnt good customer contact as well as how to display goods and products in an attractive way, manage the stocks efficiently and supervise financial transactions with the customers. I am adaptable, cheerful and hard-working, and enjoy working as part of a team. Our common interest in the environment is an added asset.
I believe I can make a real contribution to a BUYRIGHT Department Store.

I am available for interview at any time and I look forward to hearing from you. Thank you very much for considering my covering letter and CV.

Yours sincerely / Yours faithfully

X

Sarah Jones

Achevé d'imprimer en Espagne par Dédalo Offset
Dépôt légal : Août 2012 - N° de projet : 10183788